AN INTRODUCTION TO ASIA

An Introduction to
Asia

JEAN HERBERT

TRANSLATED BY MANU BANERJI

New York
OXFORD UNIVERSITY PRESS
1965

PRINTED IN GREAT BRITAIN
in 10 pt. Pilgrim type
BY EAST MIDLAND PRINTING CO.
BURY ST. EDMUNDS

CONTENTS

7

AN INTRODUCTION TO ASIA

CONTENTS

A*

CHAPTER I

Preliminaries

Oh, when will the West understand or try to understand the East?
OKAKURA KAKUZO

UNTIL very recent times the study of Asian cultures was above all an intellectual pastime. It was either an escape into intriguing and entertaining exotism, full of the unexpected, or an arbitrary way of confirming preconceived theories, or else a collection of so-called 'scientific' information which was often as minute as it was sterile and which, moreover, remained largely hypothetical.

It seems that now a knowledge of Asia, its spirit and its soul, has acquired a completely different significance in the eyes of many Westerners. Not long ago, Lafcadio Hearn wrote: 'Just as we have exterminated races weaker than ours, simply because our need for a more intense life than they were capable of living drove us to monopolize and absorb quite naturally all that was necessary for their happiness, we in our turn will perhaps be exterminated by races able to live more easily and who will seize all that is indispensable to us, races that are more patient, better inclined towards abnegation, more prolific and whom Nature can support at less cost. They will perhaps inherit some of our wisdom; they will adopt our most useful inventions, they will continue the best of our industries and will perhaps perpetuate whatever is most worthy to last in our sciences and arts; but our disappearance will cause them hardly more regret than we feel at the extinction of the dinotherium or the ichthyosaur.'

It is regrettable and even mortifying that we should have waited until we felt ourselves in danger before adopting the correct approach to the culture of such an imposing mass of humanity. The gesture would have been infinitely more to our credit had it not been the result of an ulterior motive. But it is no use regretting this now. Misfortune serves some purpose. Let us make the most of this formidable occasion to study the immense contribution of Asia to the human heritage with all the respect that it deserves.

The aim of this work is to seek the basis for a better understand-

II

ing of our Asian neighbours with a view to mutual respect and benefit. We shall therefore not dwell upon the points of similarity between Asians and ourselves, whether they originate in imitation of one of the parties by the other or from a mere convergence due to other causes. Indeed, co-operation is hardly worth while unless each party contributes what its partners do not possess. Our endeavour in sketching the original features of this vast continent will therefore be to bring out what it can contribute to the building of the 'universe' which is approaching at an ever-quickening pace and which will soon replace the 'multiverse' in which the human race has lived up to now.

However, mutual familiarity leads more often to animosity, even to hatred, than to true friendship and fraternization. 'We think without reflecting,' wrote Masson-Oursel, 'that men would understand each other if only they knew each other,' whereas antagonism is nowhere as sharp as on borders or in small groups, families or communities where the members have no secrets from one another. Consequently, imparting information that is described as 'objective' simply because it is confined to an exclusively intellectual plane is only justified inasmuch as it goes hand in hand with an effort at 'subjective' understanding, where a force of love illuminates these facts and makes it possible to place them in their right context—in time and in space—to discern the reasons behind them and to see them with the eyes of those that they affect.

That is why, before delving into any aspect of Asia, we must make a great effort within ourselves so as to be in a position to understand and evaluate her and to open our minds, without pride or humility, to all the infinite possibilities offered by a pooling of our wealth and hers in the spheres of the mind, the heart and the soul, even more than in those of economics or politics.

This does not mean that a sufficiently enlightened understanding would enable us to admire all, like all and use all in whatever is Asian. Only a great sage, with an overall vision of the world and of mankind, of the multiple chains of cause and effect, of the final goal of evolution far beyond its hesitations, its stumblings and its failures, could see how everything could be explained and justified and why nothing should be condemned because everything is necessary. Since we remain on a plane where judgement has to be exercised on the basis of human data, we have to admit, without surprise or indignation, that in Asia as well as in the West, the human individual is not perfect. In Asia, as in our own part of the world, many deep-rooted customs are condemnable or harmful and many persons or collectivities constantly or occasionally violate the most sacred injunctions, even if we judge exclusively by local or traditional criteria. But an apple tree is not to be judged by the stunted, rotten or worm-eaten fruit that the wind has torn from its branches, and it would be just as foolish and unfair to scorn a particular Asian people for the criminals, the dishonest and the imbeciles one meets there as to condemn a great American nation on the basis of the huge number of mental cases that have to be confined to asylums or of juvenile delinquents in its special courts.

The obstacles to the type of constructive comprehension that we have in mind are many and serious. We shall consider them in three groups: those that pertain to the texts and documents at our disposal, those contributed by the Asians with whom we are in contact, and those we carry in ourselves.

Firstly, in order to understand a people it is not enough to examine it as it is; you must also see how and why it has become what it is, know its sources and its traditions. 'The soul of all Semites,' wrote Masson-Oursel, 'must be sought in their traditions rather than in their ways, in their distant past rather than in the environment where they are seen to exist.' This is equally true of the other peoples of Asia. That is why the laborious approaches linguistic, philological, historic and others which have handicapped 'Western Orientalists'[1] were nevertheless necessary. But we must entertain no illusions as to what we can learn from them.

A vast majority of the most revealing texts on Oriental culture which have been preserved not only have never been translated, but only exist in a small number of unpublished manuscripts. The State Library of Outer Mongolia at Ulang-Bator (which, incidentally, is equipped in the most modern fashion with card-index catalogue, etc.) alone has 98,000 different Tibetan titles, and there is no reason to suppose that the collection is complete. Recently, an Indian scholar was able to draw up a list of 1,500 important existing Indonesian works of which only forty-five have been printed. In Asia Minor today documents are being unearthed so fast that in order to decipher them a hundred times as many specialists would be needed as are available.

Furthermore, throughout Asia, teaching has preserved, almost to our own day, an exclusively initiative and often esoteric character. The right to education—in schools or otherwise—which to us today seems to be a fundamental prerogative of man and woman, is a concept alien to Asian tradition. The latter sees in knowledge a power only to be placed in the hands of those who are worthy and will make good use of it—just like firearms or poisons. We shall deal at greater length with this capital feature, but it has

---

[1] An expression coined by Mus in *Présence du Bouddhisme*.

to be mentioned at this point in order to show that those written works which we can obtain, copy, translate and print are very often not comprehensible to the non-initiated and are not meant to be so. Grammar, etymology and comparative philology can enable us to discern the symbolic figures used in writing, speech and even in thought, sometimes even their origin and the geographic and historic areas in which they are used, but they can never give us their actual and profound significance nor even their *raison d'être*. It would hardly be excessive to compare this absence of communication to the person who sees his neighbour make a knot in a handkerchief in order to remember something but cannot guess what it is intended to remind him of. Generally speaking, we cannot understand an important Oriental text before it has been explained to us by someone who has obtained the key to it, either from a competent source or through personal experience.

This brings us directly to the second set of difficulties, because most of the Asians who would be able to elucidate their traditions for us are in no way inclined to do so.

Those with whom we are normally in touch are the very ones who have learnt a western language and have therefore received a westernized education, which has not only altered their vision and understanding and upset their scale of values but has developed in them serious inferiority complexes. Most of them cautiously, almost shamefully, conceal whatever they have been able to retain of their cultural, religious or even artistic traditions and pretend to be interested in the same things as we are, to see them in the same light, to share our opinions and tastes, even if this means lying barefacedly in order not to be considered 'backward'. Besides, most of them sooner or later end up by really becoming what they first wanted to appear—and so their evidence loses almost all value. Unfortunately for our search, it is they who have won our confidence and who gain authority most easily.

Those who have hardly had such contacts with the West and with whom we can nevertheless talk because we have learnt their language more or less imperfectly—or because we have a good interpreter—have considerable difficulty in realizing that a certain factor in their life, thought or values surprises, intrigues or shocks us. Even when they do, it is almost impossible for them to discern the reasons for our strange reactions and even more impossible to imagine what justifications could be appreciated by an intellect as strange to them as ours.

We must also realize that the terms we are inclined to idolize to the extent that they serve as pretexts or excuses for cold or hot wars, such as 'democracy', 'liberty', etc., almost throughout Asia can neither be given the same importance nor bear the same meaning. When a people has to devote its total energy to struggling against nature as well as against its neighbours—permanent or transitory—in order merely to survive, it cannot afford the luxury of political or ideological preoccupations which while not endangering its security are not essential to its self-defence. And even if in their conversations with us, westernized Asians use these expressions—and many others—in order to be in our good books and win our esteem or even without any ulterior motive, by mere superficial and indiscriminate imitation, we must not imagine that in people's minds in Arabia, India, China, Siam, Siberia or the Philippines they play a part in any way comparable to the one we assign to them. We shall revert later to the political concepts of Asia and their *raison d'être*, but the political field is not the only one to which the above comment applies.

The situation becomes even more disconcerting not only because their logic, refined and subtle though it may be, has sometimes little in common with that of Aristotle and Descartes, but also because the borderline separating concepts is often quite differently situated for them than it is for us. We shall only mention a few examples. When a very attentive observer of Islamic countries writes: 'The behaviour of the Muslim mind must be interpreted at several levels simultaneously', it means that the Muslim, in his thought as well as in his feelings and his expression of both, remains conscious of several different planes of existence at the same time. To take a more specific case, a traditional Hindu who speaks of 'Mother' may just as well mean the woman who gave him birth as India, or even the Deity in its active feminine form, and it is not unusual for him to have all three in mind. A Japanese who replies *'wakarimasen'* to a question asked of him may mean: 'I do not understand your question' or 'I do not know the answer' or even 'I do not know the subject about which you are speaking', and he hardly makes a difference between these three concepts which are so different for us. Inversely, the God which to us corresponds to a specific idea, since we can ask, without going into further detail: 'Do you believe in God?', in a Hindu's mind is associated with such a range of different or successive planes of religious experience that it gives rise to declarations astounding in their apparent contradiction.

In addition, both types—the westernized and the non-westernized—have other reasons for not wishing to lay themselves open to us. Long and painful experience has taught them that outsiders who asked them apparently innocent questions often had hostile or dangerous ulterior motives; military invasion, economic exploitation, destruction of local traditions and religions, dislocation of social units or simply slanderous publications were often the undeserved result of their confidences. That is why it was possible to speak of 'the secretiveness of the Muslim' and it has been noted with melancholy that all we know about Chinese classical scholars is 'what these scholars have been good enough to tell us', which is neither complete nor accurate. An exceptionally well-informed Frenchman confessed bitterly: 'One cannot imagine all the wiles used by orientals, after years of intimate acquaintance, in order to block the way to an understanding which to them always seems a possible source of danger.'

Even when they do not suffer from this misgiving, Asians are inclined to consider us—and not without reason—incapable of grasping anything but the superficial in them, and they prefer to let it remain at that rather than to embark upon laborious explanations which even at best might only lead to serious misconceptions, particularly because we would accuse them of not conforming to a logic which is ours but not theirs.

Finally, and still more important, is their fear of sacrilege. Whether it be a matter of personal or family customs, social organization or legal notions, historic or cultural traditions, arts or even games, metaphysical theories or religious experiences, at their basis we always find concepts so time-honoured that they have become sacred and it would be disrespectful and painful to expose them to incomprehension, discussion, criticism or ridicule against which one would remain powerless. One Asian trait is a delicate sensitivity which often attaches itself to the most unexpected objects, and when it is hurt, however involuntarily, the Asian recoils timorously and hides for a long time behind the opaque curtain of a smiling and implacable courtesy.

To all this must be added still further obstacles, the most difficult to surmount, those which result from our nature, our living and thinking habits. Up to fairly recent times, among the people whom we complacently call 'coloured'—simply because we fail to realize that our skin is as far from 'white' as that of a Chinese or an Iranian—we have known only those elements which, although heterogenous, are not representative: apprehensive and therefore hypocritical servants[2] taken from the lowest social strata, well-disciplined soldiers recruited for our armies and under the jurisdiction of ruthless military courts, petty officials—'collaborators'—tied to the apron-strings of the occupying powers, grand

[2] 'The class of people who, for us, are the first and often the most important representatives of the Chinese nation, i.e. our servants.' (A. Smith.)

lords become servile in order to keep or regain the right to oppress and exploit their compatriots, converts who deserted their Gods in order to be in the good graces of the all-powerful conqueror, students selected for our schools and universities to the extent to which they considered—or pretended to consider—us as superiors and disavowed their ancestral traditions. All these contacts could not but confirm in us the superiority complex to which we were only too inclined.

All our family, school, religious, political and social education combines to convince us that the group to which we belong—race, country, church, party—is superior to any other, if not in number and in strength, at least in quality and in virtue. When we are faced with habits and behaviour, ideas and tastes, ideals and creeds which differ from ours, without necessarily being opposed to or incompatible with them, our surprise soon gives way to disdain and inner condemnation when it does not go as far as repulsion, horror or overt hostility. It is quite obvious that the westerner who approaches Asia in such a spirit will never understand anything of it whatever be the mass of knowledge he has accumulated on geography, history, ethnography, languages, artistic and political expressions, morals and creeds or economics. 'Linguists, archaeologists, students of the past only accede to outside information on it.',[3] said an author already quoted. It is even worse when this outside and fragmentary knowledge of the past is claimed to be sufficient basis for knowledge of the present. Replying, perhaps unwittingly, to the melancholic remark of a Japanese: 'The western attitude is not favourable to the comprehension of the East',[4] an eminent Italian orientalist made a painful but sincere and unfortunately true admission: 'We westerners, full of complacency, are unfortunately still ignorant or mistrustful of Asia'.[5] Most of us are not so very keen to admit that there are in Asia some deep values from which we could profit for our own development. Our best Sankritists of today who translate the *Upanishads* or the *Bhagavad-Gita* systematically refrain from bringing out the spiritual significance of these works; and it is from this same 'Europeo-centric viewpoint' that more than a century ago Barthelemy-Saint-Hilaire could write that trans-gangetic India 'hardly deserved to be taken into account by history'.

Before we can even embark upon a study of these peoples so different from us, we must rid ourselves of the prejudices that blind us, a task which requires not only an overall intellectual

[3] Masson-Oursel.
[4] Okakura Kakuzo.
[5] G. Tucci.

resolution to keep our minds open but a long, tiring and scrupulous discipline in order to discriminate for every point between what is a local habit, physical or mental, peculiar to our group, and what is a truth or a necessity for the whole human race. Such propaedeutics is all the more arduous because we are suddenly left without any criterion and have to go beyond any accepted idea in order to reach a stage where we must perform actual acrobatics of impartiality. Does polygamy really correspond to a less advanced stage of development than monogamy? What about monotheism, polytheism, ancestor worship, different styles of clothing and food, various systems of personal hygiene and medicine, different methods of soil cultivation, and over and above everything, various scales of values which are so difficult to compare?

It must also be frankly admitted that most of those who established contact with Asia in our name were not well placed to understand it themselves—military men instructed to crush ruthlessly all that went against our material interests, missionaries whose task it was to wipe out local religions and replace them by our own religion, scholars eager to catalogue within our historical, philosophical, ethical, esthetic, economic and linguistic concepts, sections of life which do not fit into our modern western classifications, tradesmen trying to get rich by transforming the peoples' way of life, administrators responsible for enforcing order and obedience on the subject people. Of course, there were many and admirable exceptions to which we shall come back frequently, but they remained a quantitatively negligible minority and their long-stifled voice hardly ever perturbed our self-complacency.

If the westerners who have had to study Asia for professional reasons are left aside, most of us may be divided into three main groups: those who seek in Asia all that is different with the purpose of vilifying it and of strengthening our conviction that we are superior to all others; those who are also on the look-out for everything that is different but seek in it a source of relaxation and entertainment through the exotic and the extraordinary; and finally, those who, in a spirit of 'tolerance' and 'charity', are eager to find in Asia all that resembles us in order to prove that, after all, these people have *some* good in them and that they should not be indiscriminately condemned. None of these three attitudes can lead to real understanding. Their most famous exponents, the Pierre Lotis and the Rudyard Kiplings, even when they stirred small emotional waves in us, have always reached the sad conclusion, 'East is East and West is West and ne'er the twain shall meet'. Basil Hall Chamberlain faithfully echoed the opinion of Japan when he wrote of the 'egocentric and unsympathetic attitude which made Pierre Loti incapable of understanding Japan'. As for Kipling who, in India, hardly ever mixed with anybody but soldiers in the service of England and servants in the service of the English people, he believed—and made his readers believe—that those people were India!

One fact which must be remembered, for it seems unimportant but has a seriously paralysing effect: while we do have admirable monuments of Asian antiquity, temples and palaces, sculptures and miniatures, poems and philosophic teachings, we mostly avoid drawing conclusions from them as to the culture and turn of mind of our Asian contemporaries. Between old and modern times we draw a dividing line that is seldom justified by facts. Even in the cases where there seems to be an almost complete breach, many traditions subsist on a plane which may remain unconscious but which has a very real influence on present everyday life. For this same reason, we hardly ever compare the writings of Westerners who visited the East of old and what these countries are in our days. Herodotus seems irrelevant to us, we do not imagine that Marco Polo or the Ambassadors of the Republic of Venice can teach us anything on the subject—unless, of course, we go to the other extreme and we take the wrong but widespread view that Asia is ever unchanging or, at least, had remained so until we rendered her the inestimable service of arousing her from her torpor. Even Byzantium, which could supply us with such a wealth of information, has in most Western languages acquired a derogatory flavour.

Does this mean that we should despair of ever understanding each other? Certainly not, for we have today considerable opportunities and it is only up to us to take advantage of them.

Firstly, for over two centuries, our orientalists have accumulated an enormous quantity of original documents now stacked in our libraries. While exclusive concentration on historic and linguistic criticism in the western manner and the contempt shown for 'indigenous' interpretations has often led them to wrong or merely superficial translations, nevertheless, we now have at our disposal, thanks to them, work which we only need to correct and supplement.

Furthermore, the sudden disappearance of colonial regimes and the accession to independence of almost all the Asian peoples in the course of the last twenty years has broken down many of the barriers to which we have referred or has at least lowered them. Now that we can and must, willingly or otherwise, live as equals with these nations and races, the inferiority and fear complex which rendered them silent and the superiority complex which rendered us deaf have, in any case, been greatly attenuated. Now, to our greater advantage, many writers, scholars and sages of Asia express themselves quite freely on all subjects, in books and periodicals and often try even to convert us to their views—which anyway helps us to a better understanding of them.

The conversations which opened after the last war for purposes of co-operation have, to a great extent, further facilitated personal contacts. Whether it be at international gatherings held at different levels and on the most varied subjects or in other spheres—scientific or technical, professional or labour, cultural or literary, commercial or industrial—the elite of the two continents now have frequent opportunities to meet in order to discuss whatever interests them most directly, without being hampered by the famous 'colour bar'. It is not rare for these personal relationships, which generally begin in a strictly limited field, to develop eventually into friendships which may deepen till they reach the innermost regions of family or religious life. Of course, such an evolution still remains difficult and exceptional and can hardly affect Asians who do not already feel drawn towards the West or at any rate, esteem it enough to seek or accept contact with those of us who have the same interests; but many of them have carefully kept pure traditions deep within themselves and, while at the beginning they almost always conceal these from their newly-met colleagues, they are ready, sometimes, to lift the veil a little after they have watched us critically for some time. Apart from such confidences, their way of approaching problems of joint interest often reveals tendencies and conceptions very different from ours, and even when we do not understand them easily, at least we must acknowledge that they exist and that our own are therefore not the only ones conceivable among people worthy of our respect.

A recent trend has developed, however, which tends to stem the flow of such confidences: Asians feel increasingly hurt by the mental distinction we draw between 'westerners' and 'orientals'; they insist that we drop this terminology and think only in terms of human beings. It happens more and more often that at international gatherings held with the best of intentions to facilitate mutual understanding, official representatives of some Asian country rise to protest against a discrimination that they resent as offensive. This is understandable, of course, and has to be excused, but by acting in this fashion they hardly contribute to the solution of problems from which they suffer more than anybody else.

Another kind of research and cultural relationship likely to gain considerable importance is now rapidly developing among the peoples of Asia themselves. Great scholars from Japan, China, India, Soviet Asia have initiated very thorough studies on the other countries of their continent; they are combing libraries, art collections and universities, engaging in archaealogical research, exchanging visits and publications, sending each other rare documents on microfilms and so on. In most cases they are perfectly familiar with our methods and techniques of study and they apply them to the extent and under the conditions they deem appropriate, but in addition they are naturally more apt than we are to understand and explain to each other and they are not met with the same mistrust as our western scholars; among them the unwritten law that obtains throughout the East—that a thing belongs to him who deserves it most—comes into play much more easily. Through them we have already been able to avail ourselves of information and views of the greatest value. Other Asian countries are gradually joining in the research. It is the Japanese who are responsible for the publication of the text of the Tibetan *Tripitaka*; in India, the International Academy of Indian Culture—whose name does not in any way correspond to its activity—has published immense collections of works, particularly Shata-Pitaka in the 'Indo-Asian Literature' series.

Finally, there are the Europeans—not many, it must be admitted —who have completely immersed themselves in the life of Asia, either for a time or for always, who have adopted Asian ways, have founded a family there and have sat at the feet of the sages with all the open-mindedness and humility expected of a disciple. Not long ago their evidence was still treated with complete contempt and it was not rare for them to be accused of religious and cultural apostasy, national or political treason. Now they can make their voice heard freely, and among them is to be found an unexpectedly large proportion of highly cultured individuals capable of understanding and explaining what they have learnt.

Certain colonial groups, particularly among the Dutch and the Portuguese, had long ago agreed to mix with the local population through marriage (for the French and the English, it was almost exclusively a matter of temporary concubinage), but in nearly all cases the European husband considered it his duty to keep his wife and especially his children away from local religious and cultural traditions. Such associations, therefore, more often resulted in creating communities without roots rather than in any true opportunity of mutual understanding. The European women who married Asians were in a much better position to create real bonds, but most of them, unfortunately, came from a very simple environment and had not sufficient knowledge of their own culture to

make adequate comparisons; moreover, they were so much ostra-
cized by the other westerners that it was impossible for them to
make their voices heard even if they had felt a desire to do so and
their husbands had allowed them.

On the debit side, we have of course the impressions collected by
the unenlightened travellers who now pour into Asia either as
tourists or in any other capacity and who fall an easy prey to
shameless guides only too anxious to satisfy their conscious or
unconscious appetite for sensational, horrible or scandalous sights.
When they return, these people can unfortunately speak with
authority of what they have actually witnessed, and they describe
these age-old cultures just as an American may describe France
after having lunched at his Embassy and spent a night in the
Folies-Bergère quarter. And they do a great deal of harm.

One further addition to this list of difficulties and possibilities:
when we try to ascertain in what this continent differs from ours,
we often forget that the differences may have various sources. The
peculiar features that we see may be a direct consequence of the
climate or physical environment and may be found identical or at
least similar in purely European regions placed in the same conditions. They may also be characteristic of a stage of non-indus-
trialization similar to what was ours only a very few centuries ago
and we could doubtless find them also in thirteenth century or even
in seventeenth century Europe, especially in regard to family relationships, social life in town and country, the significance of religious preoccupations.

Many of the features that we shall mention as differentiating
the traditional Asia of yesterday from the Europe of today will
not therefore be specifically Asian. As this, however, affects neither
the importance nor the effects of these contrasts, we shall bring
out the fact only when it is of special interest.

What exactly is Asia? Firstly, how do we define its geographical
boundaries? While these are clearly marked to the north by the
Arctic Ocean, to the south by the Indian Ocean, to the west by
the Ural river and mountains, the Caspian, the Black Sea, the
Mediterranean and the Red Sea, some of its other confines are more
controversial.

According to most specialists, it is the principal chain of the
Caucasus which separates Europe from Asia between the Caspian
and the Black Sea; but the opinion of Russian geographers
seems to have varied considerably during the last hundred years.
While in 1890 the border was marked on the very spot by a

large cross planted upon the highest pass in the route connecting Tiflis with Orjonikidze, named for this very reason the Pass of the Cross, Krestovie Pereval, a little later it was shifted 300 kilometres to the north along a line which followed the Manich and ended south of Rostov. Now, on the contrary, the Soviet authorities adopt as a boundary line the political frontier between Turkey and the USSR some 300 kilometres to the south of this same Pass of the Cross, thus claiming Georgia, Armenia and Azerbaijan for Europe.

In ancient times, it was considered that Africa began and Asia ended at the Nile, while now the continental frontier is normally taken to be the Suez Canal or a line near this Canal.

To the south-east the separation between Asia and Oceania is very vague; there is general agreement, however, to adopt the 'Wallace Line', which leaves the Celebes and the other large islands of Indonesia on one side, the Moluccas and New Guinea on the other. Rather an arbitrary distinction, this, since it is based on two facts not very decisive in themselves: on the one hand, that the infiltrations starting in India did not go further than this line, and, on the other hand, that marsupials are to be found on only one side of it. Besides, some authors leave to Oceania the Celebes and all the islands to the east of Bali.

Finally, as regards the Pacific Ocean, it is mostly considered that Micronesia, Melanesia and Polynesia are not a part of Asia proper.

It has to be acknowledged that these different lines imposed by nature or chosen by man do not always separate clear-cut human groups. There is obviously less difference between an inhabitant of Pera and someone from Scutari of Asia than between a Turk of any kind and a Dutchman. Very homogeneous tribes may be found also astride the borderline of the Ural mountains.

Since a choice has to be made, for the purpose of our study we shall include in Asia all that lies to the south of the Caucasus and the whole of the present territory of the Indonesian Republic, but not the small Pacific islands.

Thus delimited, Asia represents some twenty-five million square kilometres or less than a third of land above water, but it bears over 1,500 million men, i.e. considerably more than half (55%) the population of the globe—and the number of its inhabitants is increasing at the rate of some forty millions per year.

Like Europe, this continent is doubtless even more remarkable by its diversity than by the features common to the whole of it. And it is a grave mistake—unfortunately all too frequent—to generalize conclusions, however justified, originally drawn from observations made only on one part of it.

In physical geography Asia has all the extremes. Immense

luxuriant forests are still practically unexplored there while deserts extend over hundreds of leagues. Its steppes cover a quarter of the globe's girth. Mountains exceed 8,000 metres (24,000 feet), plateaus spread themselves out at over 5,000 metres' altitude and vast depressions are to be found below sea level. Some river deltas cover thousands of square kilometres, some lakes extend over more than 500 kilometres—and some, even at high altitudes, are more salt than the Dead Sea.[6]

Annual rainfall varies between less than 50 millimetres in the Tarim Basin (Turkestan), in Arabia and even less in the central desert of Iran—'the driest point on earth'[7] and 7.50 metres in Northern Formosa, 11 metres in the Khasi Hills (Assam) and sometimes more. For instance, the town of Cherrapunji (Bengal), in 1861 received 22.60 metres of rain, of which 9 metres fell in a single month.

The extreme of cold is also to be found there to the south of Irkutsk where temperatures of −70° C. have been noted while Jacobabad (Sind) or Baghdad frequently register 50° C. (122° F.) in the shade and the Persian Gulf even more.

Our geographers sometimes divide the continent into two parts —green Asia and brown Asia—or Monsoon Asia and the rest of the continent. Rialle divides Central Asia itself into two 'completely dissimilar' parts by a line drawn from north to south and roughly following the 67th meridian.

This naturally results in extreme variations in population density. 'The lunar landscapes of the Hindu Kush, like a living remnant of prehistory, seem to be awaiting the birth of the animal world or perhaps even foreboding its end. Man appears almost completely alien there',[8] while elsewhere are to be found some of the most densely populated regions of the world.

The diversity of races is in no way less than that of the physical features. Indo-Aryans, those whom we call white, especially in the north and the west, Mongoloids, whom we call yellow, especially in the east, Negroids in South India and Ceylon, Negritos from the Andamans to the Philippines, Malayans in the Far-East, live side by side and often mix. Furthermore, within each one of these large families of races may be distinguished a considerable number of groups fundamentally different from each other. A guide to Soviet Asia published in 1928 lists twenty-eight important races there, the numbers of each varying at that time between a few hundreds and

[6] The Lake of Urmia, in Iran, for instance, which has an area of 40 sq. kilometres and is situated at 1,230 metres above sea level.

[7] Clement Huart and Louis Delaporte.

[8] R. Dollot.

over six million people. In their physical constitution, their language, their ways, they are greatly different from each other—and the guide-book did not embrace Transcaucasia! Some of these races are subdivided by ethnographers into a dozen or more sub-groups. On the territory of Viet-Nam alone, five great prehistoric races have been noted, sometimes mixed together.

As for cultural levels, these also go from one extreme to the other with all conceivable intermediate stages. While Iran, India, China and Japan have in the course of the centuries produced some of the most refined civilizations in which the human race can take pride, the Kelabites in Northern Borneo are still in the Megalithic era, the Pandaram tribe of south India still lives completely naked in rock hollows or tree trunks, certain groups do not possess the wheel and have never had domesticated animals; cannibals are also less rare than we like to think. Moreover, such violent contrasts can sometimes be seen within a few miles, as for instance in Formosa, the Philippines and India.

Nevertheless, however bold or utopian our attempt may seem, we shall endeavour here to bring out some general features which apply, if not fully to the whole of Asia, at least to a very large part of its immense population. It is quite obvious that on almost all points, the description offered will be subject to many and important exceptions which will vary in their geographical extension. We shall only mention the main exceptions.

In order to keep this volume within reasonable limits, we shall supply in support of our assertions only the most characteristic examples from one or two countries and we shall indicate variants only for the most fundamental subjects or when the variants themselves are of particular interest.

We have been encouraged in this task firstly because certain great orientalists have admitted that it can be done and above all, because we feel that it could meet a real need. Among us, at present, many thinkers are trying to define Europe—taken either as a whole or only in its politically 'western' side—in order to bring out its characteristics, define its place in today's world and forsee its possible role in the future. Now, it is possible to define what is peculiar to a country or a continent only by comparing it with other countries or continents; only thus can one distinguish what is 'local' from what applies to the whole human race or, at least, to a large part of it. It is to be deplored that the people who should have approached this task of defining Europe—a task so necessary and so potentially full of practical consequences—did so in ignorance of other continents and particularly of Asia which, along with Europe, has written most of the richest pages of history.

These well-meaning authorities therefore often do no more than repeat commonplaces—observations which could hardly remain valid after a more attentive study. The result has frequently been either the appalling superiority complex of which it is so hard to rid ourselves, or a violent return of the pendulum, a sort of masochistic idolatry of everything oriental—which is just as disastrous.

Of course, we can do no more here than broach the subject, but we hope that those who will continue this research will find in the following chapters a number of general ideas—some of them rather novel—which are worth verifying, exploring, analysing, even if they cannot be confirmed in their present form.

One more admission—it is quite obvious that I do not have personal experience of all aspects of life in all the countries of Asia. I have therefore had to supplement the information obtained directly on the spot with abundant literature provided by travellers and scholars, old and new, who have gone into these problems, and even more with all that has been patiently explained to me by my numerous friends who have been brought up in various Asian traditions and have remained faithful to them. It would need several pages to list even the main contributors. The best I can tell them by way of thanks is that I have honestly endeavoured to show their civilizations, their creeds, their tendencies as they see them themselves and as they would have us understand them. It is up to them to say how far I have succeeded.

PART ONE

Man and God

CHAPTER II

Religion

Religion was created at the same time as the created being
BUNDAHISN

METAPHYSICAL, religious, spiritual and mystical preoccupations, with all the ritualism that goes with them, are the main foundation of traditional Asian life; they impregnate all its spheres from family and social life to science and art. Without much exaggeration, one may apply to the whole continent the definition given by two authors for one of its regions: 'A theocentric aggregate where the profane is absorbed by the sacred.'[1]

To take as an example the case of Islam—which does not substantially differ from many others—the Muslim's sensitivity, his intelligence, his way of reacting to the world, are in fact entirely determined by his religion; the 'sacred' for him remains a structure of fundamental consciousness. Cultural expression, whether it be philosophy, literature, history, science, education or art, bears the imprint of God to such an extent that it is conceived within the single framework determined by a divine horizon, and in function of that horizon; culture is not to be distinguished from the religious phenomenon. Even for politics—one of the greatest modern reformers of Islamic religious thought, Sir Mohamed Iqbal, recognized explicitly: 'It is not true to say that Church and State are two aspects of the same thing: Islam is a single reality, defying analysis, which is one or the other according to our varying point of view just as the unit called man is a body when it is seen acting towards what is known as the outside world and a soul when considered acting towards the ultimate goal.' Therefore, for the Muslim, religion always remains topical; it impregnates the smallest details of day-to-day existence as well as the concepts regarding the cosmos and the existence of man; for him, the word 'profane' or 'lay' is totally devoid of meaning. Even the recruitment of candidates for the highest as well as the most humble offices is done in Islam

---

[1] Garelli and Leibovici.

in accordance with a criterion of piety, and fear of Hell certainly plays a bigger part than fear of the police in the observance of the most diverse injunctions.

Practically the same may be said of the other Semitic religion that has spread in Asia: Judaism. A man who has spent many years among the nomads of the Near East aptly wrote: 'The Semitic religion—which becomes such a cold and strange plant in the idolatrous soil of Europe—with the peoples of Moses and Mohammed is like a passion which circulates in their blood.'[2]

Even men and people whose behaviour, according to the historians, would make us think that religious preoccupations were foreign to their nature, were practically haunted by them. The letters written by Genghis Khan to Taoist religious leaders offer clear proofs of that deeply-rooted trait.

The Asian people that has been most often described as purely materialist or at least interested exclusively in things of this world —which does not mean the same thing—the Chinese, are not free from them—quite on the contrary—but, in them, religious feeling manifests itself differently. As Marcel Granet has pointed out, 'At first sight, the distinction between the sacred and the profane is less apparent in China than in our case. According to observers, therefore, the Chinese are said to be the most positive and the most superstitious people on earth'.[3] The authors who stress the Chinese preoccupation with things 'of this world' must admit nevertheless that they remained profoundly religious. A very attentive observer of very recent China wrote that 'the Chinese see a golden thread of spiritual life running through every form of existence and binding together, as in a living body, everything that subsists in heaven above and on the earth below'.[4]

Even those groups that now turn towards an atheist materialism do so still in a religious spirit and with aims of a spiritual nature. As accurate an idea as possible of the religious basis of a group is therefore a prerequisite for one who wishes to understand its action and its attitude under any circumstances.

[2] Charles Doughty.

[3] 1951. Rather than 'according to observers' one could say 'according to the observer's approach'. Granet himself, who knew the Chinese soul so well and has given such an extraordinarily living and true synthesis of it, seems often to contradict himself. In 1934, he wrote: 'The Chinese adopt an attitude of quiet familiarity . . . towards the sacred—hence the feeling of its immanence'. Elsewhere, 'Chinese life seems to be turned towards an ideal that is profane only. . . . In a world which is the result of the interaction of sacred forces, the Chinese live without any apparent religious preoccupations' (La religion des Chinois 1951) and elsewhere again, 'One may say that the daily life of a Chinese nobleman was entirely spent in religious exercises' (1956).

[4] V. R. Burckhardt.

Asia—this is a commonplace—is the birthplace of the great religions of the world and of many others that are not so widespread. In order to facilitate a study that must needs remain very summary, we shall group them into six large categories:

1. The religions with a more or less animist or pantheist foundation, traces of which may, of course, be found everywhere but which in many regions constitute the entire body of beliefs and are adopted as such by the whole population. We are now inclined to apply to them all the generic name of Shamanism which formerly was reserved for certain groups from Siberia and neighbouring areas.

2. The pre-Islamic religions of the Near East, including Christianity; to the latter we shall make only few references in later chapters because its main impact has been to create or widen a gulf of incomprehension between Asia and us.

3. Islam.

4. The pre-Buddhistic religions of the Middle and Far East, i.e. those that Buddhism found already in operation in the various countries where it penetrated; we have included Jainism in this group although it developed simultaneously with Buddhism.

5. Buddhism.

6. The various syncretic sects and movements.

In this and the next chapter, devoted to individual religions, we shall not touch upon their teaching nor upon details of their influence on the behaviour of their devotees, for we shall deal with it on the occasion of each specific problem. This teaching and these influences vary considerably, moreover, from one region to another. Very generally speaking:

In India and in Tibet religion is essentially metaphysical, deals with the afterlife more than with the present and indirectly results in a rigid social organization that leaves the individual perfectly free in his religious and spiritual strivings.

In Japan, the main object of that which plays the part of religion seems to be to build up the inner discipline of the individual, to strengthen his will-power and to provide him with a strong moral foundation.

In China and in Viet-Nam, religion above all aims at setting up a perfectly harmonious social organization and is inclined to ignore the individual whom it leaves to build up for himself his own individual harmony, within the framework supplied by society.

In the Semitic countries religion manifests itself mostly on the legal or quasi-legal plane through injunctions and prohibitions of all kinds, observance of which permeates the whole life of man.

In spite of such differences, religious influence is everywhere a decisive factor. Masson-Oursel very pointedly noted that the man of the East 'is above all *homo religiosus*'. The Dean of the Faculty of Medicine of Saigon declared quite recently: 'Religion is the most complete expression of human nature'.[5] It has been rightly said that Cambodia, in the era of universal suffrage as in that of the Bayon is still the identical religious people with the same thirst for spiritual life. The man who recently tried to achieve land reform in India, Acharya Vinoba, wrote that 'the concern for afterlife is a sign of maturity'. In order to have the radio accepted in Saudi Arabia, it was necessary to use the first broadcasts for verses from the Koran. The manufacturer of the best Japanese cameras has named the most perfect of them after a great deity of the Buddhistic pantheon. Arabs, Persians, Hindus and many another people of Asia still show a real passion for interminable discussion on theological subjects. We shall see later how religious pilgrimages cause vast population movements throughout Asia.

To take a more remote instance which is all the more striking because modern Hindus can see nothing strange in it, the all-powerful Emperor Akbar abandoned his magnificent capital of Fatepur Sikri very largely because a sage had complained to him that the bustle caused by the presence of the court disturbed his meditations.

Whatever we may think of it, this religious attitude towards life is not a matter of pure form made up mainly of rites and superstitions. Asians believe their religiousness to be much deeper than ours; they are inclined to think that we have only a 'second-hand' religion, the object of which is the intellectual acceptance of doctrinal orthodoxy, rather than spiritual experience. Anticlerical revolts, which are frequent throughout Asia, are aimed not at rejecting religion but at removing the decadent clergy that has become formalist or grabbing and stands in the way of genuine spiritual development.

What misleads us and disconcerts us somewhat is that in most Asian religious groups there is hardly any clergy or ecclesiastical hierarchy in the sense of the Roman Catholic Church. With rare exceptions, the priests who serve the temples and perform the cult do nothing but conduct it without having any authority over the devotees; they are neither directors of conscience nor even qualified to interpret the sacred texts—this latter task falls upon monks, scholars, lay people, etc., who act on a purely individual basis and whose opinion need not be taken as authoritative by anybody. In certain religions such as Hinduism, the priests are appointed and

[5] Phiem-Bien Tam at South-East Asia Round Table.

paid by the lay owners of the buildings used as temples and the latter are free to dismiss them or to replace them as they wish.

Islam considers itself to be a strictly 'democratic' religion without any ecclesiastical hierarchy—one may say almost without any clergy; and the Ulemas have little other than moral influence. (For the orthodox and more particularly for the Wahhabites, the granting of spiritual authority to the clergy would be tantamount to an anathema.) In China, the representative of the Jade Emperor on Earth, the one who, by a very far-fetched assimilation is called the Taoist Pope by westerners, has hardly any function, in his 'Mountains of Dragons and Tigers', other than to issue magicians' or exorcists' diplomas. Generally speaking, throughout China, the temple priest is only an intermediary imposed by custom, and, in theatrical performances, the part of the villain quite naturally falls to the Taoist or Buddhist priests—which does not mean to imply anti-clericalism any more than the comical part played by the sergeant-major on our stage implies anti-militarism. In Japan, priests were not held in very high esteem because they were government officials and in India they are held in some contempt because they have so degraded religion as to use it for earning their daily bread.

Since nobody has authority to define or interpret the essentials of dogma, the idea of a cut-and-dried *credo* is thoroughly alien to Asia. Where we are tempted to see doctrinal conflicts which would provoke religious wars for people like us, those concerned mostly see complementary concepts that throw light on each other.

A modern Hindu philosopher (Raghu Vira) has summed up this situation very well in the following terms: 'In Oriental religions, philosophy is in most cases an important element which has far more weight than dogmas and rites. In this sense, these religions have the same attitude as science. They set out to *discover* the ultimate reality of existence, not only of human beings, but of all existence, material or non-material.' It has to be pointed out, moreover, that four of the greatest Asian religions—Jainism, Buddhism, Taoism and Confucianism—do not in any way present themselves as *revealed* to man but as invented or discovered by man.

There are, however, quite a few notable exceptions. The Manichaean clergy formed a strict hierarchy and the Mazdaean clergy was as powerful as it was fanatical. Even within Buddhism there can be a hierarchy, when it is the State religion as in Tibet, Mongolia, Laos and Cambodia—where there are even two parallel hierarchies since two sects, independent of each other, have official recognition.

Out of all the great religions which flourish in Asia, only three—Buddhism, Christianity and Islam—seek to gain proselytes. The others—Judaism, Parseeism, Jainism, Hinduism, Shintoism, as well as their underlying cults, look upon the arrival of new converts with mistrust, and sometimes even close their doors to them altogether.

In their work of proselytism, the three great missionary religions, as we shall see, resort to methods that are very different. Buddhism strictly abstains from any intolerance or recourse to violence; it puts up quite happily with the simultaneous presence of other religions that have come before it and readily shares spiritual and moral influence with them; very often, it lends itself to a sort of syncretism which may go as far as merging with them. Islam and Christianity, on the contrary, refuse to share and systematically destroy, as far as they can, any religious practices or concepts other than their own; they readily resort to any amount of pressure or violence in order to make their own supremacy exclusive.

The silence of the authorities in matters of dogma has certainly contributed to an astonishing multiplication of sects, which is so much in keeping with the general aspiration of Asia, with its thirst for religion as well as its impatience with any constraint in the matter. The humorous statement that Asia produces religions just as an apple tree produces apples is not an over-statement. Around 1900, when Swami Vivekananda was asked what, in his opinion, should a religion be in order to become universal, he replied: 'The ideal is not to have the same religion accepted by all but that there should be as many religions as individuals.' All the large religious groups, from Christianity to Islam and from Hinduism to Buddhism have, in the course of their history, broken up into innumerable sects and sub-sects; this tendency is being even further accentuated in our days. Hence new religions, which either claim to be independent of all the previous ones or to unite two or more of them, spring up incessantly throughout Asia.[6]

It is not easy to form an idea of the way in which Asia imagines the Divine, for her conceptions can hardly fall within our usual categories.

Thus, while in the West, and more generally in Semitic religions, we are accustomed to seeing fierce opposition between monotheism, polytheism, pantheism and atheism, Asia beyond the Arab world sees in these various conceptions just so many partial and mutually complementary truths which correspond to the various planes of consciousness; they may not be taken to rank exactly alike, but all are believed to be authentic and equally valid in their respective spheres. The same believer may affirm successively without contradicting himself: 'There are millions of gods', 'There is

[6] See Chap. III.

only one God', 'God is in everything' and 'God is only a creation of my mind'. It may be said that the Asian is monotheistic in his philosophy, polytheistic in his worship, pantheistic in the details of everyday life and atheist in his effort to delve into himself spiritually.

Even materialism is not banished from the spiritual field. In India, the atheist *charvakas* were allowed to preach in Brahmin temples; Ramakrishna called the Western search for the most material power a cult of Shakti, the Divine Mother. Vivekananda was wont to say that in the modern West it is in the laboratories that saints can be found.[7] In Islam, Bedreddin Simavi, for whom life was nothing but a set of biological activities, nevertheless considered himself a good Muslim (although his opinion on this point was not shared by his most orthodox contemporaries, since he was executed in Mohamed I's reign). The devotees of Elohim of Sinai, who manifested himself to Moses, were neither monotheists nor polytheists but revered in their master 'the infinite multiplicity of the supra-natural, mainspring of all nature'[8] and, when in regard to the nomadic Hebrews, Masson-Oursel spoke of transcending 'the unicity as well as the multiplicity of the sacred', he was describing a phenomenon common to the bulk of Asia.

For the same reasons and under the same conditions, for the Asian devotee God is alternatingly and according to the practical needs of each phase and each aspect of his search, immanent, transcendant or within man, and as Ramakrishna said, 'still very much more than that'; for all that man can imagine or see, even in his most sublime ecstasies, does not exhaust all the possibilities of God.

Asia nevertheless brings out the concept of the divine at each of the levels that man's mind is capable of reaching. While each religious group, whether it is included in one of the present day world religions or not, emphasizes one particular level or one particular aspect for a particular purpose, it may nevertheless be affirmed that, in the immense majority of cases, this same group also admits the other levels and aspects without any hesitation or difficulty and does not deny the possibility that relationship with them can be effective and fruitful.

The most comprehensive table of this veritable 'scale' is given to us by Hinduism which progressively descends from the Absolute (*nirguna* Brahman) to the total personal God (Ishvara), to original duality (Purusha and Prakriti) or Trinity (the three Divine faces, Trimurti: Brahma, Shiva, Vishnu)—down to the quasi-innumerable

---

[7] This idea is already found in Ramakrishna.
[8] Masson-Oursel.

hierarchy of infra-divine and extra-terrestrial forces and entities such as spirits, ghosts, etc. This vast pyramid is further supplemented in at least four ways: first by admitting that capping the ultimate polarity formed by the Absolute on the one hand and the Multiple on the other (where 'personal' gods are found with whom we may have relations) there is still a supreme plane, that of Purashiva or Purushottama; secondly, by believing that the god is accompanied by his 'power of manifestation' or 'Shakti' which takes the form of the goddess; thirdly, by acknowledging the terrestrial incarnations, in human or other forms, of many gods; and finally by affirming that the human sage may rise even higher than the most sublime gods.

The Absolute, the original source of creation by his own self-multiplication, is evidently too remote from the human being and the world to be the object of worship or of figurative or symbolic representation. All that the Hindus can say of the Absolute Brahman is that 'he is not this, he is not that', *neti neti*. This Absolute may be found again, with variants, even in the Tao of the Taoists, which gives birth to the original duality of the *Yin* and the *Yang*.

Normally, on the first 'rung of the ladder' below this Absolute, as soon as one enters the potentialities of creation and multiplication, there appears a supreme personal God, distinct and distant from the Creation for which He is responsible; He is almost as difficult to pray to and to represent as the Absolute. He holds a preponderant place in the so-called monotheist religions of the Semitic group: Samaritanism, Judaism, Christianity, Islam, with their innumerable variants; but he may also be found in the official religion of pre-Muslim Persia, or in Nepal, where he is worshipped in the form of a flame, etc. Among the inhabitants of Nias and Borneo, it is clearly explained that, in order to reach the higher deities, it is necessary to go through the lower ones. Among the Shamans of Siberia, the supreme God, Tangara (in Southern Siberia) or Ai-Toion (in Northern Siberia), is above good as well as evil and expects neither prayer nor sacrifice. In Siberia also let us mention the Samoyeds, who believe in one eternal God named Num, of whom no image can be made, the Yakuts for whom the Lord of Lords, An-ya-Daidyn, is so far above them that they cannot make any offering to him, the Votiaks who honour him whom they consider as the one god, Yumar, and the Ostiaks; of the latter, we have an interesting account by Grigory Novitsky who, at the beginning of the eighteenth century, accompanied the orthodox metropolitan Philophey on a visit to these people. He tells us that they, like the Voguls and other tribes, worshipped under the name of Tornim a God of whom they had no image and to whom they had never offered sacrifice, so that when they were converted to Christianity it was not even necessary to change the name of the God; it was enough to make them forget or ignore the other lower anthropomorphic deities and to shift these latter to the demonology of the new faith. We have seen that in Hinduism, this part is played by Ishvara; all the Dravidians, whatever their type of worship, recognize a Supreme Being, omnipresent, spiritual, personal—Kadavul—that is, He-who-is, to whom there is neither temple nor worship; among the Kols, the supreme God, Bhagavan, 'is of no practical interest'.[9] This concept is much less obvious among the Chinese and the Japanese, although in China, for example, Yu Ch'ing was born 'before all beginnings'; his substance is imperishable; it is formed essentially of uncreated air, invisible and without perceptible limits. Originally he stood even higher than the great Taoist Triad.[10]

On the basis of this fundamental monotheism and often holding an infinitely greater place in religious practice, Asia, with very rare exceptions, knows an immense multitude of distinct entities and extra-human forces which are as many 'gods'.

According to the scriptures, the Hindu pantheon has 300 millions, although the most detailed texts have never even remotely tried to give a complete list of them and not even a list of the general categories in which they fall. The Bon Tibetan pantheon, in addition to the twenty top-ranking gods and goddesses, claims seventy thousand second-rank deities.

According to certain Taoist texts, there may be up to thirty-six thousand (i.e. a hundred times three hundred and sixty which is a sacred number) gods within the body, but since it is up to each man to discover for himself the number and hierarchy, the rank and name of these gods, it is not surprising that we cannot find a complete, nominative register. The Chinese, who are endowed with great curiosity for what is intellectually new, naturally feel that there can never be too many gods or practical rites. In order to widen the possibilities even further, not only do they establish

---

[9] W. G. Griffiths, *The Kol Tribe of Central India*, 1946, p. 129. The case of Brahma to whom India, so tremendously rich in temples, has only devoted two or three sanctuaries in all, is very different; if he does not receive more homage, it is rather because, in creating the world, he really played us a nasty trick and because the object of man must be to extricate himself from this sort of original curse. In French East Africa, in most cases, the supreme deity is conceived as a very schematic personality without any part in practical liturgy. The worshipper only rarely makes direct offerings to him. Besides, the creator of the earth with whom he is often identified generally evinces no interest in the functioning of the earth after creation has been completed. (Holas in *Guide AOF*.)

[10] Marcel Granet.

a kind of judicious rotation in their pantheon, but they grant only a local and temporary value to most of the gods.

The Japanese pantheon is perhaps even more complicated. Not only does it comprise, according to the texts, eighty or eight hundred 'myriads' of gods—*yaoyorozu no kami*[11]—each of whom may have several different names, but these gods are divided into categories that cut across each other: national and local gods, the latter being subdivided into family-gods or *ketsuen-shin*, greater family-gods, *dozoku-shin*, village-gods, *chien-shin*, gods that are at the same time family and local gods, *uji-gami*, *chinju-no-kami*, and *ubusunano-kami*. Quite different from these, we have nature gods, gods who mould and beget things and men, country gods, ancestors of the Imperial House and of the whole Japanese people. Again we have earthly and celestial divinities to which are connected, nobody knows how, 'wild' divinities. These deities are sometimes transformed into each other,[12] even if this should imply a change of sex;[13] what is more, they may divide themselves into their two distinct activities, *ara-mitama* and *nigi-mitama*, so that one of the two can go to one place while the other goes elsewhere. To this is sometimes added a third separate activity, that of *saki-mitama* and these two or three aspects as a whole form a fourth, also separable aspect, the *zentai-no-mitama*, the spirit of the entire body. Furthermore, a divinity may, by scissiparity, produce *waki-mitama* or separate spirits which thenceforth have their own existence. According to Hirata, divinity may be compared to a fire that can be communicated to several lamps without the original flame undergoing any change.

For the Avesta, the number of gods is quite simply 'incalculable'.

Even this, however, is not sufficient to quench the thirst for gods felt by the people of Asia. Below these countless gods, they further place a multitude of spirits and jinns of all kinds that have relations with human beings. Some belong to a race quite apart from ours, others have souls which, more or less recently, have inhabited human bodies and will possibly take that form again. It is impossible to classify them as we do in Christianity and similar religions into good and bad, divine or demoniacal entities. The Hindu sacred scriptures even explain that at the beginning, Prajapati, the

---

[11] According to the modern theologian Hirata, the number has considerably increased since the time when the holy scriptures were composed and now there are apparently a thousand five hundred myriads of them.

[12] Thus Yama-no-kami, in spring, comes down from the mountains to the fields and becomes Ta-no-kami, the rice-field divinity. (J. Mock, *Quaint Customs and Manners of Japan*, 1951-5, iv, p. 48.)

[13] Her Augustness the Heavenly Alarming Female, becomes the Male Deity, the Prince of Saruta. (*Kojiki*, XXXV.)

father of the gods, was unable to distinguish between *devas* and *asuras*, those we call gods and demons.[14] Although various groups of them are well disposed towards us and others tend to be harmful, it is rare for them not to do good to men sometimes and evil at others according to circumstances, just like the physical forces which have been more or less identified by Western modern science.

To quote only a few examples of these ambivalent beings: among the Laotian *p'i*, there are extra-terrestrial ones which are not necessarily wicked and others, proceeding from human beings who have died a violent death, which are active and evil-doing; but the good and the bad live together. In Cambodia, the *néak-ta*, territorial spirits that are clearly graded in a hierarchy, are normally the spirits of ancestors, but some of them are born as a result of the fulfilment of wishes addressed to a particular big tree.[15] The *bhutas* of Southern Canara, whose chief is Brahmeru, are a mixture of demons and ancestors. For the Veddas of Ceylon, the *yakas* include dead human beings as well as beings who have nothing in common with men. Among the Buryat Lamas, certain *tengris* live without a body and others in the body. Among the Tunguz, the only essential distinction between the good and the evil spirits lies in that the former live in the south and the west, the latter in the east and the south (sic). The Taoist pantheon itself, apart from its many gods, is full of jinns and spirits and the Chinese Buddhists count their dragons in number equal to the fish of the great deep. Finally, for all the monotheism they proclaim, the Muslims acknowledge the existence of countless demons and the Koran itself recognizes the existence of the *jinns*. Almost nowhere is it possible to draw the line between gods, jinns, spirits and demons.

It would not be possible to deal, even briefly, with the concept of God in Asia, apart from the Iranian and Semitic creeds, without mentioning the 'Divine Mother'. She is often placed well above the gods, is sometimes their mother, like Aditi in Hinduism, in some cases is identified with the Absolute, or even is the Absolute. In China, we have the Mother of Non-Birth in the Kuei-i Tao and the Ikuan Tao. Thus in the most secret cults of Benares, the monks who have reached the highest ecstasy, *the nirvikalpa-samadhi*, in the most exacting disciplines of non-dualism are the only ones allowed to worship the supreme Mother, *Rajarajeshvari*. In the Far-East, the goddess Kwannon or Kwan-yin has, to a great extent, supplanted Buddha himself in the hearts and minds of Buddhists.

[14] Taittiriya Brahmana. The same in Japan.
[15] The names or images of many of the most powerful seem to prove, according to S. Bernard Thierry, that they are old Brahmanic deities.

Lao Tse gave the name of the Universal Foster Mother to the 'Principle', and in Taoism Siwang-mon has become the most popular personality in the pantheon. According to V. R. Burckhardt, the Jade Lady had been invented under the Sungs in order to compete with Kwannon. Nearly all the Chinese syncretic sects have a Goddess-Mother as their supreme divinity. Even where she is not elevated to such heights, the Divine Mother exercises such powerful action of such a scope that in one and the same religion she receives a series of names, each of which corresponds to the different aspects under which she manifests herself. A great temple in Kyoto, the Sanjusangendo, displays a thousand identical statues of the supreme Kwannon, each holding an eye in her hand; they are the Senju Kannon, Saharabhuja-Saharanetra-Avalokiteshvara. There are nine Divine Mothers in Hinduism, twenty-one Salvation Mothers in Tibet. Apart from these very high deities, in almost all the Asian pantheons we find a multitude of goddesses. Most of the ancient Shintoist temples are devoted to female deities and in those that are devoted to male gods, goddesses are also worshipped. The explanation generally given—viz., that man born of woman sees in the female entity the primary origin of all that is—certainly carries great weight. But, on the plane of practical piety, it must not be forgotten either that man entrusts himself more readily to maternal tenderness than to paternal severity, even when he turns to God.

Under the pressure exerted by Christian missionaries, supported in turn by the Jews and the Muslims, we have untiringly made fun of the trans-Islamic Orientals who, in their ignorant and primitive 'idolatry', represent and worship God in human or animal forms—forgetting perhaps too easily the works of our greatest Christian artists who, in churches and museums, show us God the Father in the form of a hoary, old man, the Holy Ghost in the form of a dove, the angels and archangels with highly anthropomorphic faces.

It cannot be denied that Asia overflows with anthropomorphic, theriomorphic or monstrous images, painted or carved, smiling, grimacing or menacing, before which the faithful prostrate themselves, pray or meditate.[16] Their variety defies the imagination and a description would fill a whole library.

The gods represented with normal, human bodies, like the Japanese *sennin*, are in a small minority. But countless are those with human bodies 'improved' by the addition of supplementary organs, like our winged angels. Some have a larger number of arms (Vishnu, Tibetan deities, etc.), or eyes (most of the Hindu gods and their Buddhist counterparts have the third eye in the middle

[16] 'Idolatry is an evil, but not the worship of idols' (Gandhi).

of the forehead), or legs (in India, Agni has three), or heads
(especially in Cambodia, but also Ravana and Karttikkeya in India),
or mouths (among the Kol, Chandika has one mouth in front and
one behind). Others have deformed organs: the Chinese *kuei* have
their eyes on top of the head, the Afghan *jinns* have them as vertical slits throwing out flames, the Churel of the Kol people has
turned-up feet, the Japanese Yamba-Omba has its mouth on top of
the head. Others have one part of the body replaced by the corresponding organ of an animal like Ganesha with his elephant head.
Others again are mutilated like Rahu, who is only a head; and
various others have no legs like Aruna, the Suns's coachman, in
India, but also Ortik, Yelan, Long and Meik among the Ostiaks.

Some gods simply have an animal's body, like Hanuman and
often Garuda in India, and many others are deified animals which
have kept their original form like the Iranian gypaetus or *houma*,
the Inari fox in Japan. Certain animals, as a result of being devoted
to various gods, participate in their divine character and in the end
are worshipped for themselves, sometimes in temples devoted exclusively to them; e.g. in India, Shiva's bull, Yama's buffalo,
Ganesha's mouse, Karttikkeya's peacock; in Japan, Kompira's
tortoise, the doe of the great divinity of Kasuga, Daikoku's rat,
the tai fish of Ebisu, the white snake of Kenten and Bishamon's
centipede; among the Kolymyans, the brown bear incarnating Ulu-
Tayon.

Some of these animals are themselves 'improved' like the
elephant Airavata with his five heads, and the horse Uraishchravas
with seven in India, and the winged horse among the Muslims, etc.
Very many deities are represented by monstrous images that can
hardly be compared to a human or animal body. To cite only a
few examples taken from Afghanistan: the Madar-i-Al (that are to
be found also in Iran) are female monsters who can in turn rise up
to the height of an oak-tree or shrink to that of a frog; their eyes
are vertical, they have upright quills instead of hair and fleshless
breasts; they sometimes attack men and sometimes knock them
down, but they may be overcome; one of their hairs or a charm
they wear on the arm may be wrung from them and this brings all
prosperity to the possessor. The sanguinary *dehos* are monsters of
a fearful size, with tails and horns, a mixture of ogre and satyr,
that devour human beings and carry off the fairies whom they
make their concubines. The *ghouls* are female demons that are
capable of metamorphosis and feed on human flesh and blood, like
the *rakshasis* of Hinduism. Another example of fanciful representation taken this time from India: in their invocations to the Goddess
Pallyamma, the Velan describe her in the following terms, 'Oh

thou, Pallyamma, Mother with knife-like teeth, who in thy de-moniacal form appearest on the cremation ground known as Omkara, surrounded by flaming logs, with one of thy breasts thrown over thy shoulder, the other with which thou playest as with a ball, with thy hanging tongue which goes round thy head, with beans and pepper in thy left hand and seeds in thy right . . .'

If enlightened devotees are questioned about such odd peculiar-ities, it is almost always found that every detail of the icono-graphy has a symbolic significance which is of philosophical, ritual and often even magical value.

While the Asians have gone further than us in the wild luxuri-ance of their imagery, they have also been more exacting than us in their choice of simple symbols and abstractions. An instance is the purifying flame in which the Parsis and others see the 'least imperfect possible' representation of the Supreme. Another is the round stone, the Hindu *salagrama*, chosen because it has no peculiar features or distinctive attributes. The mirror—one of the summits of religious abstraction—is venerated above all else in Japan, among the Buryat lamas and elsewhere. It is also worth noting that in China the sky, god of oaths and treaties, is the only one to be given human features.

But there are also the 'empty temples' sung by Sarojini Naidu, like that of Shidambaram in India, the earliest Buddhist temples, Jewish synagogues and Muslim mosques, the temples of Kota, the Mon-golian onbones and many others, where nothing comes between the worshipper and his own visualization of the god with whom he is in communion. In Japan there are various temples, such as the Miye Jinja, a *sessha* near the Mishima Jinja, where the deity to whom the temple is dedicated is not specified, and even when this is done, one may ignore it; thus, in verses that are still famous, the Shintoist priest Saigyo, in the twelfth century, before the altars of Ise, the greatest and most important of the country, cried out: 'Who lives here? I do not know and yet I shed tears of gratitude.' And in any case, why should there be any representation at all, since a god can take any form at any time, as the Nambutiri of South India insistently declare.

However, in the case of an 'idol', whatever the raw material used, what gives it its ritual value and its miraculous power, if any, is what has been put into it psychically, either by the wor-shipper himself or else in the course of a ceremony such as 'anima-tion' in India, 'eye opening' also in India (*netra mangalya*), in Japan or in China, written prayers or relics in Lamaism, etc.

This para-divine character may also invade the image without any particular ceremony, just by the spontaneous will of the god who comes to inhabit it. Japanese dolls, which were originally not toys but either symbols of God, *kami*, or man, or else charms, are even now said to acquire a soul and even psychic powers when they have been sufficiently loved by several generations of children —and this makes the Muslim fear that children's dolls might turn into idols seem less naïve.

To complete the picture, it must be added that violently icono-clastic sects have appeared at different times in almost all the regions of Asia, and not only in those practising Semitic religions.

Whether the Asian produces painted or sculptured images of the divine or whether he visualizes It only in his thought, we know that he is ceaselessly and intensely preoccupied with It. This leads in particular to three consequences:

In the first place, the relation between man and the gods is so intimate that it is no longer possible to draw a hard and fast dividing line between them. We shall return to this point when we study the concept of space.

In the second place, the spiritual seeker can take fusion or assimilation with the divine as a practical goal that is quite attain-able and not just mere fancy. It is remarkable that in the greatest theistic religions of Asia and doubtless also in some of those to which we do not attach so much importance the greatest mystics an-nounce that they did, in fact, achieve such an assimilation or even identification with the divine, the absolute or the supreme. The great sufi Al Hallaj used to cry *an al-haqq*, 'I am the Truth'. The Skanda Purana of the Hindus writes: 'I am Thou and Thou art I'. The Adi-Granth, the sacred book of the Sikhs, proclaims 'Thou art myself and I am Thee' which is also a common theme among the Persian mystics. The Hindus repeat *Aham Brahmasmi*, 'I am the absolute Brahman' or *Shivo'ham*, 'I am Shiva'. The famous Japanese *myokonin*, our contemporary Saichi who died a quarter of a cen-tury ago (1849-1933), used to affirm, 'Amida (Amitabha) is Saichi and Saichi is Amida'.

Finally, the Asian feels towards God a familiarity which is some-times reflected in attitudes and actions that we might be tempted to deem blasphemous. In Hindu as well as Japanese temples and in many others, the 'idol' (*ishta* in India, *shinzo* in Japan) is offered not only prayers, music, singing, dancing, incense, but also food, clothing and even the daily bath. The Japanese and Chinese 'in-form' the gods of all the important events concerning them even before telling other human beings—and when a Japanese calls the Buddhist God Amida or some Shinto god 'Parent' or 'Oya', he really treats him as his father or mother. It is said that Shomatsu, a shin Buddhist of the last century, was lying down comfortably in a

temple of Amida; as someone expressed surprise at this, he retorted :
'As for me, I am in my parent's house; doubtless you are only a
stepson?'

This attitude is the source of a great joy that pervades the relations of man with his God. In India, a stern face is not considered
a sign of religiousness but, on the contrary, a proof that the person
bearing it 'knows not God'—and is therefore in no way qualified
to speak about Him, even less to impose on others his concept of
Him. From Thailand to Hong Kong, and in many other parts of
Asia, the faithful have no scruples in having gay picnics in the
most sacred temples. In Japan, where the joyful appearance of the
people's faith had so struck Lafcadio Hearn, the Tenri-kyo calls
the divine service 'the gay service', *yoki-zutome*.

But this closeness that amounts almost to a family tie also per-
mits the worshipper to revolt against his 'parent' when the latter
denies him his favours, just as a child would revolt against its
human parent. In India, the Valan insult the goddess Bhagavati and
the Kols threaten the goddess Kali if they do not receive the protection required of them; in the event of prolonged drought, the
Malayali bury a statue of Ganesha in a cess-pit and take it out only
after the rain has come; Vivekananda himself recounts that one
day he had threatened the Divine Mother to turn Muslim if she
did not accede to his prayer. Among the Tunguz, when the event
does not live up to the expectations of the idol's owner, he throws
it down several times, leaves it lying for a long time without
honours, sometimes he even drowns it.

In China, where the Emperor had full powers to grant gods promotion or retrogression, not only could one curse the god who had
not acceded to his worshipper's wishes, but one could also, at a
time of great drought, expose his image to the sun in order to
make him feel the torrid heat; and the magistrate could condemn
him and fine him, and his statue could even be broken. The Taoists
resort to similar sanctions. If their prayers are unsuccessful, the individual Taoists themselves, without having recourse to the
authorities, stop offering gold or perfumes to the gods, and throw
a dead pig or woman's shoes at them. In Japan, the Emperor, while
he could confer rank, *shinkai*, on the Shinto gods, could also punish
them : in the first century of our era, the Emperor Sujin asked for
severe sanctions to be taken against the gods of heaven and earth.
In Vietnam, some gods and spirits are officials, and as such, may be
subject to promotion or retrogression by the earthly sovereign or
his qualified representatives having authority over them.

One can understand that, under such conditions, most religious

groups in Asia often combine extremely complex and infinitely
subtle theologies with very simple practices; the latter, most often,
tend simply to foster a real obsession with the divine. We shall
examine some of these practices.

The most striking one is meditation, which has been made a real
science by the Hindus and Buddhists. They use a great variety of
methods, each of which comprises successive carefully described
stages, but all the other groups also resort to meditation with great
conviction.

The technique by which one rises from unconsciousness to consciousness of self and knowledge of God, to 'this state of immobile reason where one is no longer moved by anything', is sometimes very arduous. The adepts of Zen Buddhism, for instance,
must twice a year remain seven days and seven nights consecutively seated in meditation without lying down or dosing—and
cases are not rare in which this terrible experience makes some of
them lose their reason or even their lives.

We shall see later the use that is made in the classical Orient of
these methods of concentration, not only for introspection[17] but
also for scientific as well as artistic research and study. Let us
simply say here that this 'dream-like mortification' has contributed
to sharpening the intellect of Asian people in all spheres.

We should not a priori regard with contempt the accessories to
meditation which we are tempted to consider as childish and fanciful: mastery of the positions and movements of the body (Hindu
hatha-yoga with its asanas, dance of the Chinese old men so ad-
mirably illustrated in the film 'The Wall of China', gymnastics of
prostration which among the Muslims precedes silent meditation
and supplication and gives the latter greater efficiency, dancing
sects, etc.), breathing discipline among the Hindus and the Taoists,
material objects (incense among the Hindus and Buddhists, the
kusha mats of the Hindus and prayer carpet among the Mohammedans).[18]

But what plays the most important part in meditation is, in
general, the visual aid, i.e. the image or symbol of God which we
have already mentioned, and the audible aid, i.e. the more or less
complex composition of sounds, words and phrases forming a
sacred entity—what the Hindus call a mantra. We shall return to
the power of words, of the Word, of the mantra. Let it suffice here

[17] 'It is not in flowing water that (men can see themselves) but in stationary
water; this alone, standing still, can stop those who stop at it (to see themselves)', Tchoang Tse.
[18] Raymond Charles has said correctly, 'The carpet is a means of approaching the Absolute; it is that which is used by the believer in order to separate
himself from things at the time of prayer.'

to quote the words of an authority on Tibetan Buddhism, for it is there that the most complete science of the *mantra* has been elaborated. The *mantra*, we are told, has the 'capacity of applying not on one, but on all the planes of reality and opening a new avenue into each of them until, having many a time gone through these different degrees of experience, we are able to grasp the full body of mantric experience'. The same author adds what goes without saying: 'The purely historical or philological evaluation of a mantra is, in fact, a superficial and absurd process.'

This enables us better to appreciate the practice, so widespread in India, of repeating the *mantra* as many times as possible, or, what amounts to the same, one of the names of God. The greatest sages throughout Asia are almost unanimous in ascribing extraordinary efficacy to this process which seems to us somewhat childish. It is doubtless the Hindus who have evolved the most detailed technique in this sphere, if we are to judge from what has already been published. In India, among the sages who, in the opinion of their peers, have reached the highest spiritual level, not a negligible number have used no other method than this *japa*. Swami Ramdas is the best-known exponent of this method, but Ramakrishna himself strongly affirmed its supreme value. The Hindus, however, hold no monopoly. The same technique is to be found among the Buddhists with the *nembutsu* (Namo Amida Butsu—I prostrate myself before Amitabha Buddha) or the *shomyo* (sho—repetition, myo—name) of the Japanese; also in China among the worshippers of Ti Tsang Pusa, among the Mohammedans with the *dhikr* and in most of the other groups.

Of course, it is difficult for us to go any further and to admit that any 'repetition value' may be attached to the *mantra* offered mechanically by means of a gadget such as the prayer wheel used in Tibet, among the *tendai* and *shingon* sects in Japan (in Japan, it is known as *gosho-guruma*) and elsewhere. But we have to place on record what the actual users say about it and it is difficult to prove them wrong.

The Asian religions make considerable use of temples and altars. Throughout Islam, there is hardly a hamlet without its mosque. The town of Seiyum, in the Hadramaut, has fifty mosques for one thousand five hundred houses. In India there is a real mushrooming of altars, so much so that one town is said to have a million temples. In China it is relatively rare for a village, however small, to be without its pagoda and not to have several places of worship. In Japan, there are, on an average, twenty shinto altars or temples —*jinja*—per village. In Bangkok, pagodas, monasteries and their gardens apparently occupy a fifth of the town's total area. In Viet-nam as in Thailand, small altars or pagodas—*cai trang*—are erected in the courtyard of each house. And a veritable devotion is shown towards all the temples; it is not rare in many Asian countries to see men devote all their fortune to them and remain content with a mere pittance given back to them as alms. However, with a few exceptions, notably in the non-Semitic religions, temples are places where one goes to 'see' the image of the divine, make offerings to Him and seek His blessing and above all to perform rites, to give oneself up to meditation; collective worship of the kind familiar to us in Christianity is often completely absent; and when it does exist, it would occur to nobody to feel an obligation to take part in it.

There are also cases—very exceptional, it is true—where no recourse whatsoever is had to shrines. Thus, the Achemenides had no temples, nor the *bon* deities of Tibet, no more than certain Japanese gods such as Sujin-Sama or Mizu-ha-no-me-no-mikoto, well-gods. The same is true of regions where temples enjoy a somewhat doubtful reputation; thus, in China, Buddhist and Taoist temples are said to be haunted by evil spirits, and if a marriage procession passes in front of them, their gate is hidden from view by a screen.

On the contrary, a visit to a temple, especially at the time of its own particular festival, normally confers blessings on the visitor. That is why pilgrimages play such an important role throughout Asia.

We know the prestige that has always been attached in Islam to devotees who have succeeded in fulfilling the veritable obligation of a pilgrimage to Mecca (the *hajjis*). Even more holy are the *shahud*, those who have perished during this journey which, formerly, used to be long, dangerous and exhausting. Those who cannot perform it derive consolation from visiting, on certain special days, the tombs of great saints, honoured throughout Islam, or of local saints revered by a particular group.

From the remotest times, the roads of India have been trodden by countless troops of men and women who, while chanting hymns, walk interminable distances and climb to most difficult and dangerous places for the sole purpose of seeing holy men or of reaching the temples in various parts of the country. Some long pilgrimages such as that of Panch-Kroshi in Benares, have to be performed 'flat on one's stomach', i.e. prostrating oneself completely on the ground after each step or after every third step, or every time one has covered a distance equal to one's height. Some journeys take much longer. The Jains climb and circumambulate the sacred mountain of Politana or some temple town for seven, ten, twelve or even hundred days consecutively, subsisting exclusively on water. The great Ganges pilgrimage, the Ganga-pradakshina, takes six years.

Only a few years ago the Mongol or Tibetan pilgrims took five years to perform the Wu T'ai pilgrimage, and many of them devoted years to journeys of the same type, where they threw themselves to the ground at every third step. Immense convoys of pilgrims from Chinese and Russian territories crossed the cold Tibetan deserts in order to visit Lhassa and thus acquire the enviable title of *djo*. The Buryats cover enormous distances in order to prostrate themselves before a living Buddha at Ugra or elsewhere.

Pilgrimages are one of the great activities of Chinese Buddhism. In traditional China, not to have made a pilgrimage was considered such a calamity that probably a majority of Chinese belonged to a Mutual Loan Society the sole purpose of which was to facilitate such an enterprise. There were two kinds of such societies: *hing-shan-hui*, to enable members to undertake the actual journey, and *tso-shan-hui*, to enable them to perform the rites which could replace the journey for those who could not hope for anything better. Even recently, old Chinese women with bound feet could be seen scaling holy mountains, ten thousand feet high, on their hands and knees.

Buddhists in general gladly devote a good part of their time and fortune to visiting places that the Buddha has sanctified by his presence, places where his relics are kept, or the mausolea of great Buddhist saints.

In Japan, the poorest peasant, even if he is too poor to eat the rice he has grown himself, can always afford the luxury of a pilgrimage lasting a month or more. While the Shin sect imposes on its adepts a tour of twenty-four temples, the *Jodo* sect requires twenty-five and the worshipper of Kwannon must visit thirty-three. The Shikoku pilgrimage, however, comprises eighty-eight temples over a distance of 1,200 kilometres requiring forty to fifty days. As for the enormous Sengaji, the thousand-temple pilgrimage of the Nichiren sect, it is started in youth and ends only at a ripe age; but there are still many people in Matsue and elsewhere who have accomplished it in full. In Shintoism even the gods go on pilgrimages; nineteen thousand of them spend the month of October at Izumo.

In some cases pilgrims leave visible traces of their passage in order to prolong the contact thus established. At Bhubaneshvar in Orissa everyone builds a little 'temple' by piling up a few stones in the form of a pyramid; in Japan the Shintoists give an account of their visit on a small board or a sheet of paper, *ofuda*, which they place in the temple.

Of course, all these pilgrimages, whatever be the undeniable devotion with which they are accomplished—and the sacrifices
accepted are a conclusive evidence of it—are somewhat in the
nature of rites. But this term and all that it implies does not have
the same somewhat derogatory flavour easily ascribed to it in the
West. To mention only a few instances, a very clear-sighted
observer of Islam has described the Muslim prayers thus: 'repeated several times a day with the subtle alternating of prostration and contemplation, they project the worshipper outside his
physical continuum beyond space and duration'. One of the
greatest saints of modern Hinduism, Ramakrishna, used to say:
'Rites and ceremonies . . . are the husk which contains the grain
of truth. Consequently, every man must go through rites and ceremonies before he can reach the central truth contained therein. . . .
Let each one accomplish with faith the rites of his own creed.' In
China, it is considered that a system of rites is necessary and that
any rite can be profitable, and one of the five great Imperial
Ministers was the Minister for Rites. In Japanese Shintoism, it is
acknowledged that there is a great principle of unity between
ritual, on the one hand, politics and government on the other.

These examples will doubtless suffice to make clear that the
whole of Asia attaches considerable value to rites; their study and
practice is the substance of an actual science wherein, on the basis
of methodical experiments performed for thousands of years, it has
been possible, according to those who practise them, to discover
laws and to lay down practical rules. The concern for accuracy
and precision is just as keen as in Roman law and any mistake can
be equally grave in its consequences. The Shintoist pantheon even
has two gods, Kamu-naho-bi-no-mikoto and Oho-naho-bi-no
mikoto, who are especially responsible for correcting errors made
in incantations before these reach their destination. In later
chapters we shall consider quite a number of widely different
spheres of activity where Asians often resort to rites. Let us, in
conclusion, mention a very relevant observation made by a great
Western specialist in Oriental religions: he points out that while
worship enables one to *request* a higher entity to intervene in a
certain way, rites, by their magic power, *compel* that same entity
to submit to the worshipper's will.

Another discipline, which is credited with great virtue and very
special power by most of the non-Semitic Asian religions, is that of
chastity, more or less associated with asceticism and often placed
within the context of monastic life. Hinduism, Buddhism, Jainism
and Lamaism encourage their adepts to become monks, and many
are those who see in this kind of life the only way to final liberation.

Therefore, the monastic population is impressively large. The Hindu *sadhus* number millions and the present government of India, more concerned with raising the material standard of life than with maintaining the spiritual standard, is deeply concerned by the economic handicap imposed on the country by this huge number of non-productive people; only recently there were still towns such as Uttar-Kashi where monks made up considerably more than half the population. In Outer Mongolia, where four out of ten men were lamas, the number of these lamas was on the rise even recently: it went up from 87,000 in 1925 to 94,000 in 1928; in 1820, according to Erman, any family with more than three sons had to dedicate at least one to priesthood. At the same period, among the Buryats, one-sixth of the population that had embraced Buddhism had taken holy orders and there were over ten thousand lamas in 1910. Tibet, out of some four million inhabitants, has over three hundred thousand monks and thousands of nuns; some very reliable authors put the figure even higher and think that these monks and nuns represent a sixth of the population. In Turkestan, at Horbuksen, even recently there were eight hundred lamas out of a total of two thousand men. At present, in the town of Bangkok alone, there are four hundred Buddhist monasteries.

This insistence on chastity is often explained, in India, for instance, by a theory according to which the energy, *ojas*, spent on the sexual plane is exactly the same that can be used, if suitably channelled, on the spiritual plane. Similar preoccupations obviously go to explain the custom of reserving certain religious and ritual functions for young virgins; thus, in Japan, it is young boys and girls in a state of chastity, the *mono-imi*, who serve the temple of the Goddess at Ise, and in the rice ceremony it is a virgin, Saka-tu-ko, who plays the most important part in the distilling of the black and white wine. Among the Baydaru, little temples are erected for the men who died without being married and who thereby became *virika* or heros. Similarly, the Medara have a ceremony for boys, *vurullu*, and for girls, *bala perantalu*, who died in a state of virginity; and the Nayar venerate girls who die before being betrothed.

Austerity and self-mortification of all kinds, going sometimes to incredible extremes, are frequently practised. In India, to this day, there are still men and even women who force themselves to remain standing all the time, while others keep an arm up until it is paralysed and withered, others who remain still, surrounded by burning fires under a burning sun,[19] and so forth. These ascetics are regarded with boundless respect and an admiration often tinged

[19] This is the famous *panchagni tapas*.

with envy. In many groups, the most flattering compliment is to
say that somebody is 'rich in austerities'.

Monasticism, however, is not necessarily adopted for a whole
life-time. It may be only a preparation for adult life. In traditional
India, before he was allowed to found a family, the young man
had to spend a number of years in a state known as *brahmacharya*,
which is very similar to that of a novice in a Christian monastic
order. In Burma nobody really becomes adult unless he has worn
the saffron robe, even if it is only for a few days; and village people
are not quite sure whether an Englishman who has not undergone
such a training is really a man. The same is true for Thailand
where a man becomes 'ripe', *khon-suk*, only after three years of
monastic life; until then he is 'green', *khon-dip*. The same, more or
less, holds good for Laos, Cambodia, etc. Inversely, the custom of
embracing monastic life only after a certain age is very widespread
in many countries. It is the normal sequence for Hindus after they
have married off their children: they successively become *vana-
prastha* and *sannyasin*, which are two different stages of ascetic
life. Even recently, it was frequent in Japan to see the head of a
family, at the age of forty, renounce all his prerogatives, all work
as well as all income in order to become *inkyo*. In China and Japan
it was not rare even for emperors to abandon the throne in order
to take Buddhist orders.

Even when one becomes a monk with the intention of remain-
ing so till the end of one's life, it is always permissible to change
one's mind. The Hindu *sadhu* may always return to normal life;
and he derives a certain prestige from his former way of life. In
Burma and Thailand one may leave the orders up to three times.
In China, however, renouncing even once is shameful.

As a matter of fact, in China, while Buddhism is still monastic-
ally inclined, Taoism is less amenable to it and Confucianism is
clearly hostile to it, which means that monks there do not enjoy
as much consideration as in the countries of Central and Southern
Asia. The duties towards the ancestors, the obligation to secure
continued progeny, are for them so mandatory that to neglect
them is an extremely serious fault for which no amount of
asceticism can make up. We find similar circumstances in India, but
we shall deal with this problem when we speak of the family
group.

It is in Islam, however, that we see the most violent opposition
to chastity in general, and to monasticism in particular. Mohammed did not allow any of his companions to take vows of celibacy:
'Every time you indulge in the carnal act, you actually give alms'.
And in olden days, those who prided themselves to be misogynists

risked torture for such blasphemy. We find only few Moslem sects among which asceticism has a truly spiritual purpose. On the other hand, abstinence from sexual relations is generally a compulsory accessory to the religious period of fasting. The Parsis do not recognize vows of chastity or poverty either. It has to be noted further that Buddhist monastic orders for women have now disappeared from all the countries following Theravada, the Southern school.

CHAPTER III

Religions

'In my Father's house are many mansions.'
ST JOHN, XIV, 2

SHAMANISM

BY shamanism we mean here religions that have long been called primitive, whether they have remained unchallenged in areas which have not been penetrated by the 'great religions' which we shall review in the following sections, or they have been more or less completely supplanted by the latter.

They are generally characterized by a close communion with the forces and laws of nature which are often personified and with which man tries to attain harmony in order to enjoy their beneficial influence and to escape the dangers to which any conflict with them would expose him. In the communities following these religions, some individuals, men or women, whom we generally designate by the name of 'shamans', are subject all their life to extremely severe disciplines through which they obtain certain charisms and are able to go into states of ecstasy where they have direct contact with the entities representing these natural laws and forces; thus, to a certain extent, they are capable of foreseeing their action, which gives them the power of sooth-saying, and also to channel it, which makes them doctors and magicians. Various travellers and explorers have left us detailed descriptions of shamanist ceremonies which they have been privileged to attend.

The shamanistic peoples generally believe in a partial and temporary survival of the human being after death; during this period the deceased continues to experience needs and feelings similar to those in his lifetime; he can communicate with the living and exercise direct action on them. This is the essential feature of what is known as animism—and, naturally, ancestor worship plays an important part.

Because of a deep-rooted belief in the continuity of life, the shamanistic peoples hardly draw the line between the living and

53

the inanimate, between men and animals (a fact which engenders totemism), between man, the gods, the demons and the spirits, between matter and mind, between heaven and earth. On the other hand, the practical nature of the relationship to their environment makes the kind of abstract generalization to which we are accustomed useless for them. This is reflected in their vocabulary. The Norwegian Orientalist Swen Konow has cited two typical cases in Burma : that of the Lushei language, which has nine different terms to describe as many different species of ants and twenty to indicate as many types of baskets, but does not possess a single word meaning 'ant' or 'basket' in general; that of the Tadho language which can say 'my father' or 'your father' but cannot say simply 'father'. It is probably for a similar reason that these people are especially attached to the polytheistic and pantheistic aspects of religious thought and action and are little inclined to monotheistic sublimations, except perhaps when they try to explain the origin of the world and to claim absolute superiority for the particular god that acts as champion of their own tribe.

In general, shamanism claims neither founders nor dogmas; it appears as a spontaneous product, both strict and flexible, of the implantation of a certain people in a certain land.

These religions are hardly ever to be found in their unadulterated state except among people as yet untouched by industrialization; most of them possess no literature. As a general rule, they are not sufficiently strong to resist the assault of the big missionary religions or that of modern living, and they soon fade out in the face of invading Buddhism, Christianity, Islam or even atheism. It sometimes even happens, as in the Philippines or in Formosa, that their adepts take the initiative of turning to one of the more powerful religions in order to resist the devastating pressure of technology. These religions are usually linked to a particular tribe or group and almost never proselytize. Owing to their very nature, they can hardly accept converts. The Germans often give them the name of *Stammesreligionen*.

Nearly all the shamanistic peoples have a very low standard of living, not only because any substantial improvement makes them turn to other faiths, but still more so because they have been driven out by people better organized and more powerful materially, who have appropriated their fertile lands and compelled them to seek refuge in remote and barren mountain areas.

In Asia, the main groups of the shamanistic type are to be found in the forests, the tundras and the steppes of Siberia among the Samoyeds, the Tunguz, the Chuktches, the Buryats, the Ostiaks, the Yuraks, the Yakuts, the Lamuts (whose religion, Horro, penetrated even as far as China under the Di-tyn dynasty under the name of Tyau-Shen), in Turkestan, in China (notably Miao-tse, the Limus, the Lolos), in Tibet (where the Bon may be considered as very largely shamanistic), in India among the mountain tribes (the Nagas, the Kondhs, the Todas, etc.), in Ceylon among the Veddas, on the Indo-Chinese peninsula with the Pemsiens, in Borneo with the Dayaks, in the Philippines with the Ifugaos, in Formosa with the Hakkas, in Northern Japan with the Ainus. But there are countless other nucleii, less important, throughout the continent. In Hindustan alone, the official census of 1941 showed a total of about 25,400,000 persons belonging to tribes of which by far the great majority were 'animists'. Altogether, the peoples openly and exclusively practising these religions represent an imposing number —many tens of millions of individuals—and it is not permissible to ignore them in a study of Asia.

What is still more important in Asia, however, is the survival of shamanistic beliefs among people who pretend to be free from them and to belong to other faiths. Not only have the main religions adopted many of these beliefs immediately and incorporated them in their own fundamental dogmas and ritual, but the farther they have moved away from their place of origin the more they have come to terms, more or less consciously, with the local customs, putting up with the ancient traditions. It is indeed difficult to understand the 'great religions' and the influence they wield, unless one bears in mind the shamanistic currents which underlie them.

By a curious trick of fate, materialistic westernization which now saps the major religions and deprives them of the allegiance of the elite, also discredits them in the eyes of the masses who are then often inclined to return to the most elementary concepts, feelings and practices involved in shamanism. Thus, in Soviet Asia the Government's anti-religious policy was able to eliminate the influence of the Christian orthodox priests without much difficulty, but in so doing it strengthened to some degree the authority of the *kholduns* (*shamans*) with whom the priests until then shared the work of dispensing religious, spiritual and mystic guidance. In Laos and in other Indo-Chinese societies there is a new wave of attraction to shamanistic magic which is less hampered than it used to be by Buddhist belief. Indeed, throughout history cases of an individual or collective return to the 'primitive' religions are not rare. Thus, in the early fifteenth century, the king of Chiengmai (Thailand) abandoned Buddhism and returned to animism.

Moreover, as a result of the tolerance shown by these religions, these reconverts normally do not reject, with anger and contempt, the great church which they have abandoned, as is generally the case with Christian or Muslim neophytes. Sven Hedin mentions the case of a Chuktche who, reverting to the religion of his forefathers, ceremoniously and respectfully set up his Christian ikon in the forest, in a place where a Russian could find it—and apologized to the ikon for having abandoned it.

Whether these beliefs derived from shamanism have been openly kept up, concealed more or less deliberatley or rediscovered, they are, in general, deeply rooted in the mind, heart, soul and body of those who hold them; they influence to a large extent the whole or a great part of life for most Orientals. We shall have to revert to them in many chapters of this book. It is impossible to have a very clear vision of Asia, from Turkey to Japan, from the Arctic to Indonesia unless they are constantly borne in mind—just as it would be impossible to explain why western airlines are loth to give the number thirteen to a seat if one is not aware of the superstitions connected with this number.

THE PRE-ISLAMIC RELIGIONS OF THE NEAR-EAST

Apart from shamanism, throughout Asia there have existed a large number of more or less independent local religions which have long since ceased to have any following and have therefore lost all living tradition, even if some of their temples and books have come down to us. The contacts they had with the Roman Empire, the texts left by the Hebrews and also the excavations made by our scholars have enabled us to know more of the former religions of western Asia than of those in the rest of the continent. We know that they were many and varied and that some of them went with a high level of civilization. Generally speaking, they are now only of historical interest, and their influence does not seem to have left notable traces in the present behaviour of the people of these regions. It will be sufficient to mention here the religions of the Semites (Amorites, Aramaean, Moabites, Minaean, Nabataeans, etc.), those of the Babylonians, the Assyrians, the Sumero-Akkadeans, the Phrygians, the Hittites, the Philistines, the Phoenicians, etc. Doubtless our archaeological research will lead us to discover many others whose existence we do not even suspect.

Certain other religions subsist to this day among very restricted groups which are fast disappearing despite all their laudable efforts to resist the flood of religious—or atheist—concepts which assail them on all sides.

We may mention, more particularly, the Samaritans of Jordan

and Israel, who number only two or three hundred today, who remain faithful to the first six books of the Old Testament and for whom the transfer of the Temple to Jerusalem was the first great heresy. They regard the Jews almost exactly as the Jews regard the Christians.

We must also mention the Sabaean group, disciples not of Christ but of John the Baptist. Six thousand of them still remain, notably in Baghdad and Amara, where many of them are goldsmiths.

Zoroastrianism, also called Parseesm and Mazdaism,[1] has, as the first name indicates, a founder by the name of Zoroaster who lived at least five centuries before our era. It also has a dogma and holy scriptures—which are interpreted in various ways (in particular, by the Shahinshai and the Kadmi). On the other hand, it has hardly any images representing the Divine[2] and until relatively recent times it had no temples. 'The Divinity was not visible—it was worshipped in the form of a symbol . . . it is to a fire flaming on a stone altar that the king's homage is addressed; and the sun lights up the scene which takes place outdoors'. In the highly 'purified cult' of this 'superior religion', the 'least pagan of the pagan world', as Renan called it, any teaching tends to produce . . . what an apt Zende saying calls *humatem, hukhtem, huarestem*—good thoughts, good words, good actions. Whatever be the estate of the man—priest, warrior, farmer, craftsman—this condition has to be sought and reached by the pure man.

Zoroastrianism in olden days had considerable influence which spread from China[3] to Armenia and to Cappadocia. Although it took nearly a thousand years to spread among the Iranians, it proved a serious rival to Christianity (with which it combined to form Manicheism) and to Buddhism and Jainism; and it must have had some influence on the way in which these religions were born.

After having held absolute and intolerant sway in Persia, where it had been born (in Bactria, to be more precise), it was finally driven out by Islam; one hardly finds more than seven or eight thousand *guebres* in Teheran and Yezd in spite of a recent attempt at revival under the inspiration of Dinshah Irani. On the other hand, about ten thousand Parsis at present live in India, in the Bombay area, where they play a considerable social and economic role; they do not proselytize and they do not admit converts, and they refuse to admit children of mixed parentage. Zoroastrianism

---

[1] There are slight shades of difference between the three terms.
[2] In fact, only that of Ahura-Mazda, inherited from the Assyrians, is still in use.
[3] In 677, a great Mazdean temple was built at Tch'ang-ngan.

does not therefore exercise any religious influence outside the re-stricted group.

Another formidable rival to Christianity at its inception was Mithraism. There was a violent clash between the two in Africa, in Rome and even in the Rhone Valley and Brittany, and the latter supplanted the former as the official religion of the Roman Empire under Julian and Eugene in the fourth century. A religion of mysteries, it had probably originated in the Middle East, and we have only very indirect, partial, and therefore not always reliable information on it. Mithraism seems to have granted paramount importance to ethical problems. Many of its elements were em-bodied in Manicheism.

Judaism has no founder, but it does have both a dogma and bulky and consistent scriptures, which regulate the minutest de-tails of material life and lay down moral and judicial rules. It is above all a doctrine of life, a way of organizing an inspired society according to a religious ideal. It is a religion that presents itself as the result of divine revelations made on several different occasions and yet to be completed. Its mythology is relatively poor. Its ritual is imperative. It does not allow for monastic life. It claims to possess the absolute truth and accepts no compromise with other creeds.

It nevertheless does not indulge in proselytism and only reluct-antly receives new converts. It seems, however, that formerly Jews tried to convert their Christian slaves. It exerts hardly any religious influence outside the circle of its adepts. However, numerous groups have settled in different regions in Asia, particularly in Yemen, Irak (70,000 in the country, of which 40,000 in Baghdad), and in India, where they are held in high esteem.

Christianity has both a founder and a dogma, the latter con-tained in the clearly circumscribed scriptures that are further de-fined through interpretation by a recognized authority. It does not go into the small details of everyday life and limits itself to general rules; injunctions of a legal nature have been added only as a later and subsidiary development. The creed arose from a single revela-tion which took place once and will not be repeated. Like Judaism, it claims to possess the absolute truth. Its mythology, which is also very poor, is almost entirely borrowed from Judaism, but it is sup-plemented with abundant hagiography. Its ritualism, which is com-plex, hardly goes out of the context of religious ceremonies.

Like another great missionary religion, Buddhism, it has retained little influence in its country of origin. Born in Asia, it soon became Europeanized in its fundamental attitudes as well as in its geo-graphical extension. That is why, when it sought to conquer the continent that saw its birth, it could only effect a very marginal penetration.

Apart from the island of Cyprus, more Mediterranean than Asian, where the population is mostly Greek and consequently Orthodox, the only country in Western Asia where Christianity plays a role is the Lebanon, where Maronites, Catholic and Orthodox Armenians, Syrian Christians, etc., are collectively on an equal footing with Islam; even political power is equally divided between them.

At the other end of the continent, the Philippines, which conquerors, first from Spain and then from the United States, wished to convert to Catholicism and Protestantism respectively, claims to be a Christian country; but only a small Westernized minority has actually shown any interest in Christianity.

Throughout the Asian part of what is now the U.S.S.R., the Russian immigrants since the seventeenth century have brought their own religion with them and, while they have converted extremely few Muslims or Buddhists, they have more or less kept their Orthodox faith and the domes of their church have sprung up wherever they have settled. Several Russian churches had already been built in Siberia in 1601. The first Russian religious building on the eastern side of Lake Baikal dates from 1681—the Troitskoy Monastery.

Even more than in Europe, in proportion to its following, Christianity in Asia has been subdivided into countless rival sects and sub-sects. Thus the Nestorians, Jacobites, Armenians and Greeks are all divided in two, Catholics and Schismatics. Only the Maronites are all Catholics. In Palestine we find Melchite, Syrian, Maronite, Armenian, Greek Orthodox and Georgian Armenian Christians. In itself, this fact neither surprises nor shocks the Asians, who are accustomed to seeing such divisions in all the religions, great and small, known to them; but it certainly has deprived Christianity of much of the prestige it could have secured. This is partly why, apart from the cases listed above, Christians in Asia only constitute minorities that are numerically almost negligible.

If Christians are generally regarded with mistrust throughout Asia, it is for different reasons. It is particularly on account of their more or less conscious and close ties with the colonizing country and their missionaries. Asians are always tempted to regard the latter as 'collaborators' of the military occupants, past or present, to whom it is tempting to shift responsibility for all evils. The political part that, on many occasions, Christians in religious orders or groups sought to play in most Asian countries has, unfortunately, often confirmed their suspicions and has been the almost exclusive reason why they were persecuted in pure self-defence or retaliation.

Also, the behaviour of Christians has often done little credit to the faith they profess. 'Conversions' were often obtained by force,[4] or by cunning,[5] or in a purely mechanical way,[6] or even by swindling,[7] and they were often purchased.[8] Such instances have naturally created the most deplorable impression. They have certainly not helped to bring the best people into the fold. The spiritual level of the Christians did not always distinguish them from the devotees of the other religions; the Christian Cossack laughed ostensibly at the Buryats who believed in the spirits of the Lake Baikal, but their own explanation of the storms was that they were caused by the anger of a certain devil who lived at the bottom of the lake. For many Asians who observed the lay Christian foreigners and still more their priests, to belong to this imported religion merely meant a thirst for material comfort and the enjoyment of this comfort—which was rather repugnant to people naturally inclined to mysticism and austerity. One Christian author aptly referred to this as a disease of smugness which the Oriental Christians often seem to take over inadvertently from the Pharisees. Intolerance towards other religions was also more often considered as a proof of unfitness for spiritual experience (or, at least, as a proof that this type of experience had been lacking) than as evidence in favour of the doctrine; and this intolerance extended to all fields. Darmsteter noted with sorrow: 'Nowhere in India did I come across minds more hard and closed than among the well-

---

[4] Thus the conversion of the Tartars and the Voguls of Siberia:— 'Some of them were obstinate in refusing what was to procure them eternal happiness and as it was undesirable to make them undergo too much violence, the soldiers were made to throw them into the river (the place was convenient for baptizing them) and this was regarded as a baptism according to the rules; . . . a cross was tied round their necks and they were Christians' (J. G. Gmelin, *Voyage en Sibérie*, 1767, II, 241 and I, 170). Therefore it is not surprising to learn that when 'Tsarism was overthrown, most of the natives of Western Siberia were still heathens even if they had been baptized', (K. Donner, *La Sibérie*, 1946, p. 157).

[5] In Maduray, a missionary writing for the edification of his fellow-priests, explains that a very simple and practical way is to pretend to be a doctor: this provides an opportunity for the Cathechist to place a few drops of holy water on the forehead of young people, pretending to treat them, and meanwhile to mutter a few appropriate phrases . . . and then they are Christians.

[6] As in the case of the Woliaks.

[7] The Siberian Pope received a small bonus for each convert on record and one and the same man could be baptized twice under two different names (P. Labbé.)

[8] Throughout the Far East the term 'rice-Christian' designates those who have let themselves be baptized in exchange for suitable payment.

paid servants of Christ.' Gobineau was even more severe: 'As for the Christian (in Persia) it is best not to speak of him at all. In the complete abjectness into which he has fallen—along with his clergy—it would be desirable, for the sake of the name he desecrates, that he should disappear altogether.' Of course, Asians are too polite to express themselves as bluntly—in writing, at any rate —towards the foreigners who are their guests, but we might mention the moving appeal of an Indian, Keshub Chandra Sen, who had long meditated upon and applied Christian teaching: 'If you bring us Christ, do not show Him to us as a civilized European but as an ascetic Asian, whose fortune is communion and whose wealth is prayer.'

Finally, the people of Asia are under the impression that they already possess in their own religions all that Christianity can bring them, whether it be on the plane of ethics (we shall revert to that at greater length) or on that of miracles. A Japanese Buddhist monk explained that, if in the fourteenth century, Brother Oderic of Pordenone had failed in his efforts to bring about conversions in Tibet, it was above all 'because the Tibetans of his time had nothing to learn from him, for in Tibet, there were already many monks who could do much the same things that Jesus is said to have done'. A few years ago, when the international press announced that the Pope had had visions of Jesus Christ, the news did not raise in Asian minds any of the doubts that assailed Western atheists; there was only great surprise in learning that a man could accede to high position in a Christian church without having had such visions!

This type of mistrust is less marked against those Christian sects that have not come through the West or, at least, that have not been influenced by it, and also those sects that are really exacting in the sphere of discipline, morality and austerity (Nestorians, Old-Believers, etc.).

It is more particularly through these latter sects that Christianity has exerted an influence on important groups of the Asian population. It must also be acknowledged that the social work undertaken with so much courage and perseverance by many missionaries from all Christian denominations has left a deep mark, even when it has later been abandoned and replaced by something else.

We shall see that some elements of Christian origin can at present be discerned in a number of religious syntheses which have been attempted throughout Asia over the last few centuries.

Even if we leave aside these basic transformations, it must be admitted that in many cases the Christian groups in Asia have either considerably adulterated the doctrine or else reverted to their former beliefs. In countries such as Thailand, Borneo and even India, reconversions are frequent. In India, one of the main tasks of the powerful Brahmo-Samaj organization is to help those who had deserted Hinduism but wished to be re-admitted into it; the whole of the Varap Agri caste, in the state of Bombay, has abjured Christianity, and many other cases could be cited. If statistics are to be believed, the number of Christians has gone down remarkably since India is no longer a colony of a Christian nation. 'One fact cannot be denied,' writes Maraini, 'Asia does not want Christianity.'

ISLAM

Like Christianity, Islam has a founder, Mohammed, and a specific dogma subject to varied and sometimes contradictory interprettion. Like the former, it is the result of a single revelation which is final and will not be repeated. Like the former also, it claims to possess the absolute and complete truth, does not lend itself to any compromise with other religions and is aggressively missionary. Like Christianity again, Islam has a single Holy Book, the Koran, but like Judaism, Hinduism and Buddhism, it refers also to other equally sacred texts to which it ascribes in practice, if not in theory, the same degree of authenticity.

Generally speaking, Islam is optimistic and transcendentalist; it does not favour either asceticism or extremes of ecstasy, but it does admit the concepts of gainful work, family ownership, earthly happiness and comfort. Like Christianity, it takes the soul to be immortal; life on earth is generally considered as a phenomenon which happens only once and is sanctioned by an eternity of joy or suffering. It strongly emphasizes the oneness of God.

Its injunctions and prohibitions have a compulsory character and extend to the minutest detail in all spheres of life. Its ritual is simple but strict; its mythology is extremely poor.

Its moral rules may be summed up in the following text taken from the Hadith: 'Abu Darr relates: My friend (the Prophet) has given me a sevenfold admonition—(1) Help the poor and be near to them. (2) Look at those who are beneath thee and not at those who are above thee. (3) Never ask anything of anybody. (4) Be faithful to thy parents even if they offend thee. (5) Tell nothing but the truth even if it is bitter. (6) Do not let thyself be turned aside from the way of God by the blame of those who blame. (7) Repeat often: "There is no power or force but through God for this comes from the treasure that is hidden under the Divine Throne".'

Contrary to Christianity, Islam is firmly planted in its country of origin, where no other religion has ever been able to challenge it. Born when mankind was already adult (a fact to which Muslims attach great importance), it spread with lightning speed; in less than one century it extended to the Atlantic and to Kashmir, and it pursued its course rapidly in the following centuries.[9] At present it has some 350 million devotees. To speak only of Asia, its domination is undisputed from Turkey, which was the seat of the Caliphate till the beginning of this century, to the Islamic Republic of Pakistan and Indonesia (where the President of the Republic takes his oath on the Koran). Even where it is not the leading religion, considerable and influential groups represent it; such is the case in the Asiatic part of the U.S.S.R., in India, China, Indo-China and as far as the Philippines—and its progress does not seem to have come to a stop.

We must, however, be careful not to confuse 'Muslim' and 'Arab', as is often done, generally out of ignorance, but sometimes also intentionally, for political purposes; for instance, the very name of the Arab League, some of whose members are no more 'Arab' than Greece and Turkey are 'Atlantic'. If we can be content with approximation, four concentric circles might be drawn. First, the peoples of Arab race who are found mostly in Saudi Arabia, Yemen, Irak and Jordan. Then those who use the Arabic language, including the whole of North Africa from Morocco to Egypt and Sudan, Lebanon, etc. Then those, who, although not speaking Arabic, write their own language in the Arabic script: Persian in Iran, Urdu in Pakistan, Malay in Malaya, etc. Finally, Muslims in general, including those of China, Indonesia, Philippines, Madagascar, who do not even know the Arabic script.

Besides this, Islam also enjoys immense prestige among populations that have not embraced it, and its general culture has exercised a strong attraction. 'As the Arabs of the conquest were too proud to take up service in the chanceries of the Empire and in its offices . . . all the posts were filled from the start by the cultured members of the conquered population, by the Syrians in the former Byzantine provinces, by Persians and Aramaeans in the former Persian provinces.[10] The vanquished thereby provided the scribes of the Empire; they created the Arab philosophies and set themselves zealously to studying the Koran.

[9] At the start of the ninth Century, half the population of Canton was Muslim.

[10] E. F. Gautier.

Mass conversions to Islam were obtained more often by force than by persuasion. At the end of the last century the people of Svat were still driven to the mosque with the whip, and even the gentle Swami Ramdas, incarnation of tolerance and love, tells how one day a Muslim gave him the choice between death and the acceptance of Islam. But, strange as it may seem to us, the use of this somewhat abrupt method apparently never affected the fundamental and final character of almost all the conversions. However, the purity of doctrine and practice often suffered from it and there was a multiplication of sects, schisms and heresies. Although the concept of the cosmos remains uniform throughout the Islamic world, and even schisms have been powerless to break the elective brotherhood between the people of the *kibla* (those who turn towards Mecca in their prayers), the various religious groups in Islam nonetheless show utter contempt for each other, and wars and massacres between them are almost endemic.

Three large groups can generally be distinguished in Islam—and the Sunni, the Shi'a and the Kharidji, and they in their turn are subdivided—they differ above all in their conception of the past, present and future system of succession to the caliphate. The first of these covers at least two-thirds of the population (some authors say 90%). For them the caliph must be elected from among the members of the Qurayish tribe. It is among the Sunni that the four great schools of Islamic law can be found: Hanaii, Maliki, Shafi'i and Hanbali; to the recognized sources of the dogma—the Koran and the Hadith—they add the *idjma*, the unanimity between the faithful that confirms and justifies practices and beliefs, and also *kiyas*, analogy.

The Shiites, who number hardly more than twelve million, consider Ali (the prophet's son-in-law) and his descendants as the only legitimate caliphs; the pilgrimage to Kerbela (where Hussein, Ali's son, died) has as much value for them as that to Mecca and they have traditional sacred texts other than the Hadith of the Sunnis. They are subdivided into a great number of sects among which the following may be mentioned:

The *ithna-ashariya* or 'twelvers' whose teaching constitutes the official religion of Iran and who seem to be subdivided into three different rites—*dja'fari*, *cheiki* and *crouli*. They particularly emphasize the cult of the twelve imams.

The *zaidya*, who acknowledge the authority of Zaid ben Ali, Hussein's grandson.

The *isma'iliya*, who are scattered from Syria to Afghanistan, Turkestan, India and Yemen. Their teaching seems to comprise an exoteric part—the *zahir*, and an esoteric part—the *batin*. They are divided into two groups—the *musta'liens* and the *nizari*.

The Druzes are a community living in Lebanon and in Anti-Lebanon whose esoteric teaching is reserved for the *'ukkal*, the 'learned', but is denied to the *djuhhal*, the 'ignorant'.

The *Nusairi* is the name of the extreme Shi'a sect which numbers about three hundred thousand in Syria. It is an initiatory sect which has three successive degrees of initiation—*nadjib*, *nakib* and *imam*. It admits the concept of several worlds one above the other: the great, luminous world (*'alam kabir nurani*), the little luminous world, the little world of darkness, *zulmani*, which comprises the bulk of mankind, and, finally, the great world of darkness which is composed of the 'opponents', *addad*.

We should also mention the Kharidjit or Khawaridj sect which seems to be the oldest of all. It has played a considerable part in the history of Islam. For them, any Muslim, 'even a negro slave' may accede to the caliphate. They are now very few in number; in Asia, they are hardly to be found except in the Oman area.

The case of Iran must be considered separately, for 'this is a land dedicated more to what is translucid than to what is dark, in love with celestial serenity and not with a romanticism of the underworld'.[11] It is probably there that Islam has been most mixed with foreign and local elements and tradition. A great local authority has even asserted that the Iranians had turned Islam into 'Iranism'. Merely to travel through Persia makes one feel immediately how different the general atmosphere is from that of the other Islamic countries. A sensuous and refined cult of beauty—which easily leads to a mysticism of very uneven quality—is apparent everywhere and Iranian artists have obstinately refused to bow to all the prohibitions which strict Muslim tradition would have imposed upon them. It is in Persia that we find the largest group of people considered by the Muslims as true heretics, although they derive their authority directly from the Koran—the Babis (who prefer to call themselves *ahl-i-bayan*). They are the disciples of Saiyid 'Ali Muhammad of Shiraz (1821-1850). Subjected to terrible persecution, they divided into two groups, the first of which, the *azalis*, have now almost disappeared and the other, the *baha'is*, have been scattered in small groups in various countries. We shall mention them in several other chapters.

Diametrically opposed to the gentle, easy-going nature of the Iranian Muslims, we find the uncompromising puritanism of the Wahabites, who have ruled unchallenged over Saudi Arabia for more than a century and exercised considerable influence over the orthodox Islamic faith. Iconoclastic to the extreme, they do not even

[11] Masson-Oursel.

mention the Prophet's name in their prayers, and it seems that at one time, they even thought of destroying his tomb in order to cut short any chance of idolatry. They strictly forbid the use of tobacco, swearing and the razor. For them the mere utterance of the Islamic creed is not sufficient to make a man a believer, and allow orthodox Muslims to eat animals slaughtered by him! The founder of the sect, Mohammed ben 'Abd-al-Wahhab, lived in the eighteenth century (1703-1787) and towards the end of his life joined a small village chief, Mohammed ben Sa'ud, ancestor of the present Saudian dynasty.

One of the concepts familiar to Islam is that humanity periodically moves away from the true path and must be brought back to it by a man especially and individually 'guided' by Allah, a *mahdi*. Many Muslims believe that some day, perhaps near the end of time, we shall see the coming of the great Mahdi who will finally restore the true religion. For some it will be the most recent *imam* known to history, who disappeared mysteriously and, since then, has been living in hiding, waiting for the time to reveal himself once more.

In the course of the centuries, many a pretender has given himself out to be the mahdi and some of them have drawn huge and fanatical crowds which sometimes played a great political part.

The most recent of those who have claimed this title is Mirza Ghulam Ahmad Kadiani of Gujarat, who made this claim at the very end of the nineteenth century. His disciples, the Ahmadiyyas, carry out an intense propaganda which has now reached a large number of Muslim countries and even other regions. Their number was estimated at half a million in 1930 and has doubtless considerably increased since then. According to them, Jesus Christ, whom all Muslims acknowledge to be a great and genuine prophet, went after his resurrection to Kashmir, where he died at the age of hundred and twenty. The community split itself into two groups—the 'Lahore' group and the 'Kadian' group—between which there does not seem to be any doctrinal divergence.

Sufism (*at-Tacawwuf*) which infiltrates into most of the Muslim groups, although it forms a clearly distinct group in itself, is a sort of Koranic esotericism. According to its adepts, it 'can give access to the immediate knowledge of the eternal' and thereby 'bring deliverance from the inevitable sequence of individual existences'; it proclaims itself as the 'spirit' or 'heart' of Islam, *ruh al-islam* or *qalb al-islam* while, at the same time representing the spirit which, in the Islamic world, is most free with regard to the mental delineations of the latter. Its mysticism which, in its loftiest flights, reaches a sort of existentialist monism, has not failed to cause serious concern among many a Muslim group and the Sūfis were often persecuted.

Apart from these divisions among sects which accuse each other of causing splits, Islam has, of course, undergone much distortion and alteration, especially in the peripheric groups. The worship of saints, and pilgrimages to their tombs especially, obviously constitute a rather unorthodox practice in a monotheistic and inconoclastic religion, and yet it is very widespread in most of the Islamic countries. Bloody sacrifices go hand in hand with Muslim rites among many communities of Central Asia, in South Arabia and elsewhere. Very often, even within the most closely knit groups, reformers have launched rather revolutionary ideas. One of the most recent of these reformers, Sir Mohammed Iqbal, who is considered as the spiritual father of the Islamic Republic of Pakistan, has not hesitated to entitle one of his works: 'How to reconstruct the religious thought of Islam'. It is understandable, moreover, that in face of the development and spread of modern science and technology, Islam, like Christianity and Buddhism, is seeking to delve once more into its basic teaching in order to see whether it is perfectly compatible with whatever has been brought to light by recent discovery and invention.

PRE-BUDDHIST RELIGIONS OF THE MIDDLE AND FAR EAST

While in south-west Asia Islam has a preponderant place, Buddhism dominates in eastern and south-east Asia. In these areas, however, other religions still have many millions of followers, play a considerable part, and do not seem to be retreating in the face of Buddhism. They therefore deserve careful consideration.

The most compact and most substantial block is undoubtedly formed by Hinduism, which probably has 250 to 350 million followers in the territory of Hindustan, and also some large colonies, in particular in Ceylon and Bali, and a few small groups in Aden, Indo-China, etc.

Taken as a whole, Hinduism has neither dogma, nor founder, and nobody—not even Gandhi, who tried his hand at it—was ever able to define it. It considers its vision of the world—in its origin, its nature and its final fate—as the highest and most complete truth that can be conceived, or that even exists, and it regards the descriptions by the ancient sages, the *rishis*, as the revelation of specific laws that have governed the world's very creation and that had to be applied by the Creator. It acknowledges nevertheless that these revelatons have to be checked constantly

—and, if need be, supplemented and clarified—by the individual experiences of all the sages through the ages. Its sacred texts form an immense mass which it has never been possible to list fully. Its mythology is vast and complex and provides its main instrument of teaching.

It attaches considerable importance and value to monastic life, but is opposed to monasteries. One of its essential components is a rigid social organization that is minutely regulated. It rejects all kinds of proselytism (with the exception of a very few recent and not very widespread movements) and accepts within its fold only those who are born in it.

Hinduism has an enormous and ever-increasing number of sects, cults and philosophic systems; but their diversity raises no doctrinal difficulty because the Hindus view them as mutually complementary facets of one truth and as a choice of equally valid disciplines that could not be reconciled. Among the main groups may be mentioned:

The Shiva-ites or *Shaivas*, for whom the predominant aspect of the divine is Shiva, the destroyer-reproducer of the universe.

The Vishnu-ites or *Vaishnavas*, for whom the predominant aspect of the divine is Vishnu, the preserver-protector of the universe, worshipped mostly in the form of one or other of his incarnations or avatars, particularly Rama and Krishna.

The *Shaktas*, for whom the predominant aspect of the divine is the Divine Mother, Shakti, and more especially the Shakti of Shiva.

Like Buddhism, Jainism was born of Hinduism and is approximately contemporary with Buddhism. Although it is not a pre-Buddhistic religion, for the sake of convenience we shall say a few words about it here.

According to Jainism, twenty-four successive saviours, Tirthankara or Jina, come to guide humanity through the various ages. The most recent, Vardhamana Mahavira, seems to have lived in the same period as Buddha, and played a similar part.

It has a considerable mass of sacred scriptures even more voluminous than those of Hinduism, but up to now, hardly anything has been translated into western languages. It is opposed to proselytism and does not accept converts. Monastic life holds a preponderant place in it; respect for every manifestation of life is carried to the extreme. Its mythology is abundant and its ritual very detailed.

There are about a million and a quarter to a million and a half Jains, almost all in India, particularly in the larger cities and in the Malabar area. They are divided into two main sects, the *digam-*

bara, 'those clothed in sky', and the *shvetambara*, 'those clothed in white', who do not seem to be separated by any important doctrinal divergence. In the course of history there were eight important schisms, the largest of which, in the fifteenth century, gave birth to a dissident sect that is still considerable—i.e. the *dhundia* or 'seekers'.

Confucianism, like Judaism, claims to sum up the teaching of several previous sages, but it honours above all its main exponent, Confucius (550-478 B.C.), whose name it bears. Its teaching is not based on any metaphysical dogma; it is, in theory at least, devoid of mythology and ritual; its basic texts are numerous and voluminous and it does not require any clergy. Many authors refuse to consider it a religion because, in itself, it is practically atheist.

Its main object is to organize the life of society along the most satisfactory principles, and for that purpose, it relies mainly on the practice of five cardinal virtues: love, which lies at the root of all the others; justice, which assigns his rightful place to every individual; respect, by which one recognizes others' rights and performs one's own duties; wisdom, which makes it possible to discriminate between good and evil; and sincerity. It admits that man is fundamentally good and particularly emphasizes filial piety and ancestor worship.

Up to the twentieth century, it was all-important in China, where it regulated family ethics and individual behaviour as well as the state machinery and administration: for the competitive examinations giving access to government posts a knowledge of Confucianist texts was a prerequisite. In 1917, the Chinese parliament even debated at length a bill making Confucius a god and Confucianism a state religion; and in the following year, a ministerial circular laid down the ceremonies to be held in honour of the Great Sage. Confucianism has followed in the wake of Chinese culture wherever it has spread, and its influence has continued to extend ever since; thus, in Japan, the Japanese intellect from the seventeenth to the nineteenth centuries was moulded entirely by Confucian concepts; in Viet-Nam it became the state religion two thousand years after reaching the country, and so on.

Taoism, the other great religion of Chinese origin, seems to have become crystallized at about the same time as Confucianism, from the time of Lao Tse (604-517 B.C. according to Chinese tradition), the presumed author of the greatest Taoist text, the *Tao-teh-king*. This major text has been translated many times into all Western languages, and the interpretations given vary to the extreme.

Like Confucianism, Jainism and Buddhism, Taoism does not

claim the benefit of divine revelation: it sets itself up as the product of the wisdom and vision of human beings. It claims to be in possession of practical truth on the basis of a particular interpretation of the principles governing the world, but it does not claim to possess the absolute truth. Like the Hindu word *yoga*, the Chinese word *tao* means 'both the way to be travelled and its final goal, both the method and the fulfilment'.

It has become customary among Westerners to stress the contrast between a Taoist philosophy which, everyone agrees, is worthy of the highest esteem, and a 'popular religion' which is often viewed with undisguised contempt. Actually, the two aspects that are thus separated are closely linked, but their foundation is practically incomprehensible to the intellect and cannot be grasped except by those who have submitted themselves for years to the harsh discipline required. At the most, it may be noted that among the members of the intellectual and spiritual elite one finds an extremely high conception of the Universal Order which is a Reality, a specific Principle, the Primary Principle—not a Reality qualified by moral attributes and appearing in the shape of Providence, but a Reality characterized by its logical necessity and viewed as a Power of Realization, primary, permanent and omnipresent. This same elite is also deeply conscious of all the consequences arising for man out of the need to conform to this Universal Order (in particular, non-action, *wu-wei*) which leads to actual mysticism. Among the masses of uneducated believers, it produces a concern for the material necessities of life, the possibility of delaying death, etc., which manifests itself in various practices, most of which seem to us to be in the nature of superstition. But similar contrasts could easily be found within other great religions, not excluding Christianity.

Taoism has numerous temples, a vast, regular and secular clergy. It is endowed with an extremely rich mythology and a complex ritualism. It is practically impossible to assess the number of its followers as every Chinese is more or less a Taoist, at least, at certain times and in certain circumstances. Although it is a Chinese movement based on truly indigenous thought, like Confucianism, it has followed Chinese culture throughout its geographical extensions; under the name of *michi* or *do*, it is not without influence in Japan; in Viet-Nam, the Taoist pantheon led by the Jad Emperor, Ngoc-Hoang, doubtless has precedence over the Buddhist pantheon.

In practice, Taoism and Confucianism are closely intertwined; together with Buddhism, they constitute a whole to which a great

Dutch Sinologist, de Groot, has given the name of Chinese Universism.

Shintoism has a very special place among the religions of Asia. Like Hinduism, it claims to have a detailed knowledge of the world's origin and does not refer to any historical revelation. On the other hand, it does not possess any sacred scriptures as such, and the books that it takes as a basis, the *Kojiki* and the Nihongi, both from the eighth century of our era, are, in fact, compilations covering a very rich mythology and later historical chronicles; nevertheless, these texts enjoy almost absolute authority.

Shintoism does not purport to be in exclusive possession of the truth; it has hardly any metaphysics in the sense we give to the word, and it imposes no dogma upon its disciples. With the exception of a few, very recent and not yet very widespread movements, it does not proselytize and the very idea of conversion seems completely alien to Shintoism.

It nonetheless has a considerable hold on the Japanese people and to a large extent determines their social and political life, family structure and individual behaviour. An almost total assimilation of the Emperor with the gods (Kami) endowed the sovereign with absolute moral and religious authority. Within the family, the father holds practically the same place as the Emperor held within the State. But it is in the context of individual morality that Shinto influence is even more keenly felt. There it promotes discipline, both internal and external, above all—self-control and purity in all activities of life, from the most important to the most trivial—and it is regarded mainly as a means of progressing along the path of discipline.

Three different levels must be distinguished in Shintoism: Imperial Shinto, State Shinto or *Kokka-shinto*, and Shinto of sects or *Kyoha-shinto*.

This last, like Christianity, Islam and Buddhism, embraces a number of sects—thirteen of which were officially recognized, but new variants frequently stem from these. The Engishiki lists 3,132 officially recognized cults. On a common and agreed basis, the sects follow rather different practices, and their teaching varies according to the emphasis which they place on a particular aspect.

State Shinto, which was officially abolished by order of the American Authorities of the Occupation, places itself above all the Shintoist or other 'sects'. Its essential basis lies in the ties of consanguinity uniting the gods, the Emperor, who is the 'sovereign grandchild (of the gods)', *sume-mi-ma-no-mikoto*, the Japanese people and even the Japanese land. Among the Japanese it goes without saying that State Shinto can, and normally is, followed simultaneously with any other religion.

Finally, Imperial Shinto, which is highly esoteric, seems to have as its central component the mystical, personal communion between the Emperor and his divine and human ancestors.

The worship in the temples of sect Shinto and State Shinto (the *Kyokai* and the *Jinja* respectively) consists essentially of purification ceremonies which establish a harmonious relationship between the worshipper and the gods, *kami*. They require a great number of symbolic offerings, including sacred music and hieratic dancing.

BUDDHISM

Buddhism has a founder, Gautama Buddha (560-480 B.C. It must be noted that Chinese and Japanese Buddhists believe the Buddha to have been born in 1027 B.C.), and a dogma; but the latter is not the result of a divine revelation : it is the outcome of one man's clear-sightedness and no one is therefore under any compulsion to accept it as an absolute truth.

Its sacred scriptures are immense, but official and complete lists are available. Practically all of them have been couched in writing, most of them have been printed and large sections have been translated into western languages.

Its mythology, which was originally almost entirely borrowed from Hinduism, later grew and prospered much further. Its ritual is extremely complex. It attaches the greatest importance to monastic and convent life, which, to it, represents the ideal state for both man and woman. Metaphysics form its essential basis— although, as a matter of principle, it refuses to approach some of the greatest problems—and supplies the exclusive foundation for its philosophy and ethics. It deals above all with the way in which we can escape from the illusions that are the actual cause of our present life and it does not concern itself much with the details of this life.

The fundamental theories of Buddhism have been expounded over and over again in all the encyclopaedias and there is no need to recall them here. Buddhism was born in northern India, in Magadha, where at first it was a mere and not even very heterodox variant of multiform Hinduism; it spread rapidly through Hindustan but began to lose ground from the start of the Christian era under the impact of the revival of orthodoxy, and, around the sixth century, it had almost completely disappeared from its country of origin. Quite recently, only a few small and isolated groups were to be found in India, particularly near the Burmese border; however, for exclusively political reasons and under the influence of the Nehru Government, mass conversions have taken place in the last few years. These conversions only have statistical value as the new devotees neither receive nor wish to receive any religious instruction.

On the other hand, Buddhism spread progressively beyond the natural borders of India and, what is most remarkable, exclusively by peaceful means. By the third century B.C., it seems to have already reached Ceylon, Burma, the borders of Afghanistan and Central Asia (as far as Khotan). In Christ's time it reached China and Viet-Nam; around the second to the fourth centuries, Malaya, Sumatra, Java and the Celebes, in the third century Funan, in the fourth century, Korea and Siam, in the sixth Japan, in the seventh Cambodia and Tibet, in the ninth Champa and in the thirteenth century Laos. Today, it probably has as many followers as all the Christian churches put together.

Essentially 'polymorphous' in nature, since the Buddha preached his law according to the needs of beings—in which he behaved like a true Hindu sage—Buddhism mixed without any difficulty with the religions already established in the countries where it was introduced: Confucianism and Taoism in the Far East, Shintoism in Japan, the Bon religion in Tibet, Shamanism and ancestor worship practically everywhere. It also adjusted itself to the mentality of the different populations and readily accepted any alterations that were required. In Cambodia, for instance, for a long time it put up with human and other blood sacrifices. It also split up into many sects, to such an extent that now there are much wider differences between certain Zen groups in Japan, certain Tantric groups in Tibet and certain Theravadic groups in Indo-China and Ceylon than there are between the teaching of the Buddha and the creed of the Jains and Hindus.

Although they all claim to stem from the Buddha's authority, and each one purports to possess the only true tradition, each existing sect has its own metaphysics, morals and worship. It is customary to distinguish two large categories of sects and schools: the Theravada or 'Opinion of the Ancients' (known by the opposite group as Hinayana or 'Small Vehicle', but the Theravadins do not like this derogatory term) and the Mahayana or 'Great Vehicle', which appeared on the scene considerably later, probably shortly before the beginning of our era.

The basic difference between the Theravadins (and also the Sarvastivadins, who agree with them on essential points) and the

Mahayanists is the following: for the former, man has nothing else to do but to follow the example and the precepts of Gautama Buddha and thereby progress towards *nirvana*, the final liberation, by leading a disciple's, *shravaka's*, life, which finally takes him to the state of an *arhat*; to that the Mahayanists add that every individual is potentially a Buddha and must both seek *nirvana* for himself and try to adjust his 'Buddhahood' to the times by working for the good of his fellow men and by preaching the true doctrine effectively to them. The one who can reach this stage is a *bodhisattva*; and the great *bodhisattvas* wield so much power, as saviours, that it is only natural for them to be the object of fervent worship and a veritable cult. In Formosa, however, we find certain Mahayana Buddhist monks—the *t'aou t'oua*—who explicitly state that they are concerned only with their own salvation.

Doubtless, the doctrinal opposition between these two great schools has been somewhat exaggerated by our own orientalists because they have not attached sufficient importance to the central teaching common to both. But it is an equally great mistake to maintain, as has been done recently, that since one of the essential roles of Buddhism is quasi-political, if the schools seem to us to split and multiply, it is because we have made a basic error arising from the fact that our scrupulous and attentive observers have had before their eyes only a religion deprived of its state function. A highly competent Japanese wrote recently: 'Buddhism has strengthened Japanese national unity, and that in spite of the presence of the powerful national Japanese religion which existed previously it has never ceased to exert a preponderant influence.' The attitude of the followers of these two great schools is nevertheless dictated by a feeling of mutual rivalry as strong as that between Catholics and Protestants, and the conversions obtained from one group to the other are a matter of pride. After the recent Council of Rangoon, the whole Burmese press printed the photographs of two Japanese Mahayanist monks who had been converted to Theravada.

The Theravada group has a great unity of doctrine. It has been implanted mainly in Cambodia, Laos, Thailand, Burma (in these countries it embraces over 95% of the population, if one excludes the 'animist tribes') and in Ceylon (where it embraces 67% of the population).

While the Mahayanists generally use Sanskrit versions of the scriptures, translated into their local languages, the Theravadins rely on a Pali version of these same scriptures, of which abundant translations are also available. In order to celebrate the 2,500th anniversary of Gautama Buddha's illumination, the sixth Great

Buddhist Council met in Rangoon from 1954 to 1956. 2,500 venerable monks from six different countries met and compared the different Theravadic versions of the sacred scriptures in order to establish the authentic text. While the Government of the People's Republic of China lent, on that occasion, one of the most revered relics of Buddhism, the Mahayanists not only abstained from sending representatives, but, in the following year, held their own rival Council in Nepal.

The fundamental element of Mahayanist metaphysics is the theory of the void or of non-substantiality, *shunya*, which forms the basis of a great number of philosophical systems. For Ashvaghosha, the author of the Buddhacharita, the cosmic principle is *tathata*, 'thusness'; for Nagarjuna, the doctrine of *shunya* becomes a doctrine of relativity, where the truth of no separate individual entity can be affirmed. (This is the Shunyavada or Madhyamika). For Asanga and his brother Vasubandhu, who propound a kind of subjectivist idealism with mystical trends, there exists nothing other than consciousness, *vijnana*. (This is the Yogachara or Vijnanavada).

The Mahayana is the dominant form of Buddhism in China, Japan, Tibet, Viet-Nam (including the Viet-Minh) and in Indonesia, but in all these countries it appears under a variety of forms.

In China, where about a dozen important rival sects, mostly of local origin, coexist in perfect harmony, so that monks belonging to several different sects live together in the same monasteries, Buddhism seems to have forgotten a considerable part of the original teaching. To quote only one example, preoccupation with final liberation—*nirvana*—which is the final goal of every Buddhist, has slid far into the background and has given way to a complex system of hells and paradises where individual existence loses none of its reality. Devotion is directed not so much to Gautama, the Buddha of historic times, as to the Buddha Amitabha (the Dhyani-Buddha of the West) who is assisted by Kwan-Yin or Avalokiteshvara. A Chinese author—a highly westernized one, it must be admitted—wrote a few years ago that 'Buddhism, when absorbed by educated Chinese, becomes nothing but a system of mental hygiene —which is the essence of Sung philosophy'.

In Japan, where it has taken the name of Shinshu (*shin*—true; *shu*—religion), from the year 741 onwards the Emperor Shomu had temples to Maha-Vairochana Buddha built in all the provinces for the happiness of the people, in order to protect them against calamities, diseases and epidemics. Twelve officially recognized sects, many of which are split up into various schools very different from one another (thus, in the Shingo sect, the highly secret Tategawa schools seem to be Tantric), together probably have fifty million followers and over fifty thousand priests and monks. Among them, the three (Rinzai, Sodo and Obaku) which accept the theory of 'sudden' illumination, have, for many centuries, been playing a preponderant part, if not on account of their numbers, at least by the influence they exert on the mentality of the whole people and particularly on the elite. The Kegon shu school, the Hokekyo and Shomankyo groups teach what they call the Ekayana, the 'single vehicle', which claims to transcend on a higher plane the divergences between Mahayana and Theravada. Japanese Buddhism is also unique on various other points; thus, since the time of Shinran Shonin (1173-1262), Japanese Buddhist priests have been allowed to marry.

In Tibet, as also among the Mongols (including the Buryats of the Lake Baikal area, who have over a thousand gods—*burkhany*— and celebrate the great Tsame festival), it has taken a very special form which is generally given the name of Lamaism, though its followers prefer to call it Vajrayana. It is so different from the other forms of Buddhism that early in the twentieth century a traveller was told by the Khamba Lama of Maimutchen that the cult of Chigemune was 'identical with Indian Buddhism, but has nothing to do with the religion of the Fo' (which is the Chinese name for the Buddha). The Chinese and Siberian Mongols have a religious 'Buddhist' code which is peculiar to them, the Ganjur, comprising 108 parts, each of a thousand pages, which is attributed to Aiji-tain-dalam, of the Mongolian Eolets tribe.

CHAPTER IV

Syncretism

The various religions are like the five fingers of one hand.
THE GREAT KHAN MONGKA

THE tolerant character of non-Semitic oriental religions and their readiness to share activities with other religions results from a state of mind which is deep-rooted in Asia, and even the Semitic religions have not been able to ignore it entirely. Proselytism is repugnant to the Taoists; Gandhi considered it quite a crime to change religion and even a greater one to try to convert others (for Gandhi, attempts at conversion were actual insults to the dignity of man); even for the Muslims, tolerance is a Koranic obligation, although it certainly goes against their strong fighting instincts.

Besides, in Asia, whatever knowledge an individual or a group may have—or thinks it has—about God, or the real nature of man and the cosmos and their evolution, etc., it is never taken to be complete and final. We shall revert later to the consequences of this mental attitude with regard to practical life. In the field of religion it has given birth to innumerable sects trying to work out a synthesis between the teachings of several great instructors of humanity; the borderline separating dogmas of the various great religions therefore appears much more vague than we could possibly imagine.

One of the best examples of this syncretically inclined tolerance is supplied by Persia. In antiquity, not only did the Medes and Persians abstain from practising any proselytism but, on their coins, next to their own gods, appeared images of Baal of Tarsus and Pallas Athena as well as those of Indian deities, including Buddha. In the seventh century Tammariton II, King of Elam, sent three white horses to the temple of the goddess Ishtar in Uruk. Cyrus, as King of Babylon, was anxious to show that he imposed on nobody either the religion of his own family, or that of his people, and still less that of the Mede tribe of the Magi. As both the Greeks and the Bible themselves confess, the Achemenide sovereigns were not only noted for their tolerance, but they readily sought initiation into the cult of exotic deities and adoption by foreign gods; in 517 B.C., Darius I joined in the mourning for the death of an Apis bull. From east to west of the Persian Empire, it was a mixture of cults and an alliance of gods. This trend was further accentuated under the Sessanides; Shi-ite Iran, from the Abbaside times down to our days, has always behaved in the same way.

Even among the common people, from the end of the third millennium B.C., a large number of Semitic gods were worshipped in Elam. A great scholar has said that even before the settling of the Kassites in Babylon, early in the second millenium B.C., syncretism obtained and Babylonian deities were readily assimilated to the gods honoured in Lower Mesopotamia. In the first centuries of the Christian era, the population of Babylonia still practised syncretism widely.

In the sixth century B.C. many of the Jews allowed to return to Palestine preferred to remain in Persia, and when, after Constantine, the official Christian Church persecuted heretics, a number of them took refuge with the Great King, even while Mazdeism was the state religion. Moreover, the Israelites of the 'Northern Kingdom' worshipped Baal and Jehovah simultaneously.

Between the Altai and the Amu Darya, Soviet scholars have recently discovered considerable traces of a mixed religion, which they have called Shamano-Mazdean. Manicheism, which was in great vogue in Asia for a time, from Palestine to China, was an admirable synthesis of Zoroastrianism, Buddhism and Christianity.

Islam itself, in most cases, showed an attitude infinitely less rigid than it is supposed to have. The wish to enjoy certain material advantages has, of course, not always been alien to it; Islam normally treated the conquered peoples, the *dhimmi*, with a moderation all the more tolerant because their religious conceptions, their aberrant metaphysics and their salvation left the true believers indifferent and, furthermore, these latter, belonging to a race of masters, were dependent on the work and tribute of the vanquished peoples. In Irak, for instance, even to this day, in addition to the Christians and the Jews, there are many communities of Yazidi, Kurds, Assyrians, sun-worshippers, etc., who seem to live on perfectly friendly terms with the Muslims.

Apart from the more or less mixed religious groups, Islam itself, which in most countries has had to countenance the cult of saints, includes in its hagiography, besides genuine believers, a number of Christian saints and pagan deities. This syncretic trend, faciliated by the fact that the Muslims acknowledge the sacred character of the Judeo-Christian Bible—while often interpreting it in their own special way—has been strongly accentuated over the last century; this is partly due to the rapidly increasing knowledge of foreign religions.

In many places, the contact between Islam and some of these religions has led to mixtures even as regards dogma and, as a result, numerous 'mixed' sects have sprung up. On the shores of the Mediterranean, in the ninth century, the Nusairi of Lebanon, although they were Muslim, added Christian and Gnostic-pagan elements to their dogma which was strictly Koranic. In Syria, the religion of the Alaouites associates Shia' Islamism, Christianity and Paganism. The religion of their neighbours, the Druzes, is a syncretism of the Shia' Islamism, Animism and belief in transmigration. Quite recently, in Lebanon, Khalil Gibran, whose influence is still spreading, could be considered Muslim as well as Christian, and a long visit to the museum devoted to him does not help to decide what he actually was.

In India, in the fifteenth century, the same was true of Kabir, who made no effort to clarify this doubt for his disciples; when he died and some wanted to cremate him as a Hindu while others maintained that he should be buried in a Muslim cemetery, the dispute could only be settled by a miracle : when the shroud covering the body was lifted, all that could be seen was a heap of roses, half of which was buried while the other half was burnt on the funeral pyre. In the second half of the sixteenth century, the great Emperor Akbar tried to reconcile within a new religion all that he considered to be common to Hindu, Parsi, Muslim and Christian doctrines. These are by no means exceptional cases in India. The Bhangi in the Deccan, the Kachachia and Khatri, the Matia Kanbi and other tribes are both Hindu and Muslim. For instance, the Mapilla Muslims worship the Hindu Shakti just as the Tiyan shakta go freely into the mosques. The Kumbi of Berar, although Hindu, observe Muslim customs and festivals. Muslim and Hindu *fakirs* and *sadhus* readily share the same pipe—which would be unthinkable between Hindus belonging to different castes. In Hyderabad (Deccan) I myself have seen, at the height of the so-called Hindu-Muslim civil war, the priest in charge of a particularly revered mosque give a brotherly welcome to a saffron-robed Hindu monk and lead him to the heart of the shrine—while laymen, whatever their religion, had to remain outside the shrine. The vast sect of the Ahmadiyyas, which shows an amazing power of expansion, claims to be so universal that its founder, Mirza-Ghulam Ahmad (died in 1908), purports to be the successor of Mohammed (as a *Mahdi*) as well as the reincarnation of Christ and an avatar of Vishnu.

India is particularly fertile ground for such syncretism. The history of the religion that has been dominant there for thousands of years—Hinduism—is nothing but a long series of successive syntheses, carried out most openly, and the most sacred text of all, the *Bhagavad-Gita*, prides itself on being one of them. A European student of the East, who thought he was thus passing a final and terrible sentence on this heathen religion, wrote quite correctly: 'To speak of "Indian tolerance" is nonsense . . . Princes as well as their subjects . . . revere all the gods, believe in the utility of all the liturgies'. It has been said of Vishnuism—which in this hardly differs from other branches of Hinduism—that it is always ready to accommodate other religious beliefs and that it derives pleasure from taking over the religious concepts of all the peoples of the world. The Kharva of Konkan venerate the Virgin Mary and various Christian saints, the Mahar of Berar and Bombay have, in their Hindu pantheon, the archangels Gabriel, Azrael, Michael and Anadin, and they also worship the Muslim saint, Sheik Farid.

To mention two of the greatest names in contemporary Hinduism: Ramakrishna (1836-1886) preaches, and claims to have proved by his own experience, that Hinduism, Islam and Christianity are equally effective ways leading to God, although he advises that they should not be mixed in practice; after him, Aurobindo (1872-1950), while basing his faith and personal teaching much more on the Hindu scriptures than on any other (to my knowledge, he has never invoked the authority of the Bible, the Koran or any other non-Hindu sacred text) offers in his mystical philosophy what is perhaps the greatest synthesis ever achieved in the history of human thought. While both of them firmly refrained from founding new sects, one already witnesses the sprouting of essentially religious groups that claim to draw their inspiration from one or other of these two great sages.

If the Theosophical Society created by Europeans in India has been so successful in that country and has even spread to other parts of Asia, it is obviously because it met this intense thirst for syncretism.

This desire is equally evident in Indo-China. In Viet-Nam, where an essentially Confucian civilization has been subjected to important Buddhist and Christian influences, in Saigon, to give only one instance, the pagoda in the rue Saint-Pierre has, one behind the other, a Buddhist altar, Taoist shrines, and a place still used for the ancient shiam cult; the same priests indiscriminately serve the whole temple and the worshippers successively burn incense in the various sections.

One of the most striking cases of methodical syncretism is that of Caodaism, which was born in Cochin-China in 1926 and already has millions of followers; it has already split up into several rival sects like all the big religions. Following the pattern of the Catholic Church and practising techniques of ecstasies very similar to those of Shamanism, it combines Confucianism, the cult of the spirits, Catholicism, Taoism and Buddhism, and, at the same time, takes Sun Yat-sen, Joan of Arc, Victor Hugo and Pasteur as guides.

In Cambodia the famous temples of the Angkor area convincingly prove the close and friendly ties between Hinduism and Buddhism, although our archaeologists persist in trying to find traces in them of the western type of 'religious wars'. In the present-day royal ceremonies of modern Buddhist Cambodia, the *bako* or court brahmans are always in charge; the same is true of certain court ceremonies in the no less fervently Buddhist court of Siam. In both these countries, Buddhism and Hinduism are closely intertwined in all popular practices and are further tinged with older animist beliefs; in the Thai Ramakien, which is the local version of the Hindu epic, there are episodes where Hindu gods and goddesses (Mekhala, Parashu-Rama, Parjanya) are completely assimilated to Chinese deities and we even find four-armed statues of Buddha.

Just like the Buddhists of Cambodia with the *neak-ta*, the Buddhists of Burma do not have any scruples in propitiating the *nats* by means of small sacrifices.. The same holds good for the Laotian Buddhists, who in their *boun*, their feasts, always mix with their orthodox prayers propitiatory incantations and rites addressed to the *phi* (or spirits) which dwell even in statues of the Buddha. Despite the Buddhists' intense repugnance to bloodshed, Thai and Laotian Buddhists even in our day sacrifice a buffalo on the fourth day of the waxing moon of the sixth month, and eat its flesh on the veranda of a Taoist temple; it must be acknowledged, however, that a non-khmer aborigene is made to perform the actual slaughter.

Among the Laotians, tolerance sometimes borders on indifference; when Christian priests make their proselyting tours, they stop in the pagodas and it is the Buddhist bonzes who help them to collect the villagers. However, once the visitors have left, the good Laotians return to their homes saying: 'They are perhaps right, but why should we be wrong?'

The same kind of phenomenon is to be encountered on the insular prolongation of Indo-China, viz., Indonesia. In the eleventh century, in Java, at the time when the kings gave themselves out to be incarnations of Vishnu, the inscriptions reveal an actual symbiosis of Buddhism and Shivaite Hinduism. From the end of the thirteenth century at least, but doubtless already before that, the cult of the Shiva-Buddha used to be practised in Java. In 1268, the king of Kadiri (Java) was deified after his death in the form of Shiva at Waleri and in that of Avalokiteshvara (Amoghapasha) in Jajaghu. In the history of Java and Sumatra, moreover, mixed marriages were frequent at princely courts; there were never any struggles between Buddhists and Shivaites.

As for Tibet, it is practically impossible to distinguish, in the beliefs and ritual of Lamaism, between what is of Buddhist origin and what is Hindu or Bon. While the modern Bon (like Ryobu Shinto in Japan) consider the Sun God as an incarnation of Buddha, the orthodox monasteries print and sell Bon religious books—and at the time of a Buddhist wedding, a Bon ceremony is also held imploring the Dragon King not to leave the house in pursuit of the young bride. When the Temo Rinpoche, a great lamaist religious chief, and therefore a Buddhist, tried to assassinate the Bon Dalai Lama, he had a paper containing imprecations slipped into the shoe-soles of his enemy.

Such syncretism, however, goes even further. It even applies to Muslims and Christians. It is upon the personal intervention of the Dalai Lama that the Jungar Buddhist king Galdan, around 1680, restored the Muslim clergy's authority in Kachgaria. It has been noted that Tibetan Buddhists in the Chinese province of Tsing-hai live on excellent terms with the Muslims and, inversely, the Tibetan Muslims readily accept the idea of successive lives. As for Japanese Christians, a Japanese Buddhist monk recently remarked, not without a touch of satisfaction, that in all their homes one was sure to find, in some inner room, butter lamps, burning day and night, before an image of the Buddha. The compliment is returned in Lhassa where a bell, left behind by two Catholic missionaries who had tried to found a church, now occupies a place of honour in the Tsug Lha Khang, the great temple of Lhassa.

This remarkable open-mindedness does not prevent the Tibetans from being afraid that their own religion might be 'snatched away' from them; this fear is at the root of the cruel punishments inflicted upon all those who, consciously or otherwise, had helped the Hindu Sarat Chandra Das, a spy in the pay of the English who had travelled in Tibet. This must not lead us to conclude that there exists a strict orthodoxy based on a compulsory credo. The Tibetan proverb still holds good: 'To every province its dialect, to every lama his doctrine'.

We find the same syncretic tolerance in most of the religions of central Asia. Genghis Khan and his successors had already instructed their officials to tolerate and respect all the religious creeds of their subjects, whether Christian, Muslim or Buddhist, and even to take part in their ceremonies, but not to profess any particular belief openly. Marco Polo had also found the great Khan equally well-disposed towards the various religions represented at his court. One of his sons, Tulni, married a Christian princess, Sorgaqtani, who shared the throne with him, and Tulni's son, the Great Khan Mongka, used to say: 'The various religions are like the five fingers of one hand'. The Mongols showed equal tolerance towards Buddhists, Taoists, Confucians, Muslims, Manichaeans, Jews, dissident members of the White Lotus or the White Cloud sects, Nestorian Christians and Catholics. Even after their own conversion to Buddhism, they continued to indulge in fire worship, for which we still have their rituals. The lamaist temples of Outer Mongolia are guarded at their entrance by Shamanistic gods—Chingultu, Bogdo-Khan-Uli-Dundjin, Songinin-bulun, Bain-Dzurikhe.

Whatever be the broad-mindedness shown in these areas by religious circles and also by ecclesiastical circles, where the latter exist, there is one country in Asia that can more than compete with them—viz., China.

Without taking the expression 'Chinese Universism' in the rather technical sense given to it by its author, de Groot, we may consider it as a very apt description of the sort of merging that has occurred, not in mere dogma or metaphysics, but in the very minds of the Chinese who simultaneously and often indiscriminately practise Confucianism, Taoism and Buddhism—to such an extent that the ritual and the pantheons often become entangled, sometimes inextricably so. A Chinese who was trained in western intellectual disciplines points out that in our times, as before, intellectuals are reluctant to join any particular religion.

This is due not only to a fundamental indifference to any kind of dogma, which is what obviously strikes us at first, but also to a deeper vision. The common saying that 'the three religions (i.e. Confucianism, Taoism and Buddhism) are but one religion' also means that at their highest level it can be *seen* and *known* that the three are one, *t'ai chi han san wei i*. Something there, however, evidently escapes our Western logic: religions such as Taoism, and all the other Chinese 'orthodoxies', are both sectarian and syncretic in nature and the latter epithet applies not only to all that helped to build up a particular dogma or ritual originally, but to all the contributions that were or will be added later from outside.

Even at the time (third to fourth centuries) when Taoism and Buddhism were opposed to each other and vied with each other for influence, none of their adepts ever condemned the other religion as being false or diabolical; every one of them has always recognized the others as embodying a good measure of truth and anyway as being undeniably useful. On his deathbed, the Taoist Chang Yung (444-497) held the Tao teh King and the Confucian classic on purity in his left hand and the Buddhist Sutra of the Lotus in his right hand. A Chinese proverb says: 'Taoist alchemy, Buddhist relics and the Confucian moral code are identical'. Many of the deities worshipped in Chinese temples do not belong exclusively to any one of these religions—and the Buddhists who believe in the thirty-three paradises of Buddhism believe just as much in the eighty-one paradises of Taoism. While these three great faiths thus converge at the summit, their good relationship in everyday life also results to a great extent from the fact that they exercise complementary influences. It may be said, broadly speaking, that Confucianism regulates human activities in full detail, that Taoism places these activities in the context of a philosophical whole, where they are brought down to their right proportions and that Buddhism completes the vision of this earthly life with metaphysics for after-life and prescriptions pertaining to it. The three great masters, Confucius, Lao Tse and Buddha, are often represented on the same altar. In a Korean temple at Chang-an Sa, they are shown tasting vinegar together; as might have been expected, while Lao Tse, with his philosophy of non-action, finds this brew of life sweet, Confucius, preoccupied with the details of its organization, finds it sour and Buddha, anxious to escape from it, pronounces it bitter. It may almost be said that a high Chinese dignitary is Confucian when he is working, Taoist in his leisure hours, and Buddhist in his moments of contemplation.

The sects in China which profess to be essentially syncretic are legion. To quote only from the most recent instances, the Tsa-li, the religion of the 'inherent principle', which apparently goes back to the seventeenth century, claims to be equally Taoist, Confucian and Buddhist, and asserts as a dogma: 'These are three religions, but their principle, *li*, is one!' The Kuei-i Tao, 'the Way which follows the One', very active for nearly a century, draws its doctrine of the eight virtues and the six dangers from Buddhism, Taoism and Confucianism jointly. The T'ung-shan She, 'Society of Kindness', founded at the time of the first world war, within a few years established over a thousand branches in China and Manchuria; it worships, side by side, Confucius, Lao Tse and the Buddha, drawing its ethics from the first, its principles of longevity from the second and a system of meditation from the last. The Tao Yuan, the Society of the Way', which made its appearance in about 1920, had over thirty thousand members in 1927; it is philan-thropically inclined and places under the image of the Ultimate Sage and Primordial Ancestor the names of Confucius, Lao Tse and Buddha—and also adds to them symbols of Christianity and Islam. The Ikuan Tao, the 'Way of All-pervading Unity', which has de-veloped mostly in the course of the last thirty years, embraces the same five great religions. The Wu-shan, the 'Society for the In-tuition of Good', founded towards 1915, further adds Judaism. In some regions of China, the Generalissimo Tchao of the Dark Terrace, a high dignitary of the Taoist pantheon, is believed to have been Muslim.

As may be seen from the above examples, Chinese syncretism is not restricted to the great traditional religions of China; it opens its doors to others as well. Besides, the teachings of Manicheism and Nestorianism have probably contributed to the flowering of Chinese civilization and it is only natural that traces of them should be found in the realm of religion. In the Ch'uan shen miao, the Temple of all the gods, there is no clearly established priority —the name of Auguste Comte is written in Chinese with two characters, one of which means Virtue while the other is the patronymic name of Confucius.

This broad-mindedness is not without repercussions even on the followers of other much less tolerant religions in China. On various occasions, the Christian Heads of State, Sun Yat-sen and Chiang Kai-shek, like the Buddhist Liang Sou-ming, were not ad-verse to setting themselves up as champions of the basic Confucian principles. Certain eminent Christians of modern times, such as N. Z. Zia and Wu Lei-ch'uan, took up the thesis of the seventeenth century Jesuits and explicitly recommended that Christianity in China should assimilate certain essential principles of Confucian-ism or, at least, refuse to see any fundamental divergence between the two religions. Even the Jews in China practise, side by side with their own religion, Buddhism, Confucianism and the 'ancient cult'. In Communist Shanghai, the Catholics, who did not dare to go and pray in their own church, used to go to a synagogue. Under these circumstances, it is not surprising that in China there was no case of mass conversion as a direct effect of preaching.

We find such Chinese-style syncretic sects as far as Korea. The Tong-hak, founded in 1859 by Cho-chei-chou as a reaction and a defence against aggressive Christianity, is a mixture of Con-fucianism, Buddhism and Taoism. The sect was so active that in 1865 it was outlawed and its leader beheaded, but in 1893 it again gained so much influence that the king had to open negotiations with it.

In Japan, the three great Chinese religions also combined with Shintoism into a very harmonious synthesis. The agreement went so far that in the second half of the nineteenth century a considerable effort was necessary to *separate* Shintoism from Buddhism. Until then, under the name of Shimbutsu-Konko, they used to share the same temples and sometimes even the same clergy in a most brotherly fashion. Even in our day, Shingaku is a form of Shinto based on Zen Buddhism and Neo-Confucianism; the Ryobu Shinto, a Buddhist Shintoism, comprises various sects (Shingon Shinto, Tendai Shinto, Hokke Shinto) and the Yoshida Shinto adds Confucianism.

This confusion spreads to the very pantheon. In the eighth century, under Emperor Shomu, Gyogi Bosatsu declared that the Shinto gods were avatars of the Buddha; and this same Emperor, when he wanted to have the Great Buddha of Nara, the Dai-butsu, built, first asked permission to do so from the supreme Shinto goddess, Amaterasu, at her temple in Ise—and apparently she granted the authorization. The god Kompira, who used to be Buddhist, recently became Shinto as the result of a decision of the Emperor. The god Hachiman is more Buddhist than Shinto and his Sinico-Japanese name Hachiman designates no other than he who is known in pure Japanese as Yahata or Yawata, 'the eight standards'; moreover, as we shall see later, he is no other than the Emperor Ojin.

Nearly all Buddhist temples of Japan still have a Shinto altar within their precincts, since the Shinto deity is considered as protecting the Buddhist religion and its church. In Kyoto, in the great Zen Buddhist temple of Dai-Toku-ji, there are chapels dedicated to ancestors. Most Japanese families have their *kamidana* (Shinto altar) and their *butsu-dan* (Buddhist altar) in the same room and sometimes even as parts of one single altar—and while they turn to one rather than to the other at particular festivals or at particular times, the presence of both does not disturb them in the least. Out of a total of 80 million inhabitants, the 1950 census counted 63 million practising Shintoists, of which 44 million declared themselves Buddhists at the same time. Up till very recently, the funerals of the Shinto priests used to be celebrated by Buddhist priests.

As in China, this syncretism resulted in the establishment of extremely numerous mixed sects, some of which have gained considerable influence and are even represented in Parliament. The great patriot Kenzo Adachi built a 'Hall of eight saints' where Socrates, Buddha, Confucius, Lao-Tse, Jesus Christ, Mohammed, Kobo-Daishi and Nishiren are venerated side by side. One very important and revered person, an unchallenged master of the learning dispensed in several Zen monasteries of the most intransigent sect, goes every year on a pilgrimage to Mount Atago, where the Shintoist fire god is worshipped, and brings back amulets from there to his own temple.

This syncretism also has an impact upon the relationship with foreign cults. Imperial Shintoist Japan celebrates July 14th with as much enthusiasm as republican France, Christmas with as much fervour and pomp as the Christian countries. For Japanese Protestants there is nothing strange in withdrawing to a Zen Buddhist monastery. I myself have known one of the main representatives of the strictest Shinto sect who had on his visiting card the unexpected title of 'Evangelical preacher' in the most Christian sense of the term. At the southern tip of the country and also on certain islands, for about three centuries, there has been a 'Secret Christianity' sect, *kakure kirishitan*, which mixes its cult with various Buddhist and, above all, Shintoist elements.

It should not, therefore, be surprising that when a Japanese is asked whether he is Buddhist or Shintoist, he is unable to reply and sometimes even to understand the question—it is very much like asking an Englishman whether he is a married man or a gardener. One of the greatest qualities praised in the Emperor Yomei, who lived in the sixth century, is that he 'believed in the Buddha's law and at the same time followed the "Way of the Gods" of Shintoism'. The best Japanese historians are indignant at the thought that ideological differences between Buddhists and Shintoists are believed by us to have been at the origin of struggles leading to civil war.

The Czars themselves recognized the Asian tendency towards tolerance in the eastern part of their empire and they sometimes adapted their policy accordingly. They even encouraged Christian Orthodox sects which were persecuted in Europe to cross the Urals and the Caucasus, and let them live in perfect peace on the other side—for example, the Semeiski who came in the middle of the eighteenth century to settle among the Buryats, the various sects of the Old-Believers at the end of the eighteenth century, the Dukhobors in the Irkutsk region and in Azerbaijan, the Khlistovchinas or Skoptsi, who practised emasculation for the love of chastity and of whom there were over twelve hundred in 1889 in the town of Yakutsk alone, the vegetarian Molokanie in Azerbaijan, the beer-loving Susliniki in the Khabarovsk area, and so on. When the Russian Orthodox Church showed itself to be too aggressive, even in Asia, as was the case in the middle of the seventeenth century, the Czar sometimes enjoined it to temper its ardour.

Moreover, certain peoples converted to Christianity continue for a long time practices that are quite foreign to our religion, or even our customs. The Tchuktches, after they were baptized, never gave up polygamy. In the Irkutsk area, offerings to the mountain spirit may be seen hanging on the crosses of Christian calvaries. In the middle of the nineteenth century, the Ostiaks of the Obe, converted to Christianity, offered Shamanistic sacrifices at the start of the fishing season, and their women were veiled in the Muslim manner. The Kolymyan Christians believe in four gods: the Saviour of the West, the Saviour of the East, Saint Nicolas in the South, and the Holy Mother of God in the North. After a century of Christianity, the Yakuts still believe in all the gods of their former pantheon and are content to add the Christian saints as well. In the isba and under the tents, deep in the yurt, in the middle of the eighteenth century and probably much more recently, Saint Nicolas and the Virgin lived as very good neighbours with the various Buddhas and Shamanistic fetishes. So while a certain Christian veneer was fairly easily laid over shamanistic practices, it did not prevent the Siberians form considering themselves as good Buddhists or Muslims in spite of their having been baptized.

In the eighteenth century the very officials of the Czar, Russian and Christian alike, showed great interest in the 'witchcraft' of the Shamans; besides, in the middle of the nineteenth century, the most orthodox Russians of the Obe region still acknowledged the miraculous or scientific powers of the Ostiak Shamans. In the eighteenth century, the Buryats of the Transbaikal region, who had been converted to Buddhism for two hundred years, did not think that their new faith made of love and compassion prevented them from celebrating the horse sacrifice; the Tibetan lamas who had gone to convert them had presented their own religion as a mere extension of the local Shamanism and recognized the deity Begdse, worshipped on Mount Mon-dorgol-ola, as a true Burkhan (Buddha) and held grand festivals in his honour. Even Islam did not remain unadulterated. In the seventeenth century the Kazakhs were considered as Shamanistic rather than Muslim.

Furthermore, many individuals, although not actual members of a syncretic sect as such, apply similar combinations to their individual lives. In modern Chinese, the term *chu-sseu* means 'a Confucian scholar who lives the life of a Buddhist ascetic'. Siamese princes normally belong to the Brahmanic religion till the age of twenty and then become Buddhists.

On the other hand, and in some ways as a complement to this possibility of individual syncretism, in various Oriental religions with vast pantheons, it is almost obligatory for every individual to choose his own god or, more correctly, to find the one which was meant for him, and to relegate the others into the background. This was already the principle of the *ili* in Sumer and Akkad at the end of the third millenium; in our day, it is that of the *ishta-devata* among the Hindus, and the same obtains at present among certain Japanese Buddhist sects.

All this, of course, implies full freedom for the individual to join the particular group of his choice. In India, it is very frequent for husband and wife to belong to rival sects (for instance, those of the right hand and the left hand). In China, André de Perouse, Bishop of Zaytun (Ts'iuan-tsheou) noted as early as in the fourteenth century that 'in this vast Empire, where there are people from all the nations under the sky and all the sects, each and every person is allowed to live in accordance with his sect, for they are imbued with the opinion, or rather the error, that each can attain salvation through his own sect'.

Naturally, on this immense continent, many cases of persecution have occurred through the centuries. Acts of persecution carried out for religious reasons as such and not on account of the political activities of the followers of a particular sect, are, however, in a small minority, and out of these, most were the work of Muslims or Christians. For the former, the holy war, the *jihad* against the infidels of the *dar-el-harb* is a religious duty and, in spite of all the cases of tolerance which we have noted, it is quite obvious that they do not always shun this duty. The Kazakh legend of the old magician Korkut, condemned by Allah to wander for ever without respite and who, every time he stopped, found a gaping tomb before him, is probably a reminiscence of the Muslim persecutions. The persecutions were sometimes in the nature of extermination. Thus, Usbek Khan, the main introducer of Islam into the feudal nobility of the Oulouse, decreed death for the Shamans who played such an important part in the life of the Mongols as well as for the Buddhist lamas. Instances where non-Muslims had to choose between death and conversion are innumerable—and cruelty went perhaps even further between the followers of the various Muslim sects. Such was often the case among Christians. Thus, the Nestorians, persecuted by the monophysites in Edessa and Armenia and driven from the Roman Empire by Zenon, the Isaurian, in 489, had to take refuge within the Persian Empire, the doors of which were opened to them by Peroz; many a dissident Christian was persecuted in Russian Asia, etc. It must also be pointed out that in many Asian countries, Christian converts are forced or coaxed into ways of living and habits which uproot them from their own traditions, separate them from their brothers of the same race and more or less turn them into pariahs; without, however, ensuring that they be admitted among the Christians of western origin. Their situation is sometimes worse than that of children of a European father and an Asian mother. This is not true of the Muslim converts, who have little difficulty in building up a kind of elite recognized by other groups of society.

Pressure was also exerted by followers of non-semitic religions: in China, at the end of the fourteenth century, against the Manicheans, in Tibet against the Bons, among the Tartars who, in 1651, burnt the convent of Dalmatovskii Uspenskii on the Iset, in Korea, where the government in 1865 ordered that all Christians be put to death; even in India where, in the twelfth century, the Lingayat preached the complete extermination of all those—Jains or Hindus —who did not practise their particular religion.

It must be admitted that the universalist character of creed and thought which marks most of the religious groups in Asia has also had a consequence that is as unexpected as it is deplorable—i.e. each and every group is apt to believe that it has achieved the only complete and final synthesis between all the valid systems of the past. The result is that, on the one hand, it displays great animosity towards the other groups having the same pretensions, since the latter become its direct competitors and are *a priori* in the wrong, spreading false theories and harmful practices. One example in India is the hostility between the theosophists and those whom they call the 'Ramakrishnaists'. Similarly, the disciples of Vivekananda and those of Ram Tirtha—who preached roughly the same thing, in the same countries and under the same conditions— ignore each other. One other frequent consequence is that each group feels that it has been entrusted with a world mission and its founder automatically becomes the ultimate teacher of humanity with precedence over all those who have gone before him. Thus, again in India, in the temples and *ashrams* founded by the Ramakrishna Mission, the photograph or statue of the great saint hangs over the altar, and in secondary places we have the symbols of the great religions or the portraits of their founders—Jesus, Buddha, Krishna, etc. Extreme tolerance, which goes as far as assimilation, thus ends—a terrible paradox—in intolerance and virulent proselytism. Even in Hinduism and Shintoism, which are essentially national and racial religions, in the sense that they do not admit any outsiders, Neo-Vedantism and Neo-Shintoism have now made their appearance, and claim to be of universal application; and they aim at conquering the world. Thus the Japanese Tenri-kyo, of recent date, has reinvented proselytism with the formula 'Whoever saves others (i.e. leads him to Tenri-kyo) is himself saved'.

PART TWO

Man within the Universe

Man within the Universe

CHAPTER V

The Categories of the Mind
and Continuity

The great law of the world is continuity.   LIE TSE.

THE greatest obstacle to our understanding of Asia is that we seek
to apply to it the Kantian categories of the mind as we conceive
them in the West. Now, the large majority of Asians do not share
our conceptions of time, space and causality:

1. The very concept of time is not measured quantitatively by
means of clocks and calendars divided into equal units. Time, above
all, has a qualitative value. Furthermore, birth and death are not
an absolute beginning and end.

2. Space is not confined to what we are able to perceive with
our senses and imagine with our reason in a three-dimensional
framework. Its directly and normally perceptible portion may
have material limits but, on the other hand, space extends into a
variable and sometimes unlimited number of other dimensions,
which are worlds or planes to which our consciousness does not
normally give us access.

3. The concept of the individual's responsibility in action is
not the same as ours. Instead of considering himself as the 'author'
who has the duty and responsibility of choosing and executing
the action and who must then assume the moral and material consequences of it, the Asian mostly tends to regard himself either as
the instrument of one or more superior forces, or as a junior
partner who has been entrusted by the master of ceremonies with
a more or less important part, subject to specific rules and strictly
delimited—although the master of ceremonies may, at any time,
change these rules and move the confines—a part in which he is
allowed a certain degree of freedom and even initiative so far as
the details are concerned. The result is that the Asian is unable to
establish the same direct and rigid causal relation between the
action of the individual (or of a collectivity) and the fruit of this
action, either here on earth or in after life.

This is largely due to the fact that the Asian considers our vision of the world, obtained more or less directly through our sensorial organs, as very partial, mostly fallacious and often altogether false. While we draw from this vision our scientific conclusions as well as our rules of life, he hardly trusts it, and his abstract ideas as well as his practical behaviour are dictated by beliefs and considerations which completely escape us, or else seem unworthy of our attention.

For him, reality differs from appearances even more than, for us, a forest differs from a diagram representing a plant cell.

The fundamental theses of the unreality of the world, upheld by the great non-dualist schools of ancient India and by Buddhism, are well known to us. The Taoists also do not show great esteem for this universe of dimensions and localizations. In the second century B.C., the Chinese Huai-Nan Tse wrote: 'Those who rely on their ears to hear and on their eyes to see, submit their body to great fatigue and yet do not even attain clear perception.' Consequently, for most Asian philosophies, what we, in the West, call realism, does not have much to do with the genuine Reality; for them it is more an enslavement to appearances, neither faithful nor complete, which distorts the very nature of this Reality for us. As has been said quite rightly, 'for the Asian mind, reality is that which has to be transgressed'.[1]

'Nature,' the Shintoists of Japan tell us, 'is inscrutable and cannot be approached through the law of causality.' If, in India, Krishna is considered as the supreme and perfect divine Avatar—*purnavatara*—it is because he always looked upon life as a play—*lila*—and was never taken in by it.

Even there, however, we must not trust our western logic and conclude that this universe, because it is unreal, has no existence. For the Hindus and Buddhists, and for many other Asians, it retains nevertheless a certain kind of existence in unreality like the snake that we think we can see in the half-light and which is merely a piece of rope lying on the ground; the snake does not exist, but it makes our heart beat faster, makes us step aside and, if we have a heart ailment, may kill us. Even in Muslim philosophy, the world appears as intermediate between existence and non-existence. We should therefore rather think in terms of successive levels of truth, as we shall see later in connection with logic. Vivekananda used to say: 'One does not move from error to truth but from a lower truth to a higher truth'.

In all three respects—time, space and causality—the Asian possesses, to a higher degree than we do, a sense of the continuity

[1] Schwab.

and the logical unbroken sequence of things and happenings. The Taoist philosopher Lie Tse probably gave us the best key to the whole of Asia when he wrote, 'the greatest law in the world is continuity'. For him it is not possible to establish a definite distinction between This and That, existence and non-existence, life and death, etc. We shall come across this basic concept in almost all the subjects reviewed in the present work.

We must, however, mention at once one particular application of this trait. While in the west, the starting point of any psychology and also of any education is an absolute discrimination between self and non-self, between what is 'self' and what is 'other than self', this distinction is not given much importance in Asia, either in theory or in practice. The Asian is more concerned with seeking and bringing out all that shows the artificial, arbitrary and fallacious nature of this borderline; all his efforts tend towards a better perception and achievement of the integration of the 'self' in the Self, the 'Whole'. The distinction that is of greater concern to him is that between the apparent 'self' and the real 'Self', but this distinction is of a completely different kind and produces diametrically opposite effects.

Since the world, with its countless and infinite extensions, forms a whole without any discontinuity, the same must necessarily be true of human knowledge. A consequence of this is that, contrary to what we might expect in view of his ignorance of the laws of Nature as defined by modern western science, the Asian is less easily disconcerted by what he sees; his admiration, rather childlike to our eyes, has more the nature of enjoyment and is more a tribute to the Creator than the effect of a sudden revelation or impact provoked by the incomprehensible or the unexpected. His very humility in face of the omnipotence which he recognizes in the Higher Bodies makes him regard as natural all that he contemplates. What has been written about China by one of our best sinologists may be almost fully applied to the whole of Asia: 'When everything is marvellous, nothing is miraculous. The Chinese no more need a religion with miracles than they are predisposed to surprise at the miracles of science. The most pathetic inventions only leave them with an impression that they have seen it all before'.[2]

One of the most serious effects of westernization in Asia is probably that it has brought about an inevitable and irreversible disintegration of this sense of continuity, and has created conflicts, unthinkable up till then, between the different allegiances and the different duties, between religion, morality, science and political

[2] Marcel Granet.

life; it has opened rifts between the concrete and the abstract, this life and after-life, soul and body, God and the world and man, persons and things—wherever, up to the time of our arrival, there had been no demarcation-line, at least in non-Semitic Asia. Even when one critic[3]—a highly competent one—writes that the traditional view of the world held by Islam is 'an essentially discontinuous vision where everything is extrinsically decreed by God, where nothing has ontological existence but through the legal status given to it by God second by second', he actually demonstrates exactly the opposite of what he affirms. What more absolute, strict and consistent source of continuity can be imagined than the all-powerful Will of the One God who created the world and continues to direct it in all its details, second by second?

The most important manifestation of this sense of continuity is the deep feeling within almost all Asians either of actual identity or at least of a close parallelism between the life of the individual and that of the cosmos—an identity or parallelism that naturally covers the intermediate level, i.e. life within society.

This is particularly explicit in China. 'Thy life,' teaches Lie Tse in his very first pages, 'is an atom of cosmic harmony, thy nature and destiny are an atom of the universal accord.' For the Chinese, the whole of nature is considered as a well-ordered 'whole', a 'universe' in the true sense of the word. This parallel is drawn even in the details. Thus, just as society cannot be distinguished from the cosmos, the human body reproduces this cosmos: the kidneys represent the water element, the stomach the earth element, the liver the fire element, the lungs the gold element and the heart the wood element. These conceptions are actually applied—not without success—in Chinese medicine. Its practical consequences are felt in all fields, from magic to morals, from technical work to town planning, from civil law to agriculture. The Eight Winds correspond not only to departments of the human and supernatural world but also to magic powers. The Chinese sect of the Former Heaven yearly holds three secret meetings which are supposed to correspond to meetings held simultaneously in heaven. Similarly, in India, the dances of the Krishnaite *rasa* and the whole life of the *gopis* are but a reflection of what happens in heaven at the same time. In China, again, the town must be square because the earth is square. Geomancy and the calendar, morphology and physiology are common to the macrocosm and the microcosms; this is the totality of knowledge and the only rule. Knowledge is one: the geographer cannot be ignorant of anything pertaining to

[3] Louis Gardet.

mountains since he has recognized them as being the bones of the earth.

'Since all phenomena are related and since nothing can happen in heaven or the sky or even on the back of a tortoise-shell exposed to the fire that is not a sign, cause or effect with regard to human interests, the harmony of nature or disorder in the elements are the consequences of moral harmony in life or disorder in conduct . . . ethics is less a promulgated law than a rational conforming of life to the inner—and yet manifest—laws of the universe and of society'. The Chinese never consider man in isolation from society and never do they isolate society from Nature. They are conscious of an active solidarity between man and the world. They feel the need for organizing existence in conformity with the order of things and therefore oriented in time and space—hence the importance of the calendar and of geomancy, *fong-chouei*. They have the deep conviction that nothing that is human can fail to have repercussions on the whole of nature. For this universe to run well, man must fulfil his task; if he does not do so, the whole mechanism will go wrong and this will lead to great calamities, floods, droughts, destruction of harvests, etc. Similarly in India, the round of the seasons depends on the virtue of men.

This micro-macrocosmic conception, as untenable as it may seem to us from the modern scientific viewpoint, thus retains great spiritual value because of the impeccable order and strict subordination that it introduces in the different parts of the Universe and the close union that it brings about between Heaven, Earth and Man. Up to recent times, it penetrated all the acts of private and public life so that in the Far East, man, while being practical in the spiritual sphere, often shows himself to be very idealistic in actions that we consider of a purely practical and earthly nature. The Chinese will never stop asking simultaneously—and with the same rites—for more children to enrich the family and for rain to make the seed bear fruit. 'There is a Tao of Heaven, *T'ien Tao*; a Tao of Earth, *T'i Tao*; and a Tao of Man, *Jen Tao*. Yet among all three there is a correspondence and a harmony. True action is action among the three great principles of Heaven, Earth and Man and it is always spontaneous.'[4]

This same idea is to be found also in Taoism, Zen Buddhism and elsewhere.

China has made a minutely detailed science out of this system of correspondence, but she is far from having the monopoly of it.

The Japanese Shintoists know that the aim of 'sincerity' is to

[4] Cranmer-Byng.

place us in harmony with nature. A modern Japanese philosopher even pointed out that if the east is not very much interested in epistemology, it is precisely because it does not seek to draw a boundary line between the macrocosm and the microcosm. The Japanese, for instance, keep rice grains in the room where confinements take place (Kunio Yana-gida). Even flower arrangements stress the necessity of maintaining constant and perfect harmony between the Divine, Heaven and Man.

The traditional Viet-Namese considers that man is within the world and that a constant relationship therefore links the behaviour of the macrocosm with that of the microcosm; he considers that it is normal for man to have his voice heard by animals, things and the occult forces spread throughout nature.

For the Hindus, the identity between macrocosm and microcosm is an article of faith constantly confirmed by experience. For the Indonesians, there is a sense of concord which permeates the whole of nature, that nature of which humanity is only a small particle. For many other groups, the continuity between man and his environment, in time and space, is such that he cannot be healthy if his environment is not so and, inversely, the soundness of the environment will be determined by the acts of the man who lives in it.

This obligation incumbent upon men, in general, is naturally even more imperative for the chief, who incarnates the group as a whole and, at the same time, acts as its representative before the higher powers. 'If the Princes and the Emperor,' says Lao Tse, 'conform to the Principle, all beings, of their own accord, will cooperate with them; heaven and earth acting in perfect harmony will spread a sugared dew.' We shall see this in greater detail when we consider the foundations of social organization.

This constant anxiety to secure the indispensable harmony between macrocosm and microcosm creates the need to know not only the laws that govern the universe—and we shall see later how that has an influence not only on the concept of science and that of education, but also, in the absence of intimate knowledge of these basic laws, the need to find out at least the way in which they work and the details of their application. That is the purpose of the occult sciences, among which astrology, geomancy and all the methods of soothsaying are the foremost. As Gobineau has said, for the Asians the most important business is to know the supernatural well and as minutely as possible.

The observation of the heavenly bodies is therefore of the highest importance and we shall see the considerable progress made in Asia in this sphere from the remotest times. *Enuma anu enlil*, the great Babylonian book on astrology, was translated into Susian as far back as in the seventh century B.C. In the Lamaist monastery of the Lake of the Geese, out of ten years of study one full year is devoted to astronomy and astrology. According to the Yakuts, the Mongolian Buryats never engage in warfare between the full moon and the new moon. In the archery tournaments of Outer Mongolia, the arrows must be collected by a man born in the year of the mouse, *pica*, the first arrow must be shot by a man born in the year of the tiger, the results recorded by a man born in the year of the monkey and certain portions of songs in honour of the victors must be sung by a man born in the year of the dragon. In Laos one can only marry at the time of the waxing moon, just as in the west many farmers know even now that the time of sowing and transplanting must be chosen according to the phases of the moon. In China, when the moon is quite round and faces the sun, the king and the queen must unite. In Afghanistan, while the lunar eclipse predicts catastrophes of nature, the solar eclipse announces political catastrophes. In this same country astrologers are regarded as inspired beings who predict divine anger and charitably exhort the believers to ask for mercy. The Sino-Viet-Namese calendar, like the Roman one, apart from its usual purpose, has the aim of foretelling the future, and attaches the greatest importance to the knowledge of the days that are auspicious and those that are inauspicious.

Just as the study of anatomy and physiology is of little practical interest except in its application to individual diagnosis, leading to preventive and curative hygiene and medicine, it is obviously the horoscope and the conclusions drawn therefrom that give its full value to astronomical knowledge. This need for microcosm-macrocosm correspondence requires, for the plotting of individual 'heavens', an extremely accurate knowledge of the position of the stars at the time of birth. In Burma the birth certificate must specify the time with the greatest care.

Nevertheless, the actual date of birth and, in some countries, the year in which it took place (with the exception of China and Japan, where the year of birth is very important) does not seem to have more than secondary importance among many Asian peoples, for the person concerned as well as for others. This is so in Viet-Nam. A Tibetan does not know what a birthday is. The majority of Asians do not know their age. Some Loatian tribes, such as the Khmu, only have a very vague idea of their age but never forget the day on which the individual was born. It even happens, for example, that the forgotten date and hour of birth are calculated on the basis of what has been noted from the horoscope; it is in this way that it has been possible to ascertain the date of birth of the great saint Ramakrishna. It is not impossible that considerations of this kind may have given rise to traditions according to which the birth, the illumination and the death of Buddha all occurred at the time of the full May moon, and the birth and death of Mohammed took place on the same day of the year.

Whatever the case may be, astrologers make a fortune, relatively speaking, throughout Asia, and there is hardly any event regarding which they are not consulted. In India entire castes, such as the Kaniyans, make it their profession and Muslims and Christians are not their least assiduous customers.

As for the methods of sooth-saying, they are numerous and intensively used. All Buddhist temples incessantly echo to the sound of sticks and wooden chips that are thrown down in order to find out what the future holds. Specialists consult the shoulder-blades of sheep and tortoise-shells. Palm readers are never out of work. Throughout Asia, fortune-tellers of all kinds are assailed by customers—and their predictions come true oftener than we might expect.

It is not enough to discover the detailed functioning of the macrocosm by the methods indicated above. It is also necessary to ensure a close conformity of human action with the laws that govern the universe, and this requires thorough knowledge and a carefully prepared technique. This is the purpose of ritualism.

For many of the Asian peoples, ritualism is at least as important as the moral code, for it governs the relations of man with Nature and with the Gods, while ethics only determine the relation of man with man. Now, 'harmony with men is human joy, happiness on earth; harmony with heaven is celestial joy, supreme happiness'.[5] Rites, the Chinese philosopher Li Ki tells us, prevent disorder just as dykes prevent floods. Any act in life, from the most trivial to the most solemn, has to be performed according to rites, in order to preserve harmony with the cosmos. This is what we generally call superstition, but those who have observed it a little more closely call it the sense of the sacred.

These rites may also, of course, play a more active part, of a really magic nature, when they are used in order to get extra-human and invisible bodies to help man in his enterprises, keep misfortune away from him and bring him advantages—but then they can also degenerate to a pitifully low level.

According to all the authorities, the rite is anyway only a

[5] Tchoang-Tse.

secondary manifestation and its execution, important though it may be, must go hand in hand with an inner state of mind, a real communion, and must flow naturally and spontaneously from it, although the thorough knowledge of ritual is an extremely complex science that can be mastered only after long years of study.

The sage, who has reached this state of complete harmony within himself and with his surroundings, is the ideal cherished by every Asian. His desire is to be steeped in nature, be esthetically sensitive to it and live in perfect harmony with it. The Japanese Constitution of the Year 604, now thirteen and a half centuries old, lays down in its first article that the highest consideration should be given to the harmony which should reign within the people; and of all the names given to their country, the one the Japanese prefer by far is its ancient designation of Yama-to, the Great Harmony. 'Following the universal law in all its movements, the sage is the agent of heaven,' says Tchoang-Tse, who defines him further in a dialogue between Yen-Hoei and Confucius. 'Stripping my body,' explains the former, 'obliterating my intelligence, discarding all shape, shunning all science, I unite with him who permeates all.' 'Thou hast attained true wisdom,' concludes the latter. In Viet-Nam as in China, the conception of the Golden Mean, *tchong-yong* in Chinese, *trung-dung* in Vietnamese, teaches children that, through inner and outer balance, man must link the perfect harmony of his actions with the eternal order of the universe.

The Taoist saint becomes so much an integral part of nature that, like it, he performs the most difficult operations without even realizing that he is doing so. Huai-Nan Tse tells us that the virtue of men who are in harmony with Tao 'moulds heaven and earth, harmonizes the *yin* and the *yang*; it divides the four seasons from each other and brings the five elements into accord; its benign and gentle breath cherishes all things, both inanimate and alive; it enriches vegetation with moisture and permeates stones and metals'.[6] Even to this day, there are interminable discussions in India as to whether such a sage also has the divine power to create, *ishatva*.

Thus, having become like the gods whose supremacy he jeopardizes, the sage is the object of their jealousy and fear and sacred literature is full of the struggles in which they engage against him, the snares they put in his path in order to prevent him at least from reaching the highest rung of the ladder where he would become the equal of the creator himself.

[6] Cranmer-Byng.

CHAPTER VI

Time

Let us not confuse history with the past.

MASSON-OURSEL

THIS feeling of unlimited continuity which, by its very nature, is more qualitative than quantitative, reappears particularly in the Asian's concept of time. For him the very essence of time lies in this continuity and not, as for us, in succession; time is not a way of classifying. For the Buddhists, for instance, time is made up of a continuous flux, a real continuum, *samtâna*.

On the one hand, the day and the year are not divided into mathematically equal parts as our clocks and calendars would have us believe; just like the body of the tree or the animal, they are composed of various parts each of which has a function, an importance, laws, dimensions and proportions peculiar to itself. It is immaterial that an hour or a day of happiness or labour, according to us, has as many minutes as an hour or a day of darkness, suffering or meditation; in Asia there is no common measure between them. It has been mentioned quite rightly that in Islam 'the adoption of the uniform rhythm of solar time as a measure was regarded as devoid of interest'.[1]

On the other hand, beginning and end in time, whether it be for man or for the universe, does not have as clear and final a significance for the oriental as it does for us. We shall see this later.

The supreme paradox is that time may even retrogress, not only in theory and in mythology, but in the conceptions of everyday life. In Viet-Nam it may be granted that if a general has lost many battles it is because an error was committed in his funeral rites. In China, some lord was unable to secure complete power in his lifetime because human beings were sacrificed to him after his death.

Furthermore, Asia thinks in terms of several categories of time, just as our most recent psychology has accepted the idea of 'psychological time'. Mazdaean cosmology distinguishes between eternal time boundless and without origin, *zervan-i akanarak*, and limited

[1] Raymond Charles.

time, 'with long domination', *zervan-i derang xvatai*. India does not confuse 'historic time' with 'puranic time' and acknowledges the real and useful nature of both. Mythical time, which is 'unexpirable', is obviously not the same as the time we are conscious of in the West and which we are gradually imposing upon the East.

Finally, for the Asian, time has not always existed, even after the advent of the human being. According to a Japanese philosopher, there was a primordial state where 'life slept as deeply as death and there was not any time'.[2] India accepts the bipolarity of time and timelessness, *kalashchakalashcha*.[3] A great French historian has written, very relevantly, that in Asia evolution occurs, if not outside time, at least regardless of it.[4]

It has often been affirmed that for the West time is linear and irreversible, while for the East it is cyclic. It would be more correct to say that for us it is shown by a straight line while many orientals would represent it in the form of a sinusoidal line.

The Muslims think not so much in terms of the 'unravelling' of history as of its 'ravelling'; for 'while European thought processes move in a linear duration, Arab thought evolves in a circular duration where every deviation is a return, confusing the future and the past in the eternity of the moment.'[5] For the Bektashi Shias, the universe is eternal and moves in an uninterrupted rotating but cyclic movement.

For the Mazdaeans, cyclic time is not the time of eternal return but the time of return to an eternal origin. Besides, the Iranians in general consider the cosmic drama as taking place in three acts: *bundahishn*, creation, *gumecishn*, the mixture, a state of the world based on present experience, and *vicarishn*, dissolution of the mixture and return to ingenuity.

The Hindu sacred scriptures, which enjoy absolute authority, affirm explicitly that the creation, life and dissolution of the universe are recurrent, periodic phenomena where creation, *srishti*, corresponds to the projection of the multiple form outside the non-manifested absolute, Brahman, and dissolution, *pralaya*, is the return of the many to the absolute. This is the idea expressed iconographically in the very important aspect of Shiva as the god of dance, Natarajan, in the *tandava* where a whole series of fires light up and die down one after another.

Among the Buddhists and the Jains, the succession of Buddhas and Tirthankaras (the most recent are only last in date, without being, for all that, either the last of the series or higher than the others) also suggests the cyclical character of nature.

[2] K. Kanamatsu. [3] *Maitri Upanishad*, VII, II, 8.
[4] Henri Berr. [5] H. Roux.

An Afghan put it more simply to James Darmesteter:[6] 'The world is like this watch. Its hand always covers the same path although time passes; the hand always comes back to the same place when the watch is properly wound—and it is God who winds it.'

For the Chinese, who are just as categorical, 'the very nature of time is to proceed by revolution'.[7] For the Confucian, who considers himself above all as the living link between the past and the future, whatever applies to one generation applies just as much to the others. For Lao Tse 'the beginning of the contraction inevitably follows the apogee of the extension', and for his disciple Tchoang-Tse, in this incessant and majestic revolution, the recommencement immediately follows upon destruction. For Pon-Leang Yi, who belongs to another school, 'everything is in the process of destruction, everything is in the process of construction'. For Mencius, Chinese history proceeds in cycles of five hundred years as follows: (a) the possession of the country by a foreign conqueror; (b) the absorption of this conqueror by Chinese culture; (c) a period of confusion and (d) a period of national government. According to him, also, a sage must be borne every five hundred years. In India, Shri Aurobindo announced that five hundred years must also elapse before the world receives another sage of the calibre of Ramakrishna. However, these are only very small cycles covering particular events. India and many other countries think in terms of cosmic cycles which are counted in thousands or millions of centuries and cannot be studied by our historical methods.

This conception of cyclic time, however, seems to be much less important among most Semites and Japanese—although for certain Shinto groups 'the eternal centre of the cosmos differentiates by expiration and unifies by inspiration'.[8] Nevertheless, among these people as in the rest of Asia, there seems to be a great interest in natural events of an obviously cyclic character. In Japanese art, at least as much as in Chinese art, the motif which recurs most often is the succession of the four seasons; the phases of the moon regulate most of religious and civil life among the Hindus and the Chinese; the life cycle of cattle plays a major part in the life of cattle-breeding and nomadic peoples. The succession of the signs of the zodiac are of primary importance throughout Asia.

Even if time as a whole has neither beginning nor end, as asserted by the Taoists and by some Japanese mystics in particular, this cyclic conception does not preclude the fact that, even for the Taoists, every existence of the world, for instance, did have a begin-

---

[6] In the 1880's.   [7] Marcel Granet.
[8] Chikao Fujisawa.

ning which was more or less remote from present time and which is described with a profusion of detail.

It is strange to note that many cosmogonies start from the premise of a separation of earth from water or with the emergence of the earth from the water. In India, according to some religious groups, it is Vishnu who, in the form of a wild boar, lifted up the sunken earth with his snout, or Shiva who made the first land, Benares, spring forth from the waters on the spikes of his trident. According to other Hindu traditions, it is from the churning of the uniform and homogeneous mass of the ocean that there emerged the first elements of earthly creation; and for the Shintoists, the original couple, Izanagi-Izanami, had recourse to a very similar process. The same idea is to be found in the Semitic traditions. In Canaean cosmogony the separation of the waters was an essential moment in creation. Among the Akkadians, according to the *Enuma elish*, there was an indistinct matter everywhere from all eternity, the primordial waters; from this mass issued two elementary principles, Apsu and Tiamat. For the Hebrews, Jehovah separated the waters below from the waters above before creating the universe. In the Koran, it is said: 'From the water have we made all that is living', and, according to an Islamic tradition, on the first day, all was created in the liquid state and coagulated on the second day. For the Yakuts, the earth was formerly covered with water, but the Evil Spirit plunged into it and returned with a little clay in its mouth from which the Great White Spirit made the earth. Among Kalmuks also, 'in the beginning, the Earth was all covered with water'.

Among other peoples, as for example the Gond, the Bihor, etc., in India and also among the Thais, the Lao and the Tonkinese, the beginning was a separation between heaven and earth. This tradition is to be found already among the Akkadians where a cosmogonic text says: 'When heaven had been separated from earth, (its) constant and remote twin' and, among the Sumerians, we may read in the exordium of the hymn to the carob-tree: 'When heaven was removed from earth, when earth was separated from heaven'. Even in Islam we may read in the Koran, 'What of it! Have the infidels not seen that the heavens and earth were welded together and that we separated them?' and God is often designated there by the name of al-Fatir, the separator of heaven and earth, the lord of the separation. In China, according to Chou-king, the Lord of the Above, Chang-ti, 'ordered Tch'ong-li to break off communication between Earth and Heaven'; Luen heng states further: The distance between heaven and earth has grown; in olden days, when the spirits and men lived in promiscuity, they were so close together (the earth offered its back to heaven and heaven embraced it) that one could go up and down between the two at any time. Tch'ong-li, by 'cutting off the communication', put an end to these scandalous beginnings of the universe. For the Japanese, heaven and earth were not separated in the olden days and it was the wind, in the shape of a pillar or a bridge, that connected them. According to one variant that is to be found especially among the Muria, the clouds and the earth were, at the beginning, very close to each other.

When thinking of the creation of the world or of its time, Asia preferably visualizes several successive stages of materialization. I have depicted an extremely methodical and logical series in the Hindu myth of Sharanyu,[9] but the same may be said of many other myths. This conception occurs even in the earliest known religions. Among the Sumerians, life set itself up in successive stages; the Akkadian Genesis seems to be evolutive; among the Hurrites, creation took place in successive steps. The two accounts—or even three, if we isolate the first verse which in itself forms a story of creation—which appear in juxtaposition in the first two chapters of the Genesis, are perhaps not so much different versions—as held by a modern exegesis that is destructive as well as pseudo-historic, wishing to oppose 'Jehovist' and 'Elohist' tradition—as successive stages of creation, of the same order as in the Hindu cosmogonies. The Taoists distinguish four successive stages in the formation of the world : *T'ai yi*, the Principle of Mutations, *T'ai tch'ou*, the Great Origin, *T'ai che*, the Great Beginning, and *T'ai sou*, the Great Indistinctness, even before coming to concrete bodies.[10] The first chapters of the Japanese Kojiki similarly give a description of the gradual path towards earthly materiality which, while it is hermetic, is nonetheless lucid and logical; I have tried to explain it elsewhere[11]. Among the Mazdaeans, the 'first act' comprises two successive stages : the passage to the *menok* (subtle, celestial) stage which corresponds to the first three millenia and the passage to the *getik* (terrestrial) stage which corresponds to the next three millenia. Among the Muslims, God granted a covenant to the Adamic race 'prior to any co-property, in a life which was not earthly as yet but pre-existed in the divine mind'.

However this may be, in many an ancient tradition, the sacred scriptures existed before the creation of the world. For the Hindus, the creator, Brahma, had to work in conformity with the rules contained in the Vedas. For the Muslims, the Koran is an attribute of God, just like his eternity and is not just one of his works; it is either uncreated or goes back to two thousand years before creation.

[9] J. Herbert, *La Mythologie Hindoue*.
[10] Lie tse, 1.
[11] J. Herbert, *At the fountain-head of Japan : Shinto*.

Among the Hebrews, while Divine Wisdom did exist before the origin of the world,[12] and the Abyss, the Torah also, like the Muslim book, is two thousand years older than the world, and God had to consult it before creating the world—and the first verse of St John's gospel could also be given a similar interpretation.

One of the signs of this progressivity, which subsists even after the emergence of the earthly and material world in its present form, is the extraordinary longevity ascribed to the earliest men. For the Chinese, the twelve emperors of heaven and the twelve emperors of the earth reigned for four hundred thousand years, then the nine emperors of mankind reigned for forty-five thousand years, and it was then, according to the annals, that the imperial house was founded. According to the Chinese pilgrim Fa-hien, at the time of Buddha Krakuchanda, men still lived for forty thousand years, and at the time of Buddha Kanaka-muni, the penultimate one before Gautama, they used to live for thirty thousand years. In Japan the son of Ninigi lived for 580 years. The early Sumerian kings reigned on an average for thirty thousand years each, those of the first Kish dynasty, a thousand years each. The same was true of India, according to the Puranas. The Bible, more modest, has Seth live for 807 years.

Such conceptions of time naturally have repercussions on the approach to historic studies. Love of such study, as known in the west, is alien to most of Asia, and hardly any attempt is made to draw general ideas or laws based on history in the way in which it is done here. Of course, there are countries like China or Japan where the annalists have done their work so conscientiously that there are now genealogies and other data covering several millenia. Dated Chinese chronicles begin in the eighth century B.C., and the first compilation of general Chinese history, that of Sseu-ma Ts'ien, goes back to the second century B.C. This, however, did not prevent the first emperor from having all history books burnt. The Emperor of Japan can trace the origin of his dynasty back 2,600 years, without a break, and not long ago there was a direct descendant of Confucius who could trace his ancestry back for about as long a period. In India, the monks list the transmission of their professed doctrine from disciple to master (*guru parampara*), going back to legendary times. All these lists, however, generally serve to justify the authority claimed for the doctrine and do not fulfil the criteria set recently by the western science of history.

Besides this, the recounting of past events, true or imaginary, is considered as a genuine form of education, and sometimes the traditional stories are altered without hesitation when the need is

[12] This is not unlike the Shakti of the Hindus.

felt for it.[13] This is not rare, even among the Chinese who enjoy a good reputation as historians. While it is excessive to say like Granet that 'the whole history of ancient China is based on a system of counterfeit that is both ingenious and scholarly', it may be admitted that the Chinese annals aim above all at drawing moral lessons from the past and attach only relative importance to what we call historic truth. A strange consequence of this is that, according to Chinese ideas, the history of the reigning dynasty must not be the object of specific study. Even among the Muslims, to whom we owe many and important landmarks in chronology, especially for Asia, history, like many other disciplines, is devoid of intrinsic value. They refuse to adopt what we consider to be *the* historic approach, and nothing keeps an Iqbal or a Sheik Abduh from consulting a particular verse of the Koran in order to discover references to miracles in it, just as the Hindus assert quite seriously that their distant ancestors used to possess aeroplanes.

Besides, there is practically no borderline between mythology and history. According to some Asians, it is the former which gives the latter 'a life-giving significance and which makes it 'the very soul of a nation'.[14] For the Hebrews the birth of Eve corresponds to a historic date. The sacred scriptures, which are still our most detailed source of information regarding Ancient India and Persia, do not separate the struggles between the gods and the demons, on the one hand, from those between the Eran heroes and the Turan warriors on the other hand, or those between the Dravidian aborigines and the Aryan conquerors. Almost the same could be said about Indo-China; in China and Japan one goes without any transition or break from the 'divine' sovereigns to the 'human' emperors. When a great French sinologist,[15] who died a few years ago, used to begin his lectures at the College de France with the words: 'The first sovereign of China was a yellow owl. . . .', he really put his audience into exactly the right atmosphere. There is hardly an invention that does not go to the credit of some deity; there is hardly a princely family that does not claim some supernatural being as its primordial ancestors or claim that he had a miraculous birth; in stories of battles the gods intervene frequently, if not as fighters within a physical body, at least by throwing their weight

[13] The many alterations of history carried out by the Soviet leaders surprised only the west. For Asian people, this is neither an innovation of nor a sacrilege against the so-called historic data or against 'science'.

[14] C. Fujisawa. Bareau (in *Présence Bouddhisme*) says: 'Difficult, tedious work too often vain—why not recognize it?—which consists in trying to separate history from fiction.'

[15] Marcel Granet.

into the balance—just as in the case of the Emperor Constantine's march on Rome.

Moreover, it must not be forgotten that apart from the succession in time of mythological and historical eras, the life of the gods remains closely interlinked with that of men and it has been said that 'history may be summed up as a synchronization of events occurring on earth with cosmic or celestial happenings'.

That is one of the reasons for which historical dates as we understand them—that is, dates which vary as texts and ruins are discovered—and which have major importance in the eyes of our scholars, leave our Asian friends quite indifferent. Actually, it is immaterial to them whether Zarathustra lived a thousand or five hundred years before our era or whether Kwan-yin-tse was a contemporary of Lao Tse (fifth century B.C.) or belonged to the eleventh century of our era. I have elsewhere mentioned the unbelievable differences in the conclusions reached by our western scholars as regards the date of the Rig-Veda.[15] There are some five thousand years' leeway between them! This does not prevent them from asserting calmly that only our calculations are scientific and that data given in the sacred scriptures is fanciful. Regarding some of the most important Buddhist scripts, contemporary erudites, even after the most thorough research, hesitate to date them with an approximation of three centuries! Our most scholarly elucubrations are of interest only to those Asians trained in our school who wish to appear worthy of their professors.

It must not, however, be concluded that people in Asia are not interested in their past; the crowds that rush to the history section of museums, both in Baghdad and in Peking, in Sarawak and in Taipeh or Tokyo, would suffice to prove the contrary.

The essential as well as rhythmic identity between the macrocosm and microcosm naturally entails close correspondence between cosmic and individual time.

While many Asian countries from China to Babylon have, from the most ancient times, devised accurate and clever calendars—luni-solar ones, for instance in India, Laos, Cambodia, Thailand—among the Mongols and Chinese the beginning of the year is often determined by considerations of a different order related, in particular with the dynasty or with the crops. For instance, among the A-Kha of northern Laos, New Year's Day takes place as soon as the rice harvest comes to an end.

What is more, the hours of the day are defined according to daily events in the peasant's or in his cattle's life, and each hour bears a

---

[16] Jean Herbert : *Spiritualité hindoue.*

name in relation to its specific purpose.[17] In Burma, the monks must traditionally get up when the light is sufficient for them to see the veins of their hand; and the layman can tell the hour by the direction and length of his shadow.

Furthermore, duration is counted and even expressed according to acts of everyday life. Thus, in China people spoke in terms of the time needed to drink a cup of hot tea, that which is required to eat a bowl of rice, the time that an incense stick lasts when it is set alight. In Viet-Nam, the units used are the *tan mieng giau* (three to four minutes) which is the time taken to chew a mouthful of betel, *chin noi mu o î* (half an hour), the time taken to cook rice in a pot for ten persons. In classical India the basic unit, *mâtra* (about half a second) corresponded to a pulse-beat or a heart-beat. In Islam the unit of time is the recitation of the 112th *surat*. Among the Bedouins of the Hadramaut, the only time-unit less than a day is the interval between two ritual prayers. In Korea it is the duration of a pipe.

In addition to this continual awareness among many peoples of the identity between the two kinds of time, particularly among the Chinese, we also see the anxiety to safeguard this identity actively. Some historians suppose, not without justification, that at a certain moment chiefs representing opposite groups and opposing spirits came to power alternately with the seasons. In any case, it is known that the emperor was accustomed to changing his apartments in the palace at the beginning of each season in order to enable the influx from heaven to spread through him over the earth in the right way. If he forgot or neglected to effect this change, he ran the risk of starting a catastrophe. Even in our days, according to a cultured Chinese,[18] the supreme refinement consists in listening to the ticking of a clock.

With regard to his individual life, the Asian visualizes it less within the limited context of a human existence or a series of specific actions than within that of a long line of generations or an endless chain of successive lives or even as an illusion or a trick of the mind—this makes him much less liable than us to impatience or haste. For him the quality of our life has no connection with the mortality of our body and the value of our acts is not affected by their ephemeral nature.

Almost all non-Semitic Asians regard re-incarnation as an article of faith which suffers no questioning, just as the Christian regards the survival of the soul after death. However, they interpret re-incarnation in different ways. Those who give the most detailed

[17] Prince Pethsarath has listed in *Présence du Laos*, the names of sixteen vigils of 1 h. 30 min. each in his country.
[18] Lin Yutang.

description of it are perhaps the Hindus. For them there is a permanent entity, the *Atman*, which sojourns successively in different bodies following an ascending line from the most elementary living being to man or to the sage, and is finally liberated from this round of death and birth, *samsara;* between these evolutive embodiments there are static stages in the limbus, in hell, in paradise and even in the bodies of gods and demons.[19] (However, in India there are small groups such as the Linga Balija, who do not believe in successive lives.)

The Sikhs, the Jains, the Tibetans, most Indo-Chinese mountain tribes, the Mongols[20] and many others have rather similar beliefs, although these are mostly less specific and less subtly detailed.

For the Mazdaians, the time of birth and that of death are in no way the absolute beginning or the absolute end.

For the Buddhists the permanent entity, known as *Atman* by the Hindus, has no real existence and it is a conglomeration of impressions, thoughts, feelings and desires which is subjected to this long and painful experience of successive lives before it finally dissolves itself—but this leads to very little difference in practical behaviour. Even theoreticians supply abundant details on re-incarnation: 'The time lapse separating death from rebirth is infinitely brief. . . . If we have not thought or acted as men in the course of our human existence, we hardly have any chances of being reborn within a human body', and so on.[21]

While the Chinese generally admit the idea of re-incarnation and embellish its description with countless picturesque details, Confucianism, as such, places more stress on the succession of generations considering each being not as an independent and separate individual but as a link in a chain, the beginning and the end of which are lost in the obscurity of time. According to Taoism, 'man enters the weaving loom (of incessant universal revolution); in their turn, all beings come out of the great cosmic loom in order to go back into it when their hour comes'.[22] Even when the Chinese do not stress individual re-incarnation in the sense in which it is understood by the Buddhist, they retain their profound sense of continuity: 'Ultimately the parent vanishes into the children, the artist passes into his work and both may acquire immortality on earth through the race and through the recognition of generations to come.'[23]

In general, however, in the great Chinese tradition, individual

[19] Complete description to be found in J. Herbert, *La notion de vie future.*
[20] The powerful Tumed chief Altan Khan, who in 1577 officially constituted the Mongol Lamaist church, gave himself out to be a re-incarnation of Kublai (R. Grousset).
[21] C. P. Ranasinghe.
[22] Tchoang-Tse.   [23] Cranmer-Byng.

re-incarnation reaches such a degree of precision that it is normally the grandfather or the ancestor who re-incarnates himself into the infant; after a sojourn in Mother Earth, the child to be born abandons the world of the ancestors in order to penetrate into the living part of the family.

This concept of inter-family re-incarnation is not, moreover, peculiar only to the Chinese. It is to be found, for example, in India in certain Pano villages where, when a child is born, a priest is consulted in order to find out whether it is the incarnation of the grandfather or the great-grandfather.

The Japanese, who are much less affirmative and doctrinary, probably have an attitude half-way between that of the Chinese and the Hindus; here their Scriptures make no allusion to the condition of the dead, but they also regard the individual as a mere link in an immense chain.

There are even certain Jewish groups that believe in re-incarnation.

This consciousness of a close synchronism between man and the universe explains and justifies what we mostly consider as mere superstition, the belief that certain hours, certain days of the week or of the moon phase, certain months or certain seasons are auspicious or inauspicious for the accomplishment of certain special actions or for any undertaking in general. The Asian almanacs are full of practical information in this regard and the examples that have become familiar to us are too numerous to be quoted in full. It will suffice to give only a few of them.

In China the dead can wait to be buried for months or even years before the coming of an auspicious day, indicated by the almanac. In Tibet it is sometimes necessary to add an auspicious month to the calendar or to withdraw one which is harmful.

These periods, short or long, are frequently determined by the festivals of certain deities or by memories of their existence, more seldom by more or less symbolic arithmetical considerations; thus, in Laos, marriages are celebrated only in the even months, but in Thailand, where the same rule applies, a marriage can also take place in the ninth month.

The Asian differs from us not only by his abstract and passive conception of time, but also in his practical and active attitude. While our concern is to 'use' the time at our disposal in order to 'fit in' all the activities we think desirable, the Oriental is much more anxious to choose the most auspicious moment for each one of his activities, if necessary foregoing without regret those that do not fit in. For Asia, the rush and haste of our way of life, our irritation when it is impossible to act, seem strange and even ridiculous and stupid. If we cannot do something, it is because we were not destined to do it or because we had planned to do it as a result of incomplete information or an error of judgment.

Let us mention, finally, that for many Asian philosophies, time and space being only as we conceive them, only particular moods in the state of consciousness in which we happen to be living, there is a close bond between them. For the Chinese, for instance, 'Time and space form an indissoluble whole.'[24] For space is made of the opposition of the *yin* and the *yang*, and time of their alternation. For every individualized particle of duration there is a corresponding particle of space—and that is why Chinese thought never separates the consideration of times from that of spaces.

[24] Marcel Granet.

CHAPTER VII

Space

Of course, the gods exist.
SHRI AUROBINDO.

FOR practically all the Asian peoples there is absolute continuity of substance between all that exists, not only that which is material and perceptible more or less directly by the senses, but also that which is more subtle : the soul, the spirits, the gods; they all belong to one and the same 'nature which is in continuous transformation and which has never reached its final stage'.[1] Even Muslim thought does not distinguish between nature and supernature. Inversely, however, space in itself is not, as for us, (or, at least, as it used to be for us before the recent space explorations) immutable. 'Characterized by a sort of coherent diversity, (it) is not the same everywhere. Nor is it the same at all times.'[2]

Let us begin by considering the conception of the 'material' world, the world which in the West we call 'real'. We shall see later that for most of the Asian peoples, the country they occupy is traditionally either the whole universe or the whole civilized universe or, in any case, the centre of the world. They generally admit, however, that around this country, across immeasurable oceans, there are other, perhaps countless universes in infinite space.

The measuring of this physical space, as in the case of time, is not done in abstract units or out of proportion with man, like our terrestrial Meridian, but by means of units that either naturally correspond to objects[3] or by establishing a direct relationship between the measurements and the use made by man of the things measured. In China the length of the *li*, which corresponds to the ninetieth part of a day's walking, varies according to the nature of the ground, the gradient of the slope, the speed at which it is possible to advance; it is constant only near the capital, where practical reasons have made standardization necessary. Among certain groups in Eastern Siberia

---

[1] Henri Marchal.   [2] Marcel Granet.
[3] 'Things are not measured. They have their own measure. They are their own measure' (Marcel Granet).

the unit of distance is the *bukha*, the distance which should separate one from an ox in order not to see its horns any more. When recently they were measuring a new frontier in Saudi Arabia in miles, Ibn Saud wanted the distance to be expressed in terms of a day's ride on fast or slow camels. Formerly, in Elam, the area of a field was expressed by the quantity of seeds necessary to cultivate it.

Almost everywhere, as in the West of old, the units of weight, length and volume, as well as the ratio with their multiples and sub-multiples, varied not only from town to town, but also and especially according to the nature of the goods.

This 'material' whole—or, as people in India prefer to call it, 'gross matter'—represented by the universe does not, however, form the sum total of all that exists; far from it. Not only were the most recent discoveries of our psychology familiar to many traditional schools in the East, in India and also in Japan (where Shintoism made a distinction both between the conscious, *omote*, and the non-conscious, *ura*, and was aware of the spirit of unity which covers them and which links the physical with the meta-physical), but the Orient thinks in terms of a considerable number of other 'worlds' which intermingle with ours; we perceive them or rather we enter them only when we are carried to planes of con-sciousness other than the one we are in usually, but their action is apparent to us when we are in our normal state. It is a constant mixture of what we call the 'real' and the 'supernatural'.[4]

Here again, it is probably India that supplies us with the most complete and most minutely detailed pictures, pictures that are legion and, at first sight, inconsistent and contradictory; but an attentive and, if possible, experimental study reveals their inexor-able logic. Firstly, for the Hindus there are several *lokas*—a term generally translated as 'worlds'—only one of which, the *bhurloka*, embraces that which in all universes is similar to what is perceived now by our senses. There are generally supposed to be seven *lokas*, but the number may vary according to the manner in which we subdivide 'what is', just as geographers may assess the number of oceans differently according to the way in which they divide the whole.

Through our life, if not through our being, we constantly par-ticipate—often actively, even oftener passively—in a large number

[4] It is worth while mentioning here an exceptionally categorical descrip-tion of the attitude of Semitic religions. According to Bottero (in *Naissance*), 'one of the greatest conquests of the human mind and in the religious realm, a considerable step forward, consists in that Israel substituted, in the place of a single universe covering under its laws all that exists, two irreductible spheres, the Creator and Creation.' Asians faced with this theory would feel sorry for us in that we are thus isolated, cut off from God.

of these *lokas* although in our normal state we are hardly conscious of anything but our presence in the *bhurloka* and our relationship with it. However, either through subtle disciplines, the *yogas*, or through the influence of certain sages, or for other reasons, man may accede to planes of consciousness different from ours, where he is transported with the whole or part of his consciousness; he achieves this either by reaching beyond his limitations and going outside himself, or—what finally comes to the same—by delving within himself and analysing the most hidden depths of his being.[5]

In this exploration of the microcosm or of its twin, the macrocosm, man enters into direct contact with the forces that come into play in other worlds and with the various entities that people them. Whether it be in the countless spheres of the unconscious or the subconscious or the paraconscious or the supraconscious, he always finds himself again and may therefore conclude that at least a part of his being has always been more or less exposed to the influence of whatever exists and acts on these different planes.

The most accessible descriptions, for us, of this whole where each one of the myriad elements is as complex as the material world which is familiar to us, have been supplied to us by the great contemporary Indian sage, Shri Aurobindo, in his immense works. He proceeds, above all, by the experimental method, progressively dissecting the whole of human nature, known and unknown to us; but this operation gives him the knowledge necessary in order to describe these same planes or worlds in themselves, regardless of the observer.

Although certain great sages of Asia have systematically avoided stating their beliefs on the nature or even the existence of other worlds—this is the case with Confucius and also with Buddha—there are hardly any who have denied their existence. In the minds of almost all Asians unanimously, not the slightest doubt arises in this regard. Some groups, such as the Buddhists, the Lamaists, etc., have specific pictures in their mind regarding them, even down to the minutest details; others simply admit their existence without claiming to know them, but all are fully aware of being bound to them by bonds that are unbreakable.

We have seen earlier that the dead inhabit 'worlds' other than ours, limbus, paradise, hell, etc. Each of these is highly complex, like the world of the human beings, for various planes interplay simultaneously in them, but they nevertheless differ considerably from ours. Now, for all Asians there is constant communication between

---

[5] The clearest descriptions of Indian yogas, for non-initiates, have been supplied by Swami Vivekananda.

the world of the living and that of the dead and this communication should incidentally make it possible for us to find out the existence of certain 'other Worlds' and to give us information on them. What is of interest to us here, however, is not so much the detailed description of them as the influence exercised on humans by this communication with the dead.

Whatever be the form in which the dead reveal themselves to us after they have abandoned their physical bodies, they are always capable, many years afterwards, of coming into contact with the living, on the initiative of either side, and this is done sometimes with remarkable vigour. According to the Mongolian historian Sanang Setchen, it is the shadow of Genghis Khan which, in 1439, over two centuries after his departure from earth, struck dead the Oirat chief Toghon. Similarly, according to the categorical and consistent testimony of many witnesses, King Siuan was struck down with arrows shot by the ghost of one of his victims. It is therefore not a paradox to affirm that one of the most notable services rendered by Buddhism to the Chinese nation was to have 'pacified' the world of the dead. In Japan, the vengeance of ghosts is a favourite subject of drama.

In this same country, people never forget that 'the spirits of the dead subsist in this invisible world which envelops us on all sides';[6] and when a letter arrives after the death of its addressee, even if the letter belongs to one of the most modern families, it is deposited before the funerary stele of the dead person so that he may read it. The dead do not stop being of service to their masters, their parents, their wives and their children, just as if they were still living.

According to the Zoroastrians, the dead come back to earth on their birthdays, to the very place where prayers are offered in their honour. Many Muslims believe that the dead pay visits to their surviving friends and relatives, particularly on Fridays and, inversely, women go on that day to the cemetery to make offerings and libations.

This continuation of relations is obviously one of the main reasons for ancestor worship, which plays a preponderant part in China and throughout the Far East; and, of course, it is also the basis of spiritism which is so widespread throughout Asia, and which uses such a wide range of communication methods.

Some of these dead are normally evil for the survivors, such as the Viet-Namese *ma*, the *ne* among the A'Kha of Northern Laos, the *bhutas* and *pretas* in India; others, rarer, are normally beneficial. Mostly their attitude depends on the way in which the living cater

[6] Atsutane Hirata.

to their numerous and very genuine needs, thereby rendering them harmful or auspicious. Thus, in Laos, there is no condition worse than that of the *phi*, dead and doomed to an eternal life underground unless it receives ritual offering.

Well thought-out mental communication is established with these dead sometimes through the priests and sometimes through lay specialists—in Japan the *ichiko* send up prayers that are now Buddhist and now Shintoist; among the Taoists, this is done through sorcerers, *tao nai nai* or *hsien nai nai*, when it is not possible to consult the ancestors' funerary tablets directly; in Viet-Nam through men media, *ong dong*, and even more through women media, *ba dong*; among the Mongols by the *beki* and so on. Such relations make up the essential part of Caodaism.

A curious case of physical communication with the world of the dead is that of Japanese mothers who have too much milk. They pray to the god Jizo so that the excess should go to the dead children —and their lactation is visibly reduced.

Dreams—the very word calls up in us images of tell-tale and unreal illusions—are seen in a completely different light in most of Asia. In common Hindu philosophy, it is one of the three stages: *jagrat*, to be awake; *svapna*, dream; and *sushupti*, dreamless sleep; all of which are of equal importance, share out man's life among them and lead him to planes of consciousness that are different but all equally 'real'. In dreams it is possible—more easily than when awake—to have perfectly authentic communication with other worlds and other kinds of beings. The same beliefs are to be encountered throughout the Far East. 'It is extremely difficult,' notes an Englishman, 'to make a Chinese believe that dreams are subjective.'[7] The great Taoist master, Tchoang-Tse, having dreamt that he was a butterfly, explains that he cannot know with certainty which is illusion and which is reality—the butterfly or the man. In some traditions, still alive, particularly in Japan, dream reality is so close to reality when awake that perfectly tangible objects, such as a sword, may be received in a dream and then used in everyday life.

The most important aspect of this feeling of continuity in space is, nevertheless, the one which governs the ties between the world of men and that of the gods—categories which, except in purely Semitic religions, are not separated by any watertight or insurmountable partition. Among the Akkadians, divine purity and human impurity are not separate, for their world forms a whole.

[7] V. R. Burckhardt.

In Japan, between a man and a god, there is only a difference of degree and this distance is soon crossed: the great man becomes a small god; besides, the earth itself is a divine world and it is not separated from the other divine worlds by any bridgeless abyss.

First, it must be emphasized that for practically all Asians who have not been contaminated by western materialism, the gods are real in the fullest sense of the word. When Ramakrishna said: 'God alone is real, all the rest is unreal', he was not using a figure of speech, nor was he expressing an abstract idea. His mystical experience, shared by all the other saints and sages of India, enabled him to affirm that the reality of God—or of the gods—is of a higher order than that of men. Similarly, for the adepts of Tibetan Buddhism, the reality of the deities, the *khadomas*, is higher than that of physical objects. Although the persons who can speak of experience in this case are exceptions—a fact that cannot be denied—all the others believe them on their word as firmly as we ourselves believe in the reality of vitamins or hormones without ever having seen them ourselves. And they act in consequence.

Between men and gods the closest practical relationship is naturally that of consanguinity. This is frequently mentioned in practically all the non-Semitic countries. In the 'Book of Precepts', Ketab-e-Hukkam, of the Babis, 'we' designates both God and mankind collectively.

In a somewhat similar sense, Miki Nakayama, founder of the important modern Japanese sect of the Tenrikyo, sees 'Him' revealed first as God, Kami, then as Sun-Moon, Tsuki-Hi, and finally as Oya, the Parent, who has engendered human beings. Moreover, the Japanese is a son of the gods (The Japanese people is the 'surplus of the population of the heavens', *ame-na-masu-kitora*[8]) just as Japan is the land of the gods. While the imperial dynasty and, together with it, the whole Japanese people, are direct descendants of the goddess Amaterasu, each great family and each group, even a professional one, inserts between her and the men of our era a divine ancestor well-placed in the sacred scriptures, who further confirms the descendance. Thus the *sarume*, the sacred dancers at the imperial court, trace their genealogy from the goddess Uzume, who danced in order to draw Amaterasu out from the cavern into which she had retreated. The imperial family must even sometimes defend itself against claimants to the same ancestry or against theories demonstrating unwelcome similarities; thus, in 809, the Emperor of Japan had to prohibit the book *Wakan-Sorekitei-Fuzu*, which claimed that the reigning dynasties of Japan, China and Korea were descendants of Ame-no-minaka-nushi-no-Kami. There are in Japan to this day

[8] *Engishiki.*

descendants of the god Amenohohi-no-mikoto who serve in a temple dedicated to the god Okuni-nushi-no-mikoto. In the same country, the fact that the cosmic begetter, Kami, reveals himself directly in human parents is explicitly given as a justification for the religious nature of filial piety.

Sometimes, the lineage is less direct. Thus, the first Chinese sovereign, Huang-ti, established his power by calling down from the heavens his own daughter, Draught, who remained a goddess. Similarly, according to tradition, the first sovereign of Khotan, finding himself about to die childless, obtained a child from his god, Pi-Cha-Meu, who brought it forth from the forehead of his own statue worshipped in the big temple of the city; and, as the child refused the wet-nurses' breast, a mound rose up from the earth to feed it. Also in Khotan, in the seventh century, the sovereign was a descendant of the god Vaishravana.

The Tibetans regarded themselves as direct descendants of the god Hanuman, and still claim a divine ancestor. Cambodia is the son of the Nagi, goddess of the Water Country and of the maharshi Kambu. All the Lao peoples have as their ancestor Khun Borom, who descended from the heavens armed with all the insignia of royalty.

In India even the smallest sub-caste often claims a divine and miraculous origin—for instance, the Amballakaran maintain that they were born from a drop of the sweat of Parashu-Rama, incarnation of Vishnu, the Ahir that they are descendants of Krishna, and so on.

What is more, in India, strictly human demiurgic patriarchs appear in divine genealogies. Thus the god Garuda, great-grandson of the god Brahma, has as his maternal grandfather the sage Daksha, and as his father the sage Kashyapa, respectively son and grandson of the same Brahma.

Even in Islam this divine lineage is not unknown. Thus, in the Hadramaut the Murra claim to descend from a *jinni*.

In legendary history, considered as perfectly genuine by the peoples directly concerned, many figures cannot be clearly identified as human or divine. The Assyrians, for example, drew scarcely any distinction in their fabulous origins between men and gods. Much closer to us, the great Hindu religious reformer Chaitanya was sometimes the god Krishna and sometimes the worshipper of this same god. In our times, after what corresponds to enthroning, the Emperor of Japan becomes *atsumi-kami*, both human and divine, and it is not possible to draw the borderline between the two natures.[9] Eighteenth century texts, moreover, describe him ex-

[9] During the American occupation, General MacArthur ordered the Emperor to sign a declaration recognizing that he was not a god! School-

120

plicitly as 'god incarnate'. Other sacred texts recognize that there is not much difference between gods and monarchs; both share the same couch under the same roof. At a certain point it is also possible to discover a particular indentity unsuspected up to then. Thus, in the year 859, Shaku Gyoko 'discovered' that the god Hachiman was no other than the Emperor Ojin, who lived in the third century of our era; and his identity, which corresponds neither to an 'incarnation' nor to a 'deification' of the kind to be described later, has become more than an article of faith, a fact.

This does not apply only to the great figures. Doubt may be cast on the true nature of entire populations. According to the Mahavamsa, in the fifth century before our era, it was not known whether the aborigines were beings of flesh and blood or pure spirits. The abnormal thing, however, was that the question was even asked. Even to this day, there is in the Hadramaut a town that is completely human in construction—Ubar or Wabar—but it is commonly thought that its inhabitants are *jinn*.

Equally frequent are the cases of 'mixed' marriages between men and gods. In India, the Princess Kunti secretly married in succession the gods Surya, Dharma, Vayu and Indra and had children by each union. The Princess Madri in turn married twin gods, the Ashvins, and the result was. . . . a pair of twins. In 'liaisons' that are equally adulterous, but this time without the consent of the husband, Indra seduced the wife of the sage Gautama, and Soma seduced the wife of the sage Brihaspati. For the Pariahs of Travancore, Shiva had two children by a woman, Parachi, and the Guru of Rama is born of the love affair between Brahma and a dancer. The god Krishna took as wives Rukmini and Satyabhama, whose human birth was in no way miraculous—and there are other such examples.

In Japan, too, humans sometimes have children by the gods; thus the god Yae-koto-shiro-nushi turned into a crocodile in order to court Ikutamayori-hime, daughter of Mishima-mizokui-no-kami, and from this union was born Tatara-isuzu-hime, who became the legitimate spouse of the first earthly emperor, Jimmu.

What is even more frequent is that men are made divine, either after their death, or in their lifetime, and sometimes in strange circumstances. This is common in all the shamanistic religions. Each of the first five kings of the third dynasty of Ur was in his lifetime honoured as a deity and worshipped as such after his death. Ansakes, founder of the Persian dynasty of the Arsacides,

children were even obliged to write essays commenting on this declaration. Naturally the Emperor graciously signed and the children wrote what was expected of them. It is quite obvious that only the Americans took it seriously.

was transformed into a divinity during the reign of his brother Tiridatus in the third century B.C. In Tibet there are more than a thousand 'living Buddhas', that is, Boddhisattvas who have decided to re-incarnate themselves. Other examples abound.

But it is in China that the phenomenon has become almost a general rule, in the sense that the great majority of divinities bearing individual names are reputed to have lived a human life on earth and are mostly historical figures—unless, following another theory, perhaps true in a good many cases, they are gods whose mythologies have been adapted in order to identify them with historical characters. The result, however, is the same. The Eight Immortals themselves have a detailed biography of their sojourn on earth before being elevated to this supreme dignity. The Queen of the Sky of the Taoists is the daughter of a Fukien fisherman. What is more, according to one tradition, the all-powerful Kwan-Yin herself, who in Chinese Buddhism has eclipsed Shakyamuni and who corresponds to both Kshitagarbha and Avalokiteshvara, was supposed to be the Princess Miao-shan, a king's daughter who became a nun against her father's will. Shen-Nung, the Divine Ploughman, is supposed to be both an emperor of the twenty-eighth century B.C. and a general of the second century A.D. The Chinese god of the home is the sage Chang Kung, of the eighth century and the actors' god, the Emperor Ming Huang of the same period. The Spirit of the Sea, Yang Hu, was a marquis who became a god by getting drowned. Still in the Taoist pantheon, the five 'Deputy Ministers of Fire' are earthly ministers of the tyrannical Emperor Chou. As for the *ch'eng huang*, or 'City Gods', they are invariably selected from historical characters who have made a name for virtue on earth and are in an ascending scale of humanity, thus serving the higher divinities to forward petitions of the people. Confucius and his principal disciples also appear quite high up in this same pantheon. A common woman, who suffered wrongs and faced death to uphold her chastity might in an amazingly short time become a popular local goddess, prayed to by all the villagers.

Emperors do not always feel themselves compelled to wait till they are divinized—they sometimes take the initiative and decision themselves; the first to give such an example was Ts'in Che Huangli, who turned himself into a 'living god'. Whatever individual cases may be, in China we have the most perfect example of a total fusion—the term is not too strong—between the world of the gods and that of men, with the curious consequence that the living Emperor reigned over both at the same time and enjoyed the same absolute power over the inhabitants of both, dismissing, promoting and demoting as he wished along the divine as well as the human adder. In Japan almost the same phenomenon is found in Shintoism, and deification of men is not rare there. The god worshipped at Aso, for instance, Take-iwatatsu-no-kami, is the grandson of the Emperor Jimmu and the elder brother of the Emperor Suizei. There is even a special term, *ningen-shin*, to designate deified men. A great Japanese theologian, Hirata, goes as far as to affirm that all the dead become gods, although with different natures and varying influences.

Divinization of men, it must be noted, is not always permanent; it may cover only a certain period, more or less long. In India, for instance, most of the gods, even some of the greatest, are regarded less as permanent individuals than as posts, offices that are conferred for a definite period of time to souls that have accumulated the necessary merit in the course of their human existences. At the end of this term of office, these souls have to resume life in a human body in order to complete their evolution.

A temporary divinization may also, however, occur in the earthly life of those concerned, and for only a few days or a few hours, while maintaining its full value for that period. In India and Nepal a living person is often invested for one day with all the attributes of divinity, and God is worshipped through that person. When children are asked to act in a divinity play, for instance the life of Radha and Krishna, it is granted that during the performance they really *are* gods and have the same powers; and there are many examples of miracles performed under such circumstances.

A peculiar case of this temporary divinization is that of priests and sages who chant sacred invocations. In Japan the *norito*, which were originally gods' words addressed to men, became prayers addressed by men to the gods. The person who uses these formulae of blessing, when he or she fulfils the necessary conditions, assumes the sanctity and the power of blessing of the original divinity. This case should doubtless be compared with that of the *rishis*, who wrote the Rig-Veda hymns and who identify themselves to such an extent with the god invoked that they take his name.[10]

While men easily turn into gods, it also happens that gods visit our 'world', and our plane of normal consciousness, taking human shape. For most of the peoples of non-Semitic Asia, this can happen in various ways.

The most complete way is what is known as the 'incarnation' or 'avatar' where the god generally is born exactly like a man from a woman's womb, grows up, goes through different stages of human life and finally abandons his body or, as we may say in the West, dies. The most famous and most characteristic examples are the

[10] X, 38, 48, 49 and 119: to Indra by Indra; X, 84 to Manyu by Manyu; X, 124 and 140: to Agni by Agni.

avatars of Vishnu in India, whose number is given as[11] ten or twenty-two or even *ad infinitum*, without these different countings being in any way incompatible with each other.

These are not the only examples. All the great gods of India and also many minor gods incarnate themselves on occasion: Shiva, Brahma, Dharma, Lakshmi, Sarasvati, Kuvera, Agni, Skanda, Vayu, the serpent Sesha, the eight Vasus. There are even cases, such as that of Dattatreya, where several gods are incarnated simultaneously in the same human body. Incarnations of these same Hindu gods are to be found in Indo-China and Indonesia. Thus the Malayan kings traditionally gave themselves out to be incarnations of Shiva. The bas reliefs of Angkor represent the Khmer king as an incarnation of Indra. In the eleventh century, in Bali, the king, Karta Nagara, was considered an incarnation of Vishnu.

Divine incarnations are to be found in many other countries as well. In China, as well as in Viet-Nam, immortals are capable of becoming human beings or even animals in order to communicate with mortals. It is said that the Chinese god of literature, Wen-ch'ang-ti-kiun, had seventeen 'incarnations', but this was probably the case of a man who was divinized after having lived seventeen successive existences in various human bodies. On the faith of what was asserted by their master ad-Darazi, the Druzes considered the Egyptian Caliph al-Hakim, in the early eleventh century, as a divine incarnation.

Aside from these genuine avatars, who may be 'full' to a greater or a lesser degree, there are many cases where a god takes an adult human body, or rather creates one, without being forced to go through all the ups and downs of human life, for a longer or shorter period, or in order to accomplish a specific act.

Examples abound in ancient and modern Hindu texts. This was the case, already mentioned, of Indra, who wished to seduce the virtuous Ahalya; it was also the case of Vishnu, who wished to do the same with the no less virtuous wife of King Jalandhara; of Shiva, Vishnu and Brahma, desiring to test the virtue of Anusuya, of four other gods who sought Damayanti's hand, of Agni seeking help from Krishna and Arjuna; of Shiva testing Arjuna, etc.

These avatars may all take other forms—animal, plant or even inanimate. We have seen earlier the case of a Japanese god who, in order to marry a human, turns into a crocodile; another became a red arrow in order to join the woman who was his mistress. Indra and Agni change themselves into a pigeon and a hawk in order to test virtuous kings, etc.

[11] Brief descriptions of this are given in my book, *Spiritualité hindoue* and in my booklet, *Narada*.

There are also cases—even more numerous—of 'possession', where a divinity takes hold of the body and the mind of a perfectly normal human being and inhabits it for a certain length of time. This is quite common among the Shamans, the Shaktas, in Tibet[12] and in most other countries. The Tso-tchouan say that at the time of Confucius, the participants in the winter festivals were all 'like mad', that is, they felt animated by a spirit that was more or less divine.

Besides, the non-human entities that thus take possession of men and women or create human bodies *ad hoc* for themselves are not necessarily gods; they may also be inferior or even demoniacal beings. Thus, even in our own time, the Chinese believe that the *kuei*, harmful demons associated with the *yin* principle and who are all around us, may take the shape of men, women or animals. The natives of Northern Laos feel themselves constantly under a similar threat from spirits looking out for a chance to do evil.

While in some countries this temporary possession, in ecstasy, is a good omen for the subject and may even sometimes be regarded as a sort of guarantee of rebirth after death, in other countries people thus possessed are held in awe. Thus, in Laos, the law makes it possible to expel them from a village, and apparently there are communities made up exclusively of these unfortunates, the *phi-pop*.

Such possession may only end with death and then too, on condition that an appropriate ritual ceremony is performed; thus, among the Tiyan of India, the spirit of the goddess has to be 'withdrawn' from her worshipper immediately after death. The entity that thus inhabits a medium may often be identified by the tone and the accent which he uses or the accessories he requires.[13]

Finally, in order to bring out the complexity of the whole matter, we must mention that in Japan there are cases of gods who are 'possessed' by other gods superior to them.

Apart from this fusion and confusion between human and divine beings, gods of all kinds continually intervene in earthly matters, even in the smallest details, and themselves feel the impact of our own actions. This is admitted even by the Buddhists who, while stressing that gods are no more real than men, do not see why these two kinds of 'illusions' should not be interconnected as members of one and the same category.

These gods manifest themselves when they are called, such as

[12] A remarkably vivid, detailed description is to be found in Harrer's *Seven Years in Tibet*.

[13] In Laos. I have myself noted the same phenomenon in Madagascar and among the negroes of Brazil.

Avalokiteshvara, who is said to appear face to face—i.e., as a personal experience—and in a form appropriate to the circum stances before whoever seeks his help and implores his assistance But they may even come without being invoked, such as the *ne* of Northern Laos, from whom men can never conceal thei actions, which are punished sooner or later; and the Chinese *kuei* who sometimes persecute a whole quarter and give work to the police. It is not only in the ancient texts that they play their part as in the Tibetan epic of Guesar of Ling, where the main character are incarnations of gods or ghosts. Even to this day, for instance in Afghanistan, the djins, whose existence is admitted by the Koran itself,[14] inflict upon the human beings towards whom they are ill disposed a suffering identical to what they have undergone as a result of human actions, and play childish and cheap tricks or them. Moreover, there is nothing against the contracting of a really military alliance with one group against another; thus the Lamais Buryats offer guns to the gods so that they in turn might kill th evil spirits with greater certainty. Among the Jains, it is granted tha even the *vijjahâras* can enter the monastic orders of humans.

One explanation of this closeness—although in Asia no need fo explanation is felt—is perhaps that, according to various cosmog onies, it is out of boredom with his own solitude that God create the world of men. This is the case in India,[15] among the Tenri-ky of Japan, etc. It is conceivable, then, that under these circumstance gods will want to play with humans.[16].

We shall have the opportunity to see later that the Asian man an woman enjoy towards animals, plants, inanimate objects, the earth and the heavenly bodies, in fact, towards the whole of physica nature, a feeling of continuity, of unity as intense as that linkin them to the world of the gods. The main difference is obviously tha in our material world they share the same space with its othe inhabitants, obeying its laws, while the spaces where the gods, th dead, etc., move are almost totally unknown to us. We know tha they exist, since bodies and forces that can only exist in these othe worlds, on these other planes, show themselves to us here on earth but as regards their essence, their nature, their interplay, we ca only make assumptions, however well these might be supported b the sacred scriptures and also by the writings of more or less cor temporary saints and sages who, in a state of ecstasy, were able t enter these worlds. By way of example we might mention a descri

---

[14] *Encyclopaedia of Islam.*

[15] 'Out of joy were all things created', Tagore.

[16] 'After all, what is God? An eternal child playing an eternal game in a eternal garden.' (Shri Aurobindo.)

ion given in the Buddhist (Mahâyânist) Ganda-vyûha-sûtra of the
Vairochana Tower', one of the highest planes of consciousness,
where dwell those who understand the significance of the Void, of
'ormlessness, of Non-will' and where the Boddhisattva Maitreya
eads Sudhana : 'In this Tower, spacious and exquisitely decorated,
here are also hundreds of thousands of *asamkhyeyas* (millions of
nyriads, literally 'impossible to count') of towers, each one of which
s as exquisitely decorated as the main Tower itself and as vast as
Ieaven. All these towers, which are impossible to count, do not
nterfere with one another and each maintains its individual exist-
·nce in perfect harmony with the rest; and there is nothing here
hat prevents a tower from merging with others, individually or
ollectively. We have here a state of perfect interpenetration and
lso of perfect order. The young pilgrim Sudhana sees himself in all
he towers together as well as in each tower by itself, for all of
hem are contained in one and each one contains them all'.[17]

[17] D. T. Suzuki.

CHAPTER VIII

Causality

Inch' Allah

THE continuity that we have been able to observe, in time as well as in space, and which for the Asians is self-evident, naturally has a strong impact on their conception of causality. As there is no real rift between things, it follows firstly that all that has been or is done exerts a greater or lesser direct or decisive influence on all that is or will be. Furthermore, in view of the many planes that co-exist in close mutual connection, it is impossible to seek the cause of an event only on the plane where that event has become apparent to us.

If we were to go further, it would obviously be impossible even to bring out a cause to effect relationship of the kind sought by modern western science, either in individual cases or, even less, in generalizations leading to laws. The philosophers of Asia find a way out of this deadlock either with the help of cosmogonies that we have outlined or by seeking correspondences[1] or omens.

In the first place, they claim the existence—proved for them by the experience and the vision of sages—of a single primary cause which is at the origin of all things and which incidentally confirms the essential and organic unity of all that exists or may exist. According to the Hindus, this is the absolute, the Peerless One, the Brahman, the undifferentiated, who, for reasons explained in different ways, differentiated himself by exhaling the universe. Almost exactly the same concept is to be found among certain Japanese sects under the name of *fu-ni*, which corresponds to non-duality, the *advaita* of the Hindu monists. The Taoist concept of the 'total' which remains identical even when contemplated under the aspect

---

[1] Cf. Granet: 'instead of attempting to measure effects and causes, the Chinese use their wits in making a repertory of correspondences'.

[2] Cf. Granet: 'Everything deserves to be noted as an omen or as the confirmation of a sign (or a series of signs); but nothing incites one to seek an effective cause.'

of the Complete and in all the details of its composition' and 'in which the *yin* and the *yang* operate their mutations'[3] is a fairly similar concept; it is 'something indistinct, non-differentiated',[4] non-being, *wou*, from which is born the being, *yeou*. In Viet-Nam it is the Great Absolute, *thai cu c*, born of the Absolute Nothingness, *vo cu c*. For the Sikhs it is the Supreme Being, who has drawn the world from himself by a sort of expansion of his own essence, an expansion which occurs for his own diversion and is in perfect equilibrium. Even for the Zoroastrians, who put so much stress on dualities, there is, at the base, the All-Powerful, Yazdan, who has no counterpart; and it is after him and beneath him only that appears the great law of opposites, which dominates the whole of creation,[5] something very well understood by Masson-Oursel, when he writes that this dualism 'is only apparent, at most, provisional; and Zoroastrian morality implies its negation.' For the Buddhists, for whom the world is but illusion, the cause as such can evidently also be only illusory. Therefore, the starting point of all that exists in this world is Maya, the power of illusion. But as long as, in practice, we remain convinced of our own existence, we have, of course, to behave as if this world were real, and that is why one of the masters of Tibetan Buddhism has written: 'Buddha's teaching does not tend to deny multiplicity in favour of absolute unity, or to proclaim the absolute identity of all things; it does not attempt the destruction or the depreciation of contrasts but rather to discover their relativity, within the unity which is with them, in them and beyond them'.[6] It may also be said, without stretching the evidence too far, that for the Muslims, the oneness of God goes so far that it implicitly postulates "the *One* ... without whom" this "oneness remains precarious".[7]

The great sages who, through asceticism and meditation, have risen to the consciousness of this primary cause, are capable of seeing the why and the wherefore of all things. For them all is clear, logical, explicable and necessary in its infinitely manifold and strictly inevitable causal sequence, in the future as in the present and the past—provided they take the trouble to consider it, something they rarely condescend to do. This is not a more or less mythological legend; these potentially omniscient sages exist and I have myself had the privilege of being with several of them.[8]

---

[3] Marcel Granet. [4] Tchoang-Tse, 2.
[5] H. K. Iranshah.
[6] Lama Govinda.
[7] Masson-Oursel.
[8] Shri Aurobindo and Ramana Maharshi were remarkable examples, to mention but two sages who have died recently; but I have also known some in Islam.

For those who have not risen to that exalted state, the purely intellectual acceptance of the oneness of the primary cause is not of great practical interest and they have to confine themselves to a lower and later stage for reference. What follows immediately is generally a duality.

This duality may be on an extremely abstract level. This, for the Hindus, is the case in the Samkhian system where the Purusha is the inactive witness, and the Prakriti, the cause and essence of the universe, draws from this Purusha the means of acting or even of being. In Buddhism, by opposition to the Maya we have the *shunya*, which is generally only roughly translated by the word Void. This is the theory which is accepted by Shri Aurobindo who, reviving a traditional theory, sees in the Absolute the manifestation of the supreme duality, merged in the Purushottama of the Bhagavad-Gita. For the Taoists, as we have seen, this duality is Being and Non-Being. Among the Japanese this duality is represented by Kami-musubi and Toka-mi-musubi.

This duality, however, mostly takes the aspect of a polarity between two more or less antagonistic and equivalent forces and the world is merely a consequence of their struggle or, at least, of their interaction. Among the Chinese we have the *yin* and the *yang*, 'this pair of forces with their roots in a mysterious unity'.[9] Among the Koreans we have similarly the *li* and the *ki*; among the Hindus the gods, *devas*, and the demons, *asuras*; among the Jews, Muslims and Parsis, the principle of Good (Jehovah, Allah, Ahura-Mazda) and the principle of Evil (Satan, Iblis, Ahriman). The Zoroastrians do not even go as far as two different principles in order to bring out this duality, but already find in the dual name of Ahura-Mazda the indication that He jointly and simultaneously created Mind and Matter. Even the Japanese sometimes see in their two great primordial divinities, Izanagi and Izanami, the gods of the *yin* and the *yang*.

It has to be pointed out, however, that even between this pair of poles, continuity subsists. Polarity only exists between their extremes and all the intermediary stages may be found in the ladder that unites more than separates them, for contrasts meet in the principle, and it is only in their becoming that there is opposition. Thus we have these 'pairs of opposites', *dvandva*, that we come across so frequently among the Asians: long and short, heavy and light, true and false, grandeur and mediocrity, past and future, right and left, form and space, inner and outer, collection and dispersion; and also, on a less abstract plane, religion and science, the emotional and the intellectual, the vertical and the horizontal

[9] Jean Grenier.

evolution and involution, authority and liberty, progress and retrogression, peace and war, man and woman, day and night.[10]

Sometimes it also happens that the duality emerging directly from Unity is replaced by a trinity. This is particularly the case for many of the great schools of Hindu philosophy where, for instance, it is admitted that the supreme god, *Ishvara*, the human soul, *jiva*, and the world, *jagat*, appeared at the same time. Trinities most frequently mentioned, such as the three faces, *trimurti*, of the one god, *Ishvara*, or the three *gunas* (*sattva*, *rajas*, *tamas*), actually take their place after duality. The same may be said of the Taoist trinity made up of Pan-gu, Yu-houang and Lao-Tse, the 'three Pure Ones'.

Whatever the case may be, it is normally a disequilibrium between the components of this duality or this trinity that gives birth either to the world itself or to the disorder that disturbs it, or both when—as is frequent in Asia—the world of multiplicity is regarded as being doomed to eternal imperfection and incessant troubles.

In everyday life, however, while this primordial unity, the dualities or trinities are admitted theoretically, and regarded as the origin of every fact observed in the world, even in Asia the need is often felt to seek nearer and more specific causes. It is here that we have the infinite multiplicity of causes we have mentioned earlier manifesting themselves vertically and horizontally. Vertically, in the sense that the Asian would seek a cause to the cause we would ourselves normally recognize, and another cause to that cause, and so on in an unending chain. For instance, Asians generally do not ignore the facts of heredity, but they go further in order to find out why our souls came to be re-incarnated in a family where it would be exposed to such a heredity. Horizontally, in the sense that they are not content with merely ascribing a physical fact to one or more causes of the same order, but also see this fact as the consequence of many other factors that have nothing physical in the sense in which we usually understand this term. Thus, any fact is the point of convergence of countless groups of previous events—just as it is also the starting point of countless groups of subsequent events.

Besides, this is not just an abstract concept. 'In order to perform our part properly,' a modern Japanese pointed out, 'we must know the whole play.'[11] This, of course, does not stop anybody from choosing among the 'causes' the one or ones required in the context of the argument or the action, but it is known that this choice

[10] Granet mentions a particularly interesting polarity among the Chinese, that 'of the symmetrical and the centred'.

[11] Okakura Kakuzo.

is arbitrary, pragmatic, and when another choice is suggested, this is not considered as a fundamental disagreement but as a difference between two viewpoints which may, a priori, be equally and simultaneously justified.

These varied causes are not all of the same importance. Generally, in Asia, the more subtle they are, the more imperceptible to our normal sensory apparatus, the more decisive is the importance ascribed to them. Again these non-physical causes are, of course, mostly related to non-human entities, usually personified by gods, *jinn*, spirits, etc. We shall mention many curious examples of this in the chapters dealing with technology, medicine and even in those on art and literature.

To quote only a few typical cases: one of the most popular Japanese plays, a *ga-gaku* of the eighth century, representing a battle, devotes hardly a tenth of its stage time to the scene of the fighting, and the remainder to the prayers of the hero before the action and then to his acts of thanksgiving. In the same country, when a baby cries at night, supposedly under the influence of an evil spirit, it is quietened by scattering unhusked rice on the floor —and the child does stop crying. Among the Gond it is impossible for a couple to procreate children until they have received Rama's blessing. In Afghanistan, the only women to make good wet-nurses and produce healthy milk are the wives of brave men who have never fled before the enemy and have never been wounded in the back. In Annam the high mortality rate among underground mine workers is attributed to the anger of the mountain spirits who have been disturbed. In Viet-Nam the first person who enters the house at the beginning of the year has to be a lucky one, or have a good soul—*via lanh*—otherwise the inhabitants will suffer ill-luck right through the year. The same is true in the Arab countries. Even today, the daily existence of the Muslim is haunted by spirits, *jinn*, demons that may be offended at a single gesture.

This, of course, opens the door to all magic—white or black—which in the East, and particularly among the women, plays a considerable part and which we, rightly or wrongly, call superstition, often exploited by charlatans with or without occult powers. In Asia, this is easy. In many cases, however, it is difficult to doubt the effectiveness of the processes used, however strange they may appear. Let us cite a few examples among thousands that were credited by the masses.

Countless witnesses report that in Bali, in the tenth century, Ampu Barada used to walk on water, reduce trees to cinders by his very glance and move mountains. In about 1720, at the time of war, a Persian virgin repeated the sacred Muslim words '*La illaha ill'Allah'* two thousand times over a cauldron and thus rendered the Persian soldiers invisible to their enemies. In 1826, Seid Ahmed, in Afghanistan, was reputed to have reduced cannons to silence and made bullets harmless. Nearer to our own time, during the terrible floods in China the local authorities prohibited the killing of any animal for three days in order to appease the river god—as had always been done in China—and the waters drew back. In May 1934, the Tibetan Lama Nola Kotuhutu, officially invited by the Cantonese Government, stated that he could, by means of his incantations, protect the people against asphyxiating gases, and by arguments taken from astrology and necromancy managed to bring about a change in the placing of artillery in a fortress. About 1935, all the Indian newspapers reported the case of a naked ascetic who, having been stopped from boarding an express train, had, by his mental and spiritual strength, prevented the train from leaving despite all the additional engines brought for the purpose.

Of course, this can be stretched to the absurd. In China a school-child is not supposed to eat chicken feet because it might make him scratch and tear the pages of his exercise book. Moreover, it has been observed at all times, and not only today, that there are movements of reaction against these superstitions and even against magic—and this is true for all regions of Asia.

The causality relationship, as the Asians see it, is further complicated by a factor that we have mentioned earlier—namely, the identity, at least the qualitative identity, but often an even closer one, between the macrocosm and the microcosm. Inasmuch as man individually does no more than reflect the universe, it is in this universe that we must to a large extent seek the real causes of whatever happens within ourselves. 'The power of life attains its maximum when nothing hinders the endosmosis of the microcosm and the macrocosm.'[12] That is why, in order to increase or even maintain one's vitality, every being must adopt a way of life conforming to the rhythm of universal life. This also applies, as we shall see later, to our individual actions which, especially if we are in a position of leadership, have a direct influence on the fate of the world as a whole and are often even decisive.

In spite of this last factor, the multiplicity of causality is doubtless largely responsible for what, among Asians, seems to us to be a paralysing fatalism. *Mektoub*, say the Muslims; it was written on a 'well guarded tablet', *al-Lawh al-Mahjuz*,[13] which existed well

[12] Marcel Granet.
[13] Koran LXXXV, 22. This idea of the tablet, containing the world's destiny in advance, existed already among the Akkadians.

before creation, and consequently we can do nothing about it, and it is not our fault. Hindus and Buddhists, starting from diametrically opposite views, reach the same practical conclusion: it is *karma*, the result of what we have done, each one of us in our previous lives which none remember; consequently, we are not responsible for them in this life. This *karma*, which is the same as the *gam* of the Thai, the *kan* of the Burmese, is the real guiding line if we try to understand real life or even stories. However, it is even more difficult to understand since for many such as Tagore in India and for the Tenri-kyo believers in Japan, it bears fruit only after one or more lives in between. It must, however, be noted that in theory Buddhist theologians refuse to admit the all-powerful nature of *Karma*. Anguttara Nikaya says, 'It is like having the mind clouded in its vigilance to believe that whatever a man may experience in the way of pleasure or pain or feelings that are neither one nor the other—all is due to something he did previously.' But the very energy with which this doctrine is refuted proves that it is very widespread in practice. Theoretically, the law of *kamma* (a form of the Sanskrit word *karma*), however important it may be, is only one of the twenty-four conditions, *pachchaya*, listed by Buddhist philosophy; it is one of the five *niyama* or orders or processes which prevail on the physical or mental planes; *utu niyama*, inorganic physical order, *bija niyama*, organic physical order of sprouts and grains, *kamma niyama*, order of action and result, *dhamma niyama*, order of the norm or the Law, *chitta niyama*, order of the mind or psychical law.

Most often, this belief, deeply rooted in our present irresponsibility, takes the form, mostly sincere, of total submission to the divine. *Inch' Allah*, says the Muslim, 'if God wills'. It is the will of my Divine Mother, says the Hindu. It is heaven's will, says the Chinese. It is undeniable that this anticipated resignation often leads to procrastination, laziness, easily combined with the total lack of any desire to improve one's lot. Both together, while they do exercise a calming influence which the West could envy, are obviously not favourable to progress as we understand it. The Koran considers bigger harvests not as the fruit of man's labours but as the expression of the divine will, and that is perhaps why work on the land has been considered as something servile in Islam. It has been said that in Islam man is degraded to the rank of second causes.[14] I heard a Muslim say that he did not see why he should water the fruit trees that had been planted for him; Allah would deal with it himself if he wanted the trees to grow.

[14] Raymond Charles.

Very recently, in the Philippines, the inhabitants refused to dig wells because God had obviously wanted water to flow on the surface of the soil; if He had wanted holes, He would have made them Himself. Many orientals, as we shall see later, accept without protest illness or infirmity because it has been sent by God.

This belief in the uselessness of individual initiative and in the futility of action no doubt reaches its culminating point in the Taoist doctrines regarding the role of the government and individual rules of conduct:—never to intervene in any way in the natural course of things, never to use one's will-power, nor even to act. This is far from being the only instance. There is much Hindu teaching according to which man must refrain from acting. Furthermore, there are examples of sages—I have known some myself—who cannot even take food to their mouths and who have to be fed like infants.

While this conception has some effects that we deem regrettable, others cannot but meet with our approval. To quote only one instance, the Asian considers that the past also was the consequence of influences outside our action and the natural result is that he can feel no rancour at the wrong done to him nor any bitterness at what he has had to undergo. In a recent booklet of UNESCO, it is said quite relevantly: 'The events of the past, whatever their grandeur may have been, are less important than the recollection that is left of them and less so than the interpretation given to them by those who keep this recollection.'[15] Kaltenmark uses the excellent expression 'a resignation devoid of rancour'. In the Hadramaut, when peace is concluded between two tribes, the form used is: 'Let the past be the past.'

On the whole, the Asian bears no grudge against the one who has done him harm. Except in circles very much affected by westernization, it is unthinkable for Asians to write vindictive books on the horrors of a war or foreign military occupation, colonial or otherwise. For Asian historians the Mongol conquest was simply a scourge sent by God, like drought or earthquakes. Vindictiveness would indeed be tantamount to perpetuating a deplorable state of affairs which should be left behind as quickly as possible. Besides, when the great masters of the Far East and India enjoin that hate should be conquered by greater love, they do not state a moral axiom, they do not just give eminently practical advice, they conform to a cosmic law. I was told of the case of a young Chinese from Shanghai who, having had his home destroyed and his whole family massacred by a bombardment, did not complain or blame anybody, 'in order to safeguard his

[15] Fradier.

135

soul', as he said. To orientals this is all too natural and only a westerner would notice it.

While various factors intervene in changing this basic attitude—for example, the obligation to avenge the family's or one's own honour—these factors often stem from motives different from ours. In cases where 'vendetta' does exist, it is generally surrounded by all kinds of ceremonial. In Japan, for instance, where it was authorized both by law and by the Confucian moral code, the person indulging in it first had formally to notify the one he wanted to kill, as well as the governor of the district and he had to act according to all the rules of honour.

Inversely, and logically so, the concept of gratitude appears in Asia in a very different light from what we know in Europe. Many Oriental languages do not have any term corresponding to our 'thank you', and from the Mediterranean to India, even when it exists, very little use is made of it. As the cause of the benefit received is either divine will—since it is God who has given us all—or the effect of *karma*, and as the giver has only acted as an instrument, there is no reason to feel any gratitude towards him. An English traveller in the Hadramaut, having presented a Bedouin with a very fine gun—the object most appreciated in this region—received no thanks but, on the contrary, was taken to task for not having given an adequate supply of ammunition with it. The present has nothing to do with the will of the person who has given it; it is the will of Allah. If, by chance, gratitude is sometimes shown, this may be severely criticized—I have seen instances of this—because what happened has thus been placed on a personal plane, something that is almost improper. Further east the attitude is different. In the Far East gratitude is an important motivation, and a farmer to whom some service has been rendered might well commemorate it by inscribing the fact on a wooden tablet which would, from then on, be included among the sacred objects in his house.

As a counterpart to this strong tendency towards inaction, as already mentioned, there is the generally accepted teaching that what really matters for the individual is his action with its motives and not the consequences of this action. In India, this is the main lesson of the most unanimously venerated holy scripture, the *Bhagavad-Gita*. In fact, many schools in Asia preach the same doctrine. For the Chinese, 'joy is in the doing and not in the accomplishment'.[16] In Islam, 'to pursue any goal is considered rather vulgar'.[17]

[16] Cranmer-Byng.   [17] Elie Faure.

This leads to an attitude where man acts more as an artist wishing to accomplish a work of art than as a practical person anxious to obtain results. One of the most spectacular examples seen in modern times was that of Mahatma Gandhi in his negotiations with the British. At every stage, whether in his prison or in conference with His Majesty, he inexorably upheld the thesis which seemed right to him from the moral point of view—for Gandhi was essentially a moralist—without worrying about the near or distant material effects on himself or on his country. Actually, he was thus accumulating good *karma*—for his country and for himself—regardless of the fact that centuries might have to pass before this *karma* bore fruit. It was along this path that the whole of India followed him and understood him; but his British opponents thought him unpredictable and mad.

This insistence on right action, whatever its results might be, has been explained by some westerners as being the result of the powerlessness of the Asian before the magnitude of nature's phenomena, and particularly before its disasters, which are beyond the human scale. There is some truth in this theory.

Earthquakes are probably the most impressive disasters. In the nineteenth century alone over thirty-nine Chinese towns, twenty-two Japanese towns and twenty-one towns in the Philippines were thus rased to the ground by them. The 1897 earthquake in Assam and the 1905 earthquake in Kangra each shook an area equal to half of Europe. 200,000 persons were killed in Japan in 1703, 300,000 in India in 1737 and 180,000 in China in 1920. In Kashmir, in 1866, there were 2,000 victims in one single tremor. Japan registers several thousands of tremors every year and Gifu alone, every year, undergoes over 500 that are perceptible to man. In the last thousand years incalculable ravages have been wrought there by over 200 earthquakes. That of 1923 caused 105,000 deaths and destroyed three million houses. In Asiatic Russia the 1895 earthquake, which spread from Karsnovodsk to Samara and Tashkent, lasted five months. In 1948 the town of Ashkabad in Turkmenistan was completely destroyed.

There are other more or less related phenomena, e.g., the eruption of Krakatoa in 1883, threw eighteen cubic kilometres of matter into the air and killed 36,000 persons; in Japan, the tidal wave of 1703 carried away some hundred thousand human beings, and in 1657 even more apparently perished in the Yedo fire. In 1208, in spite of an admirable system of defence against fire, some 60,000 houses were destroyed by fire in Hangchow.

Floods probably claim second place after earthquakes. It is known how disastrous they are in the lower plains of the Yellow

River, where they are periodically made even worse by the deposit of enormous quantities of loess. In Siberia many villages and town quarters used to be carried away almost every year at the time of thaw—the terrible *razputitza*. Not long ago, the Amu Daria (the old Oxus, which formerly ended in the Caspian and now flows into the Aral Sea) swept away most of the town of Turkul, capital of the autonomous Mara-Kalpak Republic. In a century and a half, the Obe bed has shifted so much that the church of Tymskoie has had to be rebuilt five times. In the 1955 floods in India and Pakistan, it was never possible even to make a rough evaluation of the number of victims.

The wind also can take on terrifying proportions. In Kazakstan, in 1827, a snowstorm carried away 280,000 horses, 30,000 horned beasts, over a million sheep, and countless camels.

The cold, in Siberia and in Tibet, and the heat throughout Asia, reach peaks unknown to us. In some years the cold is so intense in the *taiga* that birds and small beasts die in hundreds; the heat there can be atrocious as well. At the end of the nineteenth century the Nent of north-west Siberia told the Finnish explorer Castren that the winter had been mild as hardly any crows had been found dead of cold.

Finally, all over Asia famines frequently acquire unthinkable proportions. That of Bengal in 1770 took away almost a third of the population. In Japan the famine in 1783-87 made over a million victims.

Apart from these calamities, nature shows itself in a terribly impressive way. Matiushkin reports the fact, rather frequent, as he says, of five suns appearing simultaneously in the sky where they were joined by rainbows.

Before such manifestations of natural forces man obviously feels powerless. It is understandable that the normal attitude of the Chinese should be acceptance rather than doubt, resignation rather than revolt. The Japanese speak very objectively about cataclysms as something meant above all to educate the individual[18] and probably the same may be said of all the peoples of Asia.

Generally speaking, the oriental does not try to avoid his fate. Throughout Asia the story of the gardener of Isfahan is found to be perfectly normal and moral. The story is as follows: A king's gardener one day met Death among his flower-beds. Death informed him that she would come to fetch him the following day. Terrified, he begged his master for protection, and his master gave

[18] One of them has actually dealt with a 'moral geometry', which is supposed to define our sense of proportion in relation to the universe (Okakura Kakuzo.).

him one of his best steeds, on which he fled at full gallop. At the end of his ride, he met Death once more. She asked him, 'How were you able to come so fast to the appointment we had here? Since I saw you in Isfahan, I have been wondering how you would manage it.'[19]

It is easy to understand that, faced with a nature as terrible as this, the Asian is more inclined to follow the current, rather than to swim against it. 'When the elephant falls', says a Siamese proverb, 'do not place yourself underneath it in order to hold it up; but once it has fallen, you may push it in order to help it to raise itself.' This is the principle of Japanese *judo* and many other disciplines: use the strength which is opposing or seems to be opposing you in order to make it produce the very results you wish to achieve. This is applied to all fields of activity. The art of Chinese politicians, Granet tells us, 'was to use destiny by tempting it'. He further adds, 'All that political folklore can teach us is that the Chinese were past-masters in the art of weakening a rival by giving him the wrong opportunity so as to have the favourable occasion on their own side.' This attitude compares better with the sailboat than with the steamer. While it is dictated by a relative feeling of powerlessness, it is nevertheless based, on the metaphysical plane, on the highest wisdom, for 'in the light of total consciousness, self-will coincides with the laws governing the universe'.[20]

It is doubtless because of these conceptions that Asians are surprised at our indignations and our rages. Among the Bedouins as well as among the aborigines of India, in China or in Japan, manifestations of wrath or even ill humour are, with rare exceptions, practically unknown and would not even be understood. A French author, Charles Vildrac, having gone to Japan to attend the rehearsal of one of his plays adapted for the Japanese stage, was surprised, at one point, to see the two main characters making the most respectful bows to each other while the stage directions required them to quarrel violently and one of them was supposed to brandish a chair, intending to hit the other. The author interrupted, saying, 'You have misunderstood', and he explained what the play required. But he was told: 'This is the way in which men quarrel here; if one of them were to brandish a chair, the spectators would not understand what was meant.' Throughout south-east Asia, when a 'white man' loses his temper, all his staff collect around him in order to look at the astonishing sight. The Bison-horn Maria of

[19] Other versions place this story in Samarkand, but it remains the same.
[20] This quotation is from Lama Govinda, op. cit., p. 379, but the same thesis is untiringly upheld by all the sages of the East. For the Muslim, the order of the world within which his action develops is a divine order.

Central India say : 'God was as furious as a *Sahib*.' For the Chinese, since harmony is the natural result of an equally natural opposition, the tragic character imprinted by Christianity upon human destiny cannot but cause surprise and seem incomprehensible.

This also leads to the use of criteria different from ours in the choice of the means. 'The criterion of truth', Mao-Tse-tung has said, 'is practice.' This does not necessarily contradict the attitude of Gandhi that we have mentioned earlier, for 'practice' does not only take account of the material or immediate results; in the East, it goes much further.

In order to 'go along with the current' in this manner, the human being must not only follow constantly a minute and specific ritual, but must also constantly make 'sacrifices'. Gandhi expressed the profound feeling of the whole of Asia when writing to his disciples : 'The world could not subsist for a specific instant without sacrifice.' Similarly, in the Iranian conception, without sacrifice the world would perish.

The most total sacrifice is of course, that of the man who gives his whole life to the divine, whatever be the shape in which he conceives God, either by devoting it completely to Him or by sacrificing himself. This latter form, which deeply shocks the modern western mentality, has, for this reason, practically disappeared—although, seen objectively, to sacrifice one's body to God is as defendable as to sacrifice it for a nationalistic ideal, a military or a sports objective, all of which is admired in the west as heroic. Besides, to sacrifice oneself—or to let oneself be sacrificed—in this way on an altar was considered in a good part of Asia as a privilege, a voluntary martyrdom (like that of the early Christians) which ensured in the other world a close union with the divine, and consequently eternal and perfect happiness.

Then we have the sacrifice of animals, chosen especially for their perfection from different points of view. Although becoming less and less frequent and often performed secretly in order to avoid the criticism of those westerners who do not understand it, such ceremonies are still commonly held in many countires. If it is repugnant for us to see bloodshed in a temple, we must realize that, in the case of most Asians, man will actually prove kinder and more religious towards the animals he intends to use for food when he has first offered these to God in prayer, instead of massacring them in gloomy slaughterhouses; the spirit of the animal will benefit from it and the food will have received a divine blessing. The explanation of substitutional sacrifice given by most ethnographers, and which they try to apply to all cases, not without stretching the texts and other data is only valid in a small minority of instances.

The essence of sacrifice, however, still consists of offering to the divine whatever is most precious to us. This is what is done consciously in Japan, where the poet Tsuyaruki is quoted as an example; caught at sea in a storm, he threw his mirror into the waves —because he only had one.

While the first two forms of sacrifice that we have listed are the most spectacular, they are not necessarily the most important or the most valid. What is untiringly stressed by all the masters of Asia is that man must constantly offer to the divine, or to his divinized ideal, all his thoughts, all his desires, all his words, all his actions. That is the true aim of this ritualism which we have christened superstition.

Let us point out, incidentally, that the very word 'sacrifice', and its synonyms in other European languages, correspond to a concept that is rather different from the one expressed in Asian languages. For in Asia it is a matter of 'rendering unto' the divine what has never ceased to belong to him, and not of 'offering' what belongs to ourselves.

We could not possibly conclude these considerations on the concept of causality in the East without a few words regarding the 'evil eye', which is held responsible for so many mishaps. Throughout and beyond the Middle East admiration and envy bring a curse upon their object. It is in order to preserve oneself from it that, in so many countries, people wear natural or artificial 'amulets', images or symbols of the divine, objects that have touched such images, sacred texts, objects blessed by a saint or a sage, etc. There is also collective protection, such as the placing of screens in staggered order at the entrance to a house, as in China, or placing a mirror reflector in front of the door, as is done in Manchurian inns. As recently as in the twentieth century, a whole Muslim village was seen to emigrate in order to flee from an evil presage. It has to be admitted, in fact, that the recent and duly authenticated examples of the very real and efficient action of curses which are seen abundantly throughout Asia are somewhat disturbing.

CHAPTER IX

Logic and Symbolics

Logic, after all, is but a rhythmic dance of the mind, nothing more.
SHRI AUROBINDO.

Truth can be attained only through the comprehension of the opposites.
OKAKURA KAKUZO

Orientals are masters of dialectics.
RAYMOND CHARLES

ONE of the preparatory efforts that is most difficult for us when we seek to understand Asians is to admit that the Aristotelian or Cartesian logic to which we are accustomed is not the only one possible, nor even the only one valid. Even Arab logic differs considerably from ours and Louis Milliot has written that in order to be able to compare thought as dissimilar as that of Islam and the West, 'you must start by closing the Discourse on Method'. As for the logic of India or the Far East, it is almost completely impossible to reduce it to our terms. Our fundamental axiom that A cannot be both identical with B and different from B does not hold the same value here. For the Buddhist, for example, there are 'at least' four possibilities: A may be identical with B, different from B, both identical with B and different from it, or it may be neither identical with B nor different from it. Certain texts even explicitly point out that there are cases which fit into none of these four possibilities and therefore remain outside them.[1] For the Taoist, the One is also two, it is also 8, and also 64, and an infinite quantity.[2] In Chinese logic, a black horse plus a white horse make three horses. The Sophists have not managed to make the Chinese accept the idea of the existence of contradictory terms, and, in fact, the Chinese do not need it, for they can dispense with the principle of contradiction as a means of bringing order into mental activity. They attribute this function to the harmony[3] of contrasts.[4]

Not only are Asians not scared by the antinomies but, for them,

---

[1] Examples: Samyutta Nikaya, IV; Ramakrishna 1294.
[2] John Blofeld.   [3] Ho=harmony.
[4] Marcel Granet.

as written by a Korean,[5] 'opposites are complementary'. For the Muslim Radd ul Muhtar, differences of opinion are a 'gift of God', an idea which is perfectly in line with the teaching of Mohammed, for whom they are 'a sign of divine compassion'.[6] It is thus that Asians interpret the words of Jesus, an Asian, as recorded by John, also an Asian: 'In my Father's house there are many mansions.' For Gandhi, 'the different truths are like countless leaves which appear different and which are on one and the same tree'. For his most faithful follower to date, Vinoba, they are 'certainly a sign of health, which is welcome'. Following the same conception, the Chinese readily proclaim that 'there is no advantage in taking sides in a discussion'.[7]

This general attitude certainly stems to a good extent from the fact that the oriental first and foremost recognizes the reality of the divine world and takes as a basis for his entire thought what he believes to be the rules governing this world, transporting these rules afterwards to the material world, while the westerner starts out from the material world, tries to discover its laws, and then wishes to apply these same laws fully and strictly to all that might exist outside this world—supposing anything does exist at all!

The very belief in the existence of an objective truth in the phenomenal world in the sense in which our modern science understands it is not very widespread in Asia. We have seen that, generally speaking, truth is something relative, which varies according to the planes of consciousness and points of view, and changes as we pass from one to the other. For the Japanese the real truth is not systematized objective truth, but only—or, more than that?—a 'living truth'.

For the Chinese, truth can never be proved, it can only be suggested.[8] They cannot conceive of the idea of law. Besides, for the Buddhists in general, a thing is neither true, nor non-true; all, including religion, is but human invention. The world created by the mind cannot indeed have greater reality than the mind itself.[9]

Another attitude that leads to the same conclusion is to identify truth with 'all that is'. This is found in Japan, in India where it is the same word, *sat*, which expresses both the fact of being and the fact of being true, and in other areas also.

This is doubtless one of the main reasons—but not the only one —why orientals do not like to contradict their interlocutor. Their

[5] Pan Ku. [6] Hadith.
[7] Marcel Granet.
[8] Lin Yutang and Marcel Granet.
[9] Lama Anagarika Govinda.

answer is mostly dictated by considerations of fitness for the occasion or by a natural courtesy rather than by any concern for truth, which would only be subjective anyway, and would require continuous confirmation through experience.

In Japan, for instance, where politeness is more important than truthfulness,[10] if you ask a passer-by, 'The station is in this direction, is it not?', he will be most unwilling to answer negatively, even if it is in the opposite direction. In China, if you look tired when asking how far you are from your destination, the reply is invariably: very near.[11]

Therefore, in far-eastern culture there is hardly any attempt to convince, even less to convert. In what would correspond to a western discussion there is no brutal opposition of theses and arguments, and the straight line followed by thought is not valued as it is among us. In Viet-Nam, for instance, one attempts 'to suggest to the other party what one desires, without expressing it clearly, but by hinting at it in a discreet and, at the same time, persuasive manner; by beating about the bush and by coming to the point in a roundabout way, *Noi quanh*'.[12] A Chinese never writes a treatise. He puts down only a note about it, leaving it to be sustained or disproved by posterity on its intrinsic merit; and when he pays someone the compliment of saying about him that he has no 'right-wrong', that means that that person knows how to preserve a divine indifference towards all matters and does not let himself get mixed up in disputes.[13]

Besides, for important matters at least, the oriental hardly lets himself be guided by logical arguments even if he seems to bow before the logic of his interlocutor—as he readily does. As a Siamese said very relevantly: you may very well convince me that ghosts do not exist, but I shall continue to be afraid of them. Of course, that is the kind of contradiction which clashes with our logic, but 'the Asian is not, like us, a rigid and undeformable block; thanks to his inner flexibility, he can be adjusted to all the intellectual games proposed to him by the westerner without suffering any durable or deep damage as a result'.[14]

Modern western logic, in the eyes of an Asian, has many serious faults. Firstly, it can only work on the basis of generalizations or abstractions and thus takes us away from concrete reality (Chinese thought refuses to distinguish between the logical and the real)[15] which is the only valid one. This is particularly true of statistics, which are exclusively quantitative and to which our

[10] Inazo Nitobe.   [11] Chanoine Detry.
[12] Pierre Huard.   [13] Lin Yutang.
[14] Jean Herbert.   [15] Marcel Granet.

logical mental process inexorably leads us. Then, it advocates a more or less linear causality, acting in a uniform manner, and this, as we have seen earlier, is not in line with eastern conceptions. Finally, it can only be placed on a single plane of consciousness at a time, which makes its basis and its premises incomplete, and its conclusions consequently false.

A corollary of this difference is that in the East philosophy cannot take the same place as among us. While in the West it is actually 'an attempt to interpret the universe rationally',[16] the Asian knows that human reason is congenitally incapable of ever finding such an explanation. A representative of modern Tibetan Buddhism has written that the intellect turned outward gets more and more entangled in the becoming, in the world of the *become* and the illusion of the isolated Self, that is, in death. When it is turned inward, the intellect loses itself in the void of pure abstraction, in the death of spiritual benumbing.[17] The Buddha himself stressed the impermanence and unstability of the discursive process in the following terms: 'Opinion, Oh disciples, is a disease; opinion is a tumour; opinion is a wound.'[18] Besides, the same Chinese character, *pai*, which means 'explain' also means 'in vain'.

It may, however, be said that for the oriental, logic, as we see it, may be applied usefully in two different ways. In the first place, it is valid for the utilization of that which has been created through it; for instance, no oriental will deny that our logic should be followed strictly when using the motor-car or the telephone system. On a higher plane, on the other hand, it can lead us up to a certain point in our spiritual evolution by protecting us against errors and false steps and, at that stage, should itself show us that it is powerless to guide us further and should encourage us to seek other means of progression.[19]

The Asian in general, from the Middle East to Japan, cannot understand why he should be locked in a dilemma; this mental process appears wrong to him and shocks him. For him, it is never compulsorily X *or* Y, for it can always be either Z, or better still, both X and Y.

One of the simplest and most effective ways of obviating the dangers of pure logic and of filling the void which is formed when one loses confidence in it is obviously to use one's common sense. It is on this common sense that the Chinese, in particular, rely. For them, it is not enough for a proposition to be logically set, it must

[16] Raymond Charles.
[17] Lama Anagarika Govinda.   [18] *Majjhima Nikaya*, LXXII, ii, 205.
[19] Ramakrishna; Vivekananda; Aurobindo: 'Reason was a help; reason is the hindrance'.

also be consistent with human nature. The Chinese word for 'reason' or the 'fact of being in line with reason' is *ch'ing-li* which is composed of two elements, *ch'ing* (*jen ch'ing*), human nature, and *li* (*t'ien-li*), eternal reason; *ch'ing* represents the flexible human element and *li* the unalterable law of the universe; it is from a combination of these two elements that you can draw criteria for any action or for any historical thesis.[20]

The pliability retained by oriental logic, without foregoing any of its exactness, makes it possible to use analogies more than we do. These, without proving rationally, suggest and allow more acute and accurate perception of what seemed obscure, incomprehensible, abnormal or contrary to the order of things. This explains the considerable use made of images and parables in the East and the value that is attached to precedents. Mohammed even advised the judges, in cases where the Koran was silent, to reason through direct analogy, *qiyas*.[21]

Here, we must quote in full a Chinese classical story because it gives an admirable illustration of the part played by images in oriental thought.[22]

'A warrior, before the start of the fighting, calls out to a friend in the other camp. He wants to give him prudent advice, enjoin him to flee through the mud of the flooded plain, hint that in such a case help could be given him . . . However, he merely tells him, "Have you any wheat yeast?" "No," replies the other (who perhaps does not understand). "Do you have any mountain (plant) yeast?" "No," replies the other once more. [In spite of the insistence on the word (yeast was supposed to be an excellent preventive against the pernicious influence of humidity), he still does not understand—or pretends not to understand—doubtless, he wishes to receive, with more explicit advice, a commitment that relief will be brought to him.] The friend then starts once more (still avoiding the essential words but suggesting it forcefully): "The fish in the river will have stomach-ache. What medicine will you give them?" The other (who finally decides), says, "Look at the wells without *water*. You will take them out of the wells." He therefore goes, in the thick of the fighting, to hide in a muddy hole and, once the danger is past, his friends find him there. The advice-giver has concentrated his attention on a word which he has taken care not to pronounce—while being able to give it a complex imperative value. ("Think of the water!—Be careful about water!—Use water! =Escape by using the flood with care!").'

If the orientals—all the way from the Taoists to the Muslims,

[20] Lin Yutang.
[21] Raymond Charles.   [22] recorded by Granet.

but primarily the Hindus and their disciples, the Buddhists—who excel in analysis and can carry it to an amazing degree of subtlety sometimes refrain from engaging in it, it is because analysis and definition, to some extent, take one away from reality. If they do not indulge in synthesis, as we do, it is not because they are incapable of it, as some excellent specialists of eastern thought suppose,[23] but because it would be without object. Since the 'whole' is known a priori, either through revelation, as with the Semites or the Shintoists, or through meditation and introspection, as with the Hindus, it is useless and even dangerous to want to reconstitute it on the basis of data that is necessarily incomplete and imperfectly observed.[24] The kind of synthesis that attracts them is more the one resulting from the confrontation of a thesis and an antithesis, which are reckoned as second principles and which serve as the basis for a logically postulated synthesis, this being the primary principle.

As for imagination, in Asia it is a supplement to logic rather than an entirely distinct, if not inferior, contradictory and incompatible operation. We have seen earlier the value attached to it in the East in the search for revealing spiritual experience.[25]

As an oriental has pointed out to me: 'You Europeans, and especially the French, you constantly correct us in order to remind us that 1 plus 1 equals 2, that 2 plus 2 equals 4, and 4 plus 4 equals 8. But we know that as well as you do. Only, it does not interest us; what is of interest to us is what goes beyond that, it is the realm of the imagination, of fancy, of poetry, of the divine, where all this elementary and coarse arithmetic is no longer valid. Even when we speak of the most down-to-earth things, we try to tear them away from the earth and beautify them', rather than avoid them, as a Chinese writer specifies.[26]

Moreover, this imagination or what appears to us as such, may easily be granted the dignity of what we would more correctly call intuition. It is through this that absolute truth may be understood and prayer and ascetic practices are the channels of access to it. In affirming this priority, Ghazzali, in the eleventh century, only confirmed a concept always recognized and did not introduce any innovation. Among the Muslims particularly, 'the heart' has always scored over logic, 'even among the most expert theologians'.[27] In these latter examples, I have almost exclusively mentioned cases pertaining to the Islamic mentality, only because

[23] Raymond Charles.
[24] The Chinese have managed to organize their thought without really thinking in terms of species and kinds. M. Granet.
[25] Cf. p. 45 above.
[26] Lin Yutang.   [27] Raymond Charles.

in the thought processes of the countries further east, these facts are even more evident and irrefutable, and are therefore, not worth quoting here.

There has been much discussion, especially among westerners who have lived in the East, regarding the propensity (or even the gift) that Asian people have for absorbing abstract ideas so dear to us, and without which our logic cannot set up the divisions and classifications it needs in order to function.

It seems that in India (not only Aryan India, as may have been expected, but also Dravidian India) there is an intensely active focus on abstract research—although it is very different from ours, since it is founded on concepts of continuity and unreality; but progressively, as you move away from India either towards Asia Minor or towards Indo-China and Indonesia, or towards the Far East, or even towards Siberia, this tendency decreases rapidly and gives way to a growing desire to establish direct contact with the individual object without the interposition of the intellectual concept. The Chinese would be about half-way between India and Japan.[28]

Carried to the other extreme, this rejection of pure intellectual logic in Japan and China, for instance, gives us Zen Buddhism.[29] Generally speaking, it may be said that the evolution of Buddhism, as it goes from India to Indo-China, Tibet, China, Korea, and Japan, is dictated by a concern to make progressively less use of abstract ideas. Inversely, in the case of Islam, the nearer it moves to India the less dogmatic it becomes and the more mystic. The Taoist is 'radically opposed to the use of reason',[30] and to a Japanese even Ramakrishna seems abstract.—[31] As for the Muslim, while he attributes a central and determinant place to the vastest of all abstract metaphysical concepts, he is sometimes suspicious of any conceptual generalization and of any abstraction from the concrete.[32]

[28] Drake
[29] Cf. the three volumes of D. T. Suzuki: *Essays on Zen Buddhism* which is the basic text. Also see a remarkable example of practical application in E. Herrigel—*Zen and the chivalrous art of Archery*.
[30] Jean Grenier.
[31] Katayama. Most western scholars seem to share this opinion regarding the Japanese. Percival Lowell (*Occult Japan*) writes: 'Another characteristic feature of the Japanese mind is a general incapacity to understand abstract ideas.' Walter Denning writes: 'One of the most marked characteristics of the Japanese mind is its lack of interest in metaphysical, psychological and ethical controversies of all kinds.' This is, however, not the opinion of all Japanese. Chikao Fujisawa holds that Japanese thinkers are inclined to engage in abstract speculations. This question still remains to be clarified.
[32] Raymond Charles.

There are, nevertheless, in the East, more than anywhere else, many schools of philosophy of all kinds, and their polemics are interminable; but, with some exceptions, they should not be regarded as oppositions of a metaphysical order. Not only in China, as Granet rightly points out, but throughout Asia, there is no doctrine that may not be identified with a way of life. Their rivalries, therefore, deal essentially with the relative effectiveness of the respective methods they use in order to attain a goal regarding which there is little divergence of opinions. In most cases, these schools are actually complements to each other. Among the Muslims, the four rites—*hanafi, maliki, shafi'i and hanbali* together constitute Sunni orthodoxy. Among the Hindus, the *darshanas* are not so much schools (which, according to the West, would be in opposition to each other) as 'points of view' or 'views' (this is the exact translation of the term) which complete each other harmoniously. The Chinese term *kia*, which is also generally translated as school, has more the meaning of method, prescription. Of course, it is obvious that rivalries bearing on the practical value of the respective methods may be further heightened by conflicts of prestige.

Much more important in the East than logic, in the sense in which we understand it, are symbolics, which are conspicuous not only in art, in language and in the religious sphere, but in all the details of everyday life. It has been pointed out quite correctly that in Islamic countries, for instance, 'the positiveness of action, the results, are never sought for themselves but always as a function of their possible symbolization according to theological and non-productive standards'.[33] The Chinese philosophers, according to Granet, profess the same trust in their national system of symbols as the West reason.

Asia is truly the world of symbols, but in a much broader sense than we generally understand it. While, to us, a symbol, as opposed to scientific truth reveals, while masking it, a meaning other than the superficial one, in the East the symbols endlessly disclose their meanings, their implications, before us. This is in line with the general law of continuity, so essential in Asia and also closely connected with the sense of ritualism and its degenerate form, superstition.

Some symbols have a value which varies according to the country; we shall see later a striking example of this with regard to *mudras* in eastern dancing. Other symbols, on the contrary, seem to have preserved a remarkable continuity of meaning

[33] Raymond Charles.

throughout Asia—and perhaps even beyond Asia. We shall mention one instance only—the mouse.

In Japan, while it is inseparable from the god Daikoku—who is given the very day of the rat, according to the old calendar—it is the symbol of an abundance of earthly possessions. In China the big rat which announces affluence in a house is welcomed like an honoured guest. In India, where it is inseparable from the god Ganesha, it represents the cunning intelligence which makes it possible to acquire possessions. Among the lamas of Siberia it is the symbol of wealth. In Kamchatka people used to practise a sort of exchange of food with mice and even believed that the latter understood human language. It is, perhaps, along these lines that we must seek an explanation for the fact that in the time of Isaiah some Jews used to meet secretly in order to eat mice ritually.

The symbolics of numbers, more particularly, that of letters of the alphabet and of colours, especially among the Taoists,[34] in Manchuria, in Lamaist cosmology, are throughout Asia of considerable importance and cover not only the religious and mystical realm as such, but extend to all spheres of life.

The symbolism of numbers in Asia could, in itself, be the subject of endless study. In India, for instance, interminable metaphysical, biological and yogic discussions take place on nothing more than the various meanings of the numbers 2, 3, 4, 5, 10, 21, 108, etc.[35]

However, it is above all in China that 'qualitative arithmetic'[36] plays a primary part in thought and even in life. 'The essential attribute of numbers is their function of classification.' Their function is not to express magnitude, but to adjust concrete dimensions to the proportions of the universe. They serve the purpose of evaluating; but it is not the quantity which counts in whatever they evaluate but the value, cosmic and social, of the groups to which they are tagged. Far from trying to turn the numbers into abstract signs of quantity, the Chinese use them in order to represent the form or estimate the value of a particular group. The numbers have as their essential *rôle*, not to make addition possible, but to connect among themselves various ways of division valid for particular groups. The utilization made of this concept by the different technical studies, far from altering this basic attitude, has rather strengthened it. Therefore, among the Chinese, arith-

---

[34] Lao Tse expresses distance by means of dark blue, as Ramakrishna does (§ 1319); further away is expressed as 'blue and still blue', *hinan yen hinan* (Schwab).

[35] Cf. *Mahabharata, passim*.

[36] The phrase was coined by Masson-Oursel.

metic has not been converted into a science of quantity.[37]

Most of the human groups in Asia attach a particularly sacred value to a given number: 2½ among the Gond, 5 among the Shia Muslims, because it is the number of their great prophets, 6 among the Ainus, 8 among the Japanese, and, generally speaking, among the Buddhists for whom the eightfold path is the way to salvation, 52 among the Jains, 108 among the Hindus and the Buddhists and for Hindu and Japanese rosaries.[38] The most remarkable case is probably that of the Persian Babis, to whom arithmetic is of the highest importance and 19 is the numerical expression of God; consequently, for them the year has 19 months, the month 19 days, the day 19 hours, the hour 19 minutes, and any numeration is done by 19. For the Iranian poet, this same number 19—this is doubtless not mere chance—'is equal to beauty, because it is the number of the chapters where it is normally described'.

As in western traditions, however, it is the figure 7, the number of days in the week, that is, the duration of a quarter of the moon, which is particularly sacred for nearly all Asians. It seems mainly associated with a 'second stage' in the creation of the world, that is, the one following the appearance of primordial duality or trinity. Thus, in the Old Testament[39] it is after God had created heaven and earth that he proceeded to carry through the creation in 7 days. According to the Babis, God could only create thanks to 7 letters or attributes. In the Persian Shah-Nama, the first human couple, Mashya and Mashyana, engendered 7 other couples. According to the Hindus, the primordial man, Manu, appears twice seven times. Innumerable other examples may be found in the tribal mythology of India; for instance, among the Rajnenji Pordham, Mahadeo, the Supreme God, sows 7 herbs for creation; among the Bhuiya and the Raja, there are 7 primordial couples, and so on. Even in China, where 4, 5, 6, 8 and 9 are much more important, 7 is mentioned explicitly: 'When Chaos, having shown some civility, proved worthy of being received among men, two friends (they were the spirits of lightning) spent a whole week, piercing one hole a day in him, in order to give him the human countenance that he deserved. On the seventh day of the operation, Chaos died.'[40] The number 7 also has this same important role in China inasmuch as it is the emblem of the young *yang* which govern the development of women, and the *yang* numbers attain their perfection at 7; it

[37] Marcel Granet.

[38] J. Mock, *Quaint Customs*, etc., II, 102 sq. In Japan, they correspond to the 108 sins against which protection is necessary. The Buddhist *kalpa* lasts 432 (4 times 108) million years (K. Kanamatsu), etc.

[39] Where the number 7 appears 370 times.

[40] Tchoang-Tse.

is also the classifying index number in matters of divination; that is, it makes it possible to find out what will be created. Among the Thai and the Burmese the god Kabil Maha Phrom (or Asi Brahma, the primordial creator) has seven daughters who play a decisive cosmogonical part, as also with the Yakuts and the seven daughters of the powerful god Jessagai Tayon. In Laos the primordial king, of divine origin, has seven sons; likewise the Pu Nycoeu Nya Nyeou, who act his part in Luang Prabang. As for Japan, the number 7 is found in their cosmogony at two different stages which partly overlap. On the one hand, the first seven divinities who were born alone and hid their persons, starting with Ame-no-minaka-nushi-no-kami, the Divine Master of the August Centre of Heaven, to Toyo-kumo-nu-no-kami, the Luxuriant and Integrating Divine Mistress. On the other hand there are the 'seven divine generations', *tenjin shichidai*, which go from Kuni-no-toko-tachi-no-kami, the Eternally Upright Terrestrial Divinity to Izana-gi-no-kami and Izana-mi-no-kami, the couple that directly engendered the earth, men and the other gods. The same figure 7 is also, as in China, related to human birth, since the divine Tentai condemns his daughter, the Weaver Goddess, Shoku-jo, never again to see her husband, the human Ken-gyu, except on the seventh day of the seventh month, the day on which Tentai himself went to bathe in the celestial river.

Accessorily, and by way of consequence, this same figure 7 represents the totality, either of all that is created, or of divinity visualized under one of its aspects. For the Taoists, 'Yi, by mutation, became One; One, by mutation, became 7; 7, by mutation, became 9; with this ninth mutation, you reach the end, and then, by further mutation, you come back to One'.[41] According to the Muslims there are 7 earths and seven heavens[42] and a great doctor of Muslim law is even more affirmative: 'Things almost remained only seven in number. The heavens are seven, the earths also; the mountains are seven, the seas also. The age of the earth is 7,000 years; the days of the week are seven, the planets also. The processions at the Ka'aba are seven in number; the same is true of the race between as-Cafa and al-Marwa. The gates of hell are seven, the steps of hell also.'[43] Among the shamans of Siberia there are seven upper strata, which make up the kingdom of light, and seven lower ones forming the kingdom of darkness. According to the Hindus, there are also seven worlds or *loka* (*bhur, bhuvar, svar, mahar, janar, tapah, and brahma or satya*) and there are also seven hells (*atala, vitala, sutala, rasatla, tatatala, mahatala and patala*),

---

[41] Lie Tse, 1. [42] Koran, II, 29 and XLI, 12.
[43] Wahb ben Munabbih.

or 21 or 28. For the Samoyed-Ostiaks, as recently as thirty years ago, 7 had the meaning of 'all'.

In Hinduism, there are seven great rishis, the *saptarshis*, whose names vary according to the various sacred texts. The chariot of Surya, the Great Illuminator, is driven by seven horses; and the God of Fire, Agni, has seven tongues. Throughout southern India, the 'seven sisters' are the most important Dravidian deities. In Mazdaism, Ormuzd and the six supreme archangels also form a heptade. To the Bedar or Boya of South India, Akkama is the spirit of the seven virgins who are represented by seven golden cups. Among the Samoyed-Ostiaks, there were seven lands governed by the national hero Itie till the day when he was attacked by the seven toothed devil. Other examples abound.

The same figure seven comes back with insistence in connection with the redemption or regeneration of the world. At his birth, Buddha took the *sapta padani*, the seven strides, under which sprang seven lotuses; and his mother, the Queen Maya, died when he was seven days old;[44] he remained seven days under the Bo tree and then seven days under each one of the following trees: the banyan, the muchalinda and the rajayatana.

This same figure is also found, as may be expected, in many bridal ceremonies. Among the Brahmins of South India seven steps are taken; among the Bonthuk seven women must preside over the event; and among the Gond, a woman must pardon her husband seven times.

The multiples of seven, particularly 14, are important in Laos, Cambodia (where, in the great epic of 'Ramakirti', the god Rama first kills fourteen demons, then 14,000), in Japan (in certain rosaries), in India (where forty-nine Maruts were born of the Mother of the Gods, Aditi), in Palestine (where multiples of fourteen, varying from one Gospel to another, relate Jesus to Abraham 'by a necklace where the pearls are the royal generations').[45] Among the Persians, Ormuzd created the earth in seventy days and man, Gayomart, also in seventy days. According to the Muslims, 'God surrounded the Throne with a serpent, *hayya*, with 70,000 wings, each of which had 70,000 feathers; with 70,000 faces, each of which had 70,000 mouths, and each mouth had 70,000 tongues'. In the realm of Buddhism, the Emperor Ashoka planned to build 84,000 stupas.

There are, however, areas where the figure 7 is inauspicious—for instance, among the Korava (India), because it is the homophone of the word 'to weep' in the Telegu language. The same is true in Japan where it shares an evil reputation with 17, 27, etc. It is doubt-

[44] Compare with St James's gospel (VI, 1) on the Virgin Mary.
[45] Schwab.

less by sheer coincidence that in this same country 49 (7 x 7) is so terrifying that it is never placed on a house, the probable reason being that 4 and 9 in Japanese have the same sound as 'death' and 'sorrow'.[46]

The three great sacred languages which have reached us in a living form and which are all three Asian—Hebrew, Sanskrit and Arabic —are essentially symbolic in nature. They are so first of all because of their mode of expression, which comprises a whole series of simultaneous meanings with different degrees of inner significance or esotericism.[47] They are also of such a nature by the very value of the individual letters used to form the words. Their symbolic significance, often closely related to an arithmetical value, is perhaps infinitely more important than their phonetic value in the word in which they appear. Each one of the characters of the *devanagari* script, still in use in a number of modern Indian languages, as also in Tibetan writing, corresponds to certain aspects of the divine and is used as such in the Hindu and Buddhist Tantras. Among the Muslims and the Israelites each letter of the alphabet, Arabic or Hebrew, has a numerical value, and the symbolism of a word or an expression is determined by the total value of the letters that compose it.

This is the reason why, apart from any meanings or succession of meanings that it may have (conveyed by the text and by the way in which it is chanted), going from the exoteric to the mystic, a sacred text comprises values and lessons that are inseparable from the sounds of the words and, by their very essence, untranslatable. That is why both Hindus and Muslims insist—which may be incomprehensible to us—that the Vedas, the Gita, the Koran, etc. are untranslatable by their very nature.

The Supreme Sheik of Al Azhar declared on February 15, 1955, in the paper *Al Ahram*: 'Any translation is impossible. The Koran has to be in Arabic according to the very words of God: an Arabic Koran without defects. Every term in the Koran has a meaning that none other could render. If translation can express anything at all, it is only the state of mind of the translator at the very moment when he did the translation. It is logically impossible for a limited mind to be able to achieve an unlimited divine object'.[48]

All this symbolism naturally attains its culmination in the myth which is the basic element in the vision of the world and of human

[46] John Gunther. On the death of a Japanese, his *souls* remain 49 days on the roof of his house (Hearn).

[47] Cf. Shri Aurobindo, *The Secret of the Veda*, passim.

[48] Quoted by Raymond Charles. Also Shri Aurobindo: 'To translate the Veda borders on the impossible.'

behaviour throughout Asia. A European author (Van der Leeuw) was somewhat indignant because some Easterner thought he understood life because he knew the myths—but such a presumption is only natural.[49]

The myth is, indeed, not only multi-purpose, it is much more, for it is the only way in which man can express the Higher Truths that existed prior to the differentiation between the various religious, moral, esthetic, scientific and other disciplines; and it is the natural source of the particular rules and regulations that apply in each one of these disciplines. The man who has really understood 'from within' an authentic myth, enjoys a clearer view in all fields and sees the interdependence and link between things which, to the unenlightened, seem to have no relation to one another. According to a Hindu tradition, every verse of the Rig-Veda has its application in each of the thirty-two sciences, from architecture to medicine, from archery to the art of governing people. Recent discoveries, in particular in the field of musicology, lead one to believe that such claims are less far-fetched than may have first been thought.

The study of Hindu, Japanese, Chinese, Indonesian, Tibetan and other mythologies, if undertaken in this spirit, would probably lead us to this integration of human knowledge which has, for a long time, been the goal of our modern Western science, but without much result to date.

What general conclusions may be drawn from these different observations? Subject to many exceptions and if we systematically ignore all that differentiates the thought systems of the very varied groups that people Asia, it may doubtless be considered:

(a) That traditional Asia does not attach great importance to our Aristotelian and Cartesian logic.[50] It recognizes that it is valid for use in connection with whatever has been designed and built on the basis of this logic, but as for the rest, infinitely more important for the Asians, other systems of logic, both subtler and more complex, must be applied. Govinda says: 'The logic of syllogistic thought, of historical and philological analysis, of abstract ideas and judgements of value is not the only one; . . . there is a logic that is just as legitimate and much deeper, a logic of growth in the realm of spiritual experience'.

(b) Oriental minds are more concerned with the qualitative than

[49] Cf. Herbert, 'Practical present-day value of the Hindu myth', and 'The aim and method of mythological studies'.

[50] 'Reason, which the rest of the world does not envy us so much', (Masson-Oursel). 'The very word, reason, *aql*, synonym of intelligence, does not appear in the Koran'. (Raymond Charles). 'The Chinese have no taste for the syllogism'. (Marcel Granet.)

the quantitative, which makes it possible to understand the considerable part played by symbolism. This attitude, which extends even to geometry and arithmetic, has its application in all spheres of life.

(c) Asians do not have the same propensity as we do for going from the concrete to the abstract through successive generalizations which, actually, deprive the individual of that which singles him out and leaves him only with that which makes him resemble his neighbour.

(d) They admit that man cannot become conscious of the macrocosm or the microcosm or their relationship through the discovery and study of laws that can lead to such generalizations. This consciousness may come either through a divine revelation (among the Jews, Muslims and also the Hindus)[51] or by means of a systematic and persistent discipline, rejecting all fallacious appearances (and the distorting attractions and repulsions that are the result) which arise out of our vision of the world obtained through the channel of our sensory organs and our 'reasoning reason'.[52]

(e) Therefore, their principal effort is aimed at discerning the essential harmony that necessarily links each entity and each event to the whole and at making this harmony ever-increasingly apparent on the plane of consciousness where we live. Their thinking, therefore, does not proceed through analysis and synthesis as we see them—although they are as capable of doing so as we are—but by constantly confronting the individual with the Whole without the interposition of any more or less abstract generalization, the latter's place being taken, when necessary, by symbols.

[51] For the latter, the proof that cows exist is that the word 'cow' is in the Vedas, and it is common to say, joking apart, that a Brahman who has lost his cow looks for it in the Vedas.

[52] These disciplines may be of several orders; domination of the physical body (Hindu *hatha-yoga*, Muslim flagellations, ascetics in the desert, various methods of continence, etc.), ritualism of social life (Hindu and other castes, Confucian etiquette, etc.), technique of dissociation from the world (Taoism, Buddhist and Shankarian rejection of Maya), utilization of our mental faculties to the extreme (he who knows a clod of earth, say the Hindu sacred scriptures, knows the whole universe) or, on the contrary, elimination and rejection of these same faculties (Zen Buddhism and its projections into Shintoism, Vedantic self-abstraction, escape into Buddhic *shunya*, etc.).

PART THREE

From Man to Society

CHAPTER X

The Individual by Himself

Man is more in truth than he is in fact.
K. KANAMATSU[1]

WHATEVER their creed may be, practically all the peoples of Asia admit that the human being is not composed only of the material body that can be perceived by our senses. However, although they do not agree with the materialist theories of certain western schools, they do not accept the Christian explanation according to which man is composed of two radically different elements, the mortal body and the immortal soul. Their analysis leads them to infinitely more complex and subtle conclusions.

Besides, generally speaking, the clear line drawn by our classical concepts between that which is material and that which is not seems much too oversimplified to them. They prefer to consider that there is an infinity of degrees in materiality, from the 'coarsest' to the most subtle, from the stone to the thought or even up to the immanent and transcendent divine.

In spite of the blurring of the present instant which results from this latter conception and from the absence of clear-cut boundaries between the different planes and the different worlds, in spite of the almost infinite extension of our evolution in time, with all the paligenetic vicissitudes that this involves, almost all Asian ethnic and religious groups recognize the continuous reality, in time and in space, of the human person that we are conscious of being. Of course, they certainly do not all have the same conception of what forms its unity, what gives it its permanent, even eternal and unalterable element, although this element is almost impossible to set apart, recognize or even define. However, they all more or less explicitly affirm the existence of an indestructible self, soul or *atman*, around which are made and unmade the various and successive aspects of the individual. (Let us note, however, that there are certain groups, such as the Domb of south India, according to whom the child is born without a soul and it is only after

---

[1] Exactly the same idea is to be found in Tagore.

its birth that the ancestor's soul comes to inhabit it.) This continuity of identity is complementary to continuity in time and continuity in space.

Those groups which have carried farthest their philosophical and experimental research on the nature of this self mostly see in it some divine spark or even the divine itself, both qualitatively and quantitatively, or even the absolute.

The most important exception lies in that, as a rule, orthodox Buddhists do not accept this concept of a central being in man; for them, everything is only a succession of isolated events unconnected with any real personality. As in the flame of the candle, everything is constantly renewed and permanent identity exists only in appearance. In practice, however, their belief in the *karma* or *kamma* is such that only real philosophers are able to draw practical conclusions from this theory of *an-atman* or non-existence of the self, and all the others behave exactly as if they believed in the existence of a stable self whose salvation must be prepared by entering a higher plane of consciousness.

Between this self and the physical, visible manifestation of the individual, there is a variable number of entities or degrees of materialization, which, for want of a sufficiently detailed vocabulary, our Orientalists call by the generic name of souls. These are specialized in their functions and are often localized in certain parts of the body; at death they undergo different fates and, according to certain races, do not even all appear or manifest themselves at the same time.

It sometimes happens that the same people have ideas—contradictory for us—regarding these souls and their relationship with each other; but we have seen that our concepts of logic do not apply wholly in Asia. One of the best examples is to be found among the Chinese. They accept the idea of two souls,[2] a lower soul, *p'o*,[3] and a higher 'soul-breath', *houen*, and this latter only comes when the child is capable of laughing or even only when it learns to walk and talk. Upon death the lower soul must go back among the 'sacred forces from which the soil draws its fertility'.[4] According to varied descriptions, the Chinese distinguish between two principles, the *kuei* and the *sheu*, which correspond to the *yin* and the *yang*, and they often count even three souls. In this case, at the time of death, the first goes into the ancestral 'tablet', the second remains in the neighbourhood of the

[2] Tchoang-Tse, 13.
[3] V. R. Burckhardt says that after death, this lower soul can attach itself to a skull or a bone and commit all sorts of atrocities.
[4] Marcel Granet.

tomb, and the third goes away to the land of the shadows. Further-more, Taoist and Confucian philosophers grant that there is in the waters and the hills, in heaven and on earth, an active and pure breath, *chinh khi*, which condenses to form the *élite* souls. Upon the death of the heroes who have received it, this breath goes back to the telluric regions whence it came. According to certain other conceptions, the Chinese 'also' have souls.[5]

A Japanese thinks he has a number of souls between one and nine, but according to a very widespread belief, when he loses one of them he goes mad. Besides, in Japan, the *iki-ryo*, which are the spirits of living persons (as opposed to the *shi-ryo*, which are the spirits of the dead), can even show themselves in full daylight without the persons from whom they emanate being aware of it, and they can even commit very serious misdeeds. A rather similar belief is current among the Kondh; according to them, half of the soul can escape and turn into a tiger or a snake, either in order to kill an enemy or in order to satisfy its appetite by feeding on big game; during this period, its human body shows a certain languor and it may happen that, if a tiger is then killed in the jungle, both the tiger and the man die simultaneously.

In Indonesia, man has a multitude of souls. In Cambodia, there are nineteen 'vital spirits' which escape upon death. Among the Laotian mountain people, the number of souls, *song-la*, is only three for the A-Kha, seven and nine respectively for men and women in the Ho tribes nine and ten for women and men among the P'u-Noi.

In India, the great modern philosopher, Shri Aurobindo, discerns in man a whole series of infinitely complex elements pertaining to various planes and worlds.[6]—this is, moreover, in line with the sacred scriptures, according to which, at the time of death, the various elements composing the human being return to the cor-responding cosmic elements. A particularly curious case is that of Dhangar in the Satara district of India: they do not seem to re-gard man as possessing a whole soul for himself; indeed, upon his death, the Dhangar becomes a *pitar*, an ancestor, and twelve of these *pitar* get together to form a spirit. On the other hand, out of their five gods, the principal, Mhasoba, has twenty-five spirits.

As for location, let us just mention by way of example that, while among the Hindus every part of the body is the place of residence of a divinity, among the Laotians, each of the thirty-two

---

[5] Maspero.
[6] Cf. J. Herbert—*L'anatomie psychologique de l'homme chez Shri Auro-bindo.*

parts of the body has a soul, and, among the Thai, the inner spirit, *khwan*, resides in the head.

One of the things that shocks the westerner most of all when he comes to Asia for the first time is to see piles of filth near living quarters, and also to note that people live in perfect harmony with countless insects which nest on their bodies and in their houses. We naturally come to the conclusion that these people are 'dirty', at least as much so as our near ancestors, before the adoption (among privileged, exceptional groups, even in the west) of bathrooms and D.D.T. As these undeniable facts are at the origin of a crushing superiority complex among many westerners, even among those of us who are most worthy of esteem, it is necessary to examine the matter more closely.

Generally speaking, it may be said that most Asians are very much concerned with cleanliness. Chamberlain notes that Japanese servants brought back to Europe by him found us not only lazy and superstitious, but also dirty. The purifying action of sunlight and fire is perhaps not among the lesser reasons for which they are worshipped.[7] However, they often ascribe to the concept of cleanliness a meaning completely different from ours, and their criteria are considerably different from ours.

To the Oriental cleanliness is primarily a matter of greater or lesser inner purification, or a defence against a more or less subtly defined pollution. Therefore the matter should be considered separately in several concentric circles, the innermost being composed of the subtle elements of the individual, the next of his food and his body, the third of his clothing and his house, the fourth and last of whatever is outside his house. The concern for hygiene and purity in Asia encourages the constant rejection of the impure from an inner towards an outer circle.

Inner purity is indubitably the kind to which Asians attach the greatest importance. All the ritual purification so widespread in different countries may be traced to this. The Zoroastrians perform ablution and purification rites prior to all their prayers and ceremonies; the Muslims wash their feet before entering the mosque, the Taoists wash their mouths before prayers, and the Shintoists wash their mouths even before approaching the temple. The Buryat Lamas wash their hands and mouths at every religious service, *khural*. In Buddhist and Shintoist austerity rites in Japan, it is customary to dive into pools or to stand under waterfalls in order to

---

[7] In Japan, people go as far as to extinguish 'old fires' because these have absorbed all the impurities in the surroundings and have thus become polluted themselves (Hirata Atsutane).

purify body and soul. In India, a complete bath, often repeated several times a day, as well as hair-washing for women (and men who wear it long!) is a strictly compulsory rite among all the upper castes. The same is true of the Babis of Persia. In India again, the mother who has the task of preserving the purity of all the members of the family is subject to much stricter rules of hygiene than anybody else. In feudal China, the vassals closest to the Emperor, before appearing in front of the sovereign, not only had to purify themselves by the severest abstinence, but also had to wash their hair and body. Finally, in a large number of Asian societies, the relations of a dead man, girls after their first period, women after confinement, etc., have to undergo lengthy purification before being allowed to resume normal life within the group.

The requirements of body hygiene as such are often very strict also, generally for religious reasons or because cleanliness of the body is considered as inseparable from purity of heart, or else because the physical body is considered as the temple of the divine or as an instrument necessary for spiritual progress. In Tibet, Padmasambhava used to teach the following: 'The body, although perishable, is the temple of the highest forces and achievements'.[8] In India, Ramakrishna said practically the same.

On the other hand, in many regions baths have no apparent connection with ritual considerations; this is so in Japan where the daily bath—laid down in the Scriptures[9]—is a practice taken for granted and where, in certain districts, people who take only one bath a day apologize for being dirty.[10] Among the aboriginal tribes of India are many who bathe at least once a day. The Malayans take a dip two or three times a day. Every Iranian village has a bathing establishment.

Complete or partial ablutions before or after meals are compulsory, or at least current practice, among the Hindus (The Nambutiri, for instance, have to take a full bath before every meal), the Burmese, the orthodox Jews, a large number of Muslims, in Indonesia and the Pacific Islands, and ever since Marco Polo's days among some Chinese.

Moreover, a number of Indians wash the inside of their stomachs every morning, *dhauti*, just as we brush our teeth, following a technique that is relatively easy to learn. Viet-Namese barbers clean the eyes by turning the upper eyelid and by scratching its inner surface. In many regions, from China to India and in the Near East,

---

[8] Lama Anagarika Govinda.   [9] *Kojiki*, LIX.
[10] B. H. Chamberlain. 'Even the poorest huts have their *o-furo*, the honourable bath', (Fosco Maraini).

'auricurists', who clean the inside of the ears, are as popular as pedicurists and manicurists among our ladies of fashion, and everyone goes to them. The Hindus rub their gums for a long time every morning with a special stick made of green wood, and the Hos do the same. It is for reasons of hygiene also that the Turkomans, various Mongol tribes of Northern Asia, the Bashkirs, the neighbouring Tatars, shave their heads and other parts of their body and that, in many countries, women remove the hair from their bodies either before marriage or periodically.

Even the blackening of the teeth, which for esthetic or hygienic reasons we think so ridiculous, was done as a justifiable precaution, and it is probably because of this practice that the Japanese, until recently, had excellent teeth. The custom is to be found from the Blue River to Java and from India to Japan. Generally, the blackening is caused neither by betel, nor by lacquer, but by a dye.

Methods of ablution vary considerably from country to country although they are always subject to certain rules or, at any rate, to certain customs that are rarely violated. Thus, while for the Hindus the very idea of sitting in a bathtub that has been used by others is repugnant, however well the tub may have been cleaned, the Japanese do not change the water, even if the bath is an individual one, after someone has already bathed in it; it is true, of course, that no soap is used in the tub and that one enters it only after having washed, soaped, rubbed and rinsed oneself thoroughly outside.

Besides, it has to be clearly noted that orientals generally do not confuse two concepts that are hardly distinct to us: the physical cleanliness of water (or whatever product is used for the ablutions) and its purity. A perfectly clear and odourless water may be considered by them as being dangerously impure while water that is muddy or full of all kinds of matter of varied origin may be deemed as ideally pure. The factors that go to decide this are often very subtle, and it is difficult for us to judge their value when they are explained to us. Thus, in streams or in pools, the clarity of the water has nothing to do with its purifying function. A few years ago the whole Ganges was considered polluted because some Muslims had thrown into it the dead body of a cow cut into pieces, but the carcass of a cow that died a natural death does not bother the bathers any more than a dead dog or cat in a European river. While the East does not yet soil its rivers by letting its sewers run into them as we do, it is not disturbed if the waters are somewhat muddy. The Tchuktches wash themselves in urine and this may in fact have a certain antiseptic value which, in their eyes, compensates for its distasteful appearance.

We shall see later the reasons for which Asians do not share our fear of contagion and do not think that the neglect of our present rules involves any danger. Some Chinese do not hesitate to say that it is not dirt but the fear of dirt that is a sign of degeneration, and that the westerner, constantly concerned with asepsis, is much more subject to disease than the Chinese in his poor hut who has never known disinfectants. Let us, however, make an exception for the Japanese who, perhaps under our influence, have become extremely concerned with hygiene as we understand it; in their country it is frequent to see people wearing a handkerchief or cottonwool over the mouth and nostrils as protection against microbes. At the beginning of the century, one Japanese who was obliged to mix with westerners always carried a piece of cotton-wool dipped in alcohol to clean his hands with after every hand-shake. This may perhaps be linked with the fear that many Asians have of any contact with a foreigner whose way of life, religion, physical and especially moral cleanliness are unknown to them or, for that matter, any contact even with another person of their own group as, for instance, among the Hindus. Even to this day, many Bedouins wrap their hands in cloth before touching a foreigner.

Nevertheless, many Asian peoples live in filth which we cannot justify, however much we may try to do so. In Tsarang (Nepal) on the Tibetan border, people laugh at those who wash 'because they are dirty'.[11] Tibetans readily boast that they never wash; they think that washing the body removes chances of happiness, and on her wedding-day a girl is proud of her dirt; if her face and hands are clean, she will have much less luck in her married life. Among the Buryats, a woman never bathes and a child should never be washed before the age of seven or eight years. Various Siberian tribes, such as the Tunguz of the Ona, never wash, nor do the Chinese of Szechuan. Mongols and Manchus seem to show no desire for cleanliness. The Mongols, in particular, wash only thrice in their existence: after birth, before marriage and at death. The Ainus practically never bathe.

As the basis of such an attitude there is often the fear of losing vitality in countries with little sunshine. It must also be remembered that in some areas water is extremely scarce and has to be kept for other purposes. That is why the Koran allows ablutions to be replaced by rubbing with sand, which acts in the same way as water by transferring bodily impurity to the mineral substance. In regions where water is normally frozen, there is not always sufficient fuel available to melt all that is needed for drinking and

[11] Shramana Ekai Kawagushi.

cooking—and sometimes water is even replaced by fat, which has the added advantage of giving warmth. It has been pointed out that the Bedouins of Arabia, while they do bathe rarely, due to lack of water, as soon as they find some, play about in it like sparrows.[12]

As for clothing, in many cases it is a matter of climate. In cold countries they have to be thick and warm and are consequently very expensive and difficult to wash and dry—especially when there is no alternative set available. Tibetans change their clothes once a year, but have a certain admiration for those who can wear them for two years before replacing them.[13] On the contrary, in warm countries—when there is no water shortage—Asians generally wash their clothes much oftener than we do. In the respectable Hindu castes, it would be unthinkable to wear a *sari* or a *dhoti* for two days running without washing off the sweat which inevitably accumulates on it—although 'clean' stains (ink, paint, etc.), however visible they may be, do not disturb anybody. In Burma, in Rangoon, which is probably the dirtiest city in the world, the gravest insult is to tell somebody, even a rickshaw coolie, that he has a dirty skirt. It is also frequent there to see a man or a woman standing before a fountain, on a stone a few inches in size, in the middle of an immense pool of mud and garbage, washing himself or herself most meticulously—and most efficiently.

After the body and the clothes, it is the house that forms the object of the most attentive cleaning operations. The scarcity of furniture or even its total absence, and the incredibly small number of other possessions keep the house from being overfilled and makes it easy to clean. Even at the Sino-Russian border, in Maimutchen, where the filth in the streets used to shock visitors, it had to be admitted that the houses were scrupulously clean inside. In Hong Kong, the immaculate cleanliness of the fishing craft which are also used as houses fills Englishmen with admiration. In India and in Burma the same observation may be made almost all over the country. Their revulsion to the dirt in the street compels the Hindus and the Japanese to remove their shoes before entering a house; and the latter even change their indoor shoes when they move from one room to another. Once or twice a year, the Japanese remove from their houses all that they possess in order to carry out a thorough cleaning. Those Asian peoples who do not keep the floors of their houses scrupulously clean, like the Chinese, do not sit on the ground while most others do. The officials of the World Health Organization, who are trying to make the Muslim countries accept our ideas of 'environmental sanitation', are able

---

[12] Charles Doughty.   [13] Shramana Ekai Kawagushi.

to base their work entirely on Koranic precepts, even to the extent of using the Friday sermons held in the mosques. Mazdaeans and Shia Muslims, as well as Hindus of many castes, high and low, must purify or even destroy anything in their homes that has been touched by a person believed to be impure.

This latter observation may be related to the constant pre-occupation among the Mongols, the Hindus and others not to soil with their breath divine images or offerings made to them.

It must be mentioned, however, that the cleansing agents for the house as well as for the body are not necessarily those which are sold in our own shops. In India, for instance, the ground is often washed with cow-dung diluted in water which, in fact, does have a definite insecticidal value.

The cleanliness of the village or town outside the house is what is of least interest to traditional Asians (again with the exception of the Japanese). They readily allow garbage to pile up outside the house, expecting the animals and the sunshine to do all that is necessary. In India, sewage work is left to the cows, the crows and the ants, and these prove most efficient! Of course, there are exceptions, like those mentioned by Marco Polo at Hang-chow. Under western influence, which insists, in particular, on the use of latrines, there is a big effort all over Asia to keep streets cleaner. It is sad to note, however, that this process also brings with it our standards of bodily hygiene. Perhaps the time is not far when, also in Asia, the little girl about to go on a visit will ask, 'Mummy, should I wash my hands or wear gloves?'—a story that simply makes no sense in Asian circles.

Considering the matter impartially, it must be noted, even if our hygiene experts and other supporters of health education may not like it, that the dirt outside the home does not always lead to a lowering of the general health standard or even to a degeneration of the race. In the last century, a Russian traveller was surprised to see that people living in gutters and cesspools (among the Tchuktches) without any clothes enjoyed excellent health and a robust constitution. Another traveller noted that in Tomsk, where conditions were hardly better, smallpox epidemics were less dangerous than elsewhere and stopped after having made two or three victims, in spite of the complete absence of doctors and hospitals.

With regard to clothes, Asia is much more traditional than the West and less vulnerable to the whims of fashion—although in India women's *sari* borders, in the Philippines, the type of embroidery, in Viet-Nam the length of the *cai-ao* (tunics), in China the colours worn by women and other items, do change with fashion. Nevertheless, it may be said that the two essential factors that condition clothing are practical needs and tradition—morality and modesty apparently only play a secondary part.

The dress shows to what community—village, province, caste or religious sect—the wearer belongs. A Hindu might, at a single glance at a woman's *sari*, guess her caste, her status and perhaps even her name. In Viet-Nam it was the Minister of Rites who prescribed the shape and colour of the clothes. The Japanese belonging to certain sects bear its name or motto woven in full on their *kimonos*. This is why Asian reformers almost always attack the typical costume with an eagerness which surprises us. In Turkey, Kemal Ataturk prohibited the wearing of the *fez*. In Persia, Reza Shah Pahlevi compelled men to wear a sort of uniform cap for a time, even though after that they were merely required to wear European head-gear. In India, Nehru imposed upon the administrative and urban circles a prudishness inspired directly from Queen Victoria, with the corresponding costume. In Thailand, Pibul Songram has prohibited the men from wearing their traditional *fanung*, this being replaced by European trousers, and they were made to wear hats if they wanted to ride on a bus or enter a post office. Sun Yat Sen stopped the Chinese from wearing pigtails and Mao Tse Tung made them change from long blue robes to dungarees.[14] In Japan, in order to abolish social distinctions, the Emperor Meiji prohibited the top-knot, *ei*. In all cases the reformer thereby seeks to break centuries-old habits and introduce ways of thinking and living that are totally different from earlier ones.

When a foreign conqueror tries to impose his culture upon the vanquished people—which is rare, for generally he prefers to go on treating this people as an inferior race distinct from his own—he obliges them to adopt his dress. Thus, in the fifteenth century, the Ming, in order to enforce their power in Annam and 'sinozise' the people, compelled men to wear their hair long in the Chinese style and women to dress in the short coat and trousers.

Inversely, some groups keep to their traditional costume or go back to it precisely in order to protect their individuality and to defend themselves against the invasion of western ways: the Viet-Namese with all their clothes, the Burmese and Indonesians with their skirt (*loongi*), Indonesians and Pakistanis with their head covering. At the same time, various countries give up their traditional costume for other reasons; for instance, because European dress costs less or can be changed more often, or because it is better suited to a westernized mode of living, or simply be-

[14] Robert Guillain (*The Blue Ants*) mentions that 'in uniformed China, the only jackets (western style) are now worn by convicts'.

cause they let themselves be infected by the spirit of standardization. Thus, most of the Japanese have spontaneously relinquished the *kimono*, the Burmese are no longer seen to sport a circular comb in a magnificent chignon, and in Kalimpong the Tibetans are buying felt hats.

The making of traditional garments, their cut, their purchase even, are often associated with a certain ritual. Thus, in Viet-Nam they used to be connected with auspicious days indicated in special almanacs and the first clothes of the new-born infant had to be made with the worn-out clothes of an old man in order to transfer the greatest possible longevity to their new owner.

In Asia, food is often the object of profound respect, not only because it is rarer than in the West[15] but, above all, because it is a means of achieving close communion with God. Therefore, it goes without saying that before being consumed food must first be offered to the gods in order to acknowledge that we received it only thanks to their generosity and their love.

It seems to us somewhat paradoxical or fanciful to see an author affirm that among the Ifugaos of Northern Luzon butcher's meat and poultry are nothing but a by-product of religious sacrifices.[16] But this is true of almost all Asian societies; we shall come back to that later. In India, a terrible curse consists in saying 'May he eat food which has not been previously offered to the gods.[17] This may, without exaggeration, be related to the fact that in many Asian societies breast-feeding is regarded as a way of ensuring physical continuity of a kind which could not be procured through any bottle, however pure and chemically perfect its contents might be.

In the Near East pre-Islamic usage has kept up the 'cult of bread' with milling permitted only on auspicious days, respectful handling of the sieve, prohibition to cut the loaf with a knife, the pious collection of pieces of bread by passers-by who would not dream of treading on them, etc. In the same region, the staple food is a true symbol of community life and it is used in religious and social rites as, for instance, at banquets where loaves of bread are displayed. In China, the individual who drops rice on the ground or treads any underfoot runs the risk of being punished by the God of Thunder, Lei Kung.

It is not just as a matter of naïve superstition, as is superficially believed, that the Chinese and Japanese deify their kitchen oven

---

[15] Professor André Mayer wrote in 1956: 'Asia, with almost half the people of the world, only has 17% of the food.'
[16] Margaret Mead.
[17] *Ramayana*, Ayodhya Khandam, XXI.

and make it an object of worship. It is the only object qualified to judge the moral value of the household and report to the higher divinities.

The offering to the gods, moreover, is not always a mere mental or vocal operation. It often takes a very tangible form; either, before eating, a portion of the meal is carried to the temple and, in exchange, whatever other worshippers have deposited there is brought back as a true gift from God, as is the case of the Japanese from certain districts and many Hindus, or else 'God is fed' materially in the person of the poor and the animals. In many countries, tradition has it that unless the meal has been 'fairly' shared in this manner, it will be difficult to find material for the next. I have known families in India that never begin a meal without having fed an unknown guest. Every day they go into the streets to look for a stranger through whom they can have the honour of 'serving God'. Mohammed used to teach that the best way of being a Muslim is to feed those who are hungry.

The selection and preparation of food is almost everywhere subject to close and demanding attention. 'He who eats is eaten by what he eats', say the Vedas, for the Asian never forgets that man is physically, intellectually, emotionally, morally and spiritually conditioned by whatever he absorbs in the form of solid or liquid food or any other more subtle form.

Prohibitions with regard to food are therefore as numerous as they are varied (on the southern coast of Arabia, for example, the foods allowed vary from one place to another). It is possible, of course, that some of these taboos were born out of considerations of hygiene, but their importance has been greatly exaggerated, and the real sources are of a completely different nature. The following examples will suffice to show this.

In India, in Japan and elsewhere, we have the example of men who have scruples about eating anything other than grass and leaves, but, of course, these are extreme. The principal prohibition covers animal products, many of which are not eaten by many groups. This applies particularly to food which involves taking the life of a born or about-to-be-born animal (butcher's and other meat, animal fat, fish, eggs, sea-food, etc.).

The most widespread reason for this is the repugnance towards killing, since the commandment 'Thou shalt not kill' is understood by the main non-Semitic Asian religions in a much stricter sense than by the Jews, the Muslims and the Christians. Sometimes, however, more detailed and unexpected explanations are given. For instance, the Japanese peasant is inclined to think that if one eats animals that move horizontally, one starts feeling and think-

ing in 'horizontal terms' and one uses modern science for destructive ends with the ferociousness of wild beasts, while, if one eats
plants that grow vertically, one treats all beings, living and inanimate, with compassion and love, in a religious spirit. In Japanese philosophical language, verticality, *tate*, which is constructive
and respectful, is opposed to horizontality, *yoko*, which is connected with destruction and perversion.[18] For certain Japanese sects,
the animals that are doomed to kill for food are under a real curse,
and we should move progressively from this state in order to find
food which does not compel us to kill. This attitude may be cognate
to that of 'the old sect' of red bonnets in Tibet for whom eating meat
is an act of compassion, since in this way the animal's soul is placed
under the influence of the *bodhi* in the man who eats its meat.

Whatever be the interpretation given, absolute vegetarianism is
prevalent among most Buddhists and most of the upper castes in
India,[19] and even other castes and tribes of the same country, such
as the Bant and the Ballal. Among the Kuruba, an interesting and
revealing example, only the village chief is subject to this re-
striction. The Jains, the Persian Mazdekites, the Ritsu-Shu sect in
Japan, in China the Taoist monks *tao-che*, the famous sect of the
White Lotus are, for instance, all vegetarian. The prohibition is, of
course, even stricter for the ecclesiastics than for laymen among
the Hindus, Buddhists, Manichaeans and others.

Certain groups, less strict, eat fish or eggs, but do not touch
meat. Eggs are a particularly interesting case, for while various
groups do not regard the consumption of an embryo as murder,
others think it even more criminal to deprive a being of birth than
to kill it afterwards. The difficulty is sometimes obviated by not
having any cocks in the hen-house.

Exceptions, i.e. fish consumption, are made in areas which have
no other source of food during a part or the whole of the year, and
that is why even the most orthodox Bengali Brahmins are allowed
to eat fish. Ceylonese Buddhists also eat fish, but only after it has
been dried. On the other hand, certain Tibetans, whose main food
is meat, regard killing fish as a sin and the Mongols believe that
eating fish makes one grow scales and fins.

For certain peoples, particular animals are excluded from the
diet: bovines for Hindus of all castes and all sects, pork for Jews
and Muslims as well as for the Veddas of Ceylon, who do not eat
poultry either, all quadrupeds for the eldest of the four priestesses

[18] Kikuchi Yutaka.
[19] There are notable exceptions. Thus in South India, the Pancha Gauda,
although Brahmins are not vegetarians (E. Thurston and K. Rangachari).

in the Japanese Imperial Shrine, and totem animals for very many groups.

Discrimination goes even further sometimes. Thus the Yuraks of Siberia eat reindeer meat except for the tongue, which is considered impure. There are also curious contradictions: in Assam, the flesh of black and white piebald pigs is feared, for the 'chin' spirits do not like them and yet, apparently, it is the black or black spotted pigs, *lo'n den* and *lo'n lang*, which, since the earlier neolithic period, have supplied the very meat eaten almost exclusively by the Viet-Namese and the Chinese.

We also frequently come across what may be called intermittent vegetarianism. Thus, in the Kyoto area, people are vegetarian on the first of January. In China, lay Buddhists are vegetarian through 4, 8 or 16 days a month or over a particular period, fixed by them, varying from one day to three years.

As for milk, various countries, particularly India, consider it as the pure and holy food 'par excellence', and great sages consume it as their only food. However, there are groups which refuse to drink any milk—even in India—such as the Savara and the hill people of Manipur; the priests of Kota who eat buffalo meat do not drink buffalo milk. Viet-Namese regard milk as an excremmental liquid and do not consume it in any form; the Chinese also are suspicious of it and in certain areas of Japan it is considered unclean. In Siberia, the Samoyeds do not drink any while the Tunguz do so readily. The Miao of China and Tonkin, who raise large herds of buffaloes and sell the surplus, do not even know how to milk them. A curious fact is that, in Saudi Arabia, certain tribes such as the Qara, the Rashid and the Awamir do not allow their women to do any milking; among the Mahra and the Al Kathir who are their neighbours, women may milk sheep but neither cows nor camels; and among the Arabs of Oman, on the contrary, only the women are allowed to do milking.

Let us mention a few more curious cases by way of example. Many Hindu spiritual groups formally exclude garlic and onion from their diet, just as the Chinese Buddhists once did because they did not like the 'strong odour'; in Viet-Nam, one must not enter a temple after having eaten onion, garlic or dog's meat. In China where the nobles of the feudal period did not eat many types of food, even today the Taoists are reluctant to consume anything but meat or cereals because, otherwise, they would feed the 'three worms' living inside their bodies and because herbivorous and fructivorous people are supposed to be stupid.

On the other hand, there is a whole series of foods that are common in Asia but to which we are unaccustomed: raw fish in

Japan and Thailand; ants' eggs, cow's placenta and dried Gaur's skin in Laos; white-ants in India, among the Mutracha and the Irula; various insects in Viet-Nam since the second century B.C.; earth in Northern Laos and some provinces of Viet-Nam; bears' feet in China; etc. The former British customs officials in China used to say that there is no animal, vegetable or mineral product that the Chinese do not know how to use as food or medicine.

It must not, however, be concluded from this that our Asian cousins are never refined 'gourmets'. The refinements of Chinese, Japanese, Thai and Indian cooking, although we can fully appreciate them only after long acclimatization, have nothing to envy in the French cuisine, and the 'gourmets' of these countries also hold long and scientific discourses on the subject. And now their recipes even appear in our bookshops.

When we are aware of the importance attached to food and the concern for physical and, even more, for psychical cleanliness that is felt by many Asian peoples, we can see that the procuring, preparation and presentation of food can hardly be treated in a casual fashion. The most characteristic and striking example is that of the Hindus, but they are far from being an exception.

The Jews, the Muslims, the Hindus and others attach much more importance to the moral or doctrinal purity of the seller or even his social rank than to the clean display of his ware, for the subtler impurities that may be conveyed are much more serious and dangerous than the others. Even today, orthodox Hindus never eat in restaurants even when they go on long journeys. Either they carry abundant supplies and do their cooking on the way or else they eat at the homes of acquaintances of their own class or, if on a pilgrimage, they beg for their food which, as a result, becomes free from pollution because it is God who offers it through the giver. To be allowed to give something to eat to a man or woman of higher caste or to someone who is regarded as more or less holy is considered a rare and signal privilege.

The place where food is prepared, the kitchen, is a sort of shrine which has to be kept free from all taint. For a Hindu, it is inconceivable to enter it wearing shoes that have collected dust outside; in the upper castes a full bath is taken and clean clothes are donned before venturing into it. The Nayar submit to this obligation not only before cooking but also before eating. The Rajputs consider their kitchen, the *chowka*, so sacred that only family members can enter it.

The preparation of food is generally entrusted to the purest person in the group—for instance, in India, to the mother of the family, who is subjected to the strictest physical and moral hygiene

—and that person performs this duty like a real priestly task. In India, the cook's profession is the exclusive privilege of the Brahmins, even more so than the priest's. In traditional China, it is the Prime Minister—it goes, of course, without saying that the best minister is the one most conversant with cuisine—who feeds the Royal Virtue, *wang tao*, in the person of the Sovereign. Among the Chinese, the kitchen is generally the cleanest room in the house. Therefore it is only in a few countries such as Japan that our concepts of the physical asepsis and antisepsis of food awaken any interest at all. Recently, United Nations experts noted, not without bitterness, that if in the Near East people agreed to drink filtered water obtained at great cost, it was only because it was cooler and had a better taste.

In those societies that are most concerned about the less apparent forms of purity, there are even serious misgivings regarding the influence of persons who may have touched or merely *seen* food before it is consumed.

In many groups, a woman must not touch the food of others during confinement and menstruation. The contact of a being, human or otherwise, tainted with legal impurity, renders water impure according to the Muslims and the Jews, and in India, different communities each have their own wells. Only a quarter of a century ago I had to leave a Brahmin hotel where I had been exceptionally admitted because the owner suddenly noticed that in going from my room to the latrines I passed in front of the kitchen, and that my glance—as I was a man who had not been subjected to Brahmin rules of hygiene for the last twenty-five generations— might affect the dishes being prepared and thus make them unsuitable for consumption by the more orthodox[20]

This is similar to the concern about not being seen when eating, which is frequent among Hindus, Muslims and many others. In India, the prohibitions regarding eating in common between the different castes or even sub-castes are considered of great importance and even Gandhi approved them—although he did not follow this rule. A plausible explanation which has been given for the Algerians might also be applied to Asia—viz. at the time of eating, the individual is particularly vulnerable, but there is not much evidence in favour of it.

The utensils used for food are themselves the object of very special attention. A Hindu touches rice only with utensils especially reserved for that purpose. He has an almost insurmountable repugnance to eating with a fork or a spoon, for he cannot know

[20] Cf. Laws of Manu, IV, 207-225.

who has used them before him—just as we would hardly buy a second-hand tooth-brush. He also avoids touching a cup or glass with his lips and prefers to pour the liquid into his throat unless, as in Bengal, everyone can break his earthenware vessel after using it. The same is true of the plates of leaves so commonly used in India and which were formerly used in Japan: they can be thrown away after use. A Tibetan considers unclean a cup which has been used by someone of inferior rank, but is not in the least concerned about the dirt which may have accumulated on it.

While at big festivals, marriages, births, funerals, religious or even civil festivities the oriental can absorb incredible quantities of food, in everyday life he is remarkably frugal. Besides, this is mostly through necessity. Not only are famines frequent, taking a terrible toll, and accepted with resignation like all other calamities, but, even in normal times, almost the whole population is seriously undernourished.[21] The daily ration of a Muslim, Indian, Chinese, Annamite or Japanese worker would not be enough to keep a European alive. Only the very few members of some privileged social classes and a few isolated mountain tribes eat enough to satisfy their hunger. An observer has picturesquely described the Chenchu who live in Southern Hyderabad (Deccan) by saying that they are thin in March and fat in May after the return of vegetation each year[22] Most Asians, however, do not even enjoy these periods of relative abundance.

On the whole, the diet is not very varied. In Thai, 'food' is simply denoted by the expression 'rice-fish'. In many other countries, rice or any other basic cereal is not accompanied by very much else.

Over a very large part of Asia the use of alcohol is practically unknown. Islam proscribes it entirely and only those Muslims drink it often on the sly who are more or less corrupted by their contact with the West. This prohibition is just as strict in Hinduism for the upper castes, which go so far as to exclude those who drink it by way of punishment. The Idiga of the Madras region and other groups show exceptional severity, but the lower castes and the untouchables there, as elsewhere, enjoy much greater freedom (similarly, those who have voluntarily left their caste, such as those converted to Christianity) and there are even some cases, very rare ones, where alcohol is recognized as having medicinal

---

[21] 'Nowhere has the art of living in frugality and sloth been carried so far as in the Middle East.' Dresch and Birot.
[22] Pierre Gourou.

virtues. (For example, the Marayan of South India think it is good for the lungs).

In some areas, on the other hand, alcohol is as serious a problem as in the West. The Siberians and the tribal populations consume large quantities of it and often are passionately fond of it. While it is rare to see drunkards in China,[23] drunkenness is hardly criticized in Japan.[24] European travellers in Persia were stupefied to see how much wine was commonly drunk there. Genghis Khan had laid down that people could be drunk only thrice a month; but once would be better, said he—and he added that the best would be not to get drunk at all, but who could hope to achieve such an ideal?

Other narcotics enjoy even greater popularity in Asia. Opium-consumption, which has been actively encouraged in China and elsewhere by westerners who saw in it an important source of income, did not always penetrate into the life of the people without meeting with violent opposition[25] The Commissioner Lin Tse Hu, who had tried to prevent its being imported and consumed, had to be revoked from his office upon orders given by the British in 1842, but once the Chinese had recovered their independence they canonized him. Therefore, the Far Eastern people are sometimes a little disconcerted to see that the consumption of the same opium is now for a quarter of a century the object of sharp indignant criticism on the part of these same westerners who have even set up a complete international machinery in order to proscribe its use. It has to be admitted, however, that a moderate use of it is both an intellectual stimulus and a 'tranquillizer' and its harmful effects, much less serious and frequent than those of alcoholism, are only felt among those who smoke to excess or cannot afford good quality.

Hashish, the Indian bhang and other narcotics have perhaps more serious consequences, although, even there, we find people who consume them habitually and are still perfectly balanced.

As for tobacco, its use has now spread throughout Asia, and

---

[23] Lin Yutang. However, the Taoist sage drinks alcohol, for drunkenness is close to ecstasy, and, besides, it is believed that alcohol, reserved for old people, 'preserves life'.

[24] John Gunther. The same in Korea.

[25] In about 1920, an English trade union offered a hundred pounds sterling per year to the Mongolian Administration in order to obtain a licence for importing opium which up to then was practically unknown in that country (Ivor Montagu), and even very recently the opium monopoly supplied the British Straits Government with a third of its revenue (John Gunther). See in Claude Roy (Into China, 1955) the edifying story of relations between the Chinese and the West and the part played therein by the 'Opium War'.

although some masters denounce its drawbacks, even the strictest monks do not hesitate to smoke it, often to great excess. Certain puritanical sects, however, such as the Wahhabites and the Senuists in Islam, continue to prohibit it. There is one curious fact: among various tribes of Central India, a veritable mythology has been created about tobacco being brought to man by the gods.

The consumption of tea or coffee sometimes acquires stupefying proportions in every sense of the term. An average Tibetan drinks fifty to sixty cups of tea per day.

In Asia, in general, illness is not considered in the same light as in the West. Many people do not see it exclusively as an evil and therefore do not fight it outright. Thus, for the Muslim it is a warning from God, reminding us of his might. For the Hindu, it is a way of expiating faults committed in previous lives and also an opportunity to assert mastery over matter. For the Buddhist, it helps towards understanding of the body and shows the impermanence of the self. For those who see it chiefly as an evil, the main and only cause of it must be sought everywhere but among those accepted by modern western science. We shall see that even when they are of a physiological order, they belong to categories other than ours—but mostly they are very different. Thus, any Chinese doctor asked to attend a patient will first ask: 'What has excited your anger to this extent?' Or else it is considered to stem from the extra-human demoniacal or even divine forces or entities, or from the influence of certain conjunctions between the heavenly bodies. Certain illnesses, particularly epilepsy and those affecting the eyes are frequently considered as special blessings and it would be childish and ill-advised to wish to cure them.

Anyway, Asians are generally much less inclined than we are to let their suffering be noticed by others. Perhaps this is partly due to the reasons we have just mentioned, but also because many of them have, since their earliest youth, been submitted to an extremely severe personal discipline, and a fair number have, through techniques of meditation and concentration, acquired over their physical body and physical pain an unbelievable degree of mastery. Besides, even those who have not reached this stage like to behave externally as if they had; whatever the reasons, their attitude is often worthy of the best Spartan traditions. Following a custom recorded since the fifth century and which has subsisted till modern times in the Fukien,[26] certain Chinese Buddhist monks had themselves burnt alive sitting in Buddha poses and reciting sacred texts.

[26] In Viet-Nam today.

As for the attitude in facing death, while the factors we have just mentioned are important, religious and metaphysical considerations are even more so. The drop into nothingness is not terrifying for people who lead a very hard life; hell, however awesome, is never eternal in Asian religions, and besides, easy last-minute manoeuvres make it possible to avoid it and to turn towards a paradise full of charm; finally, the prospect of re-incarnation makes what we call death rather similar to falling asleep at night in order to awaken rested the next morning.

While the Persian poets do see human existence as a quarter of an hour's recreation between two infinities of nothingness, and while in classic, feudal China, the common people, contrary to their master, did lose all individual existence when they died, these are exceptions.

Among the Taoists, the phases of death and life are in sequence 'like the periods known as the four seasons',[27] and death is to life what coming back is to going. The Tenri-kyo of Japan speaks almost in the same terms: as our body has been lent to us by God, the fact of restituting it is only like leaving in order to come back, *denaoshi*. In Japan, in general, where it is believed that men may live only for a period fixed in advance—at the end of which the God of Death, Shinigami, signals to us to come—people even rejoice at the thought of being able to shorten it in favour of someone else. The Japanese say proudly that when one of their soldiers wears a talisman of Hachiman or some other god of war, it is not in order to come back safe and sound, but to be brave and victorious. Their bravery, which has become legendary ('almost beyond what can be achieved', writes Chamberlain), is accompanied by the same contempt for death that is to be found among the Muslims, particularly in holy wars.

However, it is not only on the battlefield that the great majority of Asians consider death with indifference. An Afghan proverb says bluntly: 'If you have, eat. If you have not, die!'[28] In fact, Gandhi did not grant that the imminent danger of death from starvation was an excuse for stealing bread.

For the Hindus and the Buddhists, the distinction between life and death is an appearance without foundation. In Burma for instance, man cannot fear his own death, for life and death are but one and are only the stages on the road of existence; and to die is nothing more than to undertake a new life.

From this a French author has logically been led to the conclusion

---

[27] Tchoang-Tse, 18.
[28] James Darmesteter.

that the man accustomed to hold death in contempt also despises life. Here there is serious confusion. For the greater part of Asia, the actual opposite of living is not dying. The event that is death is opposed to the other event that is birth and the state that is life on this earth may be opposed either to the state that is life in another world or to this other 'state' that is the total absence of existence, nothingness. There is, therefore, between the alternating states of life here on earth and life elsewhere a continuity that is regularly punctuated by births and deaths in their proper alternation.

That is why we find in Asia two attitudes very different from each other but which are considered as contradictory or incompatible only by the Western mind. On the one hand, life here on earth and life 'elsewhere', including hells and paradises, may be considered as states of illusion or lower truth, and anyway, as something unsatisfying, and one must rise above it.[29] On the other hand, contempt of this episodic event, death, by which we move from one state to another, makes it possible to enjoy life better without being haunted by the fear of seeing it end. This explains the real cult of longevity among the Chinese.

Immortality in one and the same life, however, even if it does have a certain attraction, is not an unmixed blessing. In 219 B.C., the Chinese Emperor Shih Huang Ti had sent the magician Hsu Fu, accompanied by three thousand young men, to discover the 'Isles of the Blessed'. The expedition did not return, but it is not just jokingly that the writer Shikaiya Masobioye describes the terrible sufferings of these people who, having succeeded in their mission, have found immortality but cannot bear it and do all that is possible in order to die and are not successful.[30] Besides this, the mythology of many Asian countries includes episodes where the god of death fails to fulfil his duty, and this leads to a catastrophical situation which the other gods try to mend as quickly as possible.

This contempt for death is naturally bound to have repercussions on the attitude to suicide.

In fact, for instance in Japan, suicides are very frequent in various classes of society. It is curious to note that in a large Japanese public library,[31] the section on 'Suicide' is placed next to the section on 'Etiquette'. The motives for suicide may be the same as for us: personal despair, solitude, absence of aim in life, irresistible need (we

---

[29] The Lama Govinda expresses in the following terms an opinion that is shared by almost all the sages of Asia: 'To condemn life as evil and to deny its highest possibilities of development before having penetrated as far as consciousness of the Whole. . . . is not only presumptuous but senseless.
[30] Cranmer-Byng.   [31] Tenri-kyo.

shall come back to this later) to follow somebody dear to one. It is the frequent resort of lovers who see no way of uniting other than through death, *shinju joshi*, and who are granted the last homage of being buried in the same tomb; collective suicides are not rare. This was seen recently in Korea.

However, there are other reasons also; suicide may also be a protest—the strongest one conceivable and often the most effective one—against a fact or a situation where one feels powerless, or it may be purely and simply an act of obedience to an order received.[32] The history of Japan abounds in famous cases constantly cited as examples. This same attitude is to be found in other countries of the Far East. In Feudal China, the threat of suicide is a characteristic feature of the relationship between vassal and master and is always included, although potentially, in this procedure of disavowal which takes the form of remonstrance and is the essential duty of the son as well as the vassal.[33] In Viet-Nam, in 1882, when the French took possession of Hanoi, the vanquished general, Hoang-Dieu, hanged himself on an artificial mound, Tam-Son, which had been subject to the influence of Saturn and was a tumulus of fidelity to the sovereign.[34] Gandhi has shown the irresistible effectiveness of the pressure exercised by hunger strikes, unto death if necessary.

However, the groups which believe in re-incarnation—we have seen that in Asia they form the majority of the population—cannot look upon fleeing from life as a solution to the personal problems that they cannot succeed in solving; for them these same problems will necessarily reappear, perhaps in an even worse form, in the next existence and then something will have to be done to solve them. Therefore, it may be said of most Asians, that while they are doubtless more willing than we are to sacrifice their life spontaneously to a particular cause, they hardly ever let themselves be led as far as suicide through despair and discouragement. It has been said of the Muslims that they take life as it is given to them and, until Europe taught them the attraction of nothingness, they knew nothing of suicide.

A curious consequence of the belief in survival after death is the custom of distributing punishment and reward post-mortem. Some punishments were specifically intended to prevent the dead from enjoying in the other world a position which they could normally

[32] Moving descriptions of *seppuku* are to be found in Lafcadio Hearn's *Unknown Japan*.

[33] But suicide without a noble aim is not approved; Chinese law has even provided for repressive measures against anybody accused of having persuaded one of his fellow-beings to kill himself.

[34] Pierre Huard et Maurice Durand.

have claimed. Thus, when the Assyrian army pillaged Susa and Elam in the seventh century B.C., the bones of the kings were 'carried away to foreign soil and their spirits . . . forever deprived of their place of rest, refreshment and peace, the only property they had hoped to enjoy after death'.[35] Cyrus the Younger, in Persia, had his head and right hand cut off after death. In Viet-Nam, after death, the convicted were made to undergo posthumous tortures: exposure of the head, powdering of the bones, flagellation of the tomb. When, in China, the condemned people were cut into pieces, it was less for the physical suffering thus inflicted than in order to exclude them from the world of the spirits. In China also, titles of nobility were easily granted to deceased persons,[36] and while one of the reasons was to confer a dignity in this way upon the descendants, there was certainly also some thought of pleasing those directly concerned. To quote only one instance, Kuan Yu, the great military hero, was appointed Faithful and Loyal Duke in 1120, Prince and Warrior Civilizer in about 1330, Faithful and Loyal Great God (ti), Upholder of Heaven and Protector of the Kingdom in 1594.

The incessant increase of the needs to be satisfied, an indispensable factor in the Western system of civilization, is not an Asian ideal. There is no reason why that which was sufficient for our ancestors to live happily should not also bring us happiness. The philosophies of renouncement (Vedantism, Buddhism, Taoism, etc.) as well as those with essentially practical aims (Confucianism, Islam, etc.) reach the same conclusions, although for reasons that are sometimes diametrically opposed.

Left to themselves, the people of Asia, in general, have no desire to improve their material standard of living and, to our eyes, they show a real genius for finding perfect contentment in the situation where fate has placed them.[37] The Muslim must have the kalaf, the 'sufficient', and does not seek the superfluous. The state of contentment, uparati, santosha, is one of the essential virtues recognized by Hinduism.

Yet, their resources are incredibly meagre. With 55% of the total population of the globe, Asia has only about 10% of the world income. Among the nomads of Arabia, he who does not suffer from hunger is considered as living in state. The average income

[35] Clément Huart et Louis Delaporte.
[36] When a man is canonized, it happens that his ancestors may also be made noble (E. T. C. Werner).
[37] China: Lin Yutang and Arthur Smith. Bedouins: cf. Freya Stark.

of a Persian rural family or a poor family in India is about 70 dollars a year. In Java, 60% of the families have an annual income of less than 60 dollars. One hectare of cultivated land in Japan has to feed 25 to 30 persons while, in Europe, the food potential of the same land would be about six persons and in the United States two. China is even poorer, and the Korean vital minimum is even lower than that of the Chinese.

This contentment is one of the main reasons why the Asians feel much less anxiety about the future than we do. Another reason, perhaps still more serious, is that they are conscious of being part of a homogeneous and continuous whole where everything has to and will happen at its appointed time under the right conditions, and consequently it is no use worrying. This confidence and this resignation, which are taken to be fatalism and indifference, have made a deep impression on all Western observers who have most often condemned these qualities pitilessly.

Islam is an optimistic religion, even a hedonist one; having admitted the existence of the eternal order where everything is accomplished in advance, and having accepted his complete dependence, the servant of Allah is freed from all anxiety. Why burden oneself with plans, forecasts, when the future is always in the hands of God. Mohammed used to say: 'Be satisfied with what God has given thee and thou shalt be the richest of all.'[38] An old Hindu proverb says: 'He who sells grain is a merchant; he who hoards it is an assassin.'[39]

Much has been said about the total absence among the Burmese of this anxiety that we so closely associate with insecurity. In Thailand, economy and saving used to be considered as senseless. In Viet-Nam, submission to Nature and to the order of the universe had made absence of forethought a duty. In China, the peasants, although living under the shadow of famine, did not build granaries and did not calculate from one year to the next.

When easterners and westerners meet at a fair, one cannot fail to notice the contrast in the two attitudes. The love of old-age pensions and insurance policies is absolutely incomprehensible to almost the whole of traditional Asia. It is not the West that has the greatest confidence in Him who feeds the sparrows!

Under these circumstances, it is easy to understand why the Oriental is not ready to work more than necessary in order to satisfy his immediate needs. He prefers devoting the rest of his time to the calm enjoyment of all that God or nature has given him. According to a Kol saying, which would be supported by

[38] Hadith.   [39] A. Gulterman.

nine Asians out of ten, 'When there is enough to eat at home, why go and work?'

In Turkey and in the Middle East most of the farmers want to produce just enough farm products (including the products of animal husbandry) to meet the needs of their family and to buy a few elementary articles. In Burma, at the beginning of the century, when the peasant had harvested the quantity of rice that he deemed necessary, he left the rest to rot on the spot. The Laotian regulates the quantity of rice that he sows in accordance with the rain forecasts given in the calendar. In the Philippines, farming takes up hardly 75 eight-hour days a year and the peasant seeks no other occupation.

This is not a matter of laziness, as we are inclined to think, but a whole philosophy of life—and even a concern for honesty, as we shall see later.

CHAPTER XI

The Individual in His Environment

Do good to your neighbour and you shall be a true believer.
MOHAMMED.

WHILE in the West the essential purpose of the name is to make it possible to identify the person, to distinguish him from other individuals and to call him, the name in the bulk of Asia has quite another aim. It establishes, alters or simply mentions the relationship between the individual and the divine, extra-human or cosmic powers and may be used by one person to designate or call another only accessorily and on the strict condition that such use does not harm the person concerned. As this difference in conception has many and serious repercussions, it is worth while considering in detail the origin and the importance of the names of persons.

The personal name in Asia does not usually comprise this subdivision to which we are accustomed, between the individual first name and the patronymic or surname, between merely descriptive names and the proper name as such, the original meaning of which is forgotten. The efforts made by orientals to adjust their names to our customs often lead to the most comic results. A certain Hindu monk or swami bears on his passport the title Swami under the 'first name' heading. Another Hindu who is called Hanuman-Prasad, i.e. 'he who has been granted to his mother as a favour (prasad) from the god Hanuman', indicates: first name, Hanuman; family name, Prasad. An Arab who is called Abd-er-Rahman, i.e. 'slave (*abd*) of the compassionate (Rahman)', indicates: first name, Abdur, family name, Rahman, or he has A. Rahman marked on his visiting cards. For the Chinese, who generally have three names of varying importance, the confusion is often great.

That which corresponds to the patronymic, i.e. connects the individual to his origin, is mostly the name of a caste, as among the Hindus, or of a tribe or place of origin, or the individual name of the father or mother,[1] often also that of a mythological ancestor or

[1] A curious fact is that among certain tribes of south-east Arabia, there are men who, instead of thus connecting their names with their father, link

a totem.

As for the specific name of the individual, its nature and the way of selection vary from country to country.

In Islam, it is mostly the name of the Prophet or of one of his more or less immediate successors, or one of the holy names of Allah which is preceded by the word Slave, *abd*. However, if a child is seen to be delicate, sickly or threatened with imbecility, or if his brothers die young, he is often given the name of a strong wild animal—wolf, leopard, etc.—in order to compensate for his fragility and thus protect him.

Among the Hindus it is the name of one or more gods or epic heroes. 'Rabindranath Tagore', to take an example familiar to westerners, may be broken up as follows: Rab for Ravi (one of the names of the Sun God), Indra (the king of the gods), Nath (the Supreme Lord), Tagore for Thakur (God), in other words, four names of God.[2]

On the other hand, among certain Indian tribes such as the Gadaba and the Mattiya, which show less imagination, the child is merely named by the day of the week on which he is born; but that places him directly under the protection of the relevant divinity. A similar system was in use in China under the Yin dynasty, where the personal name was chosen from among the signs of the denarian series. Similarly, certain Indo-Chinese merely give a serial number as a name to their child: One, Two, Three, etc.[3] However, these are exceptions. In Burma, where again the name is given according to the day of birth, the choice is nevertheless more subtle: each day of the eight-day 'week' has a group of sounds allocated to it and these must be used as the initials of the name given.

In Tibet the child's name is chosen according to the date, the hour and the lunar conjunction at the time of birth; it is often the name of the planet corresponding to the date of birth. In Afghanistan, when two names are given to a boy, one of the two has to be a cleverly thought out one, for the sum of the numerical value of its letters must recall the date of birth. But apart from these particular cases, astrological considerations almost always intervene in the choice of a name. In China it was necessary to find out under which one of the five elements the child had been born, and then its name had to be in relation with this element.

Other factors, however, also come into play. In China, for in-
them with their son by placing the word *abu* (father of) and their son's name after their own (Bertram Thomas). The same applies to the Andaman Islands (Radcliffe Brown), and to Korea.

[2] Cf. Laws of Manu, II.
[3] The same in Japan formerly (Mock Joya).

stance, according to an old tradition, there must be a certain con-sonance between the name and the habitat, a fact which gave parenthood 'a deeper essence than if it had been simply founded on ties of the blood'.[4] In Feudal times, while the daughter's name was left to be chosen by the mother, that of the son, in noble families, was not only fixed after an inspection of the voice (for the voice is the soul and also the name), but also after consulting the forefathers.

In Japan, people mostly confine themselves to consulting the village priests and schoolmaster, but there are also competent pro-fessionals in the field. Among the Valaiyan of India, the name has to be given by a man in a state of trance.

In Buddhist countries in general, the child is frequently named after a virtue, and this name is a kind of programme to be followed for the rest of his life. However, there are also names which bring bad luck, and it is especially in order to avoid these that the Buryats generally consult a Lama. In many groups, children are given the most repulsive names in order to detract the attention of evil spirits. They are called 'silly animal', 'sickening beast', 'horrible and repulsive little pig', etc. This is done by the Viet-Namese and by various Indian tribes, such as the Bhondari, the Dudekala, etc., when they have already lost one child or more. In China, when the parents are afraid that evil geniuses will take away their only son, they sometimes give him a girl's name so that these same spirits may ascribe less value to the child. It is perhaps for reasons of the same nature that in Laos we find names with meanings that openly defy all decency.

Nevertheless, whatever be the precautions taken in selection, the individual name given at birth among most Asians may be completely replaced by another, whenever this is justified by circumstances. This happens naturally in India, Tibet and among the Buddhists when the person enters monastic life; but there are many other cases as well.

Among some groups this happens automatically at a certain age: at puberty for girls among the Kadirs of South India, and formerly in feudal China; for boys in Japan[5] and in Laos. Among the Chinese, in addition to the 'milk name' that is received when the child is a month old, there are successively the book name, *shu ming*, or school name when the child starts going to school, a 'big name', *pieh hao*, when he becomes a student, an official name,

---

[4] Marcel Granet.
[5] It is curious to note that in Japan rivers also change their names during their course.

kuan ming, when he becomes an official, plus a posthumous name, *shih hao*, and the nicknames. Among the Moger of India it is customary for the child, after a certain time, to give up the name which it had received. Among the Muslims, frequently the name given officially is, in fact, replaced by another soon after, for the simple reason that the former name made the child cry while the second one makes it smile and therefore is more agreeable to the genies.

In Japan, where there are eleven categories of names—only *jitsumyo* is the real name—a *kabuki* actor changes even his family name, *yago*, as the quality of his acting improves. In Laos, the name is completely changed when one goes up in the social ladder, and titles succeed in completely eliminating the original name of the individual—Mr Kham can successively become Phia Kanaraj, Phagna Sisong Sane, Chao Phagna Khamthongphet.

Safety reasons are often a determinant factor. The Kolyomyan of Siberia regard a change of name as the best way of escaping from the evil eye of the Shaman. In Japan, a whole science, *seimeigaku*, teaches how to escape from illness or even financial crises by a change of name. In Laos, the name is readily changed after a serious illness.

There are even cases where the name disappears. For the Taoists, the sage does not even have a proper name, for he is united with everything. Many Hindu sages lose their personal name for the same reasons and simply become the 'great sage', *Maharshi*, the 'naked grandfather', *Nanga Baba*, Mother, *Ma*, etc.

Furthermore, in countries of Chinese culture, the dead take on posthumous names which then entirely replace the names they bore in their lifetime. When a Japanese Buddhist dies, the temple priest who maintains the family cemetery gives him a new name, *kaimyo*, and until recently there was a custom in Japan establishing that a widow should bear part of her future posthumous name already before death. The Emperor of Japan, after his death, is designated by a name that he has chosen himself at the beginning of his reign. At his death, the Chinese Emperor received a 'temple name' by which he is named in history. In Viet-Nam the personal posthumous name, *ten huy*, which is composed of two Chinese characters summing up the qualities and defects of the defunct, is the only one pronounced in the invocations to the dead: example, *Thuan Du c*, Immaculate Virtue.

Whatever its origin and whatever the time of its bestowal, the name has a truly mystical and magic value. Even Confucians, disenchanted though they may be in regard to this type of speculation, call their doctrine *ming-chiao*, the religion of names.

According to the Sumerian Genesis, the gods themselves existed only once they had been named. For the Hindus, the name, *nama*, and the form, *rupa*, are the two components of a being's or a thing's individuality; therefore, *a fortiori*, they are inseparable. In China, the life breath, *houen*, cannot be distinguished from the personal name. It has even been said that in ancient China names possessed individuals much more than the individuals possessed names. The personal name, external soul or token of life, symbol of fatherhood, benefit conferred by marriage, principle of motherhood, title of power, ancestral patron and emblem were undistinguished equivalents. In feudal China the name expressed the being and made destiny, to such a degree that a man born a prince would become a stable groom if he were named such, and another one named 'he will succeed' could not but succeed. What is more, a child who, predestined to the name of Yu, bore on its palm, at birth, marks showing the Yu character, would have to possess the fief of Yu, whatever the royal will. In Japan, the name governs the whole life.

Even to this day, the name can, by antithesis, have a compensatory value in countries of Chinese culture; thus an evil-smelling street or a wretched bed in an opium den will be called by a flattering and splendid name—which is the opposite of the phenomenon we have mentioned above.

On the whole, it may be said that he who knows—or, even more serious—makes use of another's name has a sort of occult power over him. This is equally true for objects, spirits and even gods. That is why in many countries, and particularly in India, initiation consists precisely in communicating a secret name of the Divinity even when it is a name already known so that the person who receives it has the power to use it. We have seen that this conception is at the basis of the Hindu *japa* and similar disciplines in other religions. That is why the Hindu does not have the right to disclose this name, which is that of his chosen deity, his *ishta-devata*, when the name has been given to him by his *guru*. Similarly, the Lama may not reveal the name of the *yidam*, the guardian divinity chosen by him with whose help he expects to cross the borders of the material world. In China, the chief 'knows the name of the monsters: this name is their very soul. As soon as it is pronounced, the most fearful beast rushes to him, captivated.'[6]

Therefore the name must only be pronounced with the greatest circumspection; only a few privileged persons are allowed to use it

[6] Marcel Granet.

and then too, in particular circumstances; to do so on other occasions would not only be a lack of decency or respect but may even involve serious dangers. Among the Teleuts of Siberia, a woman may on no account pronounce the names of the near male relatives of her husband. In marriage announcements in Afghanistan, the girl is mentioned only by her parents' names; it would be indecent to designate her otherwise. In India it is unthinkable for a woman to call her husband by name and in many cases the reverse is also true. The Japanese and Chinese readily use a name other than their own; this is what the Japanese call *azana*. The personal name of the Emperor of China was never allowed to be pronounced in his lifetime, and Sun Yat Sen used to have himself called Sun Wen. In feudal China a young girl's name had to remain particularly secret, and the mutual respect between husband and wife prevented them from calling each other by name; and the mother of the family always called her husband 'Lord'. Even very recently, a well-bred Chinese woman never disclosed her personal name even before a court of law. The Chinese funeral tablets only show the posthumous name. In Viet-Nam, while the family name, titles, etc., are marked on the visible outside board, the real and personal name appears only on a hidden, inner board.

Even more than knowledge of the name, the possession of a photograph or a fragment of the body (bits of hair, nails, etc.) is supposed to confer upon their holder a real power over the person to whom they belong and enables him to exercise the much feared 'evil eye'. That is the main reason why most orientals feel a deep revulsion, even real terror, at the idea of being photographed. Even the Japanese, now so keen on photography, once believed that the photograph absorbed a part of the life and spirit of the subject.[7] It is not impossible that this belief might have something to do with the Koranic prohibition against the reproduction in sculpture, drawing or otherwise of a human person or even an animal. In Islam it is now being discussed whether phonographic reproduction should be allowed or not.

It is quite evident, however, that modesty is also at the basis of this fear of photography and of portraiture in general. Asians, and particularly women, have a highly developed sense of modesty, although this often shows itself in ways different from those to which we are accustomed in the West—and in a great variety of ways. The Chinese readily shows her legs up to the thigh and even higher through her slit dresses, but carefully buttons the same dress right up to the neck; the Hindu sees no harm in exposing her back and even her navel, but zealously hides the whole lower

---

[7] B. H. Chamberlain.

portion of her body down to her ankles. Among the Pulluvan, the Tiyan, the Nattaman and other tribes of the Malabar, among the Balinese and the Yakuts, in certain areas of Japan and elsewhere the woman traditionally remains bare to the waist, and in Japan women may bathe naked outdoors without shocking anybody; but with the arrival of westerners, who interpret them quite differently, these customs are in the process of disappearing. In traditional China, female nudity was all the more shocking since the woman is of the *yin* principle, and therefore impure. Among many communities the woman should never consent to show her hair.

In South India, while the Lambadi women sleep naked with their clothes for a pillow, the women among the Bonda Poroja must wear clothes at home but are not allowed to wear any outdoors, and among the Vellala, they have to undress completely for the cult of Ganesha. For the Nagar women, to cover the bust shows either lack of modesty or a very low caste.

The most striking external sign of modesty among women is the veil covering the face; we shall revert to this later when speaking of the woman's place within the family. In many strict societies of course, women of rank do not let themselves be seen by commoners. It has thus been pointed out that the traditional hair style worn by the princesses in Japanese *kabuki* is based on pure fancy, since the costume-maker never had the chance of seeing any.

It should also be mentioned that in the dances meant to be the most 'suggestive', the women are most often completely covered by their clothing—and also their jewellery. Make-up and tattooing also vary according to set rules, to such a degree that it is sometimes possible to guess the person's district of origin, and any deviation is considered most improper.

It would seem to us Europeans that such modesty, often so imperative, should go with a certain isolation and privacy. That is not at all the case and this is not one of the least inconveniences experienced by a westerner thrown into an Asian family. Even when the family is not large it is practically impossible for the individual or the couple to enjoy privacy, and it is practically impossible also, if not unthinkable, for the family to have secrets from each other. In a Chinese house it would be most improper to shut the door of one's room during the day, and in China again there is nothing embarrassing in a medical consultation taking place before outsiders, or in dictating a letter to a public scribe or in listening to one's horoscope out in the street before a very interested circle of passers-by. In India, even when a house has as many rooms as there are families—which is a great exception—

decision has to be taken every evening as to who should occupy which room; it is common for the women of the family to possess all their clothing, underclothing and jewellery in common, collected in the same chest or cupboard, and for each of them to choose from it every morning whatever she might want to wear. Anybody asks anybody else, within the family or outside, the most embarrassing and inquisitive questions, and if someone writes or reads a letter, it is more than possible that another member of the group will simply come and read it over his shoulder. This forced familiarity covers friends, guests, and all those who have been admitted into the family circle. In Japan, it is often said that this life where nothing can be hidden or disguised is a means of purification. In any case, it is true that it strengthens the unity of the group.

All this often entails, particularly in Chinese families, a continuous din to which all the members are quite accustomed, whether by day or night, and it no longer disturbs them. Perhaps, however, this is one of the reasons why solitude is so much appreciated in most oriental countries, where there is a yearning for 'cloisters built by men and those supplied by nature.[8] Another way of withdrawing oneself from this racket is obviously by not contributing to it, and it is not rare to find Asian people who have taken vows of complete silence varying from one day to several years. Gandhi used regularly to observe a day's silence, *mauna*, every week; and in doing so he only conformed to a widespread habit.[9]

This withdrawal, which is a moral and mental health cure, is never a sign of hostility towards one's neighbour. The great Hindu sage, Ramana Maharshi, used to say that the most effective way of being useful to mankind was to withdraw into a cave and think right thoughts which are necessarily thoughts of love because, as Gandhi said, 'Love and Truth are so closely intertwined that it is practically impossible to disentangle and separate them from each other'.

While Christians readily believe that their religion was the first to introduce into the world the concept and practice of love for the divine, they also generally think that Jesus acted as an innovator in advocating the love of one's neighbour. It is true that this evangelical principle rests on a basis quite different from the one prevalent in the majority of Asia. Instead of the brotherhood of men, sons of one and the same Father, the more oriental mystics base their beliefs more on the identity or non-duality of 'self' and 'others', refusing to admit a separation or difference between the

[8] Cranmer-Byng.
[9] There are also people who speak nothing but the name of their god.

two. This is what is preached by the Japanese *myokonin* Shotoku Taishi, by the Hindu Ramakrishna, by the Persian poets and many others. The so-called 'fatalist' Muslim school, including the illustrious Firdusi, without going as far on the metaphysical plane, considers pity for one's less fortunate neighbour a true echo—however weak it may be—of divine compassion itself.

While this does naturally result in a refusal to place one's own interest before that of others, it also leads to a reluctance to save others from their fate, whether it be a result of their past or a link in the sequence of their evolution. This might sometimes look like an apparent indifference which seems to exclude pity.

In Asia the neighbour's suffering is respected, and while he is offered all possible relief, even at the cost of great personal sacrifice, he is never under pressure to accept it. It is granted that others have the absolute right to refuse this help and to use their suffering in whatever way they think fit, whether it be for the expiation of past faults or for developing the mind or for any other purpose that need not be disclosed. It is in this sense that Filliozat's assertion may be understood. According to him, Buddhist doctrine does not ask for compassion. It is more correct to acknowledge, as Father de Lubac does, that Buddhist kindness and gentleness are superior to those forms of zeal and 'charity' that are too indiscreet or too pushing. In some countries, such as Burma or Japan, it is even impolite to offer help, for it means doubting the other's strength and at the same time wishing to acquire a certain power over him. In Japan, I once happened to have a bad fall and none of the ten or fifteen Japanese friends who were with me made the slightest gesture to help me to get up again; but I am convinced that, if I had asked them to do so, they would have done their utmost without sparing time or effort. In China, the social worker is regarded with suspicion, for he minds other people's business.[10]

The natural corollary of this attitude is that the neighbour is not criticized for his doings, however incomprehensible or blameworthy his conduct might be—provided, of course, that he does not disobey one of the laws imposed by the group for its own protection.

It is to be noted, however, that this is a form of love, and, as the Asian traditionalists would say, a form as intense but more perspicacious and generous than the Christian idea of love. Among the Hassidis, where the Rabbi Raphael, for instance, write: 'If a man sees that he is hated by his companion, let him love him more!', true love can only be 'an identification and a participation,

[10] Lin Yutang.

both active and passive'.[11] 'Do good to thy neighbour and thou shalt be a true believer; wish for others what thou wouldst wish for thyself and thou shalt be a true Muslim', taught Mohammed. Gandhi never asked for the foundation of 'charity institutions' for the untouchables, but he did found an association for the *service* of those he so lovingly called the sons of God (the untouchables), the *harijan*, and the strictest Brahmans vied with each other in their haste to join it. It might be mentioned incidentally that the Hindus fail to understand all the admiration we show for St Martin for having given away half of his mantle; their reaction is to ask why he did not give the whole of it. Even among the Chinese, 'this people formerly so disinclined to mutual help and solidarity when it came to altruism outside the family',[12] there was from the fifth century B.C., the great school of Mo-Tse which exercised considerable influence and whose master, Mo-Ti, preached universal love above all things. 'Men cannot be changed,' said he, 'except through a doctrine of love.' Even he, however, admitted that the law of justice and kindness is 'a law of return'. Five centuries before Christ, Confucius and Buddha said in identical terms that man should not do to others what he would not have done to himself, and the Rabbi Hillel, a contemporary of Jesus and one of the recognized masters of Hassidism, did not express himself differently.

Buddha also used to say, 'Never has hate been stopped by hate. Goodness makes hate stop. Such is the eternal law'. He also said, 'Oh monks, he who lets hate fill his heart while bandits saw off his limbs one by one would not be doing what I have commanded'. In the eighth century of our era, the Japanese master Zenju of the Hosso-Shu school wrote: 'To reply to hate with hate is like trying to extinguish a fire by throwing grass into it'. In our own time Gandhi comes back to the same theme: 'The toughest fibre must be softened in the fire of love. If it does not melt, it is the fire that is not hot enough'.

Another interesting attitude that is to be found for instance in Southern Arabia and in India consists in regarding the suffering of the unfortunate as an inevitable part of life on this earth, and seeing it mainly as an opportunity offered to the rich to do good deeds if they feel inclined to do so.

One of the most visible manifestations of this love for one's neighbour is hospitality, which reaches throughout traditional Asia —and retains almost throughout modern Asia—a level that is almost inconceivable in the West. Not only is the guest sacred, even if he happens to be one's worst enemy, but among many

[11] Baber.   [12] Robert Guillain.

peoples he is actually regarded as the visible representative of God, if not God in person, and must be honoured as such. He enjoys a sort of right of priority on all that his host possesses. The service of guests, say the Hindu sacred scriptures, is an eternal sacrifice offered by the master of the house to the Lord of all creatures.

The mythology of Hinduism and that of the mountain tribes of India have stories where a king cuts himself into pieces in order to feed his guests. There are also stories, probably authentic ones, where poor people have died of starvation rather than fail in their duties of hospitality towards an exacting visitor.[13]

It is said of the inhabitants of Mi Lich Ka in Armenia that they did not hesitate to stimulate a bandits' attack on the highway in full daylight just in order to attract outsiders to their homes and feast them; while this is exceptional, it causes more admiration than surprise among the Asians.

From the most primitive peoples of the Arctic to the Yakuts, the Buryats, the Siberian Russians, the Mongols, the Tibetans, the Indo-Chinese mountain tribes, the Laotians, the Burmese, from the Indonesians to the Chinese, Japanese and Koreans, in India, the Near East and Saudi Arabia, the manifestations of Asian hospitality have stupefied western visitors. The following anecdote illustrates the severity of this obligation among the Muslims. Once, when a subordinate officer delayed giving food to a poverty-stricken and unknown nomad who had stumbled into the camp, Ibn Saud ordered the offending officer to be flogged, and, after giving the nomad a regal feast, himself harnessed and led the nomad's camel —the highest honour that can be paid to anyone in Arabia.[14] The Muslim poet Mustatraf expresses nothing exceptional when he writes: 'Oh, my guest, if thou visitest me, it is I who shall be thy guest and thou the Master of the house.'[15] Among the Bedouins the Arab can undertake long journeys across the desert without provisions, simply relying on the hospitality of the nomads on the way; they are subject to the religious obligation of giving the traveller a bowl of milk even if, in doing so, they have to give up their own food; this is *kheyr Allah*, the Lord's generosity, towards *theuf Allah*, the Lord's guests. Hospitality takes precedence over every other relationship. Among the Bedouins the guest is sacred, not only while he is under his host's roof but also over a period after his departure varying from two days and the night in between to four days and four nights.

Even the concept of a paid hotel shocks easterners. In India one of the commonest forms of 'pious deeds' consists in building inns

[13] Cf. *Mahabharata*, Ashvamedha Parvan, XC; Swami Vivekananda.
[14] John Gunther.   [15] Freya Stark.

(*dharmashalas, chhatrams, chowdries*) where travellers are accommodated free of charge and canteens where a number of passers-by
are fed every day. The Government regards the considerable number of people who normally live by begging as a serious economic
problem; we shall return to that later. In the conventional type of
Japanese hotels, the meals have to be paid for, but there is no
charge for the rooms; in the *kichinyado*, the wood used by the
traveller to cook his rice is the only item charged. Under the old
régime, a Chinese going to Peking or any of the other large centres
was accommodated there, together with his family, free of charge
for the whole of his stay on a property belonging to his native
town. In Ceylon, most villages have their *maduwa*, their shelter,
at the disposal of passing travellers. In Bali, as well as among the
Buryats, the traveller has the right to demand board and lodging
from villagers on his way. The Tchuktches regard the acceptance
of payment for hospitality as a grave sin.

This absolute *obligation* to receive the stranger with so much
consideration and at such sacrifice is obviously not always respected very willingly, and it is not always as disinterested as it
may seem at first sight. Among the Muslims it may happen to be
of magic value, for the simplest gift of food places the guest in an
inferior position. Among the Chinese, the fear of being under
obligation to somebody places one in a position of submission, an
assumption that is not very convincing in view of the Chinese
habit of constantly borrowing money from each other. These explanations may also apply to the injunction that must be followed
in India by all those who practise Raja-Yoga—namely, that they
should accept no gifts. (This is the *aparigraha*.)

This deference to one's neighbour, which is manifested in such
different ways—from hospitality to abstention from helping, is
probably responsible in part for the remarkable allergy Asians have
towards any expression of refusal or even disagreement. Of course,
logical reasons, already mentioned, may account for this, but when
the questions are as simple as: 'Are there any seats free on the
evening train?' or: 'Will you be at home tomorrow afternoon?' it
does not seem that abstract considerations should prevent the
person from replying 'No' if indeed this is the truth.

In particular, a conditional or reluctant acceptance, especially if
it is obtained after insistence, is almost always a courteous refusal.
Westerners who do not interpret it as such are, in general, cruelly
disappointed and think that it is an act of bad faith, while actually
the person who answered thus did nothing but follow the elementary rules of Asian politeness!

When one of the persons involved does not have a perfect understanding of the other's language, these misunderstandings become even more frequent, for the Asian nearly always hesitates to ask for a repetition of the question that he has not understood, fearing to show disrespect or to confess that he is not clever enough; in case of doubt, he answers at random in the politest possible way, that is, in the affirmative.

Finally, it must be noted that often a question that occurs to a westerner and is asked by him of an Asian is senseless for the latter because he starts from quite a different basis, whether it be in regard to the facts themselves or the scales of values or the logical co-ordinates. There again, the reply is a very vague but very cautious approval.

All this frequently makes conversation difficult and uncertain and, as far as possible, the westerner must learn to ask questions in the Asian manner—which is difficult—or recheck several times before he can be sure that both parties have understood each other.

The difficulty is at least as formidable when trying to understand a joke made by a traditional Asian or to make him appreciate one. We tend easily to conclude from this, but quite wrongly, that Asians have no sense of humour. In fact, it is perhaps even more developed than ours, but one has to be very familiar with the language, traditions, way of life and even the history and literature of a country in order to be able really to understand its humour and, even more so, to laugh at it. However, the fear of breaking etiquette or of offending may sometimes restrain hilarity. Mohammed even recommended that one should not laugh, for 'to laugh much kills the heart'.[16]

What we have seen of the Asian's attitude when facing his own death does not apply to his attitude regarding the death of others. Asians generally take it with less resignation although the trauma suffered by a member of a large family or a mother of many children is normally less than in the case of a family of three or four persons, or the mother of an only child. While in the doctrine of transmigration there are strong chances of meeting in a later life those to whom one is bound by karmic bonds, one is generally just as sure of not recognizing them or of being recognized by them; and so, for all practical purposes, the separation is final. Therefore the survivors readily show their despair by shouting, weeping and wailing rather more loudly than is customary in the West.

Nevertheless, more thought is given them in the West to the future of the departed and this as soon as the end seems to be approaching. In Afghanistan the Muslims constantly repeat

[16] Hadith.

'*achadou*'—an invocation to Allah—to the dying, so that the latter in turn should be led to call the name of God at the time of death and thus be assured of salvation. In India the passing away of a dying man is made easier by removing him from all that can inspire attachment and by plunging his feet into a sacred river, while murmuring (or shouting) the name of God into his ear, and so on. The Chinese sage, at the bedside of a dying friend, seeing his wife and children in tears reprimands them severely by saying: 'Be quiet, go out, do not disturb his passing!'[17] For the Taoists, when friends, masters or near ones die, it is enough to meditate on the vanity of things and, if desired, to utter three short lamentations in order not to shock the common people—which nevertheless proves that this was not the usual attitude of the masses. Similarily, in Laos, it is considered that too visible regret might hold back the soul of the dead and hinder it from flying off to the blessed other world. The Buddhist nuns sing: 'Those that thou leavest behind are aware of thy happiness in liberation; they await their turn with patience, gaily; they do not miss thee; they are happy without thee; so follow thy destiny!'[18] One of the Japanese invocations to dead children is *miren-ouo-nokorazou*, 'let thyself not be invaded by the regret of this world.'[19]

While their attachment does not drive the survivors to hold back the departing, it may incite them to accompany the dying to the afterlife. Much has been said about Hindu *satis*—women who have burned themselves on their husbands' funeral pyres. It was regarded as a most barbaric custom and was, moreover, finally abandoned by the Hindus.[20] However, this is actually very little different from the Western mother who refuses to survive her child or the betrothed who commits suicide on her lover's tomb, themes that, in literature as well as in real life, provoke more admiration than blame among us. Besides, with very few criminal exceptions, these *sati* suicides were nearly always voluntary, based on strict conditions, and were performed after the person concerned had absorbed powerful drugs. Normally, only the first wife was allowed to do it, and the case of Ranjit Singh, where twenty-seven of his wives obtained permission to follow him, in 1839, is altogether exceptional.

It is, however, true that the widow was encouraged to behave in

---

[17] Tchoang-Tse, 6.
[18] Th. Nh. Abhay.
[19] Lafcadio Hearn.
[20] Upon the insistence of certain movements, both traditionalist and nationalist, such as the Brahmo Samaj, and not at all upon the initiative of the British, as has often been alleged.

this manner, on the one hand because the life of a widow is not very attractive, and on the other hand, because her memory would be highly honoured as a result and her funeral monument would probably become a place of pilgrimage; some of these are still very much frequented, especially in Kathiawar. In the Vizagapatam district, Yerakamma, who committed *sati*, has been deified. Two *satis* have been divinized among the Lambadi. The Tottiyan have special temples—the *thapanjankovil*—dedicated to women who have committed *sati*, and there are other instances.

Besides, it is not only in India that this custom was to be found. Examples of it are quoted in the Champa. In China, the widow who hanged or drowned herself with great ceremony and in the presence of a magistrate was honoured by the Emperor, who bestowed upon her a tablet of honour or a commemorative arch, *p'ailou*, and it needed the full effort of Confucianism to put an end to this custom; at the time of the Tcheou, the closest of the vassals normally followed his lord to the tomb. In Japan, where a very honourable term, *junshi*, means voluntarily escorting a dead person, there were famous cases of it not long ago. Among the Yakuts it was customary, whenever one of the great members of the community died, for one of his most beloved servants to burn himself with joy on a special funeral pyre in order to be able to serve his master in another life.

Of course, in Asia there were also groups where horses, slaves and even women were sacrificed. There were instances of this in the third millennium in Sumeria, but even more recently, under the Shang in China, among the Hiong-nu, the T'ou-kin and also among the Mongols (even the Buddhist Mongols) who sacrificed up to a hundred or a thousand women or servants on the tomb of the chief or even massacred whoever came in the way of the funeral procession; this continued, in fact, until a decree issued by Prince Sasakto-Khagan at the end of the sixteenth century, prohibited such practices. In 1265, when Hulagu, the founder of the Iranian Empire, was buried, beautiful virgins in festive attire were placed in his tomb. In Japan, at an Emperor's funeral, a number of his servants were buried alive; this lasted till the reign of the Emperor Suinin in the first century of our era. In Korea, until the year 502, five men and five girls used to be buried alive with every king who died. These instances may be compared with the famous, but no doubt exceptional cases, of Japanese Samurais who, before going to a hopeless battle, killed their wife and children in order to be ready for the *shini-mono-gurui*, the hour of the fury of death.

The methods used for disposing of the body vary considerably according to the regions, races, religions and even the sex, marital status, age and cause of death. Thus, for example, while the Hindus burn most corpses, they abandon the bodies of certain monks in the sacred rivers, and they bury various categories of other persons who, moreover, are not at all the same in the various castes and tribes. These distinctions are to be found from one end of Asia to the other. Thus, the Tchuktches, who are familiar with cremation, exposure to animals, etc., burn their shamans; and the Laotians, who in general burn corpses, do not follow this rule for persons who have died a violent death.

In many countries it is customary to give dead bodies to the animals to be devoured, and this from the remotest antiquity[21] to our day. It happens even in the twentieth century in the plains of Outer Mongolia. The Parsis leave them to the vultures, the Sogdiane to the dogs. The Persian Magi had the bodies torn to pieces by a bird or a dog before burying them. The Tibetans are even more methodical: the flesh is cut into pieces and the bones powdered and mixed with flour so that the birds can eat the corpse without leaving any of it behind; this is the *cha-goppo*, which corresponds to the Buddhist practice of leaving the body in the open air. In Malaya, in the Fu-nan, in the Lin-yi, burials 'in water, land, air and fire' were known, as we see from one of their stock expressions. The great Taoist, Tchoang-Tse, who caused surprise then—as today among us—with his habit of delivering corpses to the beasts instead of burying them respectfully, used to say with humour: 'In order to avoid having to give the corpse to the crows and vultures, it is allowed to be devoured by ants'.

The list of strange customs connected with the disposal of dead bodies may be prolonged *ad infinitum*. Let us mention only a few of them. Formerly, in Viet-Nam the bodies of chiefs killed by the enemy used to be sewn in a horse's skin. In the Philippines, among the Igarots of Northern Luzon, the dead are kept seated in chairs—the richer the person, the longer he is kept thus; afterwards their limbs have to be broken in order to place them in the coffin which is hollowed out of a tree-trunk. Among the Buryats, when a Lama has been cremated, little Buddhas are made of his ashes mixed with clay.

The importance of funeral ceremonies also varies to a surprising degree. In the same country—Laos—while the Khmu have practically no such ceremony, the Lao cremate their dead in sumptuous coffins, perfume them and hold feasts in their honour for six days and six nights in an atmosphere of merriment; the house where the dead are watched over is even called the happy house, *hueun di*, since to die is to enter a new and better life.

[21] The Jain Scriptures already mentioned this custom (*Mahanisitha*, p. 25).

It is probably the Chinese—in China and in their numerous communities in other parts of Asia—who have the longest and noisiest funeral celebrations. Families readily accept to be in debt for many years in order to be able to pay for the considerable costs of such funerals. Traditionally, moreover, there are two different burials, the first near the house, where, for a few months or even longer, the corpse is left to decompose and return to the ancestors' world, and the second, the real ceremony, when the deceased, thus treated, himself accedes to the dignity of an ancestor.

The same is true of Viet-Nam (and also, to some extent, of China and Korea) where, after having placed the corpse in the coffin at an auspicious hour—for astrology has as much to do with the future life as it does with this—the final funeral is celebrated only three or four years after death, in a grave (mo) dug according to strict rules of geomancy. Similarly, in Tibet the body is disposed of as described above, but only on an auspicious day. In Japan even a fictitious date of death is sometimes adopted, but this is done for practical, traditional and not religious reasons.

Celebrations in honour of the dead do not cease at the end of the few days following the death or the funeral; they continue for months or years—a hundred years in Japan, seven generations in China for those who follow Buddha's teaching,[22] three generations among the Bedouins, etc. It is the cult of the dead that plays an important role in the bulk of Asia, and even a preponderant part in countries like China. We shall come back to this when we see the place of ancestors in the family. On the one hand, this cult guarantees family unity and ensures a close bond between the individual and his ancestors as well as his descendants, a bond that is necessary in order to give him a real feeling of security on this earth. On the other hand, it supplies to the dead the material and immaterial things that they need in order to subsist, and, above all, to continue their evolution in the other world. Indeed, for most of these communities, as has been said in the case of Viet-Nam, 'it is not only death, bt also the ritual that opens the way to future life'.[23] Only through rites is it possible to operate the transfer of life or power that is necessary. Besides, this relationship between the living and the dead does not necessarily have a sad character. In many countries, from Turkey to the Philippines, cemeteries are places used for merry picnics, and throughout monsoon Asia the Festival of the Dead and death anniversaries, where lights are

[22] The father's death, in particular, is considered as such a serious event that, in traditional China, a civil servant automatically received three years' leave in order to fulfil the funeral duties. (M. Granet).

[23] Layard.

thrown on the water, are very gay occasions. This is easily understandable, since on the other side of death the individual continues his existence, mostly under conditions better than here on
earth. We have already spoken of the planes of consciousness
through which he passes.

The relationship between men and animals in Asia is very
different from what it is among us. Its metaphysical basis resides
in the fact that, for most Asian philosophies, no clear borderline
can be drawn between the two. In China, 'no theological prejudice
led people to imagine that man by himself formed his own mysterious reign in nature.' According to Lie Tse, no two beings with
blood and breath can be very different in feeling and intelligence.
That is why equal kindness should be bestowed upon animals and
on men, affirms the Lieou tu tsi king. In Japan, between man and
animal, there is a close kinship, a community of ties founded on
their identity of nature, just as between animals and gods. One of
the greatest Indian educationalists, founder of the Benares Hindu
University, wrote that 'the divine presence must be felt in all
creatures' and one of the most eminent leaders of the recent reform movement stresses 'the fundamental identity of all beings'.[24]
'The oneness of life', Masson-Oursel very pertinently affirms, 'establishes an equivalence between man and his lower brothers'. With
them, exactly as with the gods, there is a relationship of consanguinity, mixed marriages, transformations from one species to
another, not only at the time of death, but during life, cases of
possession and all sorts of communication.

In particular, many races, tribes and families have animals
among their ancestors. In India the Gadaba claim a cow as an
ancestor, and the Lambadi claim a monkey; in Sumatra the members of a certain clan of Mandeling claim a tiger. In Indonesia, the
inhabitants of the island of Wetar are said to descend from wild
boars, serpents, crocodiles, tortoises, dogs and eels. The Lao are
descendants of five boys born from a white crow's five eggs hatched
respectively by a hen, a nagi, a tortoise, a snake and a cow. In
China the princes of the barbarian kingdom of Tai are the descendants of a dog—and the early ancestors of Genghis Khan were
Boerthe China, the sacred wolf, and Daghoai Maral, the beautiful
doe. Some Minangkabauer of Sumatra, including the Rajah of
Indrapoera, the Malays of Patany Bay in Thailand and others regard crocodiles as close relatives; and in the seventeenth century
Captain Cook found in Java, Sumatra, the Celebes, Timor and
Ceram a deeply rooted belief that a woman sometimes gives birth

[24] Pandit Tattvabhushan.

to pairs of twins composed of one human and one crocodile, and he gave a detailed description of the ceremonies involved in such an event. Recently, in the eighteenth century, the famous Japanese philologist Mabuchi claimed to be a descendant of Yatagarasu, the crow that guided the Emperor Jimmu in his conquests.

The most frequent origin of the genealogical tree, however, is the mixed marriage between human and animal. The primordial shamanic Tunguz, ancestor of all the other shamanic Tunguzes, was born of the union between an eagle and a woman. For the Meo of Northern Laos, both the French and the Meo are descended from a Meo widow and a pig. The black Kirghiz claim to be the offspring of a red dog and the forty ladies-in-waiting of a princess. (Kirghiz, *qirqiz* in Turkish, or *qirq hiz*, means 'forty girls') Similar legends are to be found among certain Chinese races as well as in Tibet and among the Ainus in Japan. In China, the possessors of Sanglin, the mulberry forest, are supposed to be descended from a woman who conceived after having swallowed the egg (*tsen*) of a swallow, conquered in a tournament on the day of the spring equinox. Also in China, scholars sometimes found, in the middle of their libraries, charming young damsels of sixteen or seventeen who lived with them for a few days, a few weeks or even all their lives, and managed their households efficiently, gave them children and took care of them when they were ill—and these women were none other than fox spirits. According to the Rajavali, the founder of the great Sinhalese dynasty, Vijayo, was born of a princess and a lion. Korean legend says that Pak Hyuk-ku-se, the first sovereign of the kingdom of Silla, came out of an egg and his wife from a dragon's side, in the first century of our era. Sometimes the mixture is even more complex; thus tradition has it that Tibetan people are descended from the saint Chenrezi, son of the god O-Pak-Me (Amitabha), who apparently took the form of a monkey in order to unite with a rock she-devil, Tra-Sin-Mo.

This feature does not apply only to archaic, out-dated legends. In the cosmology of the Japanese Tenri-kyo sect, which only dates back to the nineteenth century and has millions of followers, even from the most advanced circles, God 'the parent', in order to create the prototypes of man and woman, utilized loaches, a merman and a white serpent, plus a sea-tiger and a tortoise, an eel, a flatfish, a black serpent and a ballfish; later, when the human race was destroyed, it was reconstituted from a female monkey.

The members of certain human groups are also supposed to be able to change into animals. The Munuvar, the Nayaka and others have the reputation of being able to change into tigers. In Northern

Laos it is believed that the Meo can become tigers only after their death, although they try not to, and there seems to have been recent cases of individuals changing gradually in their lifetime before the very eyes of those surrounding them.

The Paniyan and the Paraiyan, it is said, change into bulls or dogs, the Khmu into deer, certain tribes of the Hadramaut into wolves. For the Chinese the souls of the dead can come back to earth in the form of snakes or bears, and it seems that Kouen, the father of Yu the Great, did not even wait to die before changing into a bear. In Japan Prince Kamato-take, son of the Emperor Keiko, changed into a white bird after death. The Tibetans believe that the souls of some lamas enter the body of a fish; this is why they seldom eat any other than imported fish. Without being so specific, the Samoyeds of the shores of the Ket think that man can easily change into an animal and vice versa. Among the Lao, when the soul leaves the body temporarily, as, for instance, during sleep, it can take animal form, and, in order to make it return, it has to be called and welcomed periodically by a special feast, 'sukhuan'. In China, the first two August Ones, Fu-hi and Niu-kua (who invented marriage), formed a couple 'linked to each other by their tails', which is also a kind of theriomorphia. Similarly, the last August One, Chen-nung, like Tche-yu, had the head of an ox.

Cases of possession by animals are frequent, and in Japanese, there is even a term, *kitsune-tsuki*, which explicitly means possession by a fox or by a fox spirit; only specialists, generally priests of the Nichiren sect, can cast them out. This very special relationship played a considerable part in Japanese beliefs from the tenth or eleventh century, it seems, and it is explained how, even in our times, certain phenomena, otherwise inexplicable, are ascribed to the intervention of animals. There are also certain families, *kitsune-mochi*, very much feared, who possess such foxes or such magic dogs and can use them.

Such cases are just as frequent in China and whole volumes can be filled with such stories. A particularly strange case has been mentioned by P. Wieger: the spirit of a man who had been eaten by a tiger became the latter's slave until it could procure for its master another human victim whose spirit could replace it. The same belief is to be found in India among the Coorgi and the Kadar.

Apart from these cases of transformation or possession, orientals grant that it is perfectly possible to communicate with animals as with human beings. According to the Chinese Lie Tse, 'the ancient sages understood the language and the feelings of all beings and communicated with them all as with human people . . . with flying creatures, quadrupeds and insects'. Even in our day, some Malays can make crocodiles come to them by calling, and the inhabitants of Kamchatka believe that the whale, the bear, the wolf and the mouse understand human language. One of the loveliest stories, a part of which at least is quite authentic, is that of Han Yu, the famous Confucian of the T'ang dynasty, a great sceptic and declared enemy of all idolatry; he fell out of favour precisely because of his attitude in this matter and was sent away to the present Swatow, where he found the district infested with crocodiles; he sent them a written order in the noblest style enjoining them to leave—and they are supposed to have complied!

Relations with mythical animals are similar to those with known animals, as described above. It is in China, in connection with the dragon, that we find the most frequent examples. Pao-sseu, King Yeou's favourite in the eighth century B.C., was born of dragon foam that had fecundated a little seven-year-old girl, and, perhaps as a consequence, the love that she bore the king caused havoc in nature. Kao-Tsu, the first emperor of the Han dynasty, also had a miraculous birth connected with a dragon. One of the ancestors of Hia was changed into a dragon in a holy place after he had been dismembered.

All this is, of course, closely connected with the belief that animals have a soul which might some day migrate to a human body or may even have passed through one already. This goes without saying for the Hindus, and in practice, if not in theory, for the Buddhists. In Thailand, elephants, horses, buffaloes and cows have a *khwan*, just as men do, and the Japanese grant that animals have souls. According to the greatest code of India,[25] insects, snakes, butterflies, cattle, birds and plants reach heaven through austerity. In the same country, when the King Yudhisthira went to heaven with his brothers, he took with him a dog that had followed him all the way. Similarly in China, when Hsu Chen-chun left on the same journey, his dogs and chickens accompanied him, just as Houai-nan took his whole poultry yard to paradise.

For the Japanese Buddhists the animal state is a state of darkness of the mind which deserves our pity and our sympathetic kindness. No animal may be considered as being absolutely happy. However, in the state of the animal there are countless degrees. In China, four thousand years ago, the Sang already had cemeteries for horses, for it was thought that their lives did not end with the death of their physical bodies. Even in our own times, in Japan, fish and certain animals are buried and services, *kuyo*, are held in their honour in accordance with a custom older than Buddhism. A Japanese priest on pilgrimage in Tibet tells us, as if this should

[25] Laws of Manu, XI, 241.

be taken for granted, that the sheep used by him as a beast of burden had died, and he had, therefore, held a funeral service.

While in the West we are just beginning to suspect that animals, like men, have a psychology and a sociology, this has been obvious to the Asians since the most ancient times. It is even readily admitted, in Tibet for instance, that animal society is governed by a code as strict and severely applied as that of man, and when Hindus see one animal 'execute' another, they refrain from intervening in this administration of justice. In Cambodian stories, trials of animals—and even objects—are not uncommon and do not cause laughter among the readers, for, as one author (Bernard-Thierry) explains quite correctly, 'these animals are our brothers in destiny and placed under the same conditions of life, death and reliving'. The Japanese firmly believe that domestic animals sometimes agree to sacrifice their own lives in order to save their masters'.

Many Asian groups go even further and actually worship various animals, that are thus almost deified. This is not just the inevitable bond between man and his horse or camel; nor does this refer to individual mythological beings such as the vulture Jatayu in India, the big crow Yatagarasu in Japan and many others. But entire species such as the bullock in India,[26] the deer among the Tchuktches, the fox in Japan, the tiger among the Vagh Bhil (who prostrate themselves before it when they see one), the whale in Central Annam and among some Siberian tribes, the wild elephant among the Kadir of South India, and all elephants among the Karuva Haddi[27] and the Hathi also in the same area, the bear among the Ainus, who even feed the cubs on woman's milk, etc. The Rautias, in South India also, go into mourning when a tiger is killed. In the Nilgiris, the Todas milk their buffaloes in sacred sheds, following religious rites. Some Chinese villages set aside the first days of the year for honouring animals and particularly domestic animals, and for celebrating their 'birthdays': the first day for poultry, the second for dogs, the third for pigs, the fourth for ducks, the fifth for horned beasts, the sixth for horses; and after that, they similarly honour men, rice and various cereals, fruits and vegetables, and finally, wheat and barley. On the fifth day of the fifth moon, a most inauspicious day (the men born on that day are predisposed to suicide or parricide!) they even celebrate the birthdays of harmful animals: scorpions, wasps, centi-

---

[26] This is the animal referred to when speaking of cow worship in India. The buffalo is far from enjoying the same religious respect.
[27] Edgar Thurston and K. Rangachari. When they see an elephant's footmark, they take the dust from it and rub it on their forehead.

pedes, snakes, toads, etc. In Japan, when someone inadvertently catches a tortoise, it is gorged with sake after having been laid on its back and then put back into the sea.

Various peoples believe that certain animals have magic powers —the toad for the Japanese, for 'it knows things that the gods themselves know not';[28] the eel, the calao and a certain type of falcon for the inhabitants of Nias and Borneo. Among the Yakuts, every shaman possesses an 'animal mother' which helps him in his ministry and often takes the form of an elk, a deer or a bird which is, of course, revered by him.

In many groups, particularly among the Buddhists, the Jains and certain Hindus, there is the same obligation towards animals as to human beings—viz. to help and take care of them. There are many hospitals, not only for dogs and cats, but also for insects or snakes that may be found ill or injured. Certain Gujaratis even consider it a sin to live in a town where there is no hospital for animals, *pinjrapole*.

For many Asians it is a pious act—that is, primarily an act that brings about better harmony between ourselves and the surrounding nature—to release a captive animal. It is in this spirit that the Hindus let loose their cows, and even more so their bulls, in order to celebrate the great events of their life; that the inhabitants of Calcutta release jays at the time of their Durga Puja; that the Lao buy live animals at the market just in order to set them free; that once a year the Yakuts let loose a handsome stallion, and the Thai do the same to birds and fish bought in the market from Chinese shops; that in Japan, the release (*hojo*) of these same birds and fish is regarded as the noblest form of charity; that in China people buy shellfish and turtles, particularly on Buddha's birth anniversary (eighth day of the fourth moon), but also on other occasions, just in order to throw them back into the sea.

This attitude naturally creates serious food problems for people who do not wish to or cannot be vegetarian. There are various solutions. One of these is, of course, to offer the animal to the deity; we have seen that this is why Hindus kill goats in their temples. They are not the only ones to do so. An alternative is to celebrate religious rites at the time of slaughtering; this is done by the Tibetans, who simply read sacred texts over the animal's head so that it may gain access to the existence beyond.[29] In Japan, particularly for eels that have been caught, rites are held by the shopkeeper who prepares them for consumption. In Cambodia, pro-

[28] *Kojiki.*
[29] Shramana Ekai Kawaguchi. They sometimes also strangle sheep and yaks 'so as not to have to kill them'!

pitiatory ceremonies are held before elephant hunting and before the collection of wild beehives. Among the Khmu of Northern Laos, the members of the Quang family who trap a tiger first offer it a length of white cloth and a pinch of boiled rice as a sign of mourning. When the Arabs kill an animal at the slaughter-house or at the hunt, they pronounce the name of Allah, and to say that they do so in order to avoid the vengeance of the animal's soul is a somewhat incomplete explanation.

The Tunguz are said to have a custom which is certainly similar in origin—the animal killed by hunting has to be consumed, at least cleaned, on the spot, so that once the men and the dogs have fed upon it the remainder goes to the wild animals living in the same place—otherwise ill will befall the hunter.

In many large communities, however, there is a deep and sincere repugnance towards killing. The most extreme and the best-known example is that of the Jain monks, who wear a piece of cloth over their mouths to filter drinking water in order to avoid swallowing an insect inadvertently, and sweep before them as they walk in order to avoid treading on one. Without going so far, in India I have seen an East-Bengali Buddhist sob because the doctor had ordered her to kill the mosquitoes in her room. In certain countries it used to be almost impossible to have plague rats killed; the villagers preferred to emigrate till all the rats had left the village or even to lift the roofs of their huts so that the light would force the rats out. In the Muslim countries it is sometimes, as in Iran, feared that by eliminating a scourge sent by God, as all scourges are said to be, one might draw a worse one upon oneself. In Japan, the Minaduki tugomori-no-oho-harahe, the Great Exorcism of the last day of the sixth month, places incest and the sin of killing an animal on the same level.

The professions where it is necessary to kill or to use the remains of animals are despised almost throughout Asia, and those who exercise them are kept at a distance. In India, they are the most untouchable of the untouchables. The same almost holds good for butchers in Islam and in Korea, for cobblers among the Hindus and the Buddhists, fishermen and hunters in Burma, fishermen in Ceylon, blacksmiths who manufacture weapons in Tibet.

The reader will have noted that in all this, no distinction is drawn between 'useful' and 'harmful' animals. It is because throughout Asia such a classification is devoid of meaning. All animals like all men are an integral part of creation, have their part to play in it and are therefore indispensable to us even if their normal or exceptional activities seem unpleasant to us. But a part of the game that they and we are playing on earth sometimes involves rivalries and struggles.

The relations between men and independent animals are mostly governed by tacit agreements which arrange for the distribution of the soil and its fruits between them. Except for illicit encroachment by hunters or pillaging animals, each species respects the rights and privileges of the other. There are, however, cases of relentless fighting between men and animals; thus the Kirghiz torture the wolves which they manage to catch alive, and the wolves in turn tear apart all the sheep that they can catch.

Furthermore, cases of ill-treatment or even brutality to animals are not unusual—travellers and missionaries have complacently made an abundant collection of examples. This might seem incompatible with Buddhist piety, which is vaster than Christian love, since it extends to all living beings, and in conflict with this feeling (the strength of which can be judged from the above) of unity between the human and the animal worlds. But while we might expect orientals to treat their lower brothers as their equals, we cannot reasonably ask that they should treat them better! Now, in very poor, often cruelly exploited countries, ravaged by natural disasters of all kinds, the life of man is very hard, harder than we can even imagine, and he needs all his philosophy in order to face it. It is therefore only natural that the animal should share this hard lot.

This same fraternal attitude often extends surprisingly also to trees and plants. It is true that there are important exceptions; the Arabs do not have this feeling at all, the Chinese, the Ho and still others treat their forests without any consideration—but the rule is illustrated by many instances throughout the rest of Asia.

There are some cases of consanguinity. In China, Yu the Great was born from a plantain grain; and in India, the rishi Kaushika was born from a tuft of grass; in Tibet, Lobon Padma Chungne, founder of the 'old sect' of red hats, was born from a lotus flower in the Danakosha pond in Kabul. Among the Bontoc of the Philippines, the Koreans, the Miao-Kia, the Buryats and others, souls which have left human bodies go to live in trees.

Plants, in any case, have a soul and sensitivity. Certain Chams of Cochin-China do not wish to disturb the rice at noon because it is supposed to be asleep. While the Indonesians credit rice with a soul, the Laotian farmers hold a great festival, *boun Khoun Khao*, in honour of this same soul when they are satisfied with their harvest. In China, trees are supposed to bleed and to weep when they are hurt, and in Japan, the *enoki* and *yanagi* trees are also said to bleed when they are cut; their ghost, *ki-noo-bake*, even walks about in their immediate vicinity—for instance, in the shape of a lovely woman. For the Chinese and the inhabitants of the Celebes, the soul of plants takes a human or an animal form. The Hindus celebrate marriages between plants of different species.

Not only are some plants sacred to a particular god, like the *tulsi* to Krishna in India (in some areas, weddings are held between Krishna and the *tulsi*), but many are worshipped for themselves. This same *tulsi* is given offerings of fruits and vegetables by the Kudubi, while their neighbours, the Kudumi, worship the *peepal* tree. The three peaches, Okamizumi-no-mikoto, used by the Japanese god Izanagi in his fight against the armies of the lower world, have been given divine rank. Inversely, some plants are more or less demoniac, such as the *tamarind* in Ceylon and Bengal. Many an individual tree or plant is inhabited by deities or demons and has to be revered and respected for this reason. In Cambodian stories there are trees which become sentimentally attached to their master, and in India there have been relatively recent cases of human sacrifices being made to trees.

In India the scriptures prohibit the unnecessary cutting of trees; and the 'Siberian religion prohibits one from making a field out of a wood'.[30]

When a plant has to be uprooted or killed, often the same type of precautions have to be taken as with an animal. Cambodian nuns are not allowed to do either, and Siamese Buddhist monks are as reluctant to break the branch of a tree as to cut off the arm of an innocent man. The Batta of Sumatra, the Malays, the Siamese in general, some Indian groups such as the Kondhs, the inhabitants of Berar, the Larka Kol, etc., refuse to kill certain types of trees. Among the Hindus, generally speaking, a little religious service is held before a tree that has to be cut, and similarly among the Indonesians, before cutting down a forest for cultivation purposes. The Ilocanes and the Tagalogs of the Philippines ask for forgiveness of the tree or the flower that they are about to uproot. The Gayo of Sumatra take similar precautions. Even to this day the Japanese offer sake to Yama-no-kami before cutting down the trees in the mountains.

It is often thought necessary to show a sign of respect towards the tree before removing any part of it. In Cambodia the people who extract *rong* sap have to observe very severe rules, and they conduct a propitiatory ceremony when they find themselves before a big and beautiful tree; and the Tiyan do the same when they wish to remove sap for the purpose of making toddy.

In China flower 'birthdays' are celebrated on the twelfth or

[30] J. G. Gmelin.

fifteenth day of the second moon, and the Emperor Huen-Sung of the T'ang used to have concerts held for the flowers in his garden. The Chinese again condemned to chains the tree from which the Emperor Chung Chen, the last of the Ming, hanged himself. As for the Bedouins, even now they swear by the 'very life of this blade of grass.[31] It is also amusing to note that in Japanese the same terms are used for naming the parts of the human face and those of plants: eyes—buds, *me*; nose—flowers, *hana*; etc.

This same respect often extends to inanimate objects which may be individualized to such a degree as to have a soul, a will, a temperament. The largest number of instances are probably to be found in Japan. There, stones—the symbols of Kami—live and grow and even reproduce; certain sword-blades are supposed to be blood-thirsty and their owner can do no less than satisfy them. Certain bridges are jealous of each other, and woe betide the traveller who excites this jealousy by singing the praises of another bridge; one of them, the Kunimato bridge, is so jealous that when crossing it one must refrain from quoting a No which has jealousy as its theme, the *Nonomiya*, for otherwise this may be regarded as an insulting allusion. In China, to throw away an object that is not yet absolutely useless is an offence against Heaven—and is brought to its ears. Formerly, this 'feeling of veneration used to be addressed indiscriminately to the waters and the rocks . . . the same virtue was in everything; there was no less hope in the plucking of a grain than in the crossing of a stream'.[32] In Japan rocks used to speak just as the trees and grass did. In Malaya the local people believe that mineral ore lives, ages, moves, feels, and the same belief is to be found in Sikkim and in the Philippines, where the American forces learnt this at their own cost when they tried to force the Ifugaos of Northern Luzon to let the mines of the island be exploited.

All that we might be tempted to regard as childish superstition is actually based on extremely abstract and consistent metaphysics. Various societies indeed consider that the soul can inhabit an inanimate object or a plant, an animal or a man. For the Hassidis it is even man's duty to release the soul not only of other human beings but also those in the world of nature in all its kingdoms, among his animals and in his home, in his garden and his fields, among his tools and in his food, and he is able to do this by means of a special power within himself known as *Kawana*. For the Buddhists, the nature of Buddha is to be found in all things, in all that stems directly from the original Absolute and bears within itself the seed of the virtue which will lead it back there. Accord-

[31] Charles Doughty. [32] Marcel Granet.

ing to the Japanese Shinnyo-zuien, the eternal truth is manifested in everything, although in different ways, and for Hosshin, chief of the Ritsu school, all forms of life, however small and insignificant they may be, are born with a certain 'Buddha nature'; they may, however, have to go through many intermediary stages before being able to 'realize' this nature and attain liberation. The Japanese Buddhist school Hosso Shu, taking up the thesis upheld by a Hindu school, considers, on the other hand, that one of the five categories of men, the *ichchantika*, can never reach the Buddha state—which blurs even more the borderline between human and other beings.

Continuity, union and unity are felt even more intensely with those two fundamental and original entities which Asia recognizes as divine and which it worships as such, viz. heaven and earth. The devotion offered to the latter is sometimes intended for it in its totality, sometimes only for the features which are the most striking for man—its mountains and waters—which are often deified. Even in our day the great Indian social reformer Vinoba proclaims: 'The land should become the temple and service of the soil a sort of worship'.

Generally speaking, it may be said that the Asian seeks to reduce the distance between the earth and himself, or at least tries to prevent it from growing, while in the West, as Vincent Cronin points out, we are inclined to bury it in an immense tarred sarcophagus.

The earth is an object of actual worship in Asia. In India, the Baiga refuse to use a metal plough, for that would amount to ingratitude towards the earth, tearing its breast and opening its stomach; that is why they prefer a small, wooden spade. In Indo-China the adoption of farm machinery, according to the Annamite peasants, desecrated the earth, with the result that people abandon it now more easily and work instead in factories or elsewhere. A Laotian contemporary, describing the memories of his youth, writes, 'The Bodhisattva took the goddess Earth, Nang Thorani, as witness to his right, and her voice chased away the armies of Evil. With what fervour, then, upon the council of our mothers, did we worship the goddess Earth; . . . whenever we had to pour hot water, we asked the goddess to step aside'.[33] The Lamas of Outer Mongolia, until recent times were opposed to any farming in order not to offend the spirits of the earth.

The Asian knows that the earth is his mother. While, for the Jews, Jehovah drew the first man from dust, for the Tchuktches, who seldom see the earth uncovered, the god Sana fashioned the

[33] Th. Nh. Abhay.

first human couple out of snow. In India the Nattiya claim to be born from the earth; Tikum Serrong, ancestor of the higher Labche tribe in the Kalimpong area, was born of the earth of the Himalayas, while his wife, Domi, was born of the river Tista; the lower tribe, on the other hand, is descended from a large stone which may still be seen. Sometimes, as in the case of the inhabitants of the Leti, Noa and Lakor islands near Timor, the earth is called grandmother. It has been quite aptly pointed out that the fact of assimilating the life of humanity or of a human group with that of a tree—something that is common even among the Semites—is closely connected with such a feeling regarding descent. This origin sometimes leads to a corollary, viz. an identity of substance between the earth and one's remote ancestors; thus, in China, Tcheyou had a copper head and an iron forehead and ate mineral ore.

Many books have been devoted to the comparison between female fertility and that of the earth, and the countless rites celebrating this; it is unnecessary to revert to that here. The worship of Mother Earth, the bountiful, is not, as we often think with a strange superiority complex, peculiar to backward peoples who have to be discouraged from such childishness, but rather the expression of a consciousness deeply-rooted in all peoples that have not yet been isolated from nature by industrialization and westernization.

The feeling of unity with the earth is also manifested in various environments through a physical link between the time of birth and that of death. The most striking examples are to be found in China, but others exist throughout Asia. Among Chinese peasants, when a child was born, the first act was to deposit it on the ground. It was only 'when after three days of fasting on this domestic earth, the child, fed by Mother-Earth, had shown by loud cries the power that it drew from Her, that its mother, following the example of the earth, could pick it up'.[34] Similarly, the Chinese peasants used to place a dying man on the family soil and let death eat into him, close to the dark corner where they kept their seeds, which, sown, would then germinate; and this same corner was used for the conjugal bed where women conceived new lives. They then imagined that their conception was the fruit of fecund powers that emanated from the domestic soil, that the soil itself had produced the life that they felt stirring in themselves, and that the child had derived its substance from the very substance of its ancestors. In China, as elsewhere, the substance of the dead belongs to his motherland whence it originally came. Even in those communities where cremation is practised, the ashes often have to

[34] Marcel Granet.

212

be brought back to the homeland. Among the Savara, the body of a man is burnt in the last field cultivated by him. In fact, in many contracts for the export of labour, particularly for the Chinese, it is customary to have a clause regarding repatriation of corpses.

While in the West there is increasing reluctance to touch the earth, which we consider 'dirty', and the traces of which have to be washed quickly away from our bodies and our clothing, in many Asian countries it is the opposite feeling which explains the fear of touching it, particularly among the princely class, the priests, etc., whose contact might upset the earth, and who have such deep respect for it that they would not dream of placing their feet on it. An example is given by the gods and the great masters. The gods of India, when they take human shape, have their identity revealed by the fact that their feet do not touch the ground. Tradition says the same of Buddha and even of Jesus Christ. The high priest of the Palaungs in Burma follows the same rule; the same applies to the chief of the expedition among the Moi elephant hunters in Indo-China—and the most varied instances may be quoted.

As we have stated earlier, however, some parts of the earth and also some of its aspects are particularly sacred. This applies to mountains. From the Biblical Sinai and Ararat to the Himalayas bordering India and the Fujiyama of Japan, they are greatly revered. They are the home of the gods, the place where the gods readily show themselves to the prophets and sages in order to dispense their blessings and teachings. Doubtless for this reason, they are also a place for retirement and meditation sought by ascetics.

The same is true for water. In China it was believed of old that virgins could become mothers by the mere contact of sacred rivers. Inversely, there are many stories where the heroes go down more or less willingly to the water kingdom and wed a deity: in India for Arjuna, in Viet-Nam for Kinh-Duong-Vuong who, as a result, had a son, Lac-Long-Quan, the hero who fathered the Viet-Namese civilization, etc. The Khotanians had such veneration for the river that goes through Khotan that when it asked for a man to be sacrificed as payment for its waters, one of them volunteered. In Western Siberia, during the thaw, the inhabitants of Sredne Kolymsk are compassionate over the sufferings of the river Kolyma, and when the latter again flows freely, women know that their delivery will be easier. Finally, the fact that Asians so often affectionately give the name of 'Mother' to their great rivers such as the Lena, the Obe, the Ganges and the Jamuna, on the shores of which they live, is not a mere acknowledgment of the economic value of these rivers.

Close ties between the sky and men are less frequent and their descriptions are less detailed. In China, however, the three ancestors of the three royal dynasties were born of celestial origins. Sie, minister of the first sovereign, Chouen, and ancestor of T'ang, who was the founder of the Yin dynasty, was the son born of the sky and a virgin-mother. This was also the case of K'i, ancestor of the Tcheou dynasty.

The vast oriental feeling of cosmic solidarity and unity also embraces the various heavenly bodies. Thus in India various stars are none other than sages—or their wives—who, in this new 'incarnation', continue to deal with our fate. Many castes and dynasties in this same country claim the sun or the moon as primordial ancestor. While the Ladar of Mysore and the Sale regard themselves as sons of the sun (Surya) without specifying further, the maharajahs of Jaipur state that they are descended from Vivasvat, grandson of the sun. In China an old tradition represents Yao either as a tamer of suns, or as the sun itself. The Japanese term for designating man, *hito*, is generally interpreted as meaning a solar corpuscle which temporarily has become a man—and if the Yakuts, even in the nineteenth century, used to call the Tsar 'child of the sun', it was probably not just a simple metaphor in their minds.

In many Asian traditions, cases of union between human beings and celestial bodies are not unusual. In India, Karna is said to be the son of the sun and the Princess Kunti. In Japan, a girl made a mother by the sun's rays gives birth to a red precious stone which later becomes a princess.

These bonds can also take the form of a tender friendship. Yakut women and girls, for instance, are sorrowful over the moon's fate during eclipses and pity it.

Thus, the oriental has a feeling of deep solidarity with the whole of Nature in all its aspects. For the Chinese, Taoist or Confucian, humanity is not a kingdom apart, but, on the contrary, man and nature are interdependent. In all Japanese inventions there is this pleasant feeling of letting oneself be absorbed into nature; nature touches the Japanese through its ephemeral, fluid aspect, in its cyclic movements. While Shakespearian heroes fear the forest and its ambushes, those of the Indian dramatist, Kalidasa, run to the forest for refuge, and it is by delving into the soul of a tree that the great Bengali scientist, Jagadish Chandra Bose, discovered the sensitivity of plants.

CHAPTER XII

The Family

Women are the hindlegs of the elephant and men the forelegs.
Siamese proverb.

IN the greater part of traditional Asia, the family is not, as in the West, just reduced to two generations, parents and children, with the occasional rare addition of surviving grandparents or an unmarried or widowed sister or brother; it is essentially patriarchal, viz., under the dictatorial authority of the single ancestor, or in his absence, that of his substitute. It comprises four or five generations (in Asia, people marry young) and very many individuals, often over a hundred, living under the same roof in almost absolute community.

Even when it does not share the same house, this family is the real unit of population, and the individual is only a fragment who loses his perspective, his value and his power if he is detached from the group. This is so in the Muslim countries where, moreover, this system existed before Islam, in India and in most of Indo-China, in China, among the Manchus, in Japan, in Central Asia and in most of the autochtonous Siberian groups.

The Viet-Namese family may be taken as a fairly representative example; its organization has been defined by the Hong-Du c code of the Le and remained in force till Gia-Long. The homogeneity of the family, imbued with Confucianism, the lay-out of the house where everyone lives under the others' eyes, leads to a merging of the individual into a collective being in whom the interest and the will of the group always carries greater weight than that of the individual or the couple. Even when this family is dispersed, it continues, in spite of distances, to reunite for anniversaries.

One of the main criticisms levelled by Asians against school education and labour in workshops where the mothers cannot keep their young children with them is that this undermines relations within the family.

The family in Asia enjoys an extraordinary degree of solidarity, and these bonds are continuously strengthened and tightened by magic-cum-religious ceremonies. Charles writes: 'Among us the family remains a solidarity extending over several generations. It has its own existence, independent of successive chiefs. On the contrary, in the Islamic organization this is a life-long natural association; when the father dies, another harem begins without any link of continuity with the one who has just passed away'. This absence of continuity must not, of course, be understood in the extremely narrow sense, as we shall see from all the other texts that we shall mention later. Formerly, the family group itself used to make a large part of the objects for its own current use (pottery, weaving, etc.) and only European mass production ruined such activities as well as the skilled handicrafts that supplemented them.

Even legally and penally speaking, the family constitutes an indivisible unit. In olden days, in Japan, a serious crime was punished by the annihilation of the criminal's 'entire race'. In Fu–Sang the descendants of the man found guilty of a great crime had to be punished till the seventh generation. In China his entire family could be exterminated except for the sons who had not yet reached puberty, who were emasculated. When Han Sin, the generalissimo of Han, was accused of treason, his 'three families' were massacred —i.e. his father's, his mother's and his wife's families. The responsibility may be extended even further, not in order to intimidate, as is sometimes done in the West in times of war, but for moral reasons. Thus in China recently the governor of a province stated how, in a case of parricide, he had razed all the neighbouring houses to the ground because their inhabitants, although living so close to the place where the crime had been committed, had failed in their duty in not having had any moral and reforming influence on the murderer. The greatest disciple of Gandhi, Vinoba, points out— although it leads him to opposite conclusions—that when the head of a family is imprisoned, his wife and children are thereby punished, often harder than he is. In Islam, where the family is an essential subject of law, parents are under no obligation to bear witness against their child accused of a crime; in France this has been the case only since 1941.

Without going to such extremes, which are, after all, exceptional there are constant examples of family resources being entirely pooled, each member paying his earnings into a common fund and receiving from it according to his needs and according to the total means available. Among the Tchuktches, for example, when a big booty of game is brought back, it has to be shared among the members of the community. It must be noted incidentally that these century-old habits make the Asians much more amenable than we are to certain principles of life under the Communist system.

The first duty, then, of every member of the family is towards all the others. An important employer of skilled labour in China, seeing that his workers were undernourished, raised their wages, but the only result that he noted was that each one of the workers just maintained a larger number of relatives than before. For any Asian, this goes without saying, and that is why it is difficult for people in these countries to understand why they are blamed for nepotism when they prefer a relative to a more competent stranger, whatever the consequences of this choice.

In Sanskrit there are special terms, used to this day throughout India, to designate the destiny, the mission, the law of the family, *kula-dharma*, the law of the clan, *jati-dharma*, or of the village, *grama-dharma*. It has even been said in connection with China that endo-cannibalism, which makes it possible for a family to preserve its unity of substance, is simply a duty of domestic piety, a pure communion.[1]

This aspect of the family is reflected even in the terms used to designate relationships. Sometimes, in certain languages, the distinctions go so far that there are eight different names for different aunts and uncles according to the type of relationship involved. In other cases, as in feudal China, where, as Granet says, maternity is collective in essence, the word 'mother' is applied to an extensive group of people, not only to the real mother and all her sisters, but also to all the women married to the father. Besides, in a patriarchal family of this type, where there are necessarily many children of about the same age, the infants are passed indiscriminately from one breast to another among all the women who are capable of feeding at the time. Similarly, no distinction is drawn between the father and the paternal uncles, the sons and the nephews, and all cousins, however distant they may be, call each other brothers. The father, by decree, shares out his children among his secondary wives, who actually become their mothers. Often terms like uncle (in India), elder brother (for instance, in India and China), or even mother (in India) or father (for instance, in Thailand or Japan) become like titles used out of courtesy according to the age relationship between the speaker and the person addressed.

This apparent confusion, however, often goes together with a strict distinction drawn on the basis of other criteria. In feudal China, for instance, the father had only one single son, whose brothers by no means enjoyed the same rank and privileges, and the first wife of this son was the main daughter-in-law who directed all her sisters-in-law; but this is only one specific case of this hierarchy which was absolute and strict in all Asian patriarchal families

[1] Marcel Granet.

217

where the younger members owed profound respect and blind obedience to their elders.

It must not be concluded, however, that permanent harmony necessarily reigned in all such families. As in our own, there was many a conflict, often sharp, seldom open, sometimes even traditional.

We shall see later the case of sisters-in-law; let us mention simply that in Afghanistan the word cousin also means mortal enemy, that in India (where, in mythology, successive generations of the same family can alternate between the divine and the demoniac nature, as in the case of Hiranyagarbha, Prahlada and Bali) and in China, father and son may have antithetical geniuses; and also in China the eldest son may easily be in conflict with the father's younger brothers.

Such a family is, of course, characterized by the fact that all its members are descended from common ancestors or, in the case of women who have entered the family by marriage (possibly even sons-in-law in certain matriarchal families), have married the offspring of these ancestors. The latter therefore play a paramount role in such communities from the Bedouins to the Japanese, from Siberia to the Indonesian islands.[2]

The number of generations of ancestors that play a part in everyday life varies according to the groups. In principle, the geneology is made to go back as far as possible—even back to mythical or legendary times, as we have seen above. This is the case in Islam, in India and in nearly all the reigning families.

In practice, however, and with few exceptions, only a clearly defined number of generations are venerated. In China, ancestors' funerary tablets are buried after a few generations, when they disappear in an indistinct mass. In Viet-Nam one must not go beyond nine generations, *cu u toc*. In old Japanese cemeteries (*hakoba*) sticks (*sotoba*) are stuck behind the tombs (*haka*) at increasingly longer intervals over a hundred years. Consequently, the Japanese distinguish between the *hotoke*, the souls of those long dead, and the *shin botoke*, the recently dead. The Ostiaks keep the images that they make of their dead for only three years.

Periodic festivals are held and offerings made in honour of all these dead. As these rites have been described in great detail by all ethnographers, we shall only quote a few examples very briefly. In Siberia, the Tchuktches and the Samoyeds erect statues which are used as bodies by the souls of their ancestors. In Mongolia, Prince Sasakto Kagan had to issue a decree in the sixteenth century to

[2] It is to be noted that with two exceptions the Chinese dynasties destroyed the tombs of preceding dynasties. (E. T. C. Werner).

have the *ongott*, the ancestors' portraits, burnt and replaced by statues of the six-armed Mahakala, more in line with the beliefs of the moment. In China, where ancestor worship is the essential basis of Confucianism, temples used to be built for this purpose well before Confucius. The Japanese never begin their morning meal without having offered to the ancestors the first bowl that has been cooked.

These ancestors may, furthermore, come back periodically among the survivors. Formerly, at big festivals, the Chinese used to invite them to come and re-incarnate themselves and all of them used to come, in full formation, disguised as serpents for instance, in order to join family mourning ceremonies. For all Chinese Buddhists, the souls of ancestors are released once a year in summer from the underworld or purgatory where they sojourn in order to spend a couple of weeks on earth. The ancestors of the Japanese always return among their descendants for the O-Bon or Bon-Matsuri or Bon-ku festivals. In India, among the Savara, on the eve of the *guar* which is the second funeral festival, all the dead relatives are invited to participate.

A relatively exceptional case is that of the Tsa Khmu of Northern Laos among whom all the ancestors are assembled in one single individual who is the Spirit of the house, the *Roi Gang*.

All the important events in the family are periodically reported to all these ancestors. This is so in China and in Japan.

In this type of highly stratified, patriarchal family, the part of chief involves extremely extensive powers and responsibilities.

In Islam, the patriarchal spirit, made up of closer spiritual and physical ties than our family feeling, requires absolute submission, composed of fear as well as respect, towards the head whose blessing is sought and whose curse feared. He keeps all his descendants under his wing—whether they be unmarried, married, even polygamous —their wives and their children and, if necessary, his and their younger brothers and sisters. Even when married couples live apart because of town living conditions, the bonds of subordination with the head of the family remain intact, and even the wives and daughters have to obey his wife.

In India, when the head of the family is present, all the other members—except perhaps the grandmother—have to remain standing before him and speak only if they are spoken to.

The Chinese family, which extends to all those who had the same ancestor three generations back, is directed or rather represented by the oldest member of the oldest generation; he is known as the dean or the father—and if anyone deserves the title of priest, it is the father of the family, layman that he is! It has been pointed out correctly that his practically unlimited authority and the resulting respect that he enjoys plays a much more decisive part in his relations with the rest of the family than ties of personal affection.

In Siberia, among the Kirghiz, the Uzbek and most of the other groups, the power of the head of the family is at least as extensive, and the same may be said of south-west Asia, Japan and Central Asia.

This authority naturally entails corresponding responsibilities. Among the Tsa Khmu of Laos, when the members of the family depart from the rules laid down by the ancestors, the Spirit of the House, the Roi Gang, makes the head of the house fall ill.

In some cases the head of the family may abdicate his responsibilities and hand them over to a successor; in India it is acknowledged as something normal as soon as he becomes a grandfather and wishes to embrace an almost monastic life. He may also do so in Japan, as we have seen. In China, on the contrary, it is only recently that the family has learnt to do without its chief for a while, when necessary, if the latter becomes a soldier or an official.

Later we shall have the opportunity to examine the position of the chief in general, and nearly all that we say about him holds good for the head of the family.

Apart from the gods common to the largest religious community to which it belongs, the family often has its own gods, who are often in close relationship with the immediate or remote ancestors. In addition, there is one particular god, major or minor, taken from the common Pantheon, who is the object of especially fervent worship. This is often a fundamental element of family unity—which does not preclude an individual member of the family from having his own particular god chosen by himself, his *ishta devata*, as in India.

One of the main criticisms we launch against the traditional society of Asian countries is that the woman there is kept in a state of inferiority and subjection. It is true that she almost never enjoys political rights, that she is nearly always economically dependent on man and that her legal status is very unfavourable. It is also true that in some cases she is really treated like a domestic animal or a tool. Nevertheless in many societies, in various aspects, she holds an eminent place, higher than that of man. We shall give a number of examples characteristic of these two extremes, and we shall try to find some explanation.

Cases where the woman is hardly considered as a human being are not unusual. In the Hadramaut the woman is part of the herd. Even recently, in India, the Korava of Chingleput and Tanjore used to sell women and girls or pawn them. When a Velan of Phalgat or Chittur gets married, he receives the following ritual admonition: 'Thou mayst beat thy wife, but not with a staff. Thou mayst not accuse her of misconduct. Thou mayst not cut off her ears, her breasts, her nose or locks of her hair. Thou shalt not lead her to the pond (in order to bathe her) nor to the temple (in order to make her take an oath). Thou mayst keep her and protect her as long as thou willst. When thou willst no longer have her, thou shalt continue to keep and provide for your children for these belong to thee'. Even a short time ago, in Badakhstan, taxes could be paid in the form of women and children. In Uzbekistan hardly any distinction was made between women and the rest of the cattle. Among the Kirghiz a woman was worth four sheep while a cow was worth eight and a horse thirty-two. About 1890, in north-east Siberia, Russian traders used to buy girls from the tribes for a cup of vodka and a slab of tea, and in the early twentieth century, in northern Yakutsk, a girl was sold at a lower price than a reindeer.

Other humiliations, less tangible, were no less serious and showed a deep mistrust, an actual fear of the pernicious influence of woman. We shall only quote two instances among thousands: among the Badaga of India a woman may not enter a place, *hagottu*, where milk is kept; among the Kols, although there is true social equality between the sexes, the woman is not allowed to touch the plough.

It is, however, in the religious sphere proper that this disqualification of the Asian woman is the most noticeable—and probably where she feels it most. The most violent denunciation is doubtless that of the Tibetan religious reformer Padmasambhava, in whose story we may read: 'The unbroken current of *samsara* (subjection to the succession of rebirths) is caused by women. Within the circle of their bodiliness has been formed an infernal cauldron of fire. It is in this cauldron that all the sufferings of purification through the flames take place; . . . it is there that the good has to be separated from the bad. Woman—that is the name of this copper cauldron of hell. Woman is the name of the house of Mara (the tempter demon); woman is the trap set by the god of death'. But, while this diatribe is remarkable for its violence, the attitude which it reveals has nothing exceptional about it. The Buddha himself used to say: 'The seductions of women are like those of the demons; it is through them that kingdoms are ruined and individuals destroyed; however, foolish people pay much attention to them'. Similarly, in the Jain Jataka, we read: 'Infamous is the country that lets itself be governed and directed by a woman and infamous are the men who submit to women's domination'. In China the expression 'an article on which money has been wasted' is a common paraphrase for designating a young girl; and the most ideally perfect daughter, viz. she who possesses the virtues of the eighteen Lohans, according to a Chinese proverb, is not equal to a club-footed son. Among the Semites woman is supposed to have an evil nature, to be feared and despised at the same time; among the Muslims a girl, by her very essence, is an almost profane entity beside masculine sacredness; both the law of Moses and nomadic tradition show great contempt for the female sex.

Apart from a few exceptions in Indonesia and in the Maldive Islands, women are not allowed into the mosques in the same way as men, and they may not even join the daily prayers in the open squares and the streets; in mosques, if many men are reluctant to use the 'ablution stone', it is because it may have been fingered, and therefore soiled, by women. The same inferior status is woman's lot in Jewish synagogues and in Sikh temples, where she is relegated to a gallery. In India, among the Malayali, when certain cults are celebrated, particularly in Kollaimalai, women are not even allowed to stay in the village, and among the Toda they may not tread the ground through which the sacred herd has passed, but have to be carried over it. Nearly all over India, a woman is not entitled to read the Vedas or to hear them read. It is with the greatest hesitation that the Buddha consented to their joining the monastic orders, and we have seen that they are not allowed to do so in the countries where the Theravada prevails. Among the Buddhists, a nun, however senior she might be, owes respect to a monk, however newly initiated, and the study of the chapters on Mahaparijna and Aruno-papata as well as on the Drishtavada is forbidden to both Jain and Buddhist nuns. In Japan, it is only since 1800 that women have been allowed to undertake the pilgrimage to Mount Fuji, the most sacred mountain in the country, and even now they are not permitted to take part in the prayers for rain, *amagoi*, addressed to the god Ryu-o; besides, it is thought undesirable for them to be too familiar with the gods. Among the Ainus of Japan they may not take part in any religious ceremony.

It is, however, easy to find at least as many and equally striking examples of a diametrically opposite situation.

On the religious plane, there are women ascetics, the *Sannyasini*, among the Hindus, and nuns, *Aryangaian*, among the Shvetambara Jains. Buddhist nuns are now legion. Even Islam, at a certain period, had women's convents—in Syria, in the thirteenth and fourteenth centuries. In southern India the Koraga have some of their most solemn prayers said by a virgin, and in certain temples of the Bellary district the services have to be conducted by an old Kuruba woman. Among the Tunguz, the Yakuts and many other groups, particularly among the Mongoloids, there used to be women shamans, and in all the cults which use a medium for communication with the deity this part is often entrusted to women; this is particularly so in the Viet-Namese cult of the Chu vi, the spirits of the three worlds. In some parts of Asia women are also admitted into the secular clergy—something which Catholicism has never allowed and which Protestantism even now accepts only in extremely rare cases. Thus, in China about a third of the 1600 Taoist temples in the eighth century used to be served by nuns, and in 695 the Empress Wu Tso-t'ien herself celebrated the supreme religious ceremonies on the Middle Peak—a fact which caused a scandal. Among the Buddhists, there were priestesses from the seventh century on, and from the year 753, we are told about the arrival of three Chinese *bhikshuni* into Japan. In Japan, where the *norito* mentions a whole list of priestesses, the great Shinto temples even today are often run by women, in Ise (by the consecrated princess, Ituki-no-hime-miko) as well as at the Imperial temple, and this practice may have been much more widespread formerly; women also play an important part in the cult of the Water God, Suijin.

As we shall see later, it also happens that the priest or the layman is allowed to hold religious ceremonies only in the presence of his wife. The Patvegara of South India have a special ceremony, the *vaddap*, where they celebrate a cult in memory of their female ancestors. Among the Sondi of Vizagapatam, the sacred nature of women is such that they have to be vegetarian while men may eat meat.

In a quasi-religious field, we may quote, among many, one example taken from Japan where, when a well has been dug, the first bucket has to be drawn up by a woman; and another example taken from Ceylon, where only women may harvest millet.

On the social plane, however, countless cases may be mentioned where the position of the woman is equal or superior to that of the man. In Afghanistan, when a marriage proposal has been accepted, the young man's parents tell those of the future bride: 'We shall give our son as a slave to your daughter'. A French traveller (Legras) reports that he heard a European Russian in Siberia say: 'Here, if you hit your wife, she brings a lawsuit against you; I should like to see that at home!' Another one notes that in Tomsk women are freer than in Europe. In Khotan, before the Muslim invasion, women were admitted into society even when there were foreigners about. Ibn Batuta mentions the immense respect shown towards women by the Tatars of the Golden Horde; according to him, they enjoyed greater consideration than men. Ma-touan-li reports that in the west of the Wan country (Ferghana) till the country of the A, 'when a woman speaks, her husband hastens to satisfy her request'. Among the Mongols women who received the title of *khatuns* participated in parliaments where important matters were discussed. In India the Lingayat strongly affirm that man is not superior to woman, and among the Savara the murder of a woman is considered as a more serious crime than that of a man. In Ceylon the Veddas live on a totally and absolutely equal footing with their women, who play an important part in tribal discussions. In Burma, before the British occupation, the women were strictly equal to men and could own property and engage in trade quite independently.

Finally, it must be said that there is a great change now as compared with the hasty, pessimistic conclusions to which superficial, self-seeking or prejudiced observers had accustomed us. We know now that in Islam the woman is not just cattle sold to her husband with her dowry as the price, and that 'she not only knows how to keep her own autonomy but has a dominating influence on her husband more often than is thought'.[3]

It is not superfluous to recall here that many women have individually played a paramount part all over Asia, at all times. We shall only mention a few instances.

In the political sphere, such cases are recorded since the most ancient times—women who governed over great empires and small kingdoms, either because they were personally vested with the supreme power or because of the sovereign was only a toy in their hands.

In the third millennium B.C., the chronicles already report that a woman wine-merchant, Ku-Bau, had a reign of a hundred years during the third dynasty of Kush in Sumer. Cleophea, Queen of the Messag, was the worthy enemy of Alexander, and her armies held him back for a long time before she finally surrendered—and gave him a son. The famous Queen Zenobia, who was the glory of the Palmyranian Empire, was a dangerous adversary for the Emperor Aurelian. In about 630 A.D., when Queen Bora, disappointed by the defeats suffered by the empire, abdicated, it was her sister, Queen Azarnudokht, who succeeded her after a short time.

In Central Asia examples abound. In the eighth century Bokhara was governed by a queen. In the thirteenth century the important kingdom founded by Jaghatai was governed by Queen Orghana, and at the same period, in Tiflis, Queen Gontza was indulging in high politics. In the fourteenth century, among the Tatars, Queen Taidula, wife of Janibek, issued edicts in her own name. In the fifteenth century, for a long time it was a woman, the Khatun Mandughai,

---

[3] Raymond Charles.

who governed the empire of the Mongols, and she led her armies personally to drive away the Oirat invaders. At about the same period, Jagathai Queen Makhtun Khanim caused havoc among the royal Mongolian dynasties by having her son brought up in Islamism. In the sixteenth century still, among the Tatars, we find women on the throne—Taidula Cohenibekova first, then Eltina Khatun.

In Tibet the two wives of King Srong Tsan Gampa converted him to Buddhism and thus determined the whole future of the country. In India there were even Jain queens.

In Ceylon, early in the thirteenth century, Queen Lilavati left a deep mark on the destiny of her country. In Laos, even to this day, people tell the story of the first queen, the legendary Nang Pao, who let herself be seduced by a prince who was an elephant hunter. Nearer to us, in the seventeenth century, Nang Keo Phimpha, 'the Cruel', after having manoeuvred for some time behind the scenes and having had quite a string of young kings deposed or massacred, finally took possession of the throne—but she was only able to reign for a year before being executed in her turn. Cambodia had at least one queen in the Champa in about 650. Viet-Nam had one in the twelfth century in the person of Ly-Chieu-Hoang. Several of them are to be found in the history of Java; let us only mention Ishana-tungavijaya, who reigned over Mataram in the tenth century and Bhre-da, daughter of Yang-Wei-si-cha, who dominated most of the island in the fifteenth century.

But it is above all in China that empresses, and particularly dowager empresses, often exercised power, and it may be said that they made up an actual dynasty. The Regent-Empress Liu, at the beginning of the second century B.C., the Empress Wang, a contemporary of Jesus Christ, the Empress Teng, who governed for fifteen years at the beginning of the second century A.D., have all left a mark on their country's history. From the second century B.C. the Emperor Wou of the Han realized the grave danger inherent in this situation, but the practice nevertheless continued. In the seventh century, the Emperor Kao-Tsung let himself be completely dominated by his wife Wu Chow, former favourite of his father T'ai Tsung; and she was an admirable administrator and posthumously acquired the title of 'Wu, the equal of Heaven'. However, all of them did not display the same virtues, and in feudal China, as also later, the debauchery of the dowager empresses supplied the chroniclers with one of their richest subjects. It is even told that a queen of Wei made the king, her husband, summon the handsomest man in the country to her boudoir.

The history of Korea is not lacking either in women sovereigns:

in the seventh century, Queen Sun Dok, who was succeeded by her sister Chin Dok, and two centuries later, the Queen Shin Sung; recently, at the end of the nineteenth century, King Li-Hsi is reputed, not without grounds, to have left all his power to his wife, Queen Min.

Japan has had several empresses who, together with their husbands or reigning in their own right, have had a profound influence on their country. In about the year 200, it is the Empress Jingo who decided to organize and herself directed the war expedition to Korea. In fact, in two centuries, Japan had seven empresses out of sixteen sovereigns, which is perhaps a record. It was in the reign of the Empress Suiko, the thirty-third of the dynasty, that Prince Shotoku established Buddhism as a state religion; nor can we omit the names of the Empresses Saimei, Jito and Koken who were respectively the thirty-seventh, fortieth and forty-sixth of the dynasty.

Great women warriors and national heroines are to be found throughout history. Although a great connoisseur of Islamic life has rightly written : 'It is impossible to imagine the symbol of a Muslim Joan of Arc', there have been some in Asia and even in the Near East. In the seventh century, in Iran, it was the queen-mother who for some time took over the supreme command of the armies; about the same time, the Empress of the Eastern Turks in Mongolia, Wou-Tso-t'ien, widow of Kao-tsang, herself directed operations against the Tibetans. Even much earlier, in the first century of our era, in Viet-Nam, the Tru ng sisters were the first champions of the revolt against Chinese occupants, and temples have even been built in their memory. Two centuries later, it was another woman, Trieu Au, who took up the standard and fought for national independence. Not so remote from our times, the Rani of Jhansi was one of the keenest and most dangerous adversaries of the British in India.

In the religious sphere also, saints and high priestesses are legion. From the most ancient times, there are several women among the great Hindu *rishis*, the authors of these Vedic hymns which, even to our day, constitute the ultimate source of inspiration for all Hinduism. In the same country, Princess Mira Bai, who lived in the sixteenth century, is still deeply revered as being the most perfect model of the 'worshipper of God'. Our contemporary Ananda Moyi is considered as one of the greatest living sages of India, and the most eminent scholars sit at her feet in order to receive her teaching. The Saddharma-Pundarika Sutra recounts that a young girl, Pi Lan, became Bodhisattva. Among the Jains, according to the Shvetambara, the Tirthankara Malli was a woman and, in any case, the first disciple of the Tirthankara Mahavira was a woman : Ajja Chandana. The kingdom of Juda had a prophetess, Huldah. Even Islam had great saints like Shaika Sultana in southern Arabia. In Japan the founder of the Remmon-kyo and that of the Tenri-kyo were uneducated women.

In arts and sciences also the women of Asia have distinguished themselves. In India many castes are famous for the Sanskrit culture of their women, and one of the greatest Tamil writers was a poetess, Avvei; early in the thirteenth century the learning of the Cambodian princess Indradevi surpassed the science of the philosophers. The Korean, Djin-Y, is supposed to have been one of the best poets of her country. In China there have always been great poetesses and, under the Manchu dynasty alone, over a thousand of them had their works printed. Li Ts'ing-Chao in the twelfth century acquired immense celebrity and Chu Shu Chen under the Southern Sung; the same is true of certain accomplished courtesans such as Hsueh T'ao, Ma Hsiang-Lan, Liu Ju Shih. In the Great Chinese Encyclopaedia, out of 1,628 volumes, 376 are devoted to famous women, and out of these four chapters deal with women scientists and seven others with the literary productions of women. In Japan, the diaries of women take a primary place in literature. In Georgia the golden age of literature was in the reign of the Empress Thamara. China had great women painters in the fifteenth and up to the seventeenth centuries.

It must also be noted that even apart from individual cases like the ones we have mentioned, Asian women often aspire to and attain qualities which in our eyes seem to be the privilege of men. Among various tribes of the Hindu Kush (Hezareh), the women pride themselves on being as brave as the men; when required, they ride and use the gun and sword with as much temerity and skill as the boldest warrior. The women of Ashtarak, in Soviet Armenia, have recently built on their own a vast system of irrigation canals, and in the same country the women of Sahanin built a road several miles long hollowed out of the rock; in this region, there are even women blacksmiths.[4] In Turkestan, in rough jousts between men and women, the woman, mounted on a better horse than the man, whip him whenever she can.

If we wish to find our way clearly among all these contradictions, it must first be pointed out that in nearly all cases the position of women in the family and in society varies considerably with the acquisition of marital status.

Firstly, it must be acknowledged that in a number of Asian communities the infanticide of girls was frequent. Generally speaking, the daughter, so long as she is not married, remains entirely depen-

[4] Marietta Shaginyan.

227

dent on her parents, and while the poets sing her praises and story-tellers evoke her thwarted love, they are almost the only ones to grant her any importance whatsoever. In practice, she is a negligible quantity whose tastes and wishes are not taken into consideration because she hardly allows herself to have any; or if by chance she has any, she does not express them.

The position changes with marriage. Marriage, in most Asian societies, has a character very different from that in the West. A distinction often has to be drawn between the religious act (of varying importance with the greatest imaginable extremes) and physical consummation which does not necessarily go with the former—as we see from countless examples. In China, in India among the Komati, the Maravan, the Todas, marriage is frequently celebrated between a living woman and a dead man; among the Billava and also in parts of China, between two dead people. The reunion in the same tomb of Japanese lovers who have committed suicide is some-what sacred in nature like marriage. On the contrary, in various groups marriages are sometimes celebrated between children 'in the cradle', as among the Dhangar, the Kurmi and other farmers' castes, the Udaiyan or even (with the necessary reservations, of course) between children still to be born, as among the Gandharia and the Mang of Kathiawar, the Kadva of Ahmedabad and the Korava. Without going to such extremes, in a number of Asian societies there are these 'child marriages' which have aroused the virtuous indignation of the West to such a degree that the easterners themselves felt ashamed and tried to prohibit them. Yet their essential aim was only too laudable, for by letting the children become accustomed very early to their life's companion, they removed much uncertainty and all the accompanying temptations. In India, for instance, the practice of marriage at a young, even a very young age, was one of the main criteria for judging the prestige of a caste, and many groups, in order to be admitted into Hinduism, or in order to obtain a higher social rank within it, adopted this custom together with many others which we shall mention later. There is no doubt that this led to serious abuses, but the same may be said of any social custom. In Israel marriages were concluded before puberty.

That is why, in various societies, it is really a tragedy if a girl reaches puberty without being bound by the sacred ties of marriage. According to the Hindu and Jain scriptures, her parents go straight to hell as a result. Among the Variya, the girl herself cannot enter the temple or take part in any ceremony. In numerous cases, as among the Bilimagga, she loses caste; among the Pulaya, she has to be driven away from her home. Among the Dikshitar, for similar reasons, it is hard to find a marriageable girl over five. In Israel, the woman who was unable to find a husband was despised.

In other groups it is the consummation of marriage that confers upon the girl her new social and religious status. Thus, among the Nayar it is thought that a girl who dies a virgin cannot go to heaven.

We shall not speak here of the innumerable and infinitely varied rites that accompany marriage in Asian societies. They are the subject of very detailed studies that would fill libraries, and besides, few of these details could throw any light on the mentality of the people who practise such rites. It suffices to say here that in Asia, we find all imaginable forms and many others that are difficult for us to imagine, from kidnapping (in both directions!—it is said that the Hathari women used to kidnap men from the neighbouring tribes in order to marry them) to sacraments that take weeks to conclude, from the admission of the prospective bridegroom into his future bride's home in order to work there for some years before the marriage to the obligation for the girl's parents to pay relatively high sums to the boy's parents, from free choice to being absolutely compelled to marry someone in accordance with the decisions of astrologers and genealogists. In India, among the Bharvad, while two marriages may not be held in the same place even with a long interval in between, among the Ahir all marriages are held every year in the same place on the same day. And so on.

At this point we have to open a long parenthesis and speak of polygamy, also a subject on which much has been written. Systems whereby an individual may be married simultaneously to several of the opposite sex at one and the same ceremony, or at several different ones spread out over a period of time, have always been the normal standard almost throughout Asia.

Polygyny, where one man has several wives at the same time, is of many varieties. There is the case—the commonest one—where a man may, by means of several successive marriages, marry a variable number of women without waiting to be separated from earlier wives. This system existed, although on a rather exceptional basis, in primitive Jewish societies and is still to be found among the Jews of Cochin. It is the general rule among Muslims who are allowed four wives according to the Koran, but some exceptions are to be found in the rather backward groups such as the Qashquai Nomads of the Iranian Fars, the tribes of Borneo, the Mappilla of the Laccadives and Minicoy where, moreover, the women continue to live with their family of origin while other, neighbouring but more developed groups such as the Mappilla of the mainland, the Boir Ahmedi of the Iranian Fars, the Phillipino Moro, take full advantage of the authorization granted by the Koran. The Muslim Tatars and Tunguz have as many wives as they can feed.

Polygamy was already the rule in Persia under the Sassanides, and, while the great reform of Bab, which is quite recent, did not look upon it with much favour, it dared not prohibit it. It is also the normal state of affairs among the Kurds of Armenia, the Kirghiz, the Uzbeks, but less frequent among the Turkmen and in Afghanistan. In Siberia, the Yakuts, the Ostiaks, the Tunguz, and, generally speaking, almost all the Arctic peoples are polygamous. This is also the case with almost all the tribes of India: for instance, the Kâdir, Kols, Kota, Korava, Kummara, Lingayat and almost the whole of the Malabar. While the Paraiyan hardly ever exceed the number of two, the Savara have as many as four wives, the Dhangar sometimes have over five, the Yanadi seven and the Golla as many as they like.[5] Vidyasagar, a social reformer of the early nineteenth century, mentions a village in Bengal where only five men, *kulin-brahmins*, had between them 230 wives, while another man of the same area gave in marriage to a ten-year-old boy six aunts, eight sisters and four daughters, all at one time.

Polygamy is also normal in Indo-China, among the Manchus, the Chinese (during the feudal period, etiquette fixed the number of wives allowed to a nobleman at each marriage; at certain periods, the queen was not counted among the wives, because she was one with the king), the Nepalese; but it is a little less frequent in Tibet, among the Labche of Sikkim and the Katal Arayan of South India.

In certain groups the man is entitled to a second wife only if the first one is sterile; this is particularly the case with the Kannadiyan, the Komati, the Tiyan and other Indian tribes while, on the contrary, among the Savara he can only take a second wife after having had a child by the first, so as not to be accused by her of impotence. The Tatar may not take another wife without the consent of the first.

Various countries practise polygynic monogamy, where one man simultaneously marries several women at one single ceremony. In 1852, three years before his death, Sivaji, the last Maratha king of Tanjore, simultaneously wedded seventeen young girls. Often, the wives are sisters, as formerly in Japan, and to this day in Tibet and among the Kurumba of the Nilgiri region in India. In China, where this custom was once quite common, marriage also included the niece. Among the Medara of India the man is generally content to marry two sisters, while for the Kuruba or the Paniyan tribes it is precisely forbidden to have two wives who are daughters of the same parents.

In certain tribes such as the Vedan, polygamy does not mean that the husband has to provide for his wives.

[5] Edgar Thurston and K. Rangachari.

Monogamy is, however, prevalent among certain tribes such as the Veddas of Ceylon, the Saliyan of Tanjore, the Valluvan, etc.

Let us mention, finally, that in those communities where polygamy is practised, the women do not necessarily suffer more from jealousy than elsewhere. A European traveller in Siberia, seeing an aboriginal woman converted to Christianity, who had been sentenced to death for having murdered her husband, philosophically notes: 'This unfortunate woman became Christian and jealous at the same time, for this kind of madness is not known in countries where polygamy is permitted'.[6]

The polygamous peoples were at first very surprised at the efforts made by Christian missionaries (and no one could even tell on the basis of what texts this was done[7]) to convert them to monogamy, and if they did resign themselves to these new ways, it was mainly out of fear of arousing the contempt of those communities with which they wished to be on good terms. A modern Chinese author, Ku Hung-Ming, wittily defended polygamy, saying, 'You have seen a tea-pot with four tea-cups, but did you ever see a tea-cup with four tea-pots?' The best reply to this are the words of P'an Chin-Lien, concubine of Hsi-men Ch'ing in *Ching P'ing Mei*: 'Do you ever see two spoons in the same bowl that do not knock against each other?'[8]

Polyandry, where a woman is simultaneously the wife of several men, although less widespread than polygamy, does nevertheless exist in many Asian societies. It mostly takes the form of adelphogamy, that is, the husbands are brothers and their marriage with a common wife is celebrated at a single occasion. This is normally the case in Tibet, although not the absolute rule.[9] According to Delannoy it is apparently in force mostly among the aristocracy and the landed gentry.

In India the tradition goes back very far, for in the great epic, the *Mahabharata*, the five Pandava brothers, the great heroes who have been deified by so many castes and tribes, collectively married the Princess Draupadi.[10] The habit has survived in the Malabar, in certain groups in Kashmir, among the tribes of the Hindu Kush, among the Dhum, in practically all classes and castes of the Jaunsar-Bawar of the Dehra Dun districts and other Himalayan valleys near Tibet. Adelphogamy is the rule in Ladhak, in Kanawar (Punjab), in parts of Kashmir, in Coorg, among the Brahmins, Rajputs and Sudras

[6] J. G. Gmelin.
[7] Cf. *Catholic Encyclopaedia*.   [8] Lin Yutang.
[9] Shramana Eita Kawaguchi.
[10] Adi Parvan CLXXVI-CXCIV and *passim*. However, various other chapters of the *Mahabharata*, especially Adi Parvan CXCVIII, find it necessary to explain this polyandry as if it were a guilty act.

of Kumaon etc. while among the Bhutia, the Kammalan, the Kols, the Mannan of Northern Cochin, the Nayar of Travencore and others, the choice offered seems wider. Among the Kallan, a caste of robbers, where a woman frequently has ten, eight, six or two husbands who are all fathers to all her children, on the contrary, the marriages are not all held at the same time, but gradually, as the woman starts choosing other men in her tribe. Successive marriages are also the rule in Bhutan and in the Aleutian islands. Polyandry is also to be met among certain nomads of Northern Asia.

In certain societies, polygyny and polyandry are found together; for instance, among the Tibetans, the Daphla of the north-east frontier of India, the inhabitants of Lahul, parts of the Kangra area, the Kadar of Cochin and the Paraiyan of Travancore. Among the Muduvar of South India a man may have several wives in the same village and at the same time he may be one of the husbands of a woman in another village; but where there is polyandry, a woman may not marry several brothers. Among the Todas and the Urali, two or more brothers may together share two or more wives.

Often it is taken for granted that a wife has to be at the disposal of her brothers-in-law, without having married them, either all the time—as in the low castes in Ceylon, among the Jat in Punjab, among the Wynad, the Tottiyan (where this obligation extends also to close relatives) and in the Trichinopoly district (where it applies to the chief of the caste, the *pattakaran*)—or in the husband's absence, as among the Badaga of South India, and among the Veppur Paraiyan when the husband is in prison, and has to be replaced by someone belonging to the Udaiyan caste; or else when the husband is too young to fulfil his duties, as among the Anuppan and other groups in South India. In the same area, when the husband is too young, his duties are performer by any other member of the tribe— among the Malayali, for instance, it is the father of the young bride-groom.

In various Asian countries there are also systems—quite official ones, from both the religious and civil point of view—of temporary marriage. For instance, in India among the Turuvalar, in Saudi Arabia among the Asur, in Iran and in various countries of Islam, where the kind of marriage known as *muta* is concluded for a period up to ninety-nine years; it is not unusual to find pilgrims, particularly at Meshed, who take advantage of this system in order to brighten their temporary solitude.

Side by side with these customs, in the traditional Asian societies, we find concubines who do not have the same rank and prerogatives as the wives but do enjoy clearly defined rights, and slaves who are relegated to an even lower rank. This does not cause any shame to the parties concerned. In Babylon as well as in Sumer, it was up to the wife to choose for her husband a concubine slave, who in turn enjoyed certain rights. Concubinage is normal among the Chinese and the Muslims and in numerous castes and tribes of India. The Bedar or Boya even announce and celebrate the start of concubinage. This system becomes inevitable because of certain prohibitions; for instance, among the Nambutiri and the Muttatu only the eldest living son may contract marriage, and the others may only live in concubinage. The concubine may, moreover, be raised to the rank of wife when this obstacle is removed by the death of the married brother or if, as in China, the man has not had any children by his wife by the time he has reached the age of forty.

In most cases, the young woman who gets married goes simply from complete dependence on her parents to an equally complete dependence on her parents-in-law; in fact, her situation does not change, and nor does it by any means improve. Generally speaking, she is completely cut off from her original family. In China, 'to marry' is said in the same way as 'to return', because a woman, when she gets married, enters her real home. In Japan—which in this case is far from being an exception—when the marriage has been officially registered, the woman's name is struck from the register of her former family, and she may have no further relationship with her parents.

In her new family, her situation is hardly enviable. As a new-comer among her sisters-in-law, who are somewhat jealous of the intruder, she is inclined to be a kind of Cinderella and has to take on the most unpleasant tasks. Her parents-in-law are all the more inclined to consider her as their property since in most cases they chose her without consulting either her or her future husband, but with the sole consent of the girl's parents. This is normal among the Muslims, in India, Central Asia, Tibet, in ancient Japan where every-thing was decided between the respective fathers, in modern Japan among the Samurai families, in China, in Korea, in Indo-China, among the Laotians, even though it is not legal, and in most other societies. There are only a few rare exceptions—for instance, among the Buddhist Buryats, among the lower classes of ancient Japan, among the A-Kha of Northern Laos etc.

It is even said in China that a man does not marry a wife but the daughter-in-law of his parents and that the children born of this union are above all the grandchildren of the grandparents. In Korea, as in Japan, a clash between the woman and the husband's parents, or disobedience by the woman towards her parents-in-law, was sufficient cause for divorce. If certain poets[11] are to be believed, a

[11] The K'ong-kio tong-nan fei of the second century.

Chinese woman may even be repudiated by her mother-in-law; a Chinese who admits to having beaten his wife to death escapes any penalty if his pretext for doing so is that she failed in her filial duty towards his parents.[12]

This complete submission of the young husband to his parents prevents him from ever taking his wife's defence, however ill-treated she may be—and the wife owes such respect to her husband that she would doubtless never dare to ask for his intervention. In Japan she is not supposed to raise her eyes upon the face of her lord and master.

Apart from the part played by the husband's parents, the relationship between the partners is very different from that to which we are accustomed. Great shyness and reserve, curiously combined with the absence of privacy (as we have seen earlier), is the reason for the fact that married couples must not show their feelings in public. With a third party present, a wife behaves towards her husband exactly as if he were her father or elder brother, and it is almost impossible to guess that they are linked by marriage. A Chinese husband would blush if he were surprised in the act of conversing with his wife. In a group composed of several couples, the women always keep to themselves and the men do the same, without any communication between the two sides or any sign which would betray who is married to whom.

In Cambodia, betrothed and married couples call each other 'elder brother' and 'little sister', and similarly, in ancient Japan, the same term, *imo*, designated both 'wife' and 'younger sister'. In China, since time immemorial, one of the dominant principles of society has been that of the separation of the sexes. This is taken in its strictest sense; the partners have to live at some distance from each other and all their relationships require infinite precautions. In ancient China, husband and wife were not supposed to mix their clothes before the age of seventy.

A few words must be said here regarding two practices that are very widespread in the East and that tend to fill us with indignation —viz. that of compelling women to veil themselves and that of confining them to a separate part of the house where males are not allowed. Whatever the advocates of these systems might say about them, it is quite obvious that the most decisive reason is the man's desire to keep his wife hidden from the eyes of any other man. Jealousy and a sense of ownership, in Asia as elsewhere, are strong feelings, and that would make any other explanation redundant. Nevertheless, it cannot be denied that other factors, very different

[12] Arthur Smith. In China there were 'secret societies' of girls against marriage (V. R. Burckhardt).

in nature, do intervene. On the one hand, there is the intense shyness of the Oriental woman, a feeling which the man in most Asian countries constantly respects by avoiding any bodily contact and even any direct glance. On the other hand, there is the anxiety to protect the purity of the woman who is the moral and spiritual shield of the whole family. These reasons, of course, explain the resistance shown by most women to any attempt to emancipate them from what we regard as intolerable signs of servitude.

Whatever the importance of these various factors and whatever the historic, religious or ethnic origins of these habits, for a large part of traditional Asia it would be as inconceivable for a woman to show her face to an outsider as it would be for a European woman to uncover her breast—and she would be as severely and unanimously reprimanded for it.

There are various degrees of veiling, starting from the fine, almost transparent muslin which just blurs the features of the face to the horrible thick, black garment which covers the woman from head to foot and where the little openings for the eyes are themselves obstructed by a thick, impenetrable trellis, like the *paranja* of the Uzbeks. Generally speaking, it may be said that women are veiled among the Muslims of the Near East, Iran, Afghanistan, India, Ceylon, but not in Indonesia. They are also veiled among some of the Indian tribes such as the Razu, the Kamma, the Kevuto, etc. and also among the Ostiaks of Denjikovo and Ustsosvinsk and others.

On the contrary, women are not veiled among most Hindu and aboriginal tribes of India, among the Japanese, the Chinese, the Burmese, the Thai, the Viet-Namese, the Kirghiz, the Bab, the Philippines, the non-Muslim inhabitants of Java, etc.

Female seclusion also varies in degree; in some cases they are absolutely forbidden to leave the *zenana* and to receive men other than the husband; in others, there is the less serious obligation of going out only when escorted by the husband, a servant, or a younger brother; in still other instances, they may receive only a few members of the family. These restrictions, known under different names according to the country—*purdah* in North India, *gosha* in South India—may go so far that, for instance, among the Razu, a man may not even set eyes on his younger brother's wife; and among the Urya Korono (South India) a girl, after puberty, may not appear before her elder brother. This custom is so deep-rooted that even great progressive reformers such as Sir Mohamed Iqbal thought it quite natural to sequester their women; and when, in Iran, the veil was forbidden for women, a vast majority of them preferred to stay at home rather than do something so improper.

The event that brings about the greatest transformation is the birth of the first child. Among the Okkiliyan Gangadikara, the dowry is not paid until the birth of the first child. In the Andamans, the husband who comes home greets his wife for the first time only when she is a mother. If the Chinese woman has no son and gives birth to a series of daughters, her existence in the home becomes a hell. Indeed, the wife is entrusted with a capital mission, of which her sisters-in-law are, by definition, incapable, that of prolonging and perpetuating the race, and of ensuring the future of ancestor worship. Not to have a son is a calamity for the oriental. It is said that Mohammed, as a compensation for not having had any, enjoyed the benefit of a special bathing pool in heaven! In Japan, where a sterile woman is the worst thing imaginable, it often happens that the man has his marriage registered only after the birth of a male child. In Burma, it is only after she has brought a son into the world that the woman is regarded as a complete human being. In Viet-Nam, she is the lawful mother of children likely to be born of her husband's other unions. In China, there is an analogy of function and identity of virtue between the motherland and the fecund mother; there it is the mother who inspires veneration and respect. In Japan as in Tibet, she has considerable influence on her husband. In Thai, the language itself reflects this situation—the general is called the mother of his army, the magnet is called the iron's mother, the pliers the mother of strength. In India, this religious respect towards the mother is such that she is assimilated to the supreme Divinity, the Divine Mother, and revered as such. An Indian, whatever his age and social position may be, would not dream of disobeying his mother; before leaving the house, and after having washed upon his return, he prostrates himself before his mother and 'takes the dust off her feet' in order to put it on his forehead.

Generally speaking, children are entirely subject to their mother, at least in their early years, and the father starts handling them only later. Even among the Muslims, where on principle the children belong to their father, the mother, in fact, keeps them till the boys are seven and the girls nine years old. The Mosaic law demands from the child an even greater respect towards the mother than towards the father. 'The mother is a thousand times more venerable than the father', according to the Laws of Manu in India.

Therefore there is nothing surprising in that there are many societies in Asia where the mother enjoys, *de facto* or even *de jure*, a situation superior to that of the father. The really matriarchal societies exist, as may be expected, wherever polyandry is practised, in Tibet or in the Malabar, but they are also to be found in Indonesia and among various ethnic groups in Indo-China. It seems also that systems of this kind were in force in relatively recent periods in China, Viet-Nam, Japan, and their disappearance is even sometimes deplored.

Without going as far as such a rigid social system, there are many countries where the woman, once she is a mother, plays a preponderant part in the family. In Thailand it is the husband who works for the family income, but it is the woman who disposes of it, invests it, directs the commercial operations, etc. In Viet-Nam, she is mistress of her home, *noi tru o ng*, and tradeswomen are more numerous and more skilful than tradesmen; and besides, even theoretically, according to the Hong-du c code which dates back to the fifteenth century, woman is the equal of man. In China the peasant home used to be a feminine prerogative, and remained so as long as it lasted; practically, the village belonged to women, and the divinity that protected it was called the mother of the village. In Japan, while purity and obedience are the fundamental qualities expected of a woman, it is she, once she has become a mother, who controls the purse strings and takes all the domestic decisions; and she has long been allowed to own farmland, houses and money, *watakushi*.

Even on the religious and ritual plane, the woman who has given her husband a son enjoys important prerogatives. In traditional China, the head of a family, who is in charge of an ancestral temple, must have a wife; if he has lost his wives, he has to remarry provided that he is under seventy years old, or, if not, he has to hand over his responsibility to someone else. Similarly in India, among the Kota, he must immediately remarry, otherwise he might lose his position. Generally speaking, in Hindu families, a sacrifice offered by the head of a family, a *yajamanar*, has no value without the participation of the wife, the *sahadharmini* (she who shares her husband's fate).

It is of course in this context—where the woman is acknowledged to have a certain superiority—that we must look at the numerous cases where the husband lives with his in-laws. This was prevalent practice in ancient Japan till about the fifteenth century, among the Veddas of Ceylon, among the Thai and among many castes and tribes of India.

Although this interpretation may be challenged, it is also against this same background that we must look at the relatively frequent cases where the man must serve for a fairly long period at the home of his future wife's parents before her hand is granted to him. This system is to be found in Cambodia, in Laos, among certain Indian tribes, etc.

As the couple advances in age and as their descendants increase in number, its status in the group improves, and when the woman becomes a mother-in-law and a grandmother, she gets the chance of avenging herself on the younger generation for the humiliations inflicted on her in her youth.

However, it is when she becomes the oldest member of the family group that she assumes an extremely responsible position and acquires thereby a dignity that would be inconceivable in the West. We have an excellent illustration of this, so far as China is concerned, in the famous novel *Yeh-Sao Pao-Yen*,[13] where a single word from the hero's mother made him go down on his knees, although he was a prime minister. In Japan the grandmother assumes full authority upon the death of her husband, and nothing is decided without her, however mature or eminent her children might be. In a Hindu family nothing may be done without the permission of the grandmother, who is feared and venerated at the same time; and all those who try to change the ancestral customs know full well that the final decision is always in the hands of this mysterious and all-powerful individual who is never to be seen; the grandmother plays a part half-way between that of a mother ruler and an abbess. This dictatorial authority is all the stronger since generally it is not based on any legally specified right; is some countries, she is even supposed to be dependent on her eldest son, and in Viet-Nam she even derives her last name from her son.

The basis of this situation is completely different, and it is much more than compensated by her unique position in the family. Infinitely more than when she was merely wife or mother or even grandmother, the ancestress becomes the supreme guardian of the purity of the group depending on her; this is how she protects it and maintains its standards on the spiritual, religious, moral, traditional planes, and eventually also on the physical plane. She therefore has to live a life of very great austerity and constant sacrifice, maintaining close contact between her group and the higher powers. We find here a concept which we shall examine later when we speak of a larger social unit, viz. the hierarchy of duties which in the East is far stricter than that of rights, often ignored.

It remains for us to see the various causes for the dissolution of marriage and the consequences of the woman's new position which results from it. Quite rightly, Westerners are shocked by the fact that in many oriental communities the husband may repudiate his wife just as he pleases, without even having to give the reasons. It must, however, be noted that this custom is not general, and where it exists, there are other facts counterbalancing it.

In the first place, there are many societies where divorce is strictly impossible. Let us mention, just by way of example, the

---

[13] English translation: *The Dream of the Red Chamber* (London, Routledge, 1958).

case of Japan where 'a man who could not stand his wife had no resource other than to commit suicide',[14] that of the Tunguz and among the castes and tribes of India, the Bhadbunja, the Brahmins of the Bombay area, the Depala, the Dasari, the Ghadi and others. There are often cases, like the Holeya (also in India), where the husband may divorce his wife only for adultery. Among the Golla of Dharwar, even this is not sufficient motive.

In many groups, husband and wife both enjoy the same right of initiative if they wish to put an end to their union. This was the case with the Hittites of antiquity, and in our own time we have the example in India of the Kondh, the Korawars, the Kunnuvan, the Tiyan (for some of whom the consent of both parties is required) and others. In China divorce is granted through mutual consent.

In other groups, it is mostly the woman who takes the initiative for divorce, as for instance in Persia since the time of Reza Shah and among the Irula (India). In others, the woman has the absolute right to demand divorce, as among the Bottada and the Kol. Among the A-Kha of Northern Laos, the woman may purely and simply repudiate her husband. Among the Badaga, the Bedouins, the Kallan and others, the woman may, at will, leave her husband in order to go and live with another man. Among the Ravulo of India, she may only do so if she is ill-treated or deserted. In Islam the husband's being away for two years justifies divorce.

We shall see later that with regard to adultery, customs are equally varied from one community to the other.

Even when the man has the unilateral right to repudiate his wife, as among the Halepaik of Kanara (India), and among the Berad, for whom the woman's ugliness is sufficient motive, in the great majority of cases where it is granted, he must fulfil various obligations which are often rather heavy: maintenance, reimbursement of the dowry (which, in the East, is out of proportion with the family's resources), etc. Among the Tibetans, the amount of damages to be paid in case of divorce is even specified at the time of marriage. There are some communities, however, as in Thailand, where no such obstacle comes in the husband's way.

Special mention must be made of the widow's case; her fate has often been pitied, especially in India, and not without reason. Indeed, in many groups she is not allowed to remarry, and she is subject to rules of living even stricter than those applied to the oldest woman member of the family; very few Western women would be able to follow them or even survive them. There, as in the case of *purdah*, certain not very commendable factors have definitely played an important part, but they are not the only ones—and

[14] Mariko Mishima.

while the unenviable lot of the widow is doubtless partly responsible for the large number of suicides among them, it is certainly
not the only cause either. Besides, there are numerous communities,
particularly in India, where the widow may perfectly well remarry
and begin a new home; a list of these would be tiresome and superfluous.

However, remarriage of both the widow and the divorcee is
strictly regulated almost everywhere. A very widespread custom is
that of the levirate according to which—of course, this applies
wherever there is polygamy—the younger brother automatically
marries his elder brother's widow. This practice may be found,
starting from Siberia among the Ostiaks, till South India among the
Mali, the Rona, the Mandadan Chetti and others. There are sometimes variants of the same custom. Thus, among the Koppala Velama
it is the elder brother who may wed the younger brother's widow;
among the Savara, if there is no brother-in-law, the widow marries
her brother-in-law's son. Among the Lambadi of Mysore, she marries
her brother-in-law only if she does not yet have any children and
the children of the new couple are attributed to the deceased; this
is the custom known as *valli sukkeri*, the origin of which is supposed
to go back to the monkey king Sugriva, one of the heroes of the
Ramayana. This custom is also to be found, in a slightly different
form, among the Krishnavakakkar. According to a parallel custom,
the Paraiyan often marry the sister of the dead wife. There is
another custom that is even stranger for us; it allows a Kudiya widow
to marry her own eldest son. Finally, in certain groups such as the
Muduvar and the Maratha (also South India), we find the custom
contrary to levirate, i.e. the widow may marry whom she pleases
with the exception of her brother-in-law.

If, in addition, we see that in various groups there is the deepest
veneration for the woman who has had seven successive husbands
(the *beth-thamma* among the Gavara, for instance), that the Koppala
Velama women may remarry seven times and the Odde women
eighteen times (!), we are forced to conclude that the problem
of the widow's remarriage in India is not as simple as it is sometimes imagined. Let us add an amusing example: among the Oraon,
a divorced woman who remarries is subjected to a certain penalty,
but this penalty diminishes with each successive marriage. This
curious fact may doubtless be explained by saying that the first
infidelity is the most serious and that after this, the first husband
is less and less interested.

Nevertheless, it must be noted that among orthodox Hindus the
non-remarriage of widows, like child marriage, is considered a true
and essential criterion of morality. When a caste or a tribe wishes

to rise in the social scale, which is easier than might be thought, it
has to submit to stricter moral and physical rules—by the observation of the marriage rules mentioned above, by abstinence from
alcohol and meat and also the daily bath. All this is regarded as
being roughly on the same plane.

What should be concluded from all these customs which seem
so disparate and irreconcilable? Is it possible to discern a few fundamental ideas which would explain them at least partly?

We have already seen and shall see constantly in the rest of this
book that in all spheres of life in Asia, the dominant, ever-present,
obsessing factor is the religious one, with all its extensions into the
fields of ritual, magic, cult, philosophy, ethics, spirituality etc. It is
therefore obviously in that direction that we must look.

Now, with regard to women, it will be noted that there are two
capital concepts associated with them, both closely linked with
ritual purity. On the one hand, woman is the womb of humanity,
the exclusive creator of all that in the world concerns us most
directly. As such, she actually has a divine nature, she is the supreme
manifestation of the supreme demiurge, the most evident visible
representation of the supreme divinity. This explains the cult of
which she is the object in her capacity as ancestress.

This part however, although decisive, requires from her a total
purity, perhaps even more ritual than moral, without which the
whole group originating from her would be exposed to most serious
dangers. That is what explains the need for all the disciplines imposed upon her and all the taboos surrounding her.

On the other hand, the actual physiology of woman, and particularly her menstrual haemorrhages—above all those accompanying puberty and childbirth[15]—make her a being physically, and
therefore ritually, impure; her contact alone, even her proximity,
not only inflicts a taint which is difficult to wash away, but also
makes foodstuffs unfit for eating, seed unfit for sowing, and sometimes even affects tools and clothing, and houses, and therefore
requires protective measures that are sometimes cruel as well as
long, and scrupulous purification rites. Even in the intervals between
these particularly feared periods the woman continues to be a

---

[15] In many groups, the woman may only give birth to a child outside her
home in a hut especially set aside for this purpose, and she has to submit to
long purification rites before being allowed to return home. The midwife who
delivers the child is almost everywhere considered as an impure being (Cf.
Thurston). In some parts of China, it is absolutely forbidden even to *see* the
mother who has just been delivered or her child for forty days following the
confinement (A. Smith). In Japan, in antiquity, the women who were
about to become mothers were driven out of their homes. (Chamberlain in
Kojiki).

potential source of soiling. This is the reason for the numerous taboos, particularly of a religious nature, that she has to suffer all through her nubile life.

The sexual, moral and spiritual factors which have been described at such great length by ethnologists and religious philosophers are doubtless only of secondary importance. The most uncontrolled libertinage has never resulted in raising woman's place in society, and the needs of monastic life or any other austere, spiritual discipline, after all, concern only a very small number of men.

What should be regarded as equally important is the real need to protect the woman—who is normally physically weaker than man —in her contact with a still untamed nature and an inadequately ordered society which still prevail in many areas.

In addition, the religious needs of the woman, which are normally more intense than those of men, are frustrated, as we have seen earlier, on account of her inherent impurity; she therefore, quite naturally seeks compensation in magic and in all the superstitions connected with it. She often acquires such mastery of it that she becomes dangerous and feared as a result. We shall quote at some length the description of the Muslim woman given by Raymond Charles, for this could apply equally to many other Asian societies. 'The constant dealings which the Muslim girl has with the invisible world make her feared even and especially by her husband; she handles with diabolical skill a rich variety of spells in order to provoke love or to remove a rival or to strike a hated husband with impotence . . . the Muslim woman has thrown herself body and soul into the superstitions and the magical practices inherited from the pre-Islamic period, using it not only as inexhaustible and rich food to satisfy her greed for the sacred, but also as a way—through passionately cultivated mysterious powers—to a revenge on the superiority of man who is always disturbed and sometimes terrified by this ancestral reminder of occult powers . . . therefore, sorcery with all its pomp, its minute, almost household practices, where nail clippings and waste hair are buried and chicken livers are simmered in maleficent or beneficent ingredients, were suited to the mental level of most Muslim women'. They even seek to take over the ancestors who, as we have seen above, always have an important part to play. The same author has picturesquely written: 'In their so-called funerary escapades, the Muslim women defend their duties as wet-nurse, which they extend even to visitors from the tombs'.

These powers of witchcraft obviously form an abyss between woman and man which also leads to her being denied the satisfaction which she would normally seek in a religion less tainted with coarse magic. This forms a vicious circle which has been regarded as being largely responsible for 'the mutual and total lack of confidence between man and woman which is at the basis of the fundamental split in Muslim society'.[16]

Yet, strange as it may seem to us, the woman does not envy her male partner. In India and in most of the Buddhist countries, she knows that in society, in the eyes of the Divine and on the spiritual path, her position is normally inferior to that of man and that, for example, she must be re-incarnated as a man before being able to reach ultimate liberation—but even this does not make her revolt. Apart from a few extremely rare exceptions, in traditional Asia equality of rights between the sexes is an absolutely incomprehensible concept, an ideal that appeals to nobody; everyone has his own place, his own part to play, both resulting from various factors between which no parallel could or should be established.

Of course, traces of 'feminist' movements may be found in various countries at various times, as for instance in China in the remotest antiquity under the Empress Wu Tso-t'ien of the T'ang, or even in the ninth century, when the poet Tchang Ki displayed great interest in woman's social status—but they never roused much interest, and least of all among the women. When a social movement—mostly inspired by a blind wish to become westernized—leads an Asian group to reject a particular ancestral custom, it is the women who are most disconcerted and have the greatest difficulty in getting used to the new system. The women pioneers of new western ways in the East met with much greater resistance from their fellow women than from men, who perhaps regarded the change as being to their advantage in more ways than one.

On the whole, it has to be noted that oriental woman, whatever Loti may have written on the subject, is neither less gay, nor less serene, nor less happy than her sister in the West—which is, after all, the only valid criterion.

We have seen that, in the greater part of Asia, to leave descendants is an imperative duty, if only in order to perpetuate ancestor worship and to avoid breaking the chain of life. The Korean is really a man only after he has had a son. In China it is only when a man is a father that he is qualified to appear before his ancestors and before his creator. 'May your posterity be wiped out for ever' is the greatest curse that can be put upon a Chinese—and if Buddhist monks there are regarded with a certain contempt, it is because they do not procreate. In Hindu mythology, the ascetic Jaratkaru, going down to the other world, sees his ancestors hanging head downwards in a well and learns from them that they will be delivered

[16] Raymond Charles.

from this torture only when Jaratkaru has had a son—and he comes back to earth in order to fulfil his duty.[17]

The emotional ties between children and parents are remarkably strong and tender. The love of the Japanese for children in general is really touching, even if it is demonstrated with great reserve (parents neither kiss nor fondle their children after they start walking). There is even a special paradise, *Sai-no-Kaware*, for little children. The same is true of the Tibetans. The little Chinese boy is welcomed into the paternal home with wild rejoicing. Anything he asks for must always be granted. The Chinese mother is literally the slave of her children and they cannot be left to cry.

Islam teaches, 'He who strokes an orphan's head will see on the day of the last judgement as many lights as the hairs on that head'; also, 'Everything has its key; the key to Paradise is the love shown to children and to the poor'.[18]

The reverse is equally true. In Tibet, one of the most solemn oaths is: '*Ama tang me*', separate me from my mother (if I am not telling the truth[19]). Yet this very love often gives way to filial piety which is more a duty and a respect. The twenty-four patterns of filial piety which are so deeply admired in China are equally so in Korea and in Japan. In Viet-Nam, to be lacking in filial piety was considered to be one of the six most atrocious crimes and the same is true of Korea and China. For Afghan Muslims, the worst insult is to call someone the son of a father burning in hell. The Biblical injunction which lays down that a man shall leave his father and mother in order to devote himself to his wife is regarded as profoundly immoral in Japan and throughout Asia in general. In India, mythology and folklore are full of examples of men and women who sacrificed all, even their most imperative religious duties, even their salvation, in order to serve their fathers and mothers and were rewarded by the gods.

Obedience to the parents goes without saying, but there are very clear exceptions, for instance in Laos, among the Veddas of Ceylon, etc.

However, these very strong emotional ties do not necessarily follow the ties of consanguinity. It is obvious that delicate problems arise in the more or less officially polyandric societies. The solutions vary considerably from one group to the other. In Tibet, when a woman who has married several brothers gives birth to a child, it is the eldest husband who is considered the father, and the others are 'uncles'. In India the five Pandava brothers, the most famous epic heroes, have neither the same mother nor the same father. Among

---

[17] *Mahabharata*, Adi Parvan, XIII and XLV.
[18] Hadith.   [19] Shramana Eita Kawaguchi.

the Todas, the father of the unborn child is the one who celebrates a certain ceremony in the seventh month of the mother's pregnancy; he remains the father of the following children until another man, in his turn, has performed the same ceremony at a subsequent pregnancy; but the other brothers who share the same wife are also fathers.[20] In feudal China, a man could regard his wife's child as his own son, even if he had not engendered it, or even if the child were born after he had opened his harem to his customers; inversely, the fact of being the wife's child never entails the right of being considered by the husband as his own son. Finally, it is true that in Islam there are hardly any illegitimate children, but no detailed investigations are carried out regarding the father's identity!

Besides this, there is the very widespread custom of adoption. In Japan, for instance, it goes so far that certain families such as the Kuje forbid their members to marry and adopt children at every generation. Some of these children reach the highest positions. Adoption sometimes takes on an esoteric meaning, as in Islam, where it may be equivalent to alms, and the child thus adopted may be considered as bringing luck. It also frequently happens that Muslims, for instance, raise their nephews as their own children, but, as Mohammed has explicitly indicated, there is no legal bond between the adopter and the adopted. In China where, according to Mencius, the Ancients used to exchange their sons and everyone used to bring up his friend's son, naturally some kind of legal bond developed. The young adopted Chinese sometimes continues to call 'father' the one who really is so, but mostly he gives this title to the person, the uncle for example, who has adopted him[21] and, in such a case, he calls his real father 'uncle'. Anyway, in the *kouo fang*, the ritual adoption for the purpose of perpetuating the cult of a family, the adopted one has to take the name of the family that adopts him and conduct the cult at the appropriate times.

The custom that shocks us so profoundly and that is to be found in various groups, viz. that of selling children to other families, is also a kind of adoption—apart from the fact that the new family of the adopted child is generally wealthier than the former and the child's fate is therefore likely to improve. A Chinese may always buy a son in order to continue ancestor worship. Even recently, in Central Asia, the Mongols often sold their children to the Tibetans,

---

[20] William H. Rivers.

[21] In feudal times, the father was only allowed to adopt someone from a younger branch of the family; he had to adopt his closest nephew. (M Granet). A. Smith points out that, for a Chinese without male descendants, the adoption of children from side branches of the family cost less than a second wife.

and, on the other hand, brought children from the Tanguts.[22] In India, the Lambadi purchase children from other castes. However, this custom can lead to abuse and can be a source of supply for prostitution.

The case of twins is rather special. In certain societies their arrival is considered a serious calamity, for instance, in Japan, in Kamchatka, in Laos etc. In this last country, the A-Kha will even kill them, while the P u-Noi keep one and let the other die of hunger. The Koreans do not like them. The Kols do not attach any particular significance to them. Among the Muduvar they are supposed to bring luck. In China, if they belong to different sexes, it is said to be a good omen if the boy is born first. According to the Jain canons, in the first period, *sasumasusama*, of each cycle or *kalpa*, which is a sort of golden age, all children are born in pairs, each comprising a boy and a girl; but the texts do not specify the order in which this occurs.

The Asian child begins his apprenticeship as an adult much earlier than the European; the little boy works in the fields or in handicrafts with his father, and the little girl carries, feeds, takes care of and plays with those younger than herself and takes her share of the household work. The negligible part played up to now by book learning, the absence of any preoccupation with clothes and the almost universal non-existence of the concept of 'toys' develops the child's power of observation and his memory to an extreme, and he learns through experience to weigh his action properly beforehand and then to perform it fast and well.

Let us mention, finally, that in many Asian countries, traditionally as well as in our day, cases of child prodigies are extremely frequent.

Generally speaking, old age in Asia confers distinction. It is a proof of science, wisdom and peace, a source of authority. With the system of the patriarchal family, the old do not, as in the West, run the risk of being abandoned and isolated and being forced to rely on pensions and homes for the aged. In fact, veneration towards the old goes well beyond the boundaries of the family.

The most typical case is doubtless that of China, where the oldest generation is always right, and the older it gets the more infallible it becomes; nothing is so enviable as to become old : children at birth are deemed to be one or two years old, and a person who is past seventy claims to be eighty years old; in traditional China, no old-age pension system could be accepted, for it goes without saying that the children support their parents in their old age. A banquet

[22] Sven Hedin.

is always presided over by the oldest guest, whatever his social rank. The very name of the most revered Lao Tse means nothing but 'the old Master'. Formerly, only old people were allowed to use silk, which is warmer and more valuable than other textiles—and it is also up to the old to send to their rest all that is old; dressed in mourning and a hazel-nut stick in the hand, they solemnly escort the year to its end.

Of course, there are exceptions; among the Muslims, for instance, an old woman is the object of disrespectful remarks, and she is not always treated with great consideration; and in southern Arabia the old are mistrusted because it is thought that they could not have reached such years without dealings with the supernatural powers.[23] There are even a few small groups where the old are relieved of the burden of life once they have reached a certain age. This used to be the case formerly not only with the Massagetes, if Herodotus is to be believed, but much more recently among the Issedonians of central Asia, among the Buryats at the age of seventy, and among the Tchuktches whenever the person concerned asked for it.

There are still others who benefit from this patriarchal family structure, for, however strict its boundaries on certain essential planes, it nevertheless affords a wide welcome to various categories of outsiders. We have already seen that the borderline between brothers and more or less distant cousins is a vague one. For the Muslim, for instance, 'a cousin is a brother in the true and not the metaphysical sense of the word, since he participates in the life of the group'. We have also seen the case of the passing guest with whom, as a French author, Legras, puts it wittily, an 'improvised family relation' is established.

But there is also, and above all, friendship. It has even been said that in the Orient, friendship is 'a transcendental word, since it is hallowed by the communion of things shared, unpurchasable things, walks into the sunset, adventures beyond the moon'.[24] Among the Chinese, it largely occupies the place that love takes in the West.

This friendship may spring spontaneously from a few words exchanged and may take root for a lifetime, enveloping the greatest depths of the soul and mind. It is confirmed quite naturally by the use of familiar terms: cousin, uncle, brother, father. It may also be sanctioned as solemnly and ceremoniously as a marriage, as in Nepal or among the Kondh, who actually have a sacrament of friendship, the *mahaprasad songatho*. Sometimes an exchange of blood is performed, although such a rite is less frequent in Asia than in Africa and Australia. In certain cases there is even mutual adoption and

[23] Bertram Thomas.   [24] Cranmer-Byng.

the two men are declared to be brothers (with all the legal consequences that this involves), co-owners of all they possess and inheritors of each other's property; this custom already existed in Elam around the end of the second millennium B.C.

Friendship need not be solely individual—it may link a given person to a whole group. In India, in China, among the Muslims, among the Russians of Siberia, a family is not complete without the 'family friend' who often plays an important part which is set aside for him.

The close ties which unite the members of a family between themselves often extend also to wider communities: village, tribe, caste, clan or even religious community.

In Asia the village, which is the usual form of rural habitat, constitutes a small universe fashioned by man himself; the earth walls are shaped and flattened with his own hands, the stones carried on his own back, the palm-leaf roofs woven with his own fingers, the paths marked by his own feet. In Thailand, in traditional Burma, in Laos and in many other countries, the village is a practically self-contained unit where only true fraternal ties exist. The Moi, the Dayak, the Naga and other Indian tribes do not even know of a larger political unit. In western Asia all the villagers not only help each other and work together, but are more or less related and possess at least a part of the land on an inalienable and collective basis. In certain areas, when a couple wants a new home, the whole village helps in building it. This is true in Siam and in the Phillipines. In China, where the village is welded together by powerful political and social ties, it has been said that the system which governs it is exactly the same as the one which governs the family; the expression t'ung-hsiang-kuan-nien, so much used, means born in the same place. The Russians of Siberia feel so closely linked to the 'farm', zimka, which corresponds to the village, that they often bear names in the genitive plural showing this link.

It is on the basis of this close solidarity that Vinoba has tried to turn each Indian village into a small, quasi-autonomous republic which would become the social and political unit of India. It was the very foundation of the economic and social system, 'villagism', advocated by Gandhi.

It is obvious that this deep-rooted union is often counterbalanced by a more or less intense hostility—open and permanent—towards other villages, as has been noted, for instance, among the Lepanto of Luzon.

The same is true, a fortiori, of those tribes, clans and castes which are always ready to face an outside enemy. In Islam the 'clan', a sort of union of families, sometimes has its own meetings, its journals, its genealogical pride, and readily submits, particularly in Lebanon, to the *touiza*, a sort of voluntary, collective labour for farm and construction work. In the Middle East, as in China, the 'co-operatives' which appear as such to the unenlightened observer are often not so in reality, for they are actually units and not groups. These are entities generally subject to incredibly strict rules of endogamy and exogamy which, though they have been the subject of vast and thorough study, do not tell us anything of great interest about the life and the mentality of the various populations.

Finally, there is the vast community made up of the followers of the same religion or even of the same sect. It is obviously most clearly manifested in small or minority groups: Parsis, Sikhs, Jains, Christian enclaves, Sufis, sects which are more or less heretical in comparison with the majority religion.

However, it is doubtless in the Islamic *Umma*, which embraces all the Muslims, that we see the most remarkable example. This concept of *umma* has become like the substance of the Muslim soul; each one feels it within himself in spite of social inequalities and even recent barriers of aggressive nationalism. In everyday language, an Arab addresses as *khouya*, my brother, anyone of the same religion whom he does not know. This does not preclude the feeling of belonging to a particular subdivision of the *umma*. R. Charles has written in this connection: 'Within each one of the groups composing the *umma* the individual hardly exists in his own right, for his importance is only a function of his belonging to a tribe, a family, or, in towns, to one of the groups that are both professional and ethical: corporations and, in our day, trade unions. Let us stress the fact that this dependence is healthy for personal behaviour since it is the group that bears each one's responsibility'.

However, this union does not prevent conflict between members, any more than it prevents conflict within a family. The Muslim naturally conceives a certain mistrust for his neighbours 'and his cunning is sharpened thereby'.[25] Among the Thai, as among the Japanese, mistrust among the inhabitants of the same village seems to be the normal state of affairs.

[25] Raymond Charles.

CHAPTER XIII

Morals and Sexuality

*The Orient placed no less intensity in ethics than in worship; it has
even created moral fervour.* MASSON-OURSEL

WE are often tempted to consider certain Asian peoples as immoral just because the moral laws which they obey are not the same as ours. In order to achieve proper mutual understanding it is very important to examine the question a little more closely.

In the first place, it must be noted that all the great teachings of Asia constantly stress the absolute need to follow a strict moral code. The Koran, as well the Hadith which goes with it, is full of exhortations in no way inferior—in level or in intransigence—to the Biblical code. The Hindu, as a recent Catholic missionary[1] puts it, is *par excellence* a moral being, 'and for him the strict observance of relentless moral rules which compose the *yama* and the *niyama* (non-violence, truthfulness, continence, non-stealing, non-acceptance of gifts, compassion, patience, sobriety, purity, contentment, strict obedience of the scriptures, faith in God, in the master and in the scriptures, worship of God, charity, modesty, etc.) are a prerequisite to any practice of Yoga. In Buddhism and in Confucianism ethical teaching is considerably more developed and more categorical than metaphysical or dogmatic teaching. In China the whole life of the community, and particularly that of the State, is governed by moral principles. The whole of Shintoism strives to ensure purity of the individual, and here, of course, morals are of paramount importance. The Japanese, as Lafcadio Hearn wrote, does not live by thought or by emotion, but by duty.

Even to this day this preoccupation with ethics has remained a living thing. It is through their strict discipline that certain Japanese sects, such as the Nichiren sect, attract the youth of today. The Chinese are always ready to have interminable discussions on good and evil, on behaviour and the purpose of life, all on the basis of ethics. If Gandhi in his lifetime succeeded in drawing the whole of

---

[1] Mech.

India to himself, it is because, like Confucius, he was first and foremost a moralist.

However, the sphere of morals in Asia is not the same as in the West; we should admit this without automatically concluding that our own conception is necessarily better, in theory or in practice.

Generally speaking, it may be said that Asia extends its moral code to cover preoccupations which we would not dream of connecting in any way with morality. Thus, in Japan, the 'ethical code of life'[2] embraces all activities of life, including esthetics, and can even require suicide. For the Chinese Lie Tse, the only difference between stealing from nature—which is common theft—and stealing from others—which is private theft—is that the latter is punished by justice while the former is not. Gandhi, in India, makes us understand the exact meaning of this maxim when he proclaims that eating more than one needs is theft. For many Hindus, Jains and Buddhists, killing an animal is murder. For Confucius as well as for Gandhi, the principles of the individual's moral code have to be applied to all human relationships and can solve all political and even economic problems. It may be imagined that with such a widely applicable code of ethics, many Asians must regard western life as 'a veritable moral chaos'.[3]

On the other hand, the basic concepts also differ. Thus, a European 'finds' a lost object and tries to return it to the one who, in his eyes, is the real owner. On the contrary, for a Viet-Namese it is not the loser but the finder who is the rightful owner; and in his language, 'to find something' is *du o c*, which actually means 'to obtain for possession'.[4] Another example: a Viet-Namese, either in gratitude for a service rendered or because he has come back to ask for one, appears before his 'benefactor' with a red lacquered box, *cai qua*, containing conventional gifts; this may be considered by a westerner as an attempt at bribery which must be indignantly refused, while in Viet-Nam these are just ritual objects, *do le*, and absolutely indispensable, for to come empty-handed or even with other gifts would have been insulting; one thinks in terms of corruption while for the other it is just etiquette, which is an integral part of ethics. In the Far East, even recently, it was considered just as immoral for an employer to dismiss a worker, either for an offence or for slowing down of business, as to drive one's own son out of the house for similar reasons; and in Japan, even when there was a strike, an employer continued to pay his workers because he was still fully responsible for them.

[2] Masuo Maruyama.   [3] L. Hearn,
[4] Pierre Huard and Maurice Durand.

Even if we were to judge exclusively according to our own criteria, we are often filled with wonder at the high degree of morality shown by those Asian populations that have still remained in a more or less pure state—i.e. without any sustained contact with western people. In particular, we see a profound honesty which seems quite natural; doubtless, the law of Karma, wherever it is recognized, has a certain bearing on this question, and the feeling of unity with one's neighbour as well as the widespread prevalence of the collective property system, in the family as well as in larger communities, also have some effect, but in most cases people are not conscious of the relationship between ethics and those factors.

We might fill several pages with examples and evidence; let it suffice to mention a few. Doughty, who had certainly no particular affection for the Arabs, as we shall see later, was obliged to admit that they were the most honest of men. The Russians used to admire the honesty of the Buryat Mongols. In Siberia, the honesty, good temper and charity of the Orotchones, the honesty of the Lamuths and the Tatars, the trustworthiness of the Gholds have filled travellers with wonder. If the Tunguz, whose perfect honesty and frankness have been praised by travellers, are sometimes regarded by them as stupid, it is because they are so trusting that they can be easily cheated. Various Englishmen have noted that the Mongol maintains a child-like innocence and that nothing is easier than to abuse his trust.

For the Japanese, the Japanese moral code is only the natural one, for it issues without any problem from the depths of the heart.[5] Chamberlain, who has not spared virulent criticism, confesses naively that the absence of any moral code in Shintoism may be explained by the innate perfection of Japanese humanity. Lafcadio Hearn notes that on the island of Oki theft had never been known before a port was opened to foreign vessels. Already, at the end of the seventeenth century in fact, a traveller, Engelbert Kaempfer, recognized that the Japanese are far superior to the Christians as regards the practice of virtue, purity of living and worship. Arthur Smith, one of the worst detractors of the Chinese, admits that the Chinese is the most truthful of all the Asians.

The Mazdaean hell, *drudjo-demana*, is the 'abode of lies'. As for the inhabitants of India, the English have often paid tribute to their truthfulness, for instance, among the Nambutiri, the Koyi, the Koraga (a tribe that has remained in the wild state) and to their honesty, for instance, among the Kadar, the Kuricchan and others. An English colonel who was a magistrate in various Indian provinces for a long time, wrote: 'I had to judge at hundreds of trials where

[5] Mabuchi, *Koku-i-ko*.

a man could have saved his fortune, his liberty, his life, by telling a lie; he always refused to do so'.[6] The honesty of the Laotians is proverbial. In Burma people behave with honesty and rectitude because this comes to them naturally and not out of deference for others, nor out of any sense of social responsibility.[7] Already in the twelfth century, the traveller Edrisi marvelled at the equity, the kindness and the pleasant ways of the inhabitants of Zabag and Indian Archipelago. We could continue this list endlessly.

It has to be acknowledged, however, that there are many and important exceptions to these very widespread virtues. These exceptions may be divided into several categories.

Firstly, in a large number of communities the moral code is confined to the relationship with other persons or groups who also observe it. It can only be conceived on a basis of reciprocity that is not only absolute but also evident. When an individual has to do with someone outside his group who is not bound by the same rules, he himself no longer feels bound to apply them.

Thus, in olden days, the Tatars and the Tunguz used to regard as their enemy any man who was not their compatriot and thought that by stealing from him they were only following the natural law.[8] An Arab does not feel himself bound by an oath sworn to a *nasrawy*[9]. It is even likely that the Jews, the Chinese and even the Japanese feel considerably freer in action towards somebody who is not of their race.

This change is particularly marked in contacts with the westerners who penetrated into Asia. On the one hand, it was obvious even to the most unenlightened Asians that our basic codes of honour, morals, etiquette and politeness were very different from theirs. On the other hand, they were faced with invaders, people who had come in order to dominate, convert and colonize them, and whose strength was immeasurably superior to theirs. It is not surprising, therefore, that they should have sought refuge in bad faith and untruth, 'the heroic weapon of the subdued', as it has been called by a student of the Islamic world.

The unfavourable impression left on us has been further accentuated by the fact that westerners have mixed primarily with servants who seek above all to take advantage of the manna brought by the whites and are anxious to get the maximum profit from it, or else with converts to Christianity, who mostly show more appreciation for the new liberties allowed by the foreign religion than for the obligations that go with it, or colleagues trained in our school, more

[6] Sir W. H. Sleeman.
[7] J. S. Furnivall.
[8] J. Gmelin.   [9] Charles Doughty.

253

or less completely westernized, who reject as a whole all the traditional principles in order to unite with the conquerors, in the belief that the future belongs to the latter. Consequently none of these people, at least as they show themselves to us, are really representative, and many of the defects that we see in them are due more to our influence than to their tradition. The Japanese students of Lafcadio Hearn struck the right note when they explained that for them the great transformation which could be brought about by western influence would be to substitute law in the place of ethics —in other words, the fear of the police instead of the fear of God or of the conscience—which is certainly no improvement. Sven Hedin noted sadly that the deceit, lies and theft to be found so commonly among the Yakuts exist in exact proportion to the contact they have had with their conquerors from the West. In northern Siberia the aborigines who have been baptized are the ones who should be trusted least.[10]

Apart from this, there are groups where crime, in some form or another, is endemic. Some have gone in for such practices because they have no other way of procuring the most rudimentary means of existence. Arthur Smith himself recognizes that in China there are everywhere crowds of poor people whose only resource is theft. Others steal as a matter of principle. Thus in India there are certain castes and tribes who have been assassins by profession,[11] or thieves, such as the Dandasi, or forgerers such as the Chapparband. The Kathi of Kathiawar give genealogical and mythological justifications for their right to live on theft. Among the Kagirs theft and crime are not condemned. In Baluchistan, a proverb says: 'The Baluchi who has not been to prison is not a true Baluchi'. Among the Bedouins of the Hadramaut, murders and razzias, like all illnesses, are part of the divine plan.

There are also at the other extreme—but there again extremes meet each other—Hindu, Buddhist, or Sufist sages who have raised themselves to a level where it is no longer necessary to obey rules in order to do the right, just and good thing on any occasion; they are no longer bound by morals as such. 'If you thank the sun for driving away the shadows', explains Vinoba, 'he would reply that he does not know what they are and might even ask you to bring him some so that he may see'. While entire groups, such as the Honen and Shinra groups of Shin Buddhism, the Jodoshinshyo and the Tenri-kyo declare that they reject all obligations, place freedom above rules, and that their essential attitude is to accept all that makes up human life, *vinaya*, it must be admitted that their rate of

10 Hadling.
11 For instance, the Thugs, for religious reasons.

criminality is no higher than that of other groups.

All this diversity arises above all from the fact that the Christian distinction between good and evil is hardly to be found in Asia except among the Semites, who tend to revere, in divinity, a principle of pure justice, the basis of order in this world.

In Islam, where the distinction between good and evil is the result of a more or less arbitrary decision of Allah (in the fourteenth century Jurjani wrote: 'If Allah had declared as good all that he has declared as evil, there would be no obstacle'), sin is not a stigma as it is with us—it is the transgression of a prohibition, a rebellion against Allah.[12] However, for certain schools, such as the Mutazilites, there is absolute good and evil, and reason makes it possible to distinguish between them. That is why the child who has not yet reached puberty, like the madman or the sleeper, cannot sin. The two things are not contradictory, since the primary function of Islamic law was to classify acts according to a religious criterion of good and evil established by Mohammed. Yet, for the Muslims what counts more than the act is the intention. 'Come to me with your intentions and not with your actions', says Allah in the Hadith. Wakisha ben Mabad tells how one day he asked the Prophet what virtue was—and the Prophet answered: 'Ask your heart; virtue is whatever brings peace to the mind and to the heart; sin is whatever agitates the mind and causes turmoil in the breast, whatever men may think of it'.

This attitude is even more marked throughout the rest of Asia, where good and evil are relative, just like error and truth; we move imperceptibly from the worst to the best and the boundary line is far from being as clear as it is in the Decalogue or in our codes. When Lao Tse was asked what difference there was between good and evil, he did not answer; in Chinese thought, 'nothing is good or evil in itself; good and evil arise from the judgement of man who thinks that all that is in conformity with his ideas is good and all that is contrary is bad'. The most striking definition is perhaps that given by the Japanese philosopher Nakae Toju, disciple of the Chinese Wang Yang Ming, who lived in the seventeenth century: 'What is good today' he writes, 'may be seen to be bad tomorrow, because *ryochi*, the conscience, is more than customary morality, it is creative morality'.[13] The Chinese historian Sseu Ma-ts'ien notes that what accounted for the success of holy men is that they did not have identical customs and did not imitate each other. For the Hindu sages the act is nothing and the intention is all.

Often evil is only considered to be less real than good, or else it is regarded as an imperfect vision, a vision which may be improved

[12] Raymond Charles.   [13] Cranmer-Byng.

or even cured, but which does not call for any blame. In the context of *karma* and *dharma*, the evil actions we may commit are partly the consequence of what we have done in previous forgotten lives. In the Tenri-kyo, evil actions form the dust which collects on our mind, and it is enough to sweep it away. While this flexibility and this imprecision might seem difficult to reconcile with the moral strictness we have mentioned, this apparent inconsistency may be explained by a doctrine which India has established with greater clarity than any other country, i.e. that of *svadharma*. According to this theory, the *dharma* of each human being, i.e. the law to which he is subject and must follow, and consequently the moral rules he must observe as well as the mission he has to fulfil in life, differs for each individual according to his sex, caste, age, marital status and many other considerations. Thus, while the Brahmins must not kill on any account, the *kshatriya*, the warrior by caste, must not hesitate to kill his neighbour for the sake of justice; while the head of the family has to earn the money and fulfil the needs of those who are not allowed to exercise lucrative professions, the recluse and the ascetic must live solely on what God sends them without ever accepting any payment for anything they might do.

This is one of the most important foundations of the caste system. Each caste has its own moral code or rather its own series of codes and jealously sees to its application. The sanctions imposed in case of violation go as far as exclusion, which from one day to the next can turn the most respected Brahmin into a *patita*, whom even the lowest of the untouchables would not dare to touch. One may even wonder whether the campaign undertaken by the present Indian Government against the caste system will not sap the magnificent moral structure of the country.

Even if most of the other groups in Asia do not have such a scholarly theory of *svadharma*, this creed is nevertheless at the basis of the moral conceptions held by most of them. In China, a law which is not 'personal' enough to fit the case of a particular person is considered as inhuman and consequently illegal. This has led one author (Lin Yutang) to write that in China justice is not a science but an art. The true sages in China all admit without distinction that the primary duty of any being is to seek the development of his own genius. In Japan the concept of the *nibun* seems to be exactly equivalent to the *svadharma*. In Tibet, every individual creates and follows his own law.[14]

A particular case of this diversity in the moral law is the difference between the human and the divine moral code. Asia considers that the laws governing the gods are not the same as those for us.

[14] Lama Anagarika Govinda.

If this is true for the material plane—even when the gods are not eternal they enjoy a life incomparably longer than ours, since the laws of gravity or mechanics do not apply to them—it must be even more so on the moral plane. When we see in Hindu, Buddhist, Taoist and other mythologies, gods who are wicked, cunning or quarrelsome, libertine or drunk, we should not be indignant that they do not comply with our own standards even if we give a literal interpretation to their myths which, of course, actually have a cosmic or metaphysical significance.

Among the points that intrigue us in the Asian attitude, particular mention must be made of the extremes of non-violence or cruelty.

The example of non-violence preached and practised by Gandhi and by the millions who follow him fanatically is the one that comes the most easily to the mind. 'If blood has to be shed, let it be our own,' he used to proclaim; 'let us cultivate the calm courage to die without killing'. 'For the immortal honour of Dayananda's creed', proclaimed proudly the spokesman of another group; 'it is always the breast of the Arya-Samajist that has been stained with blood, never his hand'. But they were doing no more than conforming to an old and venerable tradition of the Buddhists, the Jains, the Brahmins and other groups. 'To kill is unhealthy', as a Buddhist theologian says laconically but aptly.

'One who is courageous is not violent,' Lao Tse used to say; and he further specified, 'The only part that is really suitable for a victorious general is that of chief mourner.' For Mö Tse war is nothing but brigandage without real benefit; it prevents the two parties from producing true wealth; it ruins the winner, for to enlist soldiers is to leave the fields without farmers, daughters without husbands. According to Tso-Tchuan, weapons exhale a dangerous virtue and should not be handled unless one is duly prepared, through abstinence, to undergo this formidable experience. Another Chinese philosopher has said, 'The greatest crime of all is to wage war'. Besides, in Chinese theatre, the old general is traditionally represented with plumes and banners, puffed up with pride, his mouth black with the corners hanging, all this representing the height of human stupidity. When King Mou, son of Tchao of the Third Dynasty, made a long journey in the Far East—which may well have been a pleasure trip or a series of pilgrimages—tradition blamed him for having undertaken a military expedition, for it was considered wrong to correct the ways of vassals or barbarians by means of arms, the only remedy being the exercise of virtue. We are told by Gernet that China, at the time of the Song, was anti-militarist. In India, quite recently, a splendid album of Chinese poems and paintings has been published to the glory of non-violence.[15]

In Japan, one of the prayers of the Samurai or warriors was 'Tenkai taihei', 'May long peace reign over the earth'. In 643, when the Soga clan massacred the family and friends of the late Prince Shotoku, the partisans of the latter responded by absolute non-violence.

The Buddhists, Jains and some Brahmins do not even have the right to kill poisonous insects, tigers or snakes, and the great warriors and heroes of the *Mahabharata*, the Pandava, after their triumph at Kurukshetra, went to do penance at Politana. The Emperor Babar used to forbid his armies from indulging in pillage, because he did not see any justification for it. Among the Tatars any violence is an unheard-of crime.[16]

Non-violence is respected sometimes even in the Muslim countries. In Irak the Kurd Yazidis may be exempted from military service if they are conscientious objectors. Among the Bedouins to hit a man is considered a sign of bestiality. In Southern Arabia the Sayyids, descendants of al-Faqih al-Muqaddam Muhammad Ali, derive some of their prestige from the fact that they do not carry arms, and certain tribes known as *mashayakh* carry none either. Besides, there are passages in the Koran that forbid recourse to violence.

Nevertheless, throughout Asia at all times, wars and massacres of all kinds have reached a degree of cruelty and savagery unsurpassed in other continents. Battle is often merciless. The Arabs, for instance, do not take prisoners; and besides, the vanquished prefer death to the slavery which would be their lot otherwise. This is taken so much for granted that when a man disappears in wartime, the *idda* of the wife's widowhood begins as soon as the fighting has ended; furthermore, death in battle is not frightening for a Muslim since it ensures him admission into paradise.

The victims indiscriminately massacred in times of war or insurrection may be counted by the million. There were 100,000 of them among the Dungans when they rebelled in 1864-1877, half a million in the Afghan rising under Abdul-Rahman at the end of the last century, a million when Genghis Khan destroyed the town of Ghazni. It was not rare for triumphal arches and pyramids to be built with the heads of the enemy. In Kabul in 1887, two hundred heads had thus been piled up; around 1801 the Afghan Duranis, after their victory against the Ghilzais (also Afghans), built a pyramid of 3,000 heads—and in 1792 the Emir of Bukhara, Rakhim Khan, even had a minaret made of them.

Another detail which may shock us but has really nothing to do

<hr>

[15] Raghu Vira.   [16] J. G. Gmelin.

with cruelty is that the victor sometimes commits cannibalism on the corpse of his enemy. Even to this day, in the heat of battle, the Arab sometimes drinks the blood of the vanquished. In the 1870's the Chinese of Si-nin-fu ate the heart and liver of the Dungan Muslims who had revolted and been massacred. In 1924 Prince Paldan Dolchi, asked by the Mongol government to pursue the 'vindictive Lama' Dambin Jansang into the black Gobi, did the same. The Ostiaks and the Samoyeds have this habit too. The practice should be interpreted above all as a tribute to the opponent and as a desire to assimilate his warlike virtues. And it seems that the Portuguese who came to Asia at the time of the Crusades did not scruple to eat the Turk!

To inflict such cruelty does not demand any exceptional circumstances. The refinement of Chinese torture is proverbial. What is more surprising is that the Jains, apostles of non-violence par excellence, should have equalled and probably even surpassed the Chinese in the punishment of criminals. Formerly in Indo-China, a Buddhist country, it was not unusual for a king, upon ascending the throne, to have all the members of his family massacred or mutilated, and particularly those, such as his brothers, who could have come in his way. In Annam, when Le-Lo i triumphed over the Ming in the fifteenth century, all the Annamite collaborators of the Chinese were killed. Cambodia and Ceylon are no less cruel than their neighbours. In India, among certain groups such as the Savara and in the Telegu country, live pigs are impaled. It is said that not very long ago, among the Kallar of South India, when two women had a violent quarrel, one of them brought and killed her own child before the other's door.

Throughout Asia the great heroes, whether human or divine, are almost all warriors. Even Vishnu, the Hindu god who preserves and protects the universe, when incarnated on earth, often indulges in vast massacres (Parashu-Rama, Ramachandra, Krishna).

All this seems to indicate that in Asia, broadly speaking, apart from the great and admirable exceptions such as those already mentioned, fighting is an integral part of life in general and human life in particular. Mö Ti, although he is the great Chinese prophet of love, devotes several chapters of his work to the art of fortification. Highly respected Hindu monks, themselves incapable of killing, told me that the reason for the butchery that broke out in India at the time of its partition was that Gandhi had exaggerated non-violence, upsetting the natural balance; a reaction had become inevitable.

Furthermore, it is self-evident that these acts, which in our eyes are undeniably cruel, have to be seen in another light if we remember the contempt with which most Asians regard death and even suffering.

Finally, in the act of killing one's fellow, and even in torture, the sense of destiny is a strong factor, the feeling that one is only ful-filling one's predestined mission by executing the divine will against which nothing can be done. 'It is not you (the warriors) who are killing, it is God,' says the Koran. 'Kill them, they who through me are already dead,' Krishna tells Arjuna in the *Bhagavad-Gita*.

In most cases this implacable behaviour is part of a sort of im-plicit code to which the adversaries have unconditionally adhered —and chivalry demands that this code be followed like so many other rules that have excited our admiration. The race of gentlemen brigands has survived much longer in Asia than in Europe.

In China under the earlier Hegemons it was impossible to refuse grain to an enemy suffering from famine; in ancient China a cup was offered to the enemy before battle in order to comfort him; in feudal China adversaries had to fight politely and vied with each other in courtesy and homage, shooting their arrows in turn; fight-ing was regarded as a tournament of moral values, an exchange of honours to be measured against each other.

The code of honour of the Japanese Samurai, the *bu-shi-do* (mili-tary-knight-way), formerly known as the *kyuba no michi* (the way of the bow and the horse), is composed of a series of rules and principles which are in no way inferior to those of our own age of chivalry at its finest. Kenshin, who had waged war against Shingen for fourteen years, when he learnt that the latter's country lacked salt, supplied it.

The Hindu epics contain numerous accounts describing how great warriors, between the battles, treated with the most regal hospitality those very enemies who came to their country in order to kill them in single combat.

This, however, did not preclude cunning from being regarded as a most commendable quality, both in war and in politics.

The Westerner who comes into contact with Asia, either through works of art or through travel, is easily scandalized—or thinks he should be—by the free and uninhibited way in which sexual matters are considered there.

Even the most sacred books such as the Japanese *Kojiki* and the Hindu *Mahabharata* contain many passages which our prudish orientalists have dared to translate only into Latin. The Germans sometimes translate them into French, but the reaction and the precaution are the same. Books on erotic technique which are regarded with respect by all, and which enter into the minutest details, abound in Islam (*el-Ktab*), in India (*Kama-Sutra*, *Ananga Ranga*, etc.), in Japan (*Shkido Okagami*, 'the mirror of the erotic way') and in China (*Ching Ping Mei*), and probably elsewhere also.

Hindu and Lamaistic temples are decorated with sculptures and paintings showing all the possible and even impossible modes of sexual union, and parents visit them with their children of any age without the least embarrassment. In Laos cremation pavilions are often ornamented with drawings that seem obscene to us; and in this same country a traveller (Wusthoff) in the seventeenth century tells the following story with apparent stupefaction : 'We went through a whole village by moonlight, but we could only move forward with difficulty on account of the horrible fornication that was being committed on all sides'. In many areas more or less collective copulation was part of certain important religious ceremonies, and it was only not to shock western visitors, who are incapable of perceiving their deeper meaning, that such practices were given up. As a traveller (Erman), visiting Maimutchen, to the south of Lake Baikal, wrote in the nineteenth century, even in the most distinguished Chinese homes it happened that the most valuable paintings and porcelain often represented the most erotic subjects. The traditions relating to the great lama Lobon Rinpoche, the venerated founder of the 'Old Sect' in Tibet, would be really difficult to print, even today. So much has already been written on these orgiastic or licentious cults of the Orient that there is no need to dwell on them here.

On the other hand, the gods of the Chinese Pantheon are remarkably modest. So much so that, in order to avoid fires, the walls and particularly those of the kitchen are covered with obscene decorations in order to frighten away the God of fire.[17]

It seems that in the eyes of the most qualified Asian thinkers there is no more connection between sexuality and morals than between gymnastics and medicine. Those among them—there are many—who go to the other extreme and recommend absolute continence, do so for reasons of a practical and ritualistic nature. Besides, those subjects in the temples or the sacred texts which seem pornographic to us usually do not suggest any sexual connotation to those who contemplate them; they are so used to the symbolism of the images that they do not associate any other idea with them. The Tibetans, as a great specialist (Govinda) of their country has pointed out, have a disarming objectivity before matters relating to sex. A Hindu is absolutely shocked when he is told that the sacred *lingam* representing Shiva may awaken in the person looking at it ideas or desires of a sexual nature. Ithyphallic statues, according to

[17] V. R. Burckhardt.

some authors, are a symbol of chastity; in the big Hindu temple of Suchindram, the great sages in meditation are represented in this position.

As for the manuals on the 'art of love' and the figures on non-religious works of art, it is obvious that they are very popular; but they doubtless owe their existence partly to the fact that most Asian women are, if not frigid as those of Siberia are reputed to be,[18] at least passive and unimaginative, and partly also because Asian man thinks that if something is worth doing, it is worth doing well.

It must be added that practically throughout Asia it would be literally obscene for a woman and a man to exchange signs of affection, even the most discreet signs, in public. We have already seen how strict are the rules imposed on the couple within the family. In the street, while two men might readily hold hands, it would be most improper for a man and a woman—even if they are most legally married—to take romantic walks together or even to walk arm in arm; not so long ago, this could be taken as a reason for arrest for immoral behaviour in the streets of Tokyo; and again in the same country the French word 'avec' is used to designate the couples who have the indecency to sit side by side in public. The kiss, particularly on the mouth, was unknown and incomprehensible for almost all Asians till it was revealed to them through American films, and even today it is regarded with a certain horror, even by prostitutes. In China, Viet-Nam and India people do not even kiss a child but 'smell' its head. However, this behaviour in public is not necessarily related to the attitude towards sexuality.[19]

In addition, if we remember what we have said about modesty, and the fact that Asians in touch with the West are deeply shocked by the constant preoccupation with sex in our books, our newspapers, our films, our publicity, it is hard to draw clear and simple conclusions—and it is not surprising that the same people give rise to considerable differences of opinion among the specialists. Thus, with respect to the Chinese, Kalgren sees phallic symbols everywhere, even in their script. Granet, while acknowledging that sexual themes abound in their literature, sees no reason to believe that the Chinese ever contemplated divinizing sex. And de Groot affirms that the Chinese never, either in their religious conceptions or in their

---

[18] 'The young girls and women of Siberia are frozen fish', wrote Chekhov; 'in order to flirt with them, one has to be a seal'.

[19] In connection with Islam, Charles points out that the prudishness which prohibits ambiguous poses in public and forbids nudity, even of the face, should not mislead us; the blunt wording of the Scriptures, the obscenity of the language used even in front of young children, and especially the number of crimes of passion in their criminal statistics, are eloquent.

practices, gave any importance to sensuality. It is better to confine ourselves to noting various facts—for instance, that the Chinese ritualists do not believe in excesses of debauchery, but even less in excesses of chastity; or that the Taoist sage preserves, improves and refines his *yin* and his *yang* by the combined use of sexual hygiene (without any continence) and respiratory exercises.[20]

With regard to virginity, adultery and incest, the conceptions of Asia are perhaps less difficult for a Westerner to understand, but they vary from one extreme to the other according to the countries and the races, even in areas fairly close to each other.

This is true with regard to the rule that a girl must remain a virgin until marriage. Generally speaking, any breach of this rule is thought extremely serious and may lead to heavy sanctions, either in Japan, China, India or Islam. In Oman, as also among the Eravallar in India, the unmarried pregnant girl was simply put to death. In China, in the thirteenth century, she would have been thrown out into the street without mercy. Among some Indian tribes, such as the Agasa, Alitkar, Bari and others, she was driven away from her caste, while among the Bajania of Gujarat the man would be heavily punished. Among the Uppiliyan to marry a virgin is so important for a man that he may not shave until he has done so. In Siberia, the Tunguz girls who let themselves be seduced are tied to a bush and flogged with twigs till these are broken.

However, adjustments may sometimes be made. In India, among the Urali, the Ahir, the Dhor and others, it is sufficient if the man who has seduced a girl marries her—which he is compelled to do—provided that they both belong to the same caste. Other groups take an even less tragic view of things. Among the Kabbera of South India, for instance, pre-marital relations are allowed upon payment of a sort of tax. The Hati of Kathiawar impose a small fine.

The Kolymyans, Yakuts and Tchuktches seem to attach no value to female virtue. There are also some Indian tribes, such as the Bhil, the Hallir of Kanara, the Helav, the Holaya, etc., where girls are allowed complete sexual freedom before marriage.

In the Central Borneo plateaux pre-nuptial promiscuity is normal; in India the Yanadi, and in Northern Laos the Khmu, attach no importance to a husbandless pregnancy. The Valaiyan of South India even consider the children that are born in such cases as legitimate. Trial marriages are permitted among the Dhangar, the Mahar and the Muduvar. Some groups even consider the child of an unmarried mother as a sort of bonus. In Yakutsk girls who already had a male child were very much sought after for marriage, for the birth of a boy among the Cossacks means a considerable additional

[20] Marcel Granet.

allowance for the father, and with a woman who has already become a mother, there were better chances of having one. Similarly, the Buddhist Buryats prefer to marry a woman who already has a child, for they are then surer of having a family; the child born before marriage calls his mother 'sister', and he is supposed to be the son of his grandparents. Among the Nayar, in India, a man does not like to take a virgin, and a girl often has much trouble in finding a volunteer. We should no doubt mention the elegant lines of an Afghan poet of the fifteenth century, Pir Rochan, who wrote: 'A woman is a flower; everyone has the right to breathe her scent.' In Shanghai we have the case of a nun who, in 1934, brought a lawsuit against a monk for infidelity! Finally there are groups like the Bandi in Kanara for whom marriage is an exceptional thing.

With respect to adultery, there are of course no statistics to establish whether it is more frequent in Asia than in the West, but it may be noted that the attitude towards it varies greatly among different societies.

Among the Arabs of the Hadramaut, the Ghiliak of Eastern Siberia, as formerly among the Jains of India, adultery is punished by death, although among the latter the sentence could be commuted to torture or mutilation. Among other peoples, although the penalty is not actually capital, it is nonetheless terrible: among the Gavada and the Nambutiri, funerary ceremonies are held for the guilty, and similarly among the Kappiliyan when the other party is not one of the caste. Among the Raniyava the woman is stripped of her jewels and regarded as a widow—which is almost as serious as death. Among the Savara, the husband who catches his wife red-handed has the right to kill her himself as well as her accomplice. In the Thai Khun Chang Khun Phaen, a woman who cannot choose between two men she loves is beheaded.

Ostracism is another punishment applied by numerous groups: the Kappiliyan, the Toreya (where both parties may be readmitted into the caste once the injured husband is dead), the Parivaram (when the accomplice is outside the caste, with a sinister addition in the last case—a mud statuette is made of the outsider and thorns embedded in its eyes). Even as late as the nineteenth century, the Samaya of the Bangalore area used to sell loose women, whatever their caste. Among the Siviyar the woman and her accomplice are flogged.

Other groups are less severe. Among the Bakuda, the Koraga and other Indian tribes, the adulteress has to go through seven huts built for that purpose, which are then burnt. The various groups of Laos, the Bavacha, the Paniyan, the Pano, and others in South India, are content to inflict a small fine. The Uppara make the wife's family pay such a fine, while the Ulladan procure it from the accomplice who is furthermore beaten, while all that the woman has to do is to drink the milk of a coconut in order to purify herself. Among the Valaiyan, the woman is simply reprimanded or slightly humiliated. The Annupan simply forbid the guilty woman to remarry as long as her husband is alive. The Savara and the Goa Kudubi punish only the man.

The womenfolk of the Buddhist Mongols are reputed to be very free in their ways and the same is said of the white Tais and the Turkmen women. It seems that the Tibetan women think it quite natural to deceive their husbands. In Irkutsk, the only prohibition regarding adultery was apparently that it should not be committed before an icon—without veiling it first with a curtain. In Japan, no doubt as a reaction against these cruel rules, there are nowadays couples in which each party keeps his full liberty.

Let us point out that conjugal fidelity hardly seems to grow with the progress of civilization or with rank. Among one of the most backward peoples of the world, the Veddas of Ceylon, adultery seems to be completely unknown; and the Nayadi, probably the lowest caste in the whole of India, has a horror of it.

As for incest, it is as rare in Asia as in the West, although the bounds within which it is permitted are not always the same as ours. Even the peoples—and there are many—who consider that the human race began with the inevitable incest between the two members of the original couple who, being born of the same divine parents were of necessity brother and sister, often endeavour to explain and excuse this as being the result of a mistake or an intoxication deliberately provoked by the gods. Some legislation and custom go further than ours. For instance, Muslim law, as regards incest, assimilates 'milk-relationship' with blood relationship by forbidding the union of the former foster-child, even if he had been fed but once, with one of his foster parents.

There are exceptions however. Under the Sassanides, marriage was allowed between brother and sister with an exorcistic value, *khwetuk-das*. This type of union was current in very ancient Japan. In our own era incest is allowed in the Lan-Xang family in Laos, among the Pulluvan in South India and among the Arunadan, where normally the father takes his eldest daughter as his second wife. We have mentioned the case of the Kudiya, where a woman may marry her eldest son. In Golla, in India, it was common for a man to marry his mother-in-law.

As may be expected, morals are less exacting in the case of men. Among the Kelabites in Borneo the number of conquests made by the young man before marriage is a feather in his cap to be displayed at festivals by the same number of grains of rice carefully piled up. Prostitution, therefore, is very much in vogue throughout Asia and men resort to it quite openly.

The women living by the sale of their bodies belong to various degrees, from the courtesan of the highest rank[21] to the woman who stands at her door and hails the passers-by and who is despised just like other men and women engaged in the humblest and most degrading labour.

With respect to women who earn their own living and often have dependants (children, old parents, brothers and sisters who are younger or have the promise of a better future), Asia does not differentiate very much between those who lend their bodies for sexual purposes with passing men and those who use their bodily strength in other physical labour, or their intellectual and artistic faculties in the service of more or less regular employers or customers. What is more important is the difference of quality between women within the same profession.

In order to explain the attitude of Jesus towards Mary Magdalene, the European or American Christian is obliged to suppose that she underwent a total and instantaneous transformation that led her from extreme vice to the diametrically opposite extreme of saintliness. But even were such a theory to be required by the Gospel, for an Asian like Jesus the courtesan's profession was doubtless a much smaller obstacle to salvation than the possession of great wealth or the hypocrisy of a Pharisee, which preclude all chances of reaching Paradise. In the Old Testament no excuse appears to be necessary in order to explain the fact that the direct ancestry of the Messiah includes the union between Boaz and Ruth, a woman who sold him her body. Furthermore, in India Ramakrishna used to place a prostitute far above the man who self-righteously criticizes his fellow being.

When in traditional Asia schools and institutions are especially set up for women of easy virtue, it is not in order to tear them away from 'sin' or to facilitate their access into a life described as virtuous, but rather in order to teach them to perfect their art. This is also the subject of some of the greatest classics mentioned earlier.

The courtesan's profession has nothing dishonourable about it. We have a fairly recent case in Japan of a prime minister who had married a woman he met in a bordello, and it occurred to nobody to blame him or to ostracize his wife.

[21] The Japanese *geishas* and the Chinese *sing-song girls*, as well as the famous *deva-dashis* of India, grant their favours only after long courting; they often have ladies-in-waiting in their service.

Some countries, particularly India, until recent times had a special category of prostitutes attached to the service of temples. These women were subject to very severe rules of living and were actually regarded as the brides of the god worshipped in the temple. In many areas, when one of them died the god was regarded as being in the state of a widower and therefore impure until the cremation, and no cult could be held in his honour until then. Inversely, the woman could never become a widow, and this was doubtless one of the main reasons why she was supposed to bring luck. Even in the highest castes it was compulsory for such women to take part—and sometimes an active part—in marriage festivals. Even a Protestant priest had to acknowledge that throughout India the *deva-dashis* are the most accomplished women. In China also, a marriage is hardly considered a fine one without the presence of 'songstresses'. At Vijayanagar prostitutes were allowed to approach the kings' wives and—a supreme honour—chew betel with them.

Much has been said about prostitution as a form of hospitality. While it is far from being as common as is sometimes supposed, it does exist among certain groups, such as the Tchuktches, the Koryaks, the Black Kirghiz, the Northern Tunguz, the Buryats, some groups of North Siam, certain Hezareh tribes of the Hindu Kush and the Malayali of India. In Tibet, reports a recent traveller, a servant is sometimes also offered to the visitor, but she is at liberty to refuse. This custom was sometimes related to that of trial marriage (as among the nobles of feudal China) or even with bloody rites of alliance.

Homosexuality also seems to be extremely widespread throughout Asia—in the Near East, in China and in Japan—and it is not frowned upon. In Tibet, in the monasteries, it is even regarded as a guarantee of chastity, and the warrior priests, the *thab-to*, sometimes fight duels for the favours of some young Ganymede. In various countries, particularly in India, we see manifestations of sacred homosexuality. Thus, in Vrindavan all the worshippers of the Lord Krishna consider themselves as his lovers. In Kuvvakkam, Kottatai and other places in South India, the people celebrate the memory of Iravan or Aravan, also known as Kuttandar, son of the great hero Arjuna who, at the beginning of the battle of Kurukshetra, spontaneously offered himself as a sacrifice to the gods in order to compensate for a white elephant sacrificed by the enemy's army; as Iravan died before being married, many men dress as women specially for the occasion and come to 'wed' him publicly at the time of the festival.

Coupling with animals is not unknown on the Asian continent. This is proved by numerous passages in various sacred texts, which lay down different punishments for this crime, as for instance in the Bible (Exodus XXII, 18; Leviticus XVIII, 23; Deuteronomy XXVII, 21), in the Japanese *Kojiki* (Section XCVII), where it is forbidden to couple with horses, cattle, fowl and dogs.

CHAPTER XIV

Social Relationships

It is by serving men that one can tame men.

LAO-TSÉ

IN the different societies of Asia the relations between individuals are marked by an extraordinary concern for dignity, honour, decorum and politeness. This is considered not merely as an optional refinement, even less as a luxury, but rather as one of the most essential foundations of life in common and often takes precedence over all other considerations.

Conversation in Arabic is punctuated with actual tournaments of politeness and compliments, which are sometimes extremely subtle and made to last as long as possible.[1] The Chinese vie with each other in humility so that their conversations sometimes become almost unintelligible. A European who has spent a long time in China told me that the Chinese constantly give us lessons in humility. The Japanese keep exchanging interminable bows among themselves, whatever be the social rank of the persons concerned. And these are only a few of the signs most apparent to the western observer. We have seen earlier to what extent rage or even bad temper are alien to Asian behaviour. The Japanese language has absolutely no swear words.

This refined politeness in most countries is being gradually destroyed by the introduction of modern western ways of living, and countless travellers note this with sorrow.[2]

Whatever may be the more or less conscious profound reason behind this, the rules of elementary and honest civility are innumerable and of infinite variety among the different races. They are often unexpected and disconcerting for us, and a breach of these

[1] For the Muslim the spectrum of shades of meaning to be observed varies every minute according to circumstances. (Raymond Charles).
[2] Harry Williams deplores this fact as regards Ceylon : 'A gentle, courteous people are becoming rude, vulgar and obstreperous, particularly where western education prevails'. Elsewhere he describes 'the standards of truth, courtesy, marital fidelity and simple kindness' of the Veddas.

rules is generally a serious offence. Here are a few instances: In Persia, India, Laos and various other countries of south-east Asia, when receiving something from a superior, the extended right hand has to be supported underneath by the left hand. Table manners regulate the minutest details. In feudal China, when boiled fish was served, its back had to be turned to the guest's right in summer and to his left in winter.

In various Asian languages, particularly in Thai, in Cambodian, Laotian and Japanese, as well as in certain South Indian languages, the vocabulary changes almost completely according to the person addressed, depending on whether he is a superior, equal or inferior. In Laos, personal pronouns follow a hierarchy similar to that of society; the Lao calls himself by the word *khoy* (slave) when he speaks to an equal, *kha noy* (little slave) when he speaks to a superior, and *kha pha chao* (slave of Buddha) in the administrative style when he speaks to the crowd. In Laos again, a very severe law inflicted a fine in money on those who publicly showed contempt of others and spoke to them with too much pride, and this could be done without any court procedure.

In Viet-Nam, even when an act is completely spontaneous, one has to pretend that it was done in deference to a fictitious order. For this purpose, the words *thu a* 'reply, report', *vang* 'to obey', *bam* 'refer, inform' are placed before the subject or the main clause of the reply. It is replaced by *dam* 'to dare' or *man phep* 'to have been impolite' whenever one does not share the opinion of the other person. One must also avoid looking into the face of the other person and, if necessary, apologize in consequence; that is why the word *trom*, 'furtively, on the sly', is used as a term of courtesy roughly in the same way as *dam*. It then means 'with your permission', 'if you do not mind'.[3]

In Burma, all the actions of everyday life are subject to the etiquette governing the relationship between inferiors and superiors. In Laos, as well as in Thailand, one is not allowed to approach a superior without crawling or walking on all fours.

For four centuries, the whole individual and social conduct of the Japanese has been determined by the rules of etiquette laid down by the Ogasaware school. *Bu-shi-do*, the code of chivalry which has exerted such a profound influence on the behaviour of the Japanese elite, is as detailed as it is intransigent. Some years ago, in a temple, when a minister inadvertently lifted the curtain hiding the shrine, he was assassinated soon after, and the murder was considered to be a heroic and virtuous deed. Suicide (*seppuku*), which we have mentioned earlier, is often made obligatory by the code of honour

[3] Pierre Huard and Maurice Durand.

even in order to expiate others' faults. But apart from these subtle and refined laws, we note among the Japanese, in all classes of society, an innate distinction, a natural politeness, a subtle and constant delicacy which fills us with wonder, all the more so when we learn to perceive and understand it better. The essence of politeness is to say only what is expected of you. The foundation for this lies in an inner pattern of behaviour which a Japanese has correctly defined by these three terms: cleanliness (in its widest sense), calm (inner calm) and complete absence of haste. We find a typical example in the fifth century in the two sons of the Emperor Seimei, who were polite to each other for so long, each one wishing to surrender the throne to the other, that finally their sister, Princess Iitoyo O, had to settle the matter by taking the power herself and keeping it until her death

It is Chinese culture, however, that has acquired, and perhaps justly so, the reputation of having turned etiquette and its rites into 'the foundation of the one and only order' which is born of civilization and presides over universal life, both social and cosmic. The books on this subject would in themselves fill a vast library, and wherever this etiquette has spread it has left its mark. The place to be occupied in a gathering, the words to be spoken, the time to do it, the minutest details of costume or dress, the tone of voice, the gait, everything had a ritual value, and the least error would have been a religious offence.

Man lives by his 'face' and the tree by its bark, says a Chinese proverb. Within the family, even the relationship between father and son is one essentially of honour between two persons. On the wider plane of society it has been said that by devoting their life to the cult of etiquette the Chinese of feudal times succeeded in avoiding the trouble that can be caused by an anarchic search for justice and truth. Another Chinese proverb says: 'If you meet an old man, call him grandfather, one who is not so old, uncle, and one of your age, elder brother'. Even the change-over from one dynasty to another can be carried out with the greatest courtesy.

It is not unlikely, however, that all this etiquette sprang from entirely different causes—firstly, that of never being indebted (in politeness) to the other party in order not to be in a position of dependency on him, and secondly the anxiety not to make oneself prominent by accepting a position that is considered as superior by any person. This latter conception is closely connected with the constant endeavour made by the Chinese to follow the 'middle way', which is in no way a compromise as we often tend to imagine but rather an effort to be in tune with nature, where we never find extreme solutions.

Besides, he who departs from this rule condemns himself hopelessly; as the person himself is aware of this, he sometimes even acts as if he were doomed; unbridled passion may then follow moderation, but this exception only confirms the rule.

This rule is specified in extraordinary detail in the I-Ching, this book which the Chinese presume, not without reason, to be fabulously ancient, since it lays down the most fundamental features of their daily behaviour. To give two instances of its application, both in the field of education: a young pupil, although he may potentially be 'the great and powerful dragon', must temporarily adopt an attitude of perfect humility before his seniors, the professor, the principal, etc. and keep quiet. When he reaches the intermediary level, he becomes more free and may complain to the principal, etc. When he reaches the third level, the higher classes, on the contrary, he is very much in the limelight and might incur serious beatings if he is too forward and too enterprising, for it is he who is held responsible by the authorities. The same holds good in the three grades of the teaching staff. When the young professor is in the lowest grade, the fourth, he owes respect and deference to his seniors, to the principal, etc. In the fifth grade he may take any initiative, display his strength, etc. But if he is rash enough to accede to the sixth grade, that is, to become the principal himself, he is once more very much exposed and in a very dangerous position.

Perhaps it is the same anxiety that leads to the total absence of ostentation among the Malays.

Indeed, it is most important of all to avoid 'losing face'. 'Keeping face' is in various Asian countries the preoccupation which might override all others. A Chinese tailor prefers to lose a sum which is considerable for him rather than confess that he has made a professional error. For a Japanese, to be despised and ridiculed is so serious that often the only solution is to emigrate to another province.

This preoccupation with decorum and courtesy goes hand in hand with a respect for authority which sometimes seems incredible to us. The Asian may consider this as a curse or a blessing, but for him it remains the divine right and may in no case be challenged. A king, says the Indian *Ramayana*, is a god visiting the earth. In Islam, since God is all-powerful, he who wields power on earth is obviously approved by Him. At the Imperial Palace of Tokyo, many women come every day asking for permission to do the household work in the various buildings and parks free of charge in order to enjoy the privilege of having served the Emperor. In India, during the British occupation, it was not unusual to see people bow whenever they passed in front of pillar-boxes because these bore the crowned monogram of the King-Emperor.

Up to recent times it would never have occurred to an Asian man or woman to claim the right of challenging the discretionary will of those in power, whoever they may have been. In some countries they were even credited with miraculous powers. Thus, for instance in Thailand, it is believed that any person enjoying authority, whether a policeman or gangster, is invulnerable. The Japanese think it quite natural for police officers to search their homes once every fortnight, and in their language the term *matsurigoto*, government, comes from *matsuri*, cult or worship.

The idea of liberty or human rights is a recent one imported from the West. The Asian used to be conscious of his duties and his powerlessness, but not of the rights he could claim from his superiors. He used to enjoy rights only over his inferiors. It seems that the Chinese language contains a term corresponding to the idea of freedom only since the early nineteenth century. The only way of avoiding compliance with an authority's order in the Far East was suicide. This acceptance of obedience to a higher rank, and a social order where the concept of equality is unknown, as in the caste system, is counterbalanced sometimes by great freedom on the spiritual and religious level, as in India, or a sort of sheltered independence and plasticity for the development of the mind, as in China.

Traditional society in almost all Asian countries is based on a strict hierarchy. However, this term should be understood to mean something quite different from the sense we give to it; and there we have, no doubt, one of the most marked and essential differences between Asia and the West. While we think primarily, if not exclusively, in terms of a hierarchy of rights and privileges, Asia thinks primarily, if not exclusively, in terms of a hierarchy of obligations and responsibilities: the higher the position within the family or the society, the more numerous and strict are the rules and the prohibitions. More than anywhere in Europe, the expression 'noblesse oblige' is true.

It is true that even in the Far East, at different periods, there were schools like that of Han Fei-tse in China 2,000 years ago which used to preach equality among all men before the law, and their theories were often applied, but it was nonetheless a fact that the rights and duties of individuals differed greatly, and each one could exact respect of those that resulted from his own personal and social position.

Generally speaking, while for the westerner a sense of individual *rights* is fundamental and is protected and developed by our conception of justice,[4] in the traditional East there is an awareness only of the duties which have to be fulfilled correctly by everyone of the social scale, from top to bottom. A human rights charter is an almost incomprehensible concept in Asia—and this does not only hold good for the Confucian, as it has often been suggested. It has been written rather relevantly and not without humour that in the West people are so preoccupied with the right to vote, the right to appear in court if arrested, the right to supervise the state budget, that they seem to have forgotten completely the simple right to happiness. Now, while the Chinese have never been very anxious about the rights that we claim, they have always shown themselves to be terribly exacting when it came to the right to be happy, and they have never allowed poverty or imprisonment to deprive them of it.

In this connection it must also be noted that the oriental in general does not suffer from any conflict between duties—the source of the richest and noblest subjects in our literature—nor the perplexity that goes with it. Neither Rama in India, nor the Confucian in China, nor the pious Muslim ever feel any doubt—although they might sometimes be wrong. There is never any conflict of allegiances either, for when there are more than one they are clearly categorized according to a scale of values which nobody would dream of challenging. Gandhi in India and Confucius in China have given clear lists to this effect, and elsewhere, even if there are no such specific documents, the concept is nonetheless quite clear.

In many societies it is considered that the hierarchy is pre-established, has been there forever and is of divine origin.

In their diplomatic protocol, Gengis-Khan and his successors used the opening formula, 'In the force of Eternal Heaven'.

The Emperor of Japan draws his power directly from his ancestor Jimmu-Tenno who has been commissioned by the gods to govern the world—and he does not even need to be crowned. The Emperor of China is the Son of Heaven. Furthermore, we have already seen that most of the sovereigns have superhuman origins.

This hierarchy of duties is most apparent in the caste system, the best example of which is to be found in Hindu society. The members of the lowest castes may eat and drink whatever they want, earn their living as they think fit, be clean or dirty as they wish, while the *dvija*, the 'twice born' of the upper castes, have to submit to incredibly strict rules of living in all spheres. In the Gaud Sarasvat one group was excommunicated for having taken a meal with Hindus who had been in Europe; they are the Landonvala. While

---

[4] Granet says that in order to understand Asia, we must rid ourselves of the idea of law imposed upon our minds by a narrow-minded admiration for the Roman world.

abuse of this system has been attacked and often corrected by great reformers throughout history—as was the case for all the other social systems—almost none of them, with the exception of Buddha —has ever attacked the principle. Gandhi himself saw the caste system as a law of Nature which had been turned into a science by the Hindus. Even the very westernized A. Coomaraswamy, who lived nearly all his life in America, regarded this system as the one which up to now has come closest to a society not aiming at equality based on competition, but where all interests would be considered as having the same value. In *Spiritualité hindoue* I myself have given a large number of facts and authorized opinions which all too often tend to be ignored. Let us simply mention a few details which will suffice to show that the problem is far from being as simple as is often imagined in the West. Firstly, it is not only the upper castes that are anxious to uphold the system; the lower castes, including the outcasts, are just as attached to it and, for instance, if a Brahmin ventures to enter the untouchables' quarter he might well be seriously molested. Then there are castes, such as the Pulayas and the Vettuvan, the Marayan and the Nayar, the Panan and the Kaniyan, that are mutually untouchable and where the members have to purify themselves if they come too close to each other. Finally, there are even Brahmins, among the Prathamasaki, who are untouchable, *paraiyan*, for one and a half hours every day.

The Jains do not disapprove of the caste system and they have it too. The same system is to be found in many other countries. In Ceylon castes still prevail not only in the villages, where they are absolute in character, but even among the westernized people in town, and one of the lowest castes, the *rodiya*, 'rat eaters', regard themselves as being of princely descent.

In Korea, not so long ago, the four castes were clearly divided and extremely important.

In Badakhstan (Tajikistan) there were five castes: the *shana*, the *seid*, the *mir*, the *akabyr* and the *ryot*.

In Tibet there are four noble castes: the *ger-pa*, sort of peers, among whom are the *yabshi* (or dukes), the *ngak-pa* ('miracle doers'; that is, the descendants of the Lamas who have wrought miracles and who are generally poor but honoured by the *ger-pa*), the *bon-bo* (descendants of the bon priests who transmit the latters' traditions), and the *shal-ngo* (descendants of former chiefs). Below this, the people are divided into *tong-ba* and *tong-du*. Even below that there are the *parias* who are fishermen and boatmen, blacksmiths and butchers. Finally, right at the bottom of the social scale we have the mixtures between different castes.[5]

[5] Shramana Eita Kawaguchi.

Japanese society also comprised four or five groups: the nobles, the soldiers, the priests, the farmers and the merchants; however, from the end of the tenth century onwards there were only the Samurai on the one hand and the remainder of the people on the other; but the Samurai were themselves divided into various strictly self-contained classes and nobody could move to a higher caste, even through adoption. There were also the famous *eta* and the other outcasts, who respectively numbered about 300,000 and 700,000 when the system was abolished in 1871.

In China, the population was also traditionally divided into four distinct groups: the *shih*, officers and scholars (which included the *ch'en* or State officials, and the *shen shih* or nobles), the *nung* or farmers, the *kung* or craftsmen, and the *shang* or merchants. In Viet-Nam, also, there were the same four classes: the *si* or scholars, the *nong* or farm labourers, the *cong* or craftsmen and the *thu o ng* or merchants. In both these countries, however, unchallenged popularity or personality, together with the right omens, made it possible for the poorest to rise to the highest social positions.

This system is to be found even in some Muslim Arab countries. In the Hadramaut, for instance, there are four castes: the *sayyid*, who are descendants of the apostle Sayyid Ahmad ibn 'Isa al-Muhajir, the *qabili*, citizens descended from tribes, the *meskin* or manual workers, and the *dha'if*. In Dhufar a distinction is made between the nobles (members of tribes), the *dha'af*, the *bahara* and the slaves.[6]

The practice of separation into castes has not always been abolished by the Christian churches in their religious ceremonies. Considerable evidence of this is to be found in north as well as south India.

The caste system naturally goes hand in hand with the conception of a class right at the bottom of the social ladder, that of the slaves. Not so long ago they were to be found all over Asia, as in the West less than two centuries ago. The Koran explicitly acknowledges their existence. In Korea slavery was officially abolished in 1911, and in a good part of Arabia it survives even now on a large scale. Nevertheless, in most Asian countries it was eliminated less than half a century after its disappearance from Europe; and there are even some countries, such as China, where we were considerably forestalled—at a very early date the Chinese Empire granted its peasants the legal status of free men, which was higher than that of European peasants up to modern times; serfdom was abolished in China two thousand years ago.

It must not be forgotten either that the West has taken a very

[6] Bertram Thomas.

active part in the white slave trade in Asia, just as in the case of the black slaves sent out to the United States, the West Indies and Brazil. The Genoese and Venetians used to provide Saxon, Slavonic and Circassian slaves to the Levantine and other Muslims in exchange for gold and thereby make large profits; in Siberia, the Russians bought and sold white slaves up to the end of the nineteenth century in Yarkand and Kashgar, particularly men of the Upper Oxus and the pretty girls from the Chitral, and inversely. Russians were frequently reduced to slavery by the nomads of the steppes.

Let us note further that, in many cases, being a slave does not in any way hinder access to power or opulence. In southern Arabia, even to this day, many a slave becomes a governor, commander-in-chief or prime minister; they may even possess their own slaves, and there are some degrading tasks, such as sweeping away the carcasses of animals, which the slaves leave to their masters.

In other Asian countries, the hierarchy is established according to a democratic election system. This is the case among the Yakuts, where the supreme head of the Ulus and the other chiefs have to be elected, although they have to be chosen from princely families. The same is true of the Kirghiz-Kaisaks, where the sultans of the three hordes, as well as minor chiefs, are elected for three years at a time and are re-eligible. This was also the case with the Ostiaks of the Obe in the eighteenth century and among the Bashkirs who used to elect their officers. Chroniclers report that in 2333 B.C. Shininn was apparently elected king of Korea under the name of Dan-Koon, and even if this is only pure legend, it nonetheless goes to show that this method of appointment had nothing surprising about it. Even the emperors of the Mongols were elected, and this was the case of the son of Gengis-Khan himself.

This method of appointment does not seem in any way to have undermined the divine nature of the head, no more than the election of the Catholic Pope raises doubts as to his infallibility. The same happens when the dynasty is overthrown and replaced by a rival lineage or even by the most unaristocratic of usurpers.

The absolute priority of duties over rights, even when one is conscious of the latter, prevails in the republican type of society just as much as in any other Asian society. This existed in India even in Krishna's day several millenniums before our era, and it was to be found in the Tobolsk area as late as the early nineteenth century. This system is not even contrary to Koranic law, and when recently the Islamic Republic of Pakistan was founded, apparently there was not a word of protest from any theologian.

In some of the most autocratic societies of Asia, popular consultation or polling was sometimes practised. The Japanese consultation of 604, promulgated by Prince Shotoku, in its Article 17 provided that the people has to be consulted on all important matters. The grave decisions of Gengis-Khan were taken after consultation with huge assemblies representing the people governed. In China, there was a Council of Censors, *Tu Ch'a Yuan*, which even criticized the Emperor.

In other countries the entire hierarchy is established exclusively on the basis of merit, regardless of origin.

Thus Burma was a real 'community of equals', and there was no class barring the way between the king and the masses; social rank was determined solely on the basis of knowledge. The same may be said of Thai society where there is no hierarchy of families.

The best example, however, is the traditional Chinese organization of the mandarinite, a political and social system which remained effective, almost unchanged, for about two thousand years. Only the sons of beggars and prostitutes and, at a certain period, also merchants' sons, were not allowed access to it, and no member was born noble. In China even the celestial mandate which authorized kings to reign, could only be the result of the merit (*kong*), if not of the individual himself, at least of a Great Ancestor.

In China under the reign of the Emperor Wou of the Han, the principal councillors were former swineherds, vagabonds, labourers, grooms. The same holds good for modern Japan : Sachio Sakurauchi, secretary general of the powerful Minseito, had begun life as a bean-curd (*tofu*) vendor; Korekiyo Takahashi, one of the most remarkable men in modern Japan, was an illegitimate child and had been a mine worker; Ugaki, in his youth, used to work for six yen per month; Hirohito was the son of a stone-cutter; Yosuke Matsuoka had been a lift-boy; at the age of fourteen Araki was an apprentice in a soya factory; General Minami, as a child, had to walk to Tokyo because he had no money to do otherwise.

In the Muslim countries, while some of the most important posts are normally reserved for the members of the reigning family and some other very great families, all the others are filled solely according to merit. Even in those areas, such as southern India, where the caste system was strictest, nothing could prevent a man of the lowest caste from having access to the highest office.

The increase of duties and responsibilities as one goes up the social scale is strikingly illustrated by the position of the chief in nearly all the Asian countries. There seems to be 'a conviction that the master of men is a reflection of the absolute Master'.

In China, 'deities and chiefs are but one'[7] and one character
designates the divine, the holy, the sage and the emperor.
The emperor had the mission of interpreting to creation the
will of the creator. According to what he is, men and plants are
said to multiply or not, rivers to flow or dry up. Rash or guilty
action on the part of the emperor may directly lead to public
calamity, and there are cases in history where, in order to save his
people, he has confessed his faults publicly. In the second century
before our era the Emperor Wou proclaimed, 'The heavenly way,
T'ien tao, would have calamity spring from hateful actions and
prosperity come as a result of virtue. The faults of all the officials
must originate in my person.'[8] The emperor reigns over nature
just as he does over his subjects; he is responsible both for the order
of the seasons and the prosperity of the country. After a long
drought, T'ang the Victorious cut off his hair and nails and probably
buried them in the ground—and the rain came. Renouvier has
written: 'Under the Empire, the Son of Heaven . . . governs the
course of time . . . In order to play this part, he should not act or
regulate, but concentrate his virtue, edify and educate, for he does
not impose order, he secretes it.' Masson-Oursel writes: 'The
sovereign ordains by his direct action rather than through commandments.' 'The chief's thoughts,' writes Granet, 'know no bounds.
He thinks of the horses and they become stronger. The chief's
thoughts are untiring—he thinks of the horses and they rush forward. The chief's thoughts are upright—he thinks of the horses and
they go straight.'

The same applies to Japan where, as we have seen, the emperor
is a god incarnate. It is his duty to enter into mystical communion with the spirit of the race, and we see much evidence of
this. In 319, the Emperor Nintoku proclaimed, 'The poverty of the
people is my poverty; the prosperity of the people is my prosperity.
For the people to be prosperous and the prince poor is something
that cannot happen.'

In one of his best-known poems, the Emperor Meiji wrote in the
nineteenth century:

> 'If the people commit any sin whatsoever,
> May the heavenly deities punish me for it,
> Since all my people is born of me.'

Emperor Hirohito not long ago gave a magnificent example of this
attitude at the time of the American occupation. If we go back
further into the past we find the Shagi No which took place at a

[7] Marcel Granet.   [8] Marcel Granet.

time when the virtues of the Emperor were such that even the animals used to obey him.

In Thailand, when there is a cholera epidemic or drought, the king accepts personal responsibility for it; in 1925, when lightning hit a peasant's buffalo, he turned against the governor of the province, 'the Lord of Heaven', who had to compensate him. In Fou-yu (Korea), if the harvest happened to fail, the blame was laid on the king.

This crushing burden of responsibility naturally implies certain moral, spiritual and psychic conditions to be fulfilled by the chief. Even those who are judged extremely severely among us according to our modern western criteria, often deserve respect from various points of view. Marco Polo wrote of Genghis Khan that he was prudent and wise and that his death was to be lamented, and Join-ville notes that he 'procured peace'.

In China it was considered that the emperor could keep himself in power only through his virtue. He had to cultivate his entire nature so that it could fulfil the spiritual, esthetic and physical needs of his people. In feudal China, a king was not allowed to open his mouth for the three years of mourning following his father's death, and the potentates, even when they seemed to be preoccupied with glory, realized that supreme power is made of expiation and devotion. Even their administrative responsibility was 'heavy'; the first emperor of China is said to have handled a weight of 120 pounds of reports per day.

Since the borders of China were identified with the confines of the universe, by travelling or by sending messengers to the four poles, or by performing ceremonies at the four gates of his capital, the sovereign used to transport his virtue to the limits of the world and used to subject the universe to the order established by him. He governed space because he was the master of time.

The Chinese lord of old was only supposed to grow melons and cucumbers, i.e. fruits that do not keep; he had to refrain from hoarding grain. Even today, the Emperor of Japan must not touch money.

It is said that Yao as well as Chouen, and to a lesser degree, Yu the Great, founder of the Chinese royal line, lived solely for the good of the people without thinking of themselves. The Emperor of Japan has to live without desires. Lao Tse gave a doctrinal explanation of this attitude by saying: 'It is by serving men that one can tame men.'

In Japan, chiefs were brought up in the strictest fashion. It is said that the last Dowager Empress, who was a Princess Fujo, was taken away from her parents when she was seven days old and entrusted for five years to a family of peasants which treated her like one of them; her foster-mother used to carry her on her back when working in the rice-fields. In Islam, it was the most worthy member of the royal family, acknowledged as such by the Ulema sages, who was entrusted with the supreme responsibility.

An unexpected and interesting consequence of this conception of the chief, his duties and responsibilities, is that when the latter no longer has the virtue required and does not fulfil his duties effectively, he loses his *right* to be chief—and this may happen even for a certain period only.

In China the power of any dynasty was born of a virtue (*to*), which goes through a time of plenitude (*tcheng*), then wanes (*ngai*), and after an ephemeral resurrection (*hing*), is exhausted and extinguished (*mie*); it must then be exterminated (*mietsiue*) . . . Any dynasty which kept power once its time had come to an end no longer possessed anything but *de facto* power. *De jure*, it was a usurper . . . The last sovereigns of a race, think the theoreticians, are essentially tyrants and rebels. Blinded with pride, they act on their own instead of conforming to the virtue that is identical with the natural order (*tao*) . . . royal virtue is obtained by obeying the celestial orders. It is ruined by the high-handedness which is typical of tyrants.

In Japan, where it is unthinkable for the emperor personally to be implicated in anything, it is the ministers who are exposed. Since the first world war, five prime ministers have been assassinated and four others have run great risks—and in most cases the murderers only received fairly lenient sentences. In Islam one may legitimately refuse to obey the monarch as soon as he is thought to have departed from the stipulations of canon law; besides, when an earthly chief suffers misfortune, it clearly shows that divine investiture has been withdrawn from him.

Another feature of Asian groups is their close solidarity and immense collective pride.

For many of these people, as we have seen, their country is the centre of the world, not only culturally and politically, but geographically—either because the rest of the universe has remained unknown to them as in the case of certain tribes shut off in their mountain valleys since time immemorial, or because creation is supposed to have begun in their land, as the Hindu Shivaites and the Japanese Shintos think, or else because their race has been chosen to receive the sole and supreme divine revelation as is believed by the Israelites, Yazidis and many others. This general thesis is often supported by the belief that the first man belonged to the particular race in question, a belief held by the Japanese,

Israelites, the Kelabites of Borneo, the Saora and Bondo of Central India and countless other groups. There is an amusing exception— the Budubudaka consider themselves to be the last race created, and a superfluous addition!

This, of course, leads those peoples to consider the rest of mankind as inferior. This is especially notable among the Chinese, who only see barbarians around them, the Afghans, the Japanese, the Hindus, the Israelites, etc. A French magistrate who lived a long time in Pondicherry, wanted to draw up a sort of list of precedence of the castes inhabiting that area; among the many people whom he questioned, he found unanimity on only one point, namely, that the caste to which the person in question belonged was superior to all the others. This group pride is nearly always accompanied by intense solidarity. Even if, in certain groups, the individual mostly distrusts his fellows, everyone is united when it comes to facing the outsider or undertaking collective work. The Japanese vocabulary establishes no distinction between military companionship and conjugal fidelity, and the words of the oath taken on both occasions are the same.

When a village is destroyed by a calamity in the Philippines or in Pakistan, all the inhabitants work together in order to rebuild it and manage to do so with amazing speed. In very many countries, when a peasant takes in his harvest, all the neighbours come to help him with all their equipment. That is why in Soviet Asia, from Tajikistan to Uzbekistan, and in China it has been easy to mobilize hundreds of thousands of volunteers in order to execute large public works—roads, canals, dams.

We have already seen how this feeling of solidarity, in a group that is more or less large but not clearly defined, may lead to conceptions of honesty that are different from ours.

Taken to the extreme limit, this solidarity can itself lead directly to an actual pooling, not only of property, but even of women and children, as preached in Persia by Mazdek in the late fifth century.

It also greatly facilitates the development of patriotism, for it is relatively easy to transfer from the family and clan to the whole nation this predisposition of the individual to sacrifice himself for the group. This has long been the case in Japan, for instance, and to a much lesser degree in some other countries that have recently become independent. The individual then easily tends to consider himself, socially and materially, as a mere cogwheel in an immense machine, which does not preclude his preserving strong independence in the higher spheres of thought, religion, spirituality—while the reverse happens in the West where we tend to conform easily in these very spheres, and at the same time claim greater freedom in economic and social matters.

The result of this close relationship is that in most Asian societies, just as in black Africa and ancient Greece, expulsion from the community is like a supreme punishment, ontologically identified with the death penalty.

CHAPTER XV

Foreign Policy

*Both in the Middle and the Far East, beyond and above all the
differences and divergences, we find against a common background
the same vision of life, a similar way of understanding the world
and man.*   TUCCI

Now that we have seen how the manifold human relationships
are organized and work within an Asian society, it is interesting to
examine the rules that govern the relations of the societies between
themselves. In this chapter we shall necessarily have to concentrate
on the situation as it is in the middle of the twentieth century, for
the intensification and transformation of the relations between Asia
and the West have eliminated the problems considered important
up to then, have profoundly changed others and have, above all,
brought forth serious new problems in the field of foreign policy
—and by that we mean all that is connected with the relations
between various human groups, whether they happen to be at the
time under the same 'national' sovereignty or divided into several
'nations'.

The first point that strikes us is that the great wave of western-
type nationalism, imported from Europe, which has strongly helped
the peoples of Asia to obtain their political independence, has not
purely and simply fallen back once this result has been achieved.
It has immediately had to seek further objectives, and one of its
main manifestations has taken the form of an aggressive imperialism
within as well as outside the national boundaries.

Outside, there has been a mushrooming of irredentisms. Everywhere where one of the newly sovereign nations can argue that
there are historic, legal, cultural or even religious ties, it noisily
claims the relevant territory—and sometimes it does no more than
present economic or strategic arguments in support of such claims.

Naturally, the first targets are the territories that are still part
of former European or American colonial empires, but we already
have frequent cases of a large state threatening a weaker one, or of
sharp disputes between two states of comparable size. Of course, in

itself, this is no novelty. In Asia as on other continents, wars of conquest have occurred throughout history. What is new is the ideological element and the fact that these disputes are placed in the context of world politics.

On the one hand, the purely material interests that mostly motivate these disputes are hidden, often clumsily so, behind grand abstract principles borrowed from western terminology, from Voltaire to Woodrow Wilson and without missing out the French Revolution. This makes it possible to seek protection from the highest international instances which are responsible precisely for defending and ensuring observance of these same principles. A side result that is not unimportant is that these fabricated pretexts can take on paramount value by stirring public opinion and turning its attention away from immediate and burning domestic problems.

On the other hand, the claimant and defendant countries, i.e. those that possess and those that do not, frequently appeal to great foreign powers—sometimes even to the metropolis of former colonial empires—which are only too glad to seize this opportunity to intervene, either in order to extend their sphere of political and military influence, or in order to secure export markets, or else to obtain privileges for exploitation and development, particularly in the oil-rich areas.

Aside from this 'external' imperialism, there is another form which, although less noticed by the world press, is no less dangerous and disquieting. It is the imperialism exercised upon national, ethnic, religious, linguistic or cultural minorities and especially upon peoples who are now supposed to be designated by the term aborigines.

The groups in power pretend to safeguard national unity, but actually they create it from scratch, a unity which is ideal rather than real. These groups sometimes represent the majority, but at other times they only reflect the minority in many ways, a minority seeking to eliminate by every means possible all the factors hindering the total uniformization of the country and the people.

The new governments, going much further than the most intolerant colonial administrations of the past, endeavour to impose their own language (christened the 'national' language) not only in the secondary and high schools, but even in the primary classes, thus compelling children to be educated in a language totally unknown to them and their families. The social legislation in force among the groups in power is imposed upon the population even if it is most unsuitable. Local customs are the object of open or hidden opposition, with the desire to eliminate or change them. All that smacks of the slightest 'regionalism' or might contribute to maintain a feeling of cultural autonomy is relentlessly driven out. Religious minorities are often oppressed more or less directly. When a government ostensibly declares its liberalism in a particular sphere —and does indeed practise it—often it does so only in order to better impose its will to centralize and standardize in all the other spheres or wherever this is in its own interest.

When the minorities thus attacked and persecuted are numerically and economically strong, and when they have reached a cultural level in every way comparable with that of the governing group, they can manage to defend themselves to some extent, although in fact they are constantly compelled to give way under various types of pressure. The situation is far more tragic when the minority groups are less numerous, economically weak, lack contact with the outside world, and when their cultural standard is not generally acknowledged as being high. This is the plight of the so-called aborigenous peoples that are to be found to a greater or lesser degree in all the Asian countries. Their entire personality, often most valuable for the common heritage of mankind, is threatened with complete extermination over a shorter or longer period of time without anybody from outside realizing this fact or taking the trouble to come to their rescue.

These groups, which vary in number between some dozens of individuals (Todas) and several millions (Gonds), generally have a traditional social organization that is completely different from that of the more evolved neighbouring population. These groups are mostly the former possessors of the country who have been progressively pushed back towards the less fertile regions by successive waves of invaders. They lead a simple and rough life, have few needs and make no extra effort to increase their material welfare; they enjoy intensely the leisure left to them after having satisfied their most immediate needs and do not take easily to mechanization. They devote a great part of their time to games, to dancing and feasting of all sorts, and they remain in close contact with the nature around them. On the whole, they seem to be perfectly happy and do not show any desire to change their way of life.

They are often accused of not having an 'organized' religion and of having as their priests and doctors people we describe as 'witches'. We blame them for being 'superstitious'—i.e. holding beliefs that we cannot explain—and for conforming their lives to these beliefs. But in the immense majority of cases, all this should not really disturb the neighbouring groups. It is true that some castes or tribes, on account of their habit of pillaging, are a danger to the surrounding people, but such cases are rare. On the other hand, some of these groups seem to have retained valuable secrets relating to physical and moral hygiene—for instance, a particular Himalayan tribe (Hunzas), which has never suffered from disease, and another important Indian tribe (Santals), which does not know what anger is!

A few courageous voices (among them a place of honour must be given to Verrier Elwyn's as champion of the Indian aborigines) have been raised in their defence, so that they may be left to live in peace the life of their choice and not be integrated against their will into a cultural and economic entity which will cost them their dearest assets without bringing them much in exchange. Indeed, in some countries such as Formosa and certain areas of Burma, it seems that the authorities have resigned themselves to non-interference, but in most cases they are subjected to brutal pressure in order to make them toe the line set by their neighbours, to use them as cheap labour for the economic profit of the country, and to make them relinquish all that is peculiar to their culture and lose themselves in the mass. Sometimes armed revolt in the form of guerilla warfare, in the areas inaccessible to the regular army, holds the central government back for a while, as, for instance, in India with the fierce Nagas, but in most cases, the rest of the world hardly ever hears of the matter or is completely indifferent to it. The surest protection of these groups lies precisely in the fact that the areas where they take refuge are too inaccessible and too poor to be attractive for development.

In order to defend themselves, some of these groups take refuge with Christian, Muslim or Buddhist missionaries who promise to secure for them greater respect in society. As a result they are converted *en masse* to the religion that holds out such promises. But this protection is an illusion, for generally the missionaries try to change their way of life for motives different from those of the central government, but with practically the same results—i.e. their social and tribal organization, their family structure, their religious practices are rapidly destroyed and they are placed at the mercy of government intervention.

Of course, from the beginning of time the peoples that had attained a higher degree of economic organization and power and a more refined culture have shown contempt for the less fortunate groups, whom they considered as barbarians. So long as the concept of slavery remains part of social ethics, it is only natural that entire populations should be reduced to complete slavery.

For the Chinese of the classical period, the barbarians were only 'game' and more like beasts than men—and at that time the foreign policy of China was animated by a true 'colonial spirit', manifested by the officers in charge of the outposts; nevertheless, as a rule, once they had surrendered, the outcasts of civilization were mostly judged according to their own customs. Not long ago, in Japan, it was legally a political crime to teach the Ainus to read. The Thais had made servants out of entire groups like the Kha, whose plight has hardly changed to this day. In India, most of the large castes or non-Hindus who are kept in a state of considerable social inferiority were originally also aborigines (although many groups of untouchables and *patitas* are descendants of high-caste persons who seriously violated the laws of their own group). In the Middle East, while the Arab nations can call themselves 'anti-colonialist', they are nonetheless nations that are supporters of slavery, and they tend to apply the system collectively to many groups.

However, at a time when the emerging nations claim to be inspired by the principles of liberty, equality, humanity, in the highest sense of the words, it is regrettable to see them adopt towards the less developed groups an attitude that is strangely similar to that of the very colonizers against whom they had revolted and from whom they are proud to be free.

Among the groups that have to suffer most from these trends towards unification and standardization, in the newest as well as the oldest states, we must particularly mention the nomads. From Siberia to Mongolia, in Turkmenia, Afghanistan, the whole Asian side of the former Ottoman Empire, Persia and many other regions, the nomads formerly made up a large proportion of the population and now, in spite of all the pressure which is brought to bear on them, there are presumably five millions left on the Asian continent, perhaps ten per cent of the total number of inhabitants of the Middle East.

Besides, it would be a mistake to think that they used to lead an entirely free life in a more or less anarchic society. Their grazing rights were strictly regulated by unwritten agreements concluded with other nomadic or sedentary groups. Within each tribe the relations between individuals, between the tents and the subgroups, were similarly governed by imperative customs, and non-observance often led to most serious punishment.

Within strict bounds, however, the nomad used to enjoy immense freedom, an extreme sense of honour and also considerable prestige. In Arabia the nomads used to be regarded as aristocrats, leading a free life without manual labour, exploiting peasants brought under servitude. The best description has perhaps been given by Hackin, citing Afghanistan. He says that permanent contact with nature develops not only the physical qualities but also a sense of liberty and responsibility. Any fault, any mistake, any excess is immediately corrected by sanctions which affect the very basis of material life—the herds, the pastures. Thus, daily experiences lead to the formation of a richer personality. The result of this type of life is worthy of admiration. We see well-built, adroit, agile, serious, very honest, very understanding men, whose intelligence is constantly alert and active and who apply our methods of induction and deduction every day to all sorts of problems. In fact, in order to be complete personalities, these men have less to learn from us than we from them. The process of sedentarization, which is pursuing its course relentlessly, certainly deprives them of much more than it gives them in all important fields; this is now beginning to be realized.

A large number of groups and tribes that were thus uprooted from their traditional way of life and driven out of their normal habitat were unable to survive. We may deplore the fact that many of them have become extinct in the course of the last two centuries. To mention only the case of Russian Asia under the Tzarist regime, the Anyula, the Kamass, the Kangienici, the Koryaks, the Mators and several other tribes (their vocabularies had been compiled by Doctor Robeck in 1791) have disappeared without leaving any traces. A similar list could be made for India (between 1858 and 1901 the Andamans aborigines seem to have lost four-fifths of their numbers) and several other regions of Asia.

One of the most visible forms of this campaign against minorities is the intense effort towards language unification undertaken within every state. It must be admitted that the number of languages used in Asia is awe-inspiring: the Philippines have eighty-seven languages, all very much alive, Borneo forty, India 225, the Chinese province of Fukien alone has 108, so different from one another as to be unintelligible from one group to another, and the 1200 Samoyeds used to have about a hundred different dialects.

The main languages themselves have many variants, according to the region; the Persian spoken in Iran is not the same as that of Afghanistan, and the Jews of Iran speak a Judeo-Persian peculiar to themselves. The greatest variety of languages mix and combine in the border areas. Thus, on the shores of Lake Baikal a variety of Russo-Chinese Sabir is spoken; in South India, Labbai and Marak-kayars speak Arabo-Tamil. Many languages have different scripts according to the region and cannot be read by a neighbouring area; thus Pali, the sacred language of the Buddhists, is written in Siam, Ceylon, Burma, Cambodia and Laos in the respective national alphabets.

On the other hand—or rather for this very reason—various parts of Asia, from the remotest antiquity, have had truly international and very widespread languages. This was so, for instance, in Babylonia in the middle of the second millennium, and with Aramaic from the eighth century B.C. till the beginning of the second century

A.D., with Sogdian, the instrument of an advanced culture in the first millennium of our era between the Indo-Iranian world and the Far East. But in no case did these languages, which were meant to facilitate relations between linguistically different countries, ever seek to supplant the local vernacular.

The campaign undertaken at present by the various central governments is very different. In the Philippines an attempt is being made to impose Tagalog as the single language of the land; in Formosa, Mandarin Chinese, which no Formosan ever spoke; in Indonesia, the Indonesian Bhasa; in Afghanistan, Pushtu, the only merit of which seems to be that it is not the national language of any other independent people, and it has therefore been adopted as a step towards the unitarian policy of the country. It has to be recognized that the large Communist countries have, on the contrary, adopted the policy of reviving and developing the national languages of the ethnic minorities, often going so far as to provide them with an alphabet that had been lacking up till them. (The Chinese publishing firm for minorities intends to publish by 1967 works in some twenty-five non-Chinese languages, seventeen of which have not had a script until now.) However, a common State language is often superimposed.

Until the beginning of the twentieth century nationalism, as we see it in the West, i.e. loyalty towards a specific community defined above all according to frontiers, was practically unknown in Asia, with the sole exception of Japan. Everywhere else the feeling of solidarity, extremely powerful as we have seen, is manifested within the context of the family, the village, the clan, the tribe, the profession, the caste, the race, the religious sect, the language group or even of a common set of ethics or else towards a particular dynasty or chief taken individually. It has nothing to do with political, administrative or other forms of dependence upon the central government of a state which is a subject of international law. Besides, the great empires—Turkish, Chinese, French, English, Dutch, Russian and later Japanese—which had for long divided and disputed territories inhabited by a variety of races, would have vigorously crushed all nationalist tendencies, had there been any. The line was drawn only between the invader or master on the one hand, and the indigenous or subject races on the other.

The question of whether a government is legitimate or not is only of interest to its rivals within and outside the country, as a pretext for challenging it. For the masses there can only be a *de facto* authority which is more or less remote and which, more or less directly, gives orders, inflicts punishment, collects taxes, sometimes

even distributes privileges. When the name of a great unit now pro-
moted (or demoted?) to the rank of a nation was the object of great
love and devotion, as was the case with India, it was on a completely different plane which had nothing to do with patriotism;
the Hindus worshipped the Goddess India, our Divine Mother India,
raised temples and statues to her and offered her flowers and incense;
Gandhi had a large temple built for her in Benares ('The Hindu
conception of the motherland is more cultural than territorial,' says
Mookerji). It is in a similar spirit that in the seventh century, Kuan
Tchong, Minister of Ts'i, declared that all the Chinese (i.e. all those
belonging to the Chinese *race*) are related.

The concepts of nation and fatherland began to attract the Asians
as soon as they saw that it is one of the component factors of the
economic and military power with which we defeated them and
held them under our yoke for so long. These very ideas have been
cultivated—by a trick of fate—as a powerful lever to raise the
colonized people against their western masters. Once this result has
been reached, the new masters have naturally continued to develop
this feeling by every possible means in order to establish their
power more firmly within the country as well as in its foreign
relations.

This nationalism, however, has not yet been driven to the
extremes known in Europe. Firstly, it has some weak points. The
nomads, for instance, fail to understand how an artificial political
border can cut off the grazing grounds which they had been freely
using for centuries, and the very idea of passports is incomprehensible to them. It is not unusual to see Asian states where the civil
servants or even the ministers are not its nationals. Many a family
that has been settled in a particular region for centuries continue
to regard themselves as belonging to their community of origin and
keep its costume, language, religious customs, food habits, and have
their brides sent out to them from it.

But above all, Asian nationalism is considerably tempered by two
opposite factors: strong emotional attachment to units smaller than
the nation, and secondly, the ideal which is related to larger units.

Most of the smaller units do not go outside the borders of what
is now termed a 'state'; this is nearly always the case with families,
castes, etc. But there are many units where a more or less large
proportion of the members suddenly enter a category new to them,
that of 'outsiders', and this creates painful problems and counteracts
the attempts to have patriotism assume its rightful role in politics.
There are units—and large ones at that—which have been divided
into similar sized pieces by means of borders fixed at conferences
held in Lausanne, Paris or Geneva. This dismembering does not make

it easy for those who are its victims to show the passive and docile loyalty required of them by the new national government, especially as its capital and its political leaders are either unfamiliar with them or are traditionally hostile. Thus, we have the Kurds torn between Iran, Irak, Turkey and U.S.S.R., the Armenians divided between Turkey and the U.S.S.R., the Thai between Laos and Siam, the Pathans between Afghanistan and Pakistan, the Kirghiz between China and the U.S.S.R., the Mongols between China and the Peoples' Republic of Mongolia, etc., not to speak of the countless small racial communities astride all the borders of south-west Asia, where their names are unknown except to specialists, but which nonetheless suffer cruelly from such separations. We must also mention those communities which, as a result of outside political provocation, have been cut in two by a frontier so arbitrary that it cannot be drawn except on maps—for example, the Koreans and the Viet-Namese.

The strongest brake to excessive nationalism is applied by an exactly opposite tendency. Emotional tendencies of loyalty towards units larger than the present states are developing in Asia with amazing speed. The two main trends—but not the only ones—are Panarabism with its more extensive variant, Panislamism, and Panasianism.

Both obviously originate in the desire or need to fight against the western countries guilty of colonialism, imperialism, capitalism, etc. and accused of having so long and so mercilessly exploited peoples who were militarily weaker. The solidarity between those who feel oppressed by a common enemy has intensified, deepened and crystallized what up to then was mainly a vague emotional feeling without any political impact. We have already mentioned the fraternity which every Muslim feels towards all his co-religionists as soon as a common front has to be shown to infidels. This trend is obviously much stronger when it is accompanied by a feeling of racial community as well, a community with boundaries that vary according to the convenience of the moment. This identification between the members of this vast community has lately even been written into the constitutions of certain Arab states—a fact that has not received sufficient notice.

Panasianism, although it is not based on such specific and ancient foundations, is rapidly reaching a position where it will oust nationalism in the various countries. It was consecrated at the Bandoeng Conference in April 1955—which embraced for its purpose some 56 million Africans as well as its 1,500 million Asians —it is constantly developing economic and cultural ties between the various national units. While it has not eliminated all the inter-

Asian disputes, (many of these, such as the Sino-Indian conflict on the Southern Chinese border and the Indo-Pakistani dispute over Kashmir, have been directly inherited from the late colonial administration) it does place them in a completely new and different perspective.

Parallel with this development of Panasianism and similar movements, strengthened by them and strengthening them in turn, we see over the last fifteen years the emergence of an Asian superiority complex, which, up to now, had not been openly manifested, and which anyway never covered such a wide field.

Of course, every Chinese, every Muslim, every Hindu knew inwardly that he was quite superior to the barbarians of the West whose domination was due only to their purely material superiority. He could not be contemptuous enough of these people—immoral, agitated, illogical, cruel, untrustworthy, lacking in self-control, materialist—and so on. With very rare exceptions, people in all Asian countries had only the strict minimum of contact required by circumstances with these dangerous and uncouth intruders. Even among the most devoted collaborators, their apparent servility ill-concealed their innermost attitude. This is, moreover, one of the main reasons why our contacts with Asians accentuated dislikes and misunderstandings instead of facilitating mutual understanding and friendship.

To be quite objective, it must be admitted that our behaviour towards the Asians has not always been above reproach. The history of the Crusades, as recorded by Muslim authors, is considerably different from the usual image painted of them—and the entire Near East has kept a vivid recollection of them even to our day. The French, British, Dutch and Portuguese colonization throughout South Asia took place under conditions which were carefully guarded from too much publicity in Europe. After the Boxer Rebellion in China there were terrible massacres in which all the Europeans took part and which were accompanied by indescribable pillage and atrocity. The atom bombs that were tried out in Japan have left scars that nothing will efface. A former lieutenant of Napoleon, the Italian Avitabile, succeeded in terrorizing even Afghanistan, which is not a country renowned for the gentleness of its customs. The contrasts between the standard of living of the colonized or semi-colonized peoples and that of the conquerers who lived among them, from the product of their soil and their labour, also led to great bitterness. It is easy for nationalists or mere anti-westerners to revive all these memories, without displaying much imagination, in order to excite the population against those who are held responsible for all its misfortunes and humiliations.

The sorrowful spectacle of our dissensions and our wars into which, under the most hypocritical pretexts, we tried to drag them, with their consent or by force, the demoralizing use we make of our material wealth and our scientific discoveries, was not likely to make us rise in their esteem. To this is added the fact that they have become our disciples in all those fields where they felt, wrongly or rightly, that they had been outdone—economic and industrial development, scientific research, political organization, armaments. Forgetting that they have benefited from our efforts over two centuries or more, they note that they are now progressing much faster than we ever did in those very fields where we used to crush them with our superiority.

There is nothing surprising, therefore, in that the situation should now be reversed and that the Asians are now rapidly approaching the point where they will regard us exactly as we used to regard them half a century ago. There again they imitate us, and while we may fear the consequences, we could at least be proud of our pupils.

It should be observed, furthermore, that the Asians do not blindly adopt all that comes from us. On the one hand, they choose what seems suitable or beneficial. On the other hand, they adapt to their own needs and their own traditions whatever they have decided to borrow. This is particularly so with Communism, where some important elements—discretionary power granted to authority, pooling of land and incomes, community life taken to the extreme —in most of Asia are nothing new and therefore nothing shocking.

While words such as Panasianism are very recent, the idea goes back to antiquity. Powerful factors of cohesion have long existed over vast sectors of the continent. Let us mention a few of them.

Firstly, mass migrations have been innumerable throughout history; they have either been imposed by the authorities for political and economic reasons, or they had been rendered necessary by famine, or they have simply been stimulated by the desire to find more fertile land and to escape from cumbersome neighbours. Such movements are far from having come to an end. In 1942, in Burma alone, there were two million first generation immigrants out of a total of 17 million inhabitants. During the partition of India and Pakistan, some twelve to fifteen million individuals emigrated to other provinces.

That is why the population is often a composite one which does not indulge in any merging of the various elements or even in many mixed marriages. Out of four million inhabitants, Cambodia has 300,000 Viet-Namese, 300,000 Chinese, 100,000 Chams and Malays; in Uzbekistan there are over a million Jews from Western Ukraine,

White Russia, Bessarabia and Southern Bukovina. Some towns, such as Irkutsk, Darjeeling and many others are so mixed that it is really impossible to find out which race is in the majority. In the seventh century Tch'ang-ngan, the capital of T'ang, was already an international town.

It is not unusual to see a single population migrating several times over a few centuries. The Kalmuk Torguts left China, settled down on the Volga, but in 1771 some 400,000 of them out of 470,000 took to the road to return to their country of origin. The Yakuts, who were formerly in Central Asia, were driven from the eastern shores of the Aral Sea by the Mongols under Genghis Khan; once they reached the Lena valley, they in turn ousted the Tunguz Mongols and the Lamuts, forcing them to emigrate to the north of the Arctic Circle.

In spite of the repugnance shown by most Asian races towards ethnic mixtures, these population movements necessarily led to many mixed unions and produced all kinds of mixed races. In Russian Asia, a good number of migrant peasants—and even intellectuals in exile—mixed with the indigenous population and often adopted their language and customs. In Yakutsk and its surrounding area, the Russians became completely 'Yakutanized'; those who had not brought their families with them readily took wives from the local tribes in spite of sporadic efforts on the part of the Tzars to provide them with wives of their own race. In the Harbin region there are many Russo-Chinese couples. Elsewhere, many Indo-Europeans and Samoyeds have been 'Turkicized'. The Chinese who came to Tibet rarely took their wives with them and they produced many mixed children although not settling permanently in the country. Marriages between Mongols and Buryats were not unusual—and even in China it seems that marriages between different races were frequent.

In addition to these population movements, contacts of all kinds between the different Asian populations have been infinitely more numerous and frequent than one would suppose in view of the difficulty of communication.

To quote one example, it is known that in the ninth century of our era the Wiguri Turks were familiar with the whole of Upper Asia from Korea to the Urals.

There was frequent exchange of ambassadors, sometimes even beyond the borders of Asia. It seems that Roman ambassadors went to China in the second half of the second century, and in 567 there was an exchange of embassies between Mongolia and Byzantium.

Commercial communications, however, played an even greater

part in creating a feeling of solidarity among the Asians. It is difficult for us even to imagine the range and scope of these communications. Much has been said about the Silk Route with its different branches across the whole continent from China to the Mediterranean, but there were many others as well. In the South, Viet-Nam was a stopping place for the Roman merchants who, under Marcus Aurelius, used to go to Canton; and the toilet sets found there have an uncanny resemblance with similar objects used 4,000 years ago in Bohemia, 9,000 kilometres from Hanoi; similar objects have been found in Mesopotamia and Tibet. Neighbouring Cambodia was itself a frequently used passage early in the Christian era, when it was a crossroad for travellers, tradesmen and pilgrims westwards from China, or in the reverse direction. In Oc-Eo, in a site dating back to a period earlier than the sixth century, objects of Roman origin have also been found. In south-east China in the thirteenth century there were large commercial markets where the volume of trade was so great that it could not even be compared with that of the large trading centres of Europe at the same time, and Chinese junks used to go from Japan to Madagascar; Hangchow used to obtain its rice supply from regions over 3,000 kilometres away. In northern Asia the Tchuktches served as middlemen for trade between the Russians and the tribes inhabiting the northern tip of America. In another direction, Siberian gold used to come to India through Bactria; in about 1880, along the route between Afghanistan and India, 50,000 men and as many camels used to pass through Dera-Ismail-Khan every winter.

All these diplomatic and commercial relations used to bring in their train innumerable cultural relations which often seem to have been considered even more important by the people concerned.

Let us mention only a few striking examples. In the middle of the second millennium B.C., important Babylonian texts 'used to be read in the cuneiform text, and some of them were translated and adapted to the language of northern Syria, Asia Minor and Egypt'. In Khmer architecture some of the motifs found are closely related to those found in Asia Minor and Mesopotamia—and there are even some motifs of Oceanian origin. The observations made by Hiuen-Tsang during his journey to India were known in Japan since the early eighth century. The Mongols have long been using two alphabets—one, known as the *phag-ta*, which came from India via Tibet, and the other, known as the *pigur*, of Phoenician origin, brought by Nestorian missionaries of Aramaic culture. Indian and Chinese culture have for thousands of years radiated an intense and wide-ranging influence; the Chinese Emperor Wu was apparently more concerned with the extension of Chinese civilization than with the creation of a state. We shall examine later the efforts made by sovereigns to have scholars, artists, works of art, literary texts, brought from far-away countries. In 1092 the ambassadors of Korea in China asked to buy a very large number of books (a request that was refused by the emperor).

In this context, religious intercommunication, resulting from visits by pilgrims and propagandists, obviously played a paramount part. We have already seen the importance of pilgrimages throughout Asia. From the second century A.D. onwards, different races, united only by their religion, the Parthian Ngan Che-kao, the Indian Chu Sho-fo, the Yue-che Tche Tch'an, took Buddhism from the Serinda to the Far East. Not only did the Buddhist scriptures and the Hindu epics, especially the *Ramayana* (which went as far as China), spread to many countries where it coloured the life of millions, but also Christian teaching in its Asian forms, Islam,[1] the Mazdaist, Lamaist and even Taoist[2] cults penetrated to the remotest places, bringing with them a feeling of close solidarity with the followers of the same religion living thousands of miles away.

The similarity of the economic situation in many regions of Asia, especially in contrast with the one revealed by western representatives in Asia, has also largely contributed to strengthening the ties between their inhabitants and has led them to display a united front against the rest of the world, the rich colonizers whose way of life, even in the most material details, is so different from theirs. Today it is a commonplace to state that the similarity of situation between the African and Asian peoples has brought them together and has led to the formation of the vast political unit known as the Afro-Asia group. People whose minimum daily needs are roughly at the same level, whose ambitions as regards standard of living are the same, who encounter similar material difficulties, understand each other much more easily than people whose problems and means of solving them are completely different. To try and rouse the pity of a Chinese, Indian or nomad audience for the poverty of the Holy Family at the time of the Nativity or the flight into Egypt is not an easy matter; for the members of the audience do not regard this as any more painful than their own daily lives.

Finally, we must mention one factor which has for some centuries taken on a paramount importance—viz. community of political interests between those who have been colonized. In addition to a

---

[1] In the fourteenth century, a king of Yemen sent caravans up to Afghanistan in order to seek comments on the Koran.

[2] Kamara, King of Kamrup, had a request sent to the Chinese Emperor for a translation of the *Tao teh king*, and some Indian doctrines such as the *sahajayana* are impregnated with Taoism. (K. M. Panikkar.)

deep resentment at the humiliation inflicted upon them and at the economic impact of colonialism, which they see only in its worst light, they are animated by the wish to unite as closely as possible in order to be able to negotiate with the West under the best possible conditions. Even the fact that certain peoples, such as the Russians and the Japanese, have also been colonizers has little effect on Asian solidarity when the latter is seen to be a trump card in international disputes.

In addition to all these factors which make the Asians feel that they belong to the same big family, there are also, of course, factors that dissociate them or bring about antagonism, but these are nearly always of secondary and passing importance and it would be wrong to overestimate them.

Foremost among the disintegrating factors are, of course, wars throughout the centuries, which we have mentioned earlier, but we must also remember what has been said regarding the attitude of the non-Semitic Asians towards those who have harmed them in the past. There are also strict hierarchies of castes and even of races which alone would suffice in Europe to provoke and justify unextinguishable hatreds, but we know that such a state of affairs seems absolutely natural to the Asian, and it does not even occur to those whom we regard as the victims that they could complain about it. When one group shows deep contempt for another (in about 1900, the Dowager Empress of China used to call the Japanese 'the island monkeys'; among the Tatars of Krasnoiarsk, the commonest curse is to say: 'May you live like a Russian') the latter is not greatly annoyed, because it pays back in the same coin. The feeling of superiority deep-rooted in every group protects it from animosity towards those who are not intelligent enough to understand what is what.

PART FOUR

The Work of Man

CHAPTER XVI

Economics and Law

Wealth is nothing but manure; the face is worth a hundred thousand pounds.
                                                          Chinese Proverb

ON the whole the Asian religions preach no more contempt for material wealth than the Christian Gospel, but it must be recognized that the proportion of people who take this teaching seriously is infinitely higher in the Orient than in the West. While the Christian draws a distinction between that which belongs to God and that which is Caesar's, Islam considers spiritual and temporal values as a whole—and this is true for the whole of the East in general, apart from the Chinese of course.

It is true that in the Muslim countries, in India, China and Japan, we find fabulous wealth side by side with incredible want, but the general attitude is totally different from ours. The following example will illustrate this contrast. Lao Tse is absolutely categorical: 'The worst fault is to want to acquire. Those who know how to say "this is enough" are always content.' (*Tao Teh King.*) But this refusal to compromise is so incomprehensible to us that a westerner who has made a serious and remarkably sympathetic study of Taoism, Wieger, feels compelled to add two words which, on the pretext of improving 'the excessively concise nature of the Chinese' text, completely distorts its meaning. He translates: 'The worst fault is [always] to want to acquire [more].

The anxiety to meet one's bare needs necessarily plays an important part in countries where poverty exceeds all that we can imagine, where only a small minority eats to its satisfaction, where only a few possess a second set of clothes. In Armenia, many old women used to die in the same clothes that they had been seen wearing all their lives. In Northern China the average income per capita per annum is estimated at less than two pounds, and this is nothing exceptional, either in the countries that had remained independent or in those that had been colonies. Confucius himself used to consider that to feed people was more urgent than to educate them, and in our times, Ramakrishna used to say that religion must not be preached to empty stomachs.

This brings out one fact with even greater force, viz. that in Asia the thirst for the superfluous that has invaded our lives to such an extent that we can no longer even identify it is mostly absent or reduced to a minimum.

In Viet-Nam, for instance, even now the traditional type of education imposes limits on the search for wealth. Until 1945, the Viet-Namese bourgeoisie, in particular, once a certain fortune had been made, considered itself satisfied and valued honours more than wealth. In Burma to make a fortune has never been a goal; the main anxiety is to increase one's merits in order to be reborn after death at a higher stage of evolution—and merits are acquired by giving, not by hoarding. Therefore, the miser is threatened with the same fate as the parricide.

In India, millions of men have taken a vow of absolute poverty, and even to this day the dream of a considerable number of Hindus is to abandon all they possess as soon as they have brought up their children and to lead a life of mendicity. The caste of tradesmen, the *vaishyas*—those whose task is to collect wealth—comes after that of the intellectuals and warriors and just before that of manual labourers. In China one emperor, in 219, prided himself on having forbidden 'the last of all professions', trade. In Japan merchants held the lowest place on the social ladder.

In India again, the goddess Araikasu Nachiyar accepts no offering greater than a pie (the smallest unit of currency, worth about a farthing). In Ceylon, as a westerner has noted with some amazement, one of the most 'backward' groups on earth, the Veddas, regard material progress 'as just so much dust'.[1]

In Omsk in Siberia, hardly more than fifty years ago, a European traveller (Legras) observed that the people there used to disdain money and honours, lived on very little, without counting their money, and shared what they had fraternally. They did not act thus because of any moral theory or religious law, but by instinct. A doctor who was there, for instance, maintained—and everybody agreed with him—that neither he nor his colleagues should be entitled to receive fees, not even from the wealthy.

Mohammed used to tell the Muslims: 'You desire the riches of this world and Allah wishes to give you the riches of the next world.' Of course, the booty collected in their early conquests may have made the Muslims forgetful of this fundamental principle, but it was revived in the seventh and eighth centuries, in Irak for instance, as a reaction against the luxury introduced by Othman and developed under the Omeyads. In our day, in Afghanistan, one

[1] Harry Williams.

of the countries least affected by westernization, there is 'this equality based on the absence of wealth, a flexible property system, a way of life that is practically the same for the great and the humble without any great differences in their culture or their needs. It is thanks to this equality that Afghanistan does not even know what class conflict is and has remained immune to the Bolshevism of its neighbours'.[2]

Besides, in those Asian countries where there is a great disparity in fortunes, this gives rise to little indignation or even protest. This is because the rich, in traditional Asia, are subject to many and heavy obligations. In fact, it is they who are responsible for nearly all public works, the building of roads, bridges, dams etc., and it is they who, as far as possible, save the people from dying of hunger in case of famine. They set up and maintain free hotels and restaurants for travellers and, in the name of the whole collectivity, offer costly sacrifices to the gods—and so on. Of course, the important item of labour is supplied by the people, but then the workers are fed by the rich, and in Asia, to be able to earn one's bread by working is in itself considered a stroke of luck.

Charity, either directly or through charitable institutions, is a heavy burden which has to be borne by income and capital. The Japanese have an interesting word, *intoku*, which means to do good secretly. The Hindu, whether rich or poor, normally has to devote a quarter of his earnings to charity, the Muslim, one-tenth. Thus, in Islam, the religious foundations, the *habus*, which collect a substantial part of the sums offered in this way, take upon themselves the task of operating most public utility services—religious services, education, hospitals, etc.

These requirements can sometimes go very far. At the time of Hiuen-Tsang, the King of Afghanistan, every year during the Wucho festival, used to give his wife, his sons and all his royal treasures plus himself as an offering. They were bought back and returned to him, but, at any rate, the gesture subsisted.

Ostentation is practically unknown in Asia except among the princes, for whom it is a sort of duty. Islam particularly has always been hostile to luxury and especially to the building of high dwellings, a symbol of arrogance. Men there are not entitled to wear gold or silver rings. In Japan luxury is a sign of vulgarity.

Finally, throughout Asia the beggar, whether man or woman, religious or lay, is the object of respect—even more so if he is old or infirm. To place oneself entirely in the hands of He who looks after the sparrows and the lilies of the field is regarded as a sign of saintliness. For countless Hindu women who have renounced

[2] René Dollot.

the world and come to await death in the holy city of Benares, begging is quite honourable, whereas they would be polluting their life of purity and renunciation if they were to accept paid work. In India there are even castes of beggars who are attached to other castes, and the latter are responsible for keeping them, on condition that they accept no alms from anyone else. For instance, the Bavani Nayakkan are the *jati pillai* of the Kapu, the Dakkali of the Madiga, the Mailari of the Komati etc. In Gujarat alone, the Audichya, Mevada and Modh Brahmins, who live almost exclusively on alms, in 1901 totalled over 230,000 persons.

While the Viet-Namese despise those who live in a shameful manner, they do respect the poor. They speak of an old beggar as *Ong lao an may* or *ba lao an may*, 'Sir, or Madam, old beggar'. In general, beggars are known as *thanh bach*, 'pure and white families'. In the Buddhists' view, a celestial spirit may be doomed to beg through one of its earthly existences in order to expiate a slight fault. This is what seems to have happened to an old beggar named Dong-Lam who died in Hanoi in about 1893 in one of the streets of the town; an altar was erected for him in the temple known as the Sword of Happiness at the Crossing of the Incense Sticks near the Street of Boxes. In India, in Benares, I myself have seen an old woman who had no name and who, according to all the sages and monks who knew her, was a minor deity incarnated on earth and pretending to be mad; it was supposed to be a signal piece of luck if she accepted a mouthful of the food offered to her. A Korean proverb says that the beggar pities the palace reader.

The beggar who asks for alms and receives them does nothing more than exercise a right which is his in the general order of things. In Islam, for example, the wealth of this world belongs no more to their owner than to the person, less favoured, who has to claim from others the share allotted to him by God. The gift made by a Muslim to a beggar is not an individual present, since everything on this earth belongs to God, but a share taken away by Allah from his own wealth entrusted to its present owners. The beggar may even be very wealthy; in the Islamic museum of Cairo, we can see a seventeenth century Persian beggar's bowl which is entirely encrusted with gold. Even in Persia today, a bus will stop on the highway with the sole purpose of giving alms to blind beggars. It is true that certain reformed sects, such as the Babis, have reacted and prohibited begging, but without much effect. In India it is not he who receives who is blessed, but he who gives.[3]

In Tibet beggars form a community apart, and the profession is

[3] Swami Vivekananda.

hereditary, as in the case of the special Indian castes that we have mentioned earlier.

It would be wrong, however, to suppose that throughout Asia asceticism is considered a virtue recommended to all; India is exceptional from this point of view. It is true that in Islam, among the Buddhists, and in Japan, profound respect is shown towards those who have made such a vow, that Arab fakirs and Persian dervishes enjoy as much prestige as the Hindu *sadhus*, that in Siam even the most unimportant novice would not stir to serve the king, and Japan is proud of her forty-fifth emperor, Shum, and of his daughter, the forty-sixth empress, Koken, who both abdicated in order to take up monastic life—but however numerous such cases may be, they are only individual cases, and the ideal of the population as a whole is to have the strict needful, or as the Chinese would say, to follow the Middle Way, which in this case amounts to much the same. Neither the Koran nor the Avesta preach asceticism.

Consequently, those who spend their time in trade without producing usable goods do not enjoy very much esteem in many Asian countries. In fact, the tradesman is very often also and primarily a farmer. Each one offers the surplus of his own production either at his door or at the local market or else at the fair held periodically, in tiny quantities, which reveals the poverty which is the lot of the immense majority of Asian societies. In order to sell their small quantity of wares, the peasants readily spend days taking them to the market or waiting patiently for the customer; but this also affords an opportunity for contact with the outside world, for conversations and visits which are often regarded as being more important than the transaction itself.

Some societies, however, have long since organized their commercial life very methodically. Addapakshu, Sukkal of Susa at the end of the third millennium B.C., had a stele built in the town bazaar showing the prices of the various goods; the indications on the bricks forming the foundation of the stele express the wish that Shamesh, the god of justice, should make everyone obtain the right price. In the year 119 of our era there was a commercial register in China and an economic system of price levelling—which was even then opposed by the partisans of free trade; certain state monopolies had already been operating for some time and their number was soon to increase.

On the other hand, wherever loans with interest had become a custom, the rates were sometimes fabulous: 50% per month in the thirteenth century in China, 500% per year not so long ago in Outer Mongolia.

The payment of services rendered to individuals and to the community by non-farmers is operated in as uncommercial a fashion as possible, in the sense that priests, schoolteachers, doctors, craftsmen and cleaners in many traditional societies are not paid according to the amount of work done over a given period but are maintained by the village, the tribe or even the patriarchal family which, inasmuch as their means allow them, supply them with whatever they need—in exchange they do whatever is expected of them. This system creates particularly close ties of fraternity and solidarity between these people and the farmers who form the bulk of the population. In Madras, barbers and washermen (two of the most untouchable castes) are 'the sons of the village'.

It is also the same kind of solidarity and interdependence that binds man to the soil. This sentiment is of a sacred nature in Asia, even in those societies where tradition does not remind men that the soil is the mother of the human race and should be the object of worship. That is why a human being cannot be the absolute owner of a plot of land as is the custom in the West. Besides, man belongs to the soil rather than the soil to the man.

According to certain groups, the soil belongs to God. This, generally speaking, is the case in Islam, where man is never called upon to share the inaccessible sovereignty of Allah on earth; he is simply invested with the power to administer the land granted to him by divine favour. According to others, it is the collective property of the community, as in China, in Yaghistan, in a large part of India, in the Siberian forest and, in practice, also in some Muslim countries like Indonesia, Saudi Arabia (where it belongs to the tribe), in various Middle Eastern countries (where it may belong to the village or to a family comprising a number of adult men), in Turkey, in Cyprus (in the case of pastures, whereas arable land is private property).

In certain areas the land is considered as belonging to the ancestors buried under it, which means that the former 'owner' can never really be driven away; that is why the Chinese are most reluctant to part with the land that they have inherited. Recent examples show that tombs sometimes resist the most powerful machinery used for their removal when, for instance, a new road has to be built. For us, writes a Japanese (Nitobe), the land is more than just the ground from which gold is extracted or grain is harvested; it is the sacred abode of the gods and of the spirits of our ancestors.

Frequently land is entrusted to farmers individually over a limited period and then redistributed. This system is to be found particularly in the Arab countries with their *musha* system. In the Levantine steppes the whole village territory is reallotted after every three-yearly cycle of cultivation. In Palmyrena and in the Hauran, the distribution is effected on a *pro rata* basis according to the number of male members in the family. In Central Java it is the municipality which is regarded as the owner and which redistributes the land. In Irak it is the Emir who gives out the land (*miri* property). In Palestine, Jordan, Syria and Lebanon, the headmen and leaders of the tribes act as middlemen. This periodic redistribution is found even in Tibet. In Assir (Arabia), there is an additional stipulation which lays down that when the rivers run dry in one valley, its inhabitants have the right, on a reciprocal basis, to farm fields in a more fortunate valley.

In Islam, the concept of the divine ownership of the soil goes together with the idea that the soil's product is necessarily a gift of God and has nothing to do with man's personal effort.

However, a small private holding is common in very many areas from western Asia to Cambodia, China and Japan.

The concept of a state budget supplied by taxes is also necessarily very different in traditional Asia from what it is in the West—and this for several reasons. Firstly, in normal times, there is no publicly-known budget so that the taxpayer cannot find out how his money is being used; then, most of the expenses which, in a modern western country, are the state's responsibility are here borne either by the community or by the wealthy; finally, the taxpayer draws practically no distinction between what is taken by the landowner, by the moneylender, by the armies camping in his province, by the bandits demanding ransom or by the state; it has to be remembered, further, that very often tax-collection is more like a raid and that such confusion is therefore excusable.

Nevertheless, various Asian countries at various times had carefully planned budgetary and fiscal systems. In seventh century China, there was a complete system of old-age pensions and maternity benefits; in the eleventh century, a system of loans to farmers and unemployment benefits had also been arranged, and it sometimes happened that in times of calamity, or in order to mollify recently conquered populations, the Chinese emperors would reduce taxes or even cancel them altogether. The same custom prevailed in Japan; in Cambodia people exercising a particularly dangerous profession were exempted from paying taxes.

As for contracts between individuals, almost everywhere in Asia they take the form of an oral commitment based on mutual trust between the parties, each of which stakes its honour and reputation on the deal. Among the peoples which have not yet been influenced by Roman or Anglo-Saxon legal concepts from the West, every member of the group is more effectively guaranteed by such a commitment than we by our elaborate machinery of signed texts and law courts that ensure their observance. A Japanese does not ask for a receipt when he lends money. The Samurai's word, *bushi no ichi-gon*, is worth more than any contract, says Nitobe. Nor does a Middle-Easterner, when he entrusts a messenger with a large sum of money to be carried to the other end of the country.

The Muslim has a quasi-instinctive dislike for any kind of contract which is, after all, the result of an independent will going against fate for private ends. 'To contract is to disturb the divine order,' they say. Besides, for them there is no clear line between the commitment undertaken before God—as are all commitments between believers—and the obligation towards God himself. In Islam, the convention is first and foremost a religious instrument and therefore oral, ritual and solemn. It consists of traditional-style clauses— the recitation of the first verse of the Koran, the *fatiha*, serves as a preamble—and it can be declared null by the *cadi* who is the religious judge.

In many countries, however, the outsider is not regarded as offering such guarantees since it is not known how his group will react in the event of his breaking his word. Furthermore, the neighbouring country remains a potential enemy which it is wiser to weaken, even through cunning, than to enrich and strengthen through full co-operation. Therefore the oral contract, when made with a foreigner, does not always have the same absolute value as the one concluded with another member of the same group.

The situation is completely reversed when a written and signed contract of the western type is required. This type of contract, we must not forget, presupposes that both parties have equal rights and duties and they may require the enforcement of these before a court of law, a concept that is alien to nearly all Asians. Not only is the distrust implied by this act insulting, producing a desire for revenge, but its very nature is an invitation to cheat in a game where, as in poker or in chess, each one has to try and beat his opponent. For the Muslim there is no divine intervention whatsoever in the *franghi*, written, private, lay contracts concluded with unbelievers.

As for legislation, while in the West we tend to think that the 'more' modern it is the better, and a century-old law that has not been brought up to date is often a cause for shame—or amusement, as an anachronism—in the Orient the attitude is exactly the reverse. The older a rule or a law the more venerable it becomes, and if its origin is lost in time it may be considered as being of divine or semi-divine origin and nobody may tamper with it.

This holds good not only for short series of general, ethical injunctions or prohibitions, like the Ten Commandments revealed to Moses, but also for extremely detailed codes of civil, administrative and criminal law with carefully specified rules of procedure. While the Sumerian codes, those of Hammurabi, which are 4,000 years old, and that of Eshnunnah, codified by Bilalama two centuries earlier, are regarded by our scholars as being the oldest, there are others, such as the Laws of Manu of India, which, according to tradition, go back even further. In Israel the Pentateuch and the Talmud are used for reference even today. Only a few years ago Professor Katsuhiko Kakei, who taught law at Tokyo, explained his whole subject on the basis of the most traditional Shinto principles. The Koran, already fourteen centuries old, still has force of law in most Muslim states. What is more, these ancient precepts are not necessarily 'backward'; an eminent French jurist (Charles) noted that, with regard to penal liability, Muslim law forestalled by twelve centuries the European legislations which used to take legal action against animals and corpses. Only living man, enjoying his full powers of discernment and possessing the same capacities as required under civil and religious law, is penally responsible for his acts under traditional Muslim law.

The same author notes that in Islam, just as there is no distinction between that which is God's and that which is Caesar's, there is also none, for principles or for social structure, between religion, ethics, ritual and positive law—consequently, for Muslim scholars and sages a prayer may become nullified and a sale may be subject to censure. But obedience to the Koranic law which defines the divine rights, always has priority over human rights. That is why, whenever an attempt has been made to apply to a Muslim people laws and codes based on those of the occupying power, there has always been one stumbling block—viz. the establishment of a satisfactory relationship between revealed law and human law.

The very concept of legislation devised by man for man is in contradiction with the divine powers or the divine delegation which the chief is normally supposed to have received. In China, publication of the law means limiting the discretionary powers of the chief and implies, furthermore, that the virtue of the chief is not sufficient to prevent crime; that is why the Legists, who at a certain period enjoyed real influence, did not succeed in putting over the concept of a permanent rule and that of Sovereign Law. Among the Muslims, 'since the State—apart from the person of the sovereign —is only a phantom', human law cannot be very much more real.

It was therefore only natural that in some countries and some schools of thought, human legislation was not only superfluous but even dangerous. It is in Taoism that we find the most characteristic example : 'The more the rules, the less wealthy the people,' Lao Tse used to affirm, and 'the more detailed the code, the more thieves there are'. Up to recent times, the Afghans had no laws. This was not due merely to the more or less open desire for a reign of anarchy which would be profitable to many (it has been said that anarchy has the same attraction for the Arab as order has for us, for it enables him to do justice to himself) but also because the existence of a detailed set of laws opens the door to procedure and thereby provides all sorts of loopholes—like the written contract which seeks to provide for every eventuality.

There is another fundamental conception which intervenes and to which reference has already been made—namely that the same rule is not applicable to all individuals since rights and duties vary considerably from one group to another. A crime committed in India by a Brahmin or against a Brahmin is judged quite differently from the same crime committed by or against a person belonging to a lower caste. Outside all personal considerations, the fact that different races co-habit in the same country makes it necessary to impose a different system of law for each race or group; thus, even in our days, in Ceylon, Roman and Dutch law were applied in Colombo, Singhalese law in Kandy, Tamil law in Jaffna, and Koranic law to all the Muslims.

For all these and other reasons—particularly, mistrust of the magistrate's honesty—going to court is regarded as undesirable and even blameworthy in many Asian communities. According to Confucius, the ethical man never has recourse to law courts. Under King Wen of the Third Dynasty, the spirit of challenge was non-existent. According to the Japanese, if there is a lawsuit between two men, both deserve to be punished. Among the Badaga of South India, to make an official complaint or to start a lawsuit was a crime not so long ago.

In any case, there was a widespread tendency to submit disputes to arbitration rather than to refer them to courts or to invoke laws. This is to be seen among a variety of peoples from the Buryats and Tunguz to the Burmese and Japanese. Besides, the distinction between the judiciary and the administrative, which is sacrosanct for us, does not seem to be necessary or even desirable in Asian society. In Islam, to decide cases is a compulsory act of worship which has to be performed by every learned and pious Muslim. Among the Confucians, the conception of justice was so paternalist that—as a European author (R. Huard) sadly points out—it stifled all development of law.

It is nevertheless true that certain races have a natural tendency to such quibbling in court. The most notable case is to be found in

some Muslim circles which actually enjoy the game of legal litiga-
tion and think that life would be empty once it ended, so that even if
judgement has already been given, whenever a new magistrate is
appointed the two parties seize the occasion to make a new presentation and ask for further judgement of the case. Of course, we must
remember that every Muslim has an acute sense of justice and any
frustration is regarded by him not only as a violation of distributive
justice, but a breach of the divine order itself, an order which determines the share assigned to every being in creation. Therefore, a
claim before court is a holy requirement and a dishonest act committed by the other party a sacrilege when it injures the claimant's
interests. This same love of wrangling is to be found among the
Chinese, especially when it comes to sacred objects and particularly
in the case of their family temples. Thus, in thirteenth century
China the accused was immediately thrown into prison, for even
were he not guilty his case disturbed the peace of the region—and
that of the judge! As for the accuser, he was also the object of
strong suspicion. To compensate for this tendency and to attenuate
its effects, the Muslim cadis are first and foremost conciliators and
even, as has been aptly observed by one of our best experts on the
subject (J. Berque), 'releasers of strength' in the sense that they
really have a 'peace-producing' power. Throughout China, also,
such 'pacifiers' used to try their influence—usually successful—in
disputes of all kinds.

It should be added that this propensity to procedure often results
from the application of laws of the western type. While in Burma,
before the British occupation, there were no courts, the study of the
new law introduced by the British includes the study of loopholes
for getting round the law or avoiding its application. The Afghans,
for instance, have now learnt all the tricks of law while some years
ago they did not even know what a law was. The same is true of the
Buryats.

State police, which is now flourishing in so many Asian countries,
to the extent that it hampers any activity, in many cases is a recent
innovation. It used not to exist in Burma; it was unknown in the
villages of India and in most other areas. The maintenance of order
was the task of the senior members of the tribe, group or caste, and
it hardly ever required coercive methods. Moral pressure, which
could go as far as ostracism, sufficed.

The nature and severity of punishment has varied in Asia both
in time and space from the most inflexible cruelty to the most
absolute leniency.

In Persia, under Artaxerxes I, judges who had passed iniquitous
sentences were skinned alive and their skins used to be spread over

the seat of their successor. In ancient Japanese law, anybody who caused a fire used to be burnt alive. In Tibet, not long ago, large numbers of men were reduced to begging because the law courts had ordered their hands to be cut off and their eyes to be torn out. The Ye-tha used to cut a thief in two through the middle of his body. Even to this day, in Arabia, a thief has his hand cut off, but by a surgeon instead of an axe-blow as of old. In Annam, before the seventeenth century, banishment was usually accompanied by the removal of several fingers or one or both hands. In Yakutsk, in about 1685, the rebel chief Djennik, chief of the Ulos Kangalook, was scorched alive and his new-born child wrapped in its father's skin while the mother was executed on the wheel. Even recently in Siberia the normal punishment for a woman convicted of having murdered her husband was to be buried alive up to her neck. As late as 1869, the Rajah of Jaipur used to have murderers' hands, nose and ears cut off—and examples could be given *ad infinitum*.

On the other hand, in the Middle Ages, Persian law allowed nobody, not even the king, to make a man suffer death for any crime whatsoever. In the second and third centuries in China, it was thought that there is no such thing as crime. Only sins were supposed to exist, and they were naturally punished by sickness; consequently the part of prisons was played by hospitals. Formerly in Laos, the king Fa Ngum, used to proclaim that it was wrong to kill murderers, that one death was enough and that to inflict a second one was an error. Besides, for the Buddhists in general the idea of inflicting punishment 'as an example' is absolutely incomprehensible, for they consider the penalty in a personal and religious context and not in that of a secular community. As an English author (Hall) has put it very strongly, to 'show an example' to them is like washing the same garment twice in order to clean another one which is not washed.

While life in Siberian prison camps was atrocious, Russians themselves, and people with authority at that, recognized that the political deportees, in the Amur region for instance, led a life which may well have been the envy of many active Russian generals. It is also recognized that Islam had the merit of having humanized the arbitrary nature of penalties and of having rejected the cruel custom of the 'question', which was abolished in France only on the eve of the Revolution.

In various societies, particularly in the Far East, the sovereign used to request the condemned to execute his own sentence, particularly when the death penalty had been inflicted on him. The victim, in complying, did no more than fulfil a duty like any other duty.

CHAPTER XVII

Education

Knowledge lies in the mind like fire in tinder.
V I V E K A N A N D A

*Fools are so scarce in the Orient that their opposites cannot be said
to form a category.* G O B I N E A U

KNOWLEDGE, and those who possess it, enjoy immense prestige
throughout Asia, and the privileged who are able to devote themselves to the acquisition of knowledge do not stop at any effort or
sacrifice. For Mohammed, the role of the believer is to 'learn from
the cradle to the tomb'.

In China, where there is 'not an inch of the country' where learning is not deeply venerated, only academic studies requiring almost
superhuman memory could open the door to administrative posts
at all levels, and the competitive examinations were organized with
the most scrupulous honesty; it was not rare to see candidates aged
eighty or ninety competing for these posts, so great was their prestige, apart from all the more tangible advantages they procured.
Every community attached such importance to the success of at
least one of its members in these examinations that it collected the
money to pay for his studies and it was impossible to have a door
in the southern wall of the local Confucian temple before a student
of the town had successfully passed the *chin-shih* examinations.
From 2,200 B.C., the Ministry of Education enjoyed more extensive
powers than any similar ministry in our day, and in the thirteenth
century Hangchow had bookstores, stalls and markets for books.

In Korea, no more than fifty years ago, all the self-respecting
families prided themselves on owning numerous and authentic
manuscripts. The profession of bookseller was the only one a gentleman could exercise, and the humblest coolie would toil and sweat
so that his son might learn to read.

In Japan, where the voracious appetite for knowledge is proverbial, the very aim of the first diplomatic relations established
with Zui (China) in 607 was to obtain the texts of the Buddhist

scriptures without having to pass through Korea.

In Tibet, a Lama's training may require sixty years of study, and in each year he may be called upon to learn by heart some thousand pages of Buddhist sacred texts. Not long ago, there were several examples of these priests who, by dint of study and examinations, managed to reach the position of Regent without being nobles or living Buddhas. The Dalai Lama himself has to pass examinations and this is not just a formality.

In India, the *pandit*, he who has a vast book knowledge of the sacred scriptures, is revered almost as much as the sage, and many a great master has had to warn his disciples against the temptation of confusing the two. Of course, it is true that the pandit's erudition is really fabulous—it is not unusual, even in our day, to find pandits who can not only recite with the correct intonation tens of thousands of verses but who are also able to add important commentaries in these texts collected over the centuries. Such knowledge, moreover, is not just mechanical, for they are capable of remembering instantaneously all the relevant passages on any particular subject submitted to them.

The same was true of China where there were real walking encyclopaedias. At the beginning of the Manchu period, the scholar Ku Yen-Wu, who went all over the country researching on the cultural geography of China, had following behind him three big cartloads of books, and every time he came across evidence which disproved a passage in one of them, he made a relevant note.

The written texts themselves were the object of profound veneration. An English traveller to Outer Mongolia reports having seen manuscripts illuminated with ink made from powdered precious stones (Montagu), and I myself have seen in North India a copy of the voluminous *Ramayana*, written and illuminated entirely with ink of the same type. In China, even recently, it was forbidden to throw away or soil any piece of paper with script on it; it had to be burnt in a temple or school—and this prohibition extended even to empty toothpaste tubes with writing on them. The same rule has been seen to exist in Japan, although it is not generalized. In some Indian castes, a person in a state of pollution may neither read nor write, so holy is writing.

However, the sages throughout Asia—and we know their great influence—have never failed to point out the dangers of an erudition so wide that by its very extent it might lack in depth. 'To wish to embrace all that may be known,' recalled Lie Tse, 'only produces a superficial science,' and he used to preach 'the return to the original ignorance' which alone can procure inner peace. He illustrated his teaching by a curious story : A man emerges from a rock, leaps into flame, plays in the smoke, and when he is asked for his secret, he replies, 'What is a rock? What is fire?' He is told, 'What you have just come out of, that is rock. What you have just crossed is fire.' 'Ah!' exclaimed the man, 'I did not know that.' Lao Tse himself was very categorical: 'He who claims to secure the good of a country by spreading learning is wrong and ruins that country.' Already, under the Ming, the thinkers used to reject erudition in favour of intuitive thought, and it has been said quite correctly that Chinese thought 'is turned towards culture and not towards pure knowledge; it aims at wisdom and not at science as we understand it.'[1] In Japan, 'the only true knowledge is the one assimilated by the learner and which is shown in his character'.[2]

Similarly, in India, Ramakrishna once uttered solemn warnings: 'The minds of the so-called learned remain attached to earthly things . . . that is why they are unable to acquire true knowledge.' 'The holy scriptures, philosophy, logic and grammar are nothing but burdens which tire the mind.' In Islam, the goal assigned by Allah for any learning is 'elevation' of the mind.

The best description of the traditional orthodox attitude of the Hindus, Buddhists and even Muslims towards education has doubtless been summed up by a contemporary English Buddhist (Blofeld). According to him, the world already has enough schools and universities where people teach you to make a minute study of such and such an infinitesimal fraction of the outer rim of existence; above all, we need monastic schools where men can acquire the secret knowledge which leads them to the very core of existence whence all rays emanate. 'The East,' according to Masson-Oursel, 'is surely the environment where the mind has been used for everything but for the acquisition of knowledge.'

These two attitudes—respect of book knowledge and the lesser importance attached to such knowledge as compared with 'wisdom' —are not as contradictory as may be thought at first sight. Traditionally, Asia endeavours, not to know the world with its fallacious appearances in all its details, but to reach the central secret and see what is the cause of the universe as it appears before us. 'Why do cocks chant cock-a-doodle-do and dogs bark bow-bow?' asks Tchoang-Tse—and he replies: 'This fact is known to all men, but even the wisest has not discovered the reason.' 'The Sage,' says Lao Tse, 'knows before having seen,' by means of higher principles. For the Taoists, with the help of the total knowledge involved in Tao, it is possible to possess the genius which leads to success in astronomy and physics, which enables one to become an immortal or to rule over a particular province of nature. He who is perfectly

[1] Berr. [2] Inazo Nitobe,

familiar with a lump of clay, says the wisdom of the Hindus, knows all the clay in the universe. This is what explains the boundless admiration felt by hundreds of millions for Gautama Buddha, this man who was the same as themselves and who, by his own forces and unaided by any revelation, succeeded in attaining full knowledge of this central secret. Once 'that' is known, it is easy to know the innumerable applications and ramifications which comprise all that is. The Buddhist 'abrupt' school, the *tuen*, have explained this doctrinally from the time of the Council of Lhassa by saying, 'Suppose that a Buddha does know the differentiations, it is only as a concession, an artifice for the good of others.'

In our time, in India, Tibet, Islam and perhaps elsewhere, there are still masters who possess this central secret and who may be asked to explain things they do not know. Once these things have been described to them with sufficient accuracy—and not necessarily with intellectual descriptions or words—they place them in their right context with their whys and wherefores, their subtle causes on various planes, their corollaries, their consequences and repercussions, in such a way as to make them a comprehensible and necessary unit of the vast universe.

Even among those who do not indulge in metaphysical research and do no more than turn life on earth into an art, the highest education aims at forming a sage rather than a scholar. Thus, traditional Sino-Viet-Namese teaching was essentially educational and introvert; it first inculcated into the children the desire to perfect themselves. The ambition of every Sino-Viet-Namese was to be worthy of the title of *kiun-tse* (in Viet-Namese *quan-tu*), i.e. a gentleman, and to escape the appellation of *siao-jen* (in Viet-Namese *tieu-nhan*) i.e. common man, who selfishly seeks his own advantage in all things. Cunfucian philosophy stresses this opposition, regardless of any idea of social class. The best is the sage, i.e. the good and generous man in whom dignity predominates over his own interests and sometimes even over equity; he is furthermore constant in his sentiments. This constancy, different from western constancy, is designated in Sino-Viet-Namese by the words *tru'o'c-sau*, 'after as before'.

This traditional teaching, practical as well as moral and religious, used to remain necessarily utilitarian and utilizable and did not fall into ridiculous anomalies which compelled Indian twelve-year-olds to study Chaucer, little Annamites to learn the history of the Merovingians and the Yakuts, who did not even know Russian, to work on Latin grammar.

Thus the path followed by classical education in the East is often nearly the opposite of the one in the West. On the one hand, teaching is traditionally given by religious masters in Islam, India and in all the Buddhist and Lamaist countries. To mention only a few examples taken from Indo-China: in Laos, the chief of the Pagoda is supposed to run the Pagoda school; in Cambodia, the clergy has an ever-growing effect on youth, and it is common to see a monk look after a dozen children, deal with their education and their other needs by means of alms received; the monasteries—their are often two or three per village—are inhabited by the monks of the same village and so are in close touch with the local population and become, as it were, schools. The same happens in Burma, where this local free education has the immense advantage of being dispensed to all children indiscriminately, while the paid school, often far away, helps to accentuate the inequalities between poor and rich.

Furthermore, the classes normally start with a religious ceremony. In India, the master writes with his finger on the child's tongue the name of a deity who protects learning. In the countries of Confucian influence, the boy, when he goes to school for the first time at the age of about six, has to offer his teacher a cock, which is sacrificed to Confucius—this is the 'opening of the intelligence'.

Finally, the first intention is to learn and only then to understand the great laws governing the universe, not through the observation of individual cases, followed by generalizations and deductions, but starting from the teaching of the great sages.

This is what explains the method which consists in having children, at a very young age, learn by heart long passages from the Koran, the Buddhist Suttas or the Upanishads, long before they are capable of grasping their meaning. These texts impregnate their minds much more effectively than modern psychological methods attempting to act on the subconscious. Later, once the pupil has attained the intellectual and spiritual development which will enable him to understand these texts, he will have them at his disposal without having to search for them laboriously in a library.

However, the method most characteristic of Asia does not consist in supplying long and numerous texts, however rich in substance they might be, nor in accumulating data from observation, experimentation and indirect documentation—but rather in deep and long meditation on particular data, which may be the observation of a fact or an object or an extremely brief sacred formula given by the master. This is particularly the case with the Muslims, the Hindus, the Zen Buddhists of China and Japan. We have already seen the part played by meditation and *japa* in religious practices; often similar methods are used in the most down-to-earth scientific research work. In school, the Chinese child is taught to concentrate on what he reads and ignore the sounds around him.

Under these circumstances the instructor obviously has a very great responsibility and the sacred aura conferred upon him (even if he is a layman) is understandable. It has been rightly said that the relationship between master and disciple, teacher and pupil is, in their highest expression, the most perfect relationship in the East whether it be among the Muslims, the Taoists, the Buddhists or the Hindus. Lao Tse noted that this relationship was 'a mystery of the gravest importance'. One of the great and relatively recent religions of India, that of the Sikhs, is actually the religion of the *guru* or master.

The master indeed communicates not only his intellectual and technical knowledge, but also the strength, intelligence and will-power necessary for receiving and using this knowledge. He really becomes the second father of the person he guides and directs. 'My parents gave me birth,' writes an eminent Japanese (Nitobe), 'and the master made a man of me.' In the Confucian conception, both in China and Viet-Nam, he comes before the real father, immediately after the sovereign. His pupil owes him an almost religious respect and manifests it by behaving like a servant or even a slave towards him; he thereby penetrates even deeper into the master's life and begins increasingly to resemble him.

Even after his studies have been concluded, he is conscious of not being able to use his learning except by the grace of his master. In Laos, the *accoucheur*, before starting his work of delivering the baby, invokes the spirit of his master so that he might remember at the right time the *gatha* or magic formulae which will enable him to succeed. In the same country, the craftsman raises an altar to the 'master craftsmen' who, in the past, have taught the techniques used by him today.

The most moving story in this connection is probably that of the untouchable Prince Nishada who, by reason of his caste, was debarred from learning archery from the master of his choice, Drona. He therefore carved a statue of Drona and begged it to teach him— and he thus became a prodigiously skilful archer. But when Drona met him and discovered the subterfuge, he demanded, in payment for 'his teaching', that his pupil's right thumb be cut off so that thenceforward Nishada was unable to bend the bow.

For this relationship can be fruitful only if the master enjoys a discretionary power over his pupil. Without going as far as the previous story, in Cambodia, when a child is entrusted for instruction to a monk, the latter is told that he may do what he pleases with the child, provided he does not return it crippled. In fact, all Asian folklore abounds in stories where the master, in order to make his teaching really sink in and to test it, imposed infinitely difficult and perilous tasks upon his disciple.

Apart from the masters recognized as such, there are the story-tellers. We shall come back to them later. It is through them that the masses learn history, mythology, geography, much of natural science and a great deal more; their tales are remembered and repeated an infinite number of times and the necessary moral and other conclusions drawn from them. Nevertheless, Asia has at all periods of its history possessed great cultural centres with abundant libraries drawing crowds of students from far and wide. Though we are accustomed to using the term 'university' only for the institutions which began to develop in the West towards the end of the twelfth century, it must be recognized that establishments for higher learning had long existed in Asia. In the first half of the seventh century A.D., in China under the Emperor T'ai Tsung, there were 5,000 foreign students in the schools of Changan alone. In the eighth century in India the Buddhist University of Nalanda (destroyed in 1197) had 10,000 students maintained at the expense of the emperor who provided each of them with two servants; besides, there were many more candidates than seats, for only twenty or thirty per cent were admitted. In Korea in the twelfth century, there were six thousand students at the university level.

This is also true of primary and secondary education. In 1894 the town of Kokand in Siberia, with 60,000 inhabitants, had some 120 schools, almost exclusively Muslim, with over 6,500 pupils.

In about the year 600, during the Sui Dynasty's reign, the Chinese Imperial library held no less than 370,000 volumes, and under the T'ang dynasty there were 208,000. Under the Emperor Yung-Lo, in the fifteenth century, a single great collection, the Yung-Lo Ta-tien, was composed of 22,877 rare and ancient works collected into 11,995 volumes. In 735 Genbo, at one single time, brought 5,000 volumes of Buddhist sutras to Japan.

In spite of such immense resources, and in spite of the considerable esteem shown towards writings and the knowledge to be drawn from them, traditional Asia has never suffered from the confusion we make nowadays between an 'illiterate' and an ignorant person —and we must not draw hasty conclusions from the extremely high number of Asians who, even very recently, did not know how to read or write.

In 1942, in Indonesia, which had been a Dutch colony for a long time, 95% of the population was illiterate. In the early twentieth century, six or seven Turkmens out of a thousand knew how to sign their name and hardly one per cent knew how to read. In 1925, three Kirghiz women out of a thousand could read. These are by no means exceptional cases. On the other hand, there is at present only one per cent of illiterates in the Japanese prisons, and it may be said that in Cambodia, thanks to the pagodas and the monks, there have for a long time been no male illiterates. In Burma, for the same reasons, a large part of the villagers know how to read. We must also observe the almost incredible fact that in the statistics drawn up by the colonial powers, or even by international authorities, all those who only know their national language and its script and are not quite familiar with the Latin alphabet are often listed as 'illiterate'!

Furthermore, many spoken Asian languages used by large groups have been given an alphabet only recently. This is the case with many languages used in the U.S.S.R. The Japanese do not seem to have had any script of their own before the introduction of Chinese ideograms.

On the one hand, intellectual development, even in the narrowest sense of the word, has no connection with the degree of book knowledge, and on the other hand, what is known as 'book knowledge' does not in any way imply knowing how to read and write. It has been seen that in South-East Asia illiterates speak four or five languages fluently, while this same achievement becomes much more difficult once they have learnt to read. In the great universities of Islam (e.g. el Azhar), India (Benares) and Japan (Tenri-kyo), I myself have seen many classes sitting with arms crossed and listening to most scholarly lectures on the most obscure subjects—and remembering them faithfully. It would seem that the fact of being able to rely on a printed work or a book of notes considerably undermines the part played by memory and leads eventually to its weakening. It is now readily agreed that the most voluminous sacred texts have been orally transmitted with strict fidelity for many centuries—in fact, much better than when successive copiers have accumulated their mistakes. In Islam the memory of the ancients makes a cadastral survey unnecessary.

Apart from this, Asians are reluctant to couch in writing, much less print and publish, texts considered as most sacred, for that would be profanation and sacrilege; only oral transmission, with the effort it requires and the possibility it offers of selecting the listeners, is considered a worthy method. It is doubtless in this spirit that we must understand the fact that the introduction of writing into Japan was in those days considered as a sign of frivolity. When Plato blamed Denys for having committed the 'crime' of wishing to write down important thoughts which should only be transmitted by word of mouth, he expressed an opinion which is still shared by most Asians who have remained faithful to their traditions. In the sphere of law, in Islam, relinquishing such oral methods is really in the nature of a revolution. This is doubtless one of the main reasons why the Asian peoples who have a written literature have, side by side with it, another non-written literature, which is often abundant and significant.

If Asia does sometimes distrust writing, this is not because it is imported from abroad; let us not forget that Asia invented writing and presented us with this valuable gift. The Sumerians used it in Lower Mesopotamia in prehistoric times, and the Chinese characters had attained the highest perfection in the second millennium B.C. It is the Phoenician script as it appears on the sarcophagus of Ahiram which gave birth to the Greek alphabet and our own modern alphabets. Besides, the alphabet itself might be of religious value, as we have seen earlier: the classic alphabet of India, *devanagari*, is said to have been created and used by the gods themselves, as its name (*deva*—gods) indicates; for the Muslims, the Arabic script is considered sacred.

CHAPTER XVIII

Science and Technology

In all fields, Asia has been the teacher of humanity.
PIERRE GOUROU

In the field of social life, arts, entertainment, institutions and technology, China was incontestably the most highly developed country in the world in the thirteenth century.   JACQUES GERNET

WHAT we have said earlier regarding education and its spirit naturally applies also, to a very great extent, to the spirit and the place of science and technology. We must, however, bear in mind the strong underlying trend in every Asian in all his activities—viz. to remain in harmony with nature, to bring out, maintain and intensify the unity between the macrocosm and the microcosm.

This leads to several important consequences. Firstly, the use of scientific methods must not entail the elimination of religion or of the sacred, but on the contrary must strengthen their action. It is, in fact, striking to see with what perseverance the Asians, instead of 'leaving God at the door of the laboratory' as Pasteur had to do, seek, and if necessary introduce, the divine in their science and technology; we shall see a few striking examples later. This endeavour is doubtless the spontaneous effect of a strong atavistic tendency, but it is nonetheless a conscious and systematic one. The Muslims argue that the divine revelation made to their prophet is not merely the last to date but also the last to be made to mankind; and for them modern science is its continuation, the next stage which confirms, perhaps adds to, but never contradicts Koranic teaching. Orthodox Hindus who, on the other hand, pride themselves on possessing the oldest revelation and therefore the most authentic one, assert with equal conviction that our most recent discoveries and inventions, including atomic fission and the jet plane, are no more than what had already been known and used by the sages, heroes and gods of the hymns and epics. However naïve these assertions might appear to us, we must acknowledge that they conform to the Hindu's cyclic conception of time. All the Buddhists are anxious to demonstrate that modern science is

322

not only compatible with all their dogmas but is their natural development; large neo-Buddhist sects even consider this as additional proof that the Buddha's teaching is the only valid one today. The Taoists themselves, although so much against the spread of, or even the search for, anything that might move man away from the original perfection, specify clearly that 'what has caused all the evils of this world and the unhappiness of all those who inhabit it is the science that goes counter to nature'.[1] In this they are much more consistent with themselves than our orientalists might think.

That is why the Chinese, for instance, although they built machines well before Europe, would never have been able to, or rather wished to, create the machine age or even adopt it, had they been left to themselves. I do not think that Taoist chemical and mathematical ideas could ever have led to technology even if they had not been frustrated by Buddhism and Confucianism.

The machine and the tool, in the traditional Asian view of things, are no more than a prolongation of the human body, which enable us to make better use of our faculties, but should never substitute us and even less dominate us. Like the simple magnifying glass, the most perfected microscope increases our visual organ's power of perception but cannot replace it.

The assimilation of the macrocosm and the microcosm means that quantitative concepts are perceived in a perspective completely different from the one we are used to and are both less important and less real than qualitative concepts.

We have seen how throughout Asia the symbolic value of numbers awakens a great deal of interest, and that even essays on the purest high philosophy, among Hindus and also among the Buddhists and the Sufis, contain so many figures that their reading often becomes tiresome. But if one wishes to use the customary expression, 'symbolic arithmetic', care must be taken not to give it a calculation value involving operations like multiplication and division. Theirs is rather a system of 'symbolic numbers' where the only authorized operation is the one deriving directly from the numbers, that is, addition. Even this addition consists of a simple juxtaposition which keeps and accentuates the individuality of the different units in a group; it is never an arbitrary assimilation resulting from abstraction where whatever is different is systematically ignored and the common element is emphasized. It is therefore exactly the opposite of statistics, which are invading all the activities of the modern Western world. In some countries even

[1] Tchoang-Tse.

the population census used to be regarded as criminal.

Granet has pointed out that the idea of quantity plays practically no part in the philosophical speculations of the Chinese, although numbers did awaken passionate interest among the sages of ancient China; theirs was an extreme respect for numerical symbols combined with extreme indifference to all quantitative conceptions.

Another consequence of this process of assimilation between the macrocosm and the microcosm is that, while keeping to the human scale and without passing beyond it, science is able to attain a macrocosmic value and truth. We have seen this illustrated in connection with units for measuring time and space. The same may be said of the musical notes and the scale in China where, although this might seem strange, both were fixed in relation to the of his cosmos.

In the West, we are prone to deplore the high rate of infant of all things, the sage of black Africa, dominated, crushed by the bush and the forest, knows that he is the measure of nothing. The Asian sage, although he knows himself to be powerless before the sudden unleashing of nature, placidly lifts up his head after the catastrophe and once more becomes the master and the standard of his cosmos.

In the West, we are prone to deplore the high rate of infant mortality in Asian countries and the short expectation of life prevalent there. The traditional Asian approach is quite different— a child who does not look as if he can live in a healthy and vigorous condition will do better to die very young rather than be diseased and invalid all his life, thus being a burden to himself and to those around him. If we ignore the children who thus die before reaching their fifth year, for instance, we would find that the expectation of life is not as different from ours as is generally imagined.

Besides, there are many more instances of very great longevity in Asia than in the West. In traditional China old age started at seventy and a sage was said to live until his hundredth year. In Laos, in the seventeenth century, according to Father Martini, there were so many old people in such robust health that a considerable army for the defence of the kingdom could have been made of the centenarians alone. In 1928, when Ivan Shopen made a census of the centenarians in Armenia, he found 108 for every hundred thousand inhabitants; he came across persons aged 120 and 130 years in the Aparan area, and 140 years in Daralogos; in the Darachirag region there were centenarians in all the villages, without exception. I myself have known in India a great sage whose recollections—very clear ones—go back to a period prior to the establishment of the British in Calcutta.

The example of Laos given above is not an isolated one; there are other cases where this longevity is accompanied by remarkable strength and resistance and a surprising alertness of the senses. The travellers who visited Northern Asia before it was affected by modern western civilization were all stupefied by what they saw in this connection. Thus, in about 1840 the scientist Wrangel noted that the Yakuts do not feel the cold, and Erman confirms this by stating that the Yakut children run around completely naked when the temperature is 10° C. below zero, that they can bear hunger to an incredible degree, that their memory of places is developed to the highest degree, that their eyesight is excellent, etc. He quotes the following example: 'One of them, as incredible as this may seem, assured us that by looking at the sky one day, he had seen a large bluish star swallow smaller ones and vomit them afterwards; it was the eclipses of Jupiter's satellites that this man had observed'. Colonel Veniukoff reports the case of a black Kirghiz who, pierced by a stroke of the lance through the chest—the weapon had struck his back, perforated his lungs and broken a rib—two days after his wound was able to return to his dwelling, fifty-three miles away, and after one month begin his riding and racing on horseback as if nothing had happened. Sven Hedin knew a Kirghiz horseman aged 111 who had had four Kirghiz and about a hundred other wives and who climbed a mountain 15,000 feet high, and he tells how the people of this race can discern the colour of a horse long before an outsider even realizes that there is a horse anywhere. Miagkoff has seen a Cossack of the Ossuri distinguish between male and female chamois at a distance of over a thousand yards and successfully shoot from this distance at the animal of his choice. The Kurumba of India are seen to have similar sharp vision. Jacquemont reports the case of a Sikh spiritual leader, a hundred years old, who in a fit of rage cut off the head of his eighty year old son with a single stroke of the sabre. Among certain Indian tribes, such as the Kathari, a woman working in the fields stops only for a short time to give birth to her child and resumes work at once. It is no different in Tibet or Arabia. In other tribes and castes resistance to pain reaches absolutely incredible proportions; according to reliable evidence, the Sharan are capable of spraying their clothes with petrol, setting fire to them and dancing till death seizes them. In China a case was reported of an infant of fourteen months who, stung on the head by thirty bees, spent a very good night and the next day showed no sign of swelling.

All these cases should make us think before showing contempt —as was done till recently by all western-trained doctors and by some even today—for the therapeutic and hygienic methods traditionally used in these countries. Of course they are empirical in the sense that they are not based on any chemical or bacteriological analysis or on our current conceptions of physiology and histology. But which doctor would ever apply a treatment based only on laboratory conclusions without first confirming them by all sorts of 'live' experiments, i.e. 'empirically'?

The Asian methods differ from ours mainly in that they ascribe complex causes to the illness where the physical element, as we have seen, is far from being the only important one and may often even be considered as negligible. When the causes are regarded as being of a physiological order, they are interpreted very differently. Thus, in Japan certain critical ages, *yaku-doshi*, are supposed to bring certain disorders in their train quite normally. In the *ayurvedic* medicine of India, the cause is a disequilibrium between certain 'humours'. In China, it is the disequilibrium between the fundamental elements—the *yin* and the *yang*, or the five elements. In both systems practised in Burma, the disequilibrium is supposed to occur between the four elements of the body. In Viet-Nam suffering is supposed to be caused by excess energy or insufficient energy at the level of certain organs; or else, as in Laos, by 'contrary spirits', and in cases of epidemic an attempt is made to amuse them with whistling kites, *dieu sao*, which at the same time spread yellow arsenic powder, *hung hoang*. Suffering is also ascribed in many cases to the evil eye of beggars or criminals—or to a contagion or pollution which is much more psychic than material and which results from the 'continuity' obtaining between the bodies of all beings. Sometimes it is death which is said to be contagious and not the disease, which explains why certain groups are unwilling to go to hospital, since the death rate there is higher than anywhere else.

The traditional school of medicine which followed Chinese culture everywhere in its vast expansion can pride itself on its illustrious traditions. Its origin is ascribed to Shen-Nung who, in the eighteenth century B.C., composed the *Pen Ts'ao*, the first treatise on medicine. Early in the T'ang period, Sun En wrote a medical encyclopaedia in thirty volumes. A Chinese school of medicine was started in 1076, and at that time official teaching was divided into nine sections: general medicine and broad medical theories (two sections), treatment of rheumatism and paralysis, ophthalmology, obstetrics, odontology and laryngology, treatment of abscesses and fractures, acupuncture and moxibustion, treatment by means of charms and amulets—without counting legal medicine, on which there is a thirteenth century treatise explaining, in particular, the system of artificial respiration for the drowning. One of the methods peculiar to this great school, acupuncture, which Soulié de Morand introduced recently into Europe and which is now practised by many western doctors, had been adopted in Japan in the sixth century and in Viet-Nam in the tenth—and it can also be applied to animals. Recently, changing its mind after a wave of westernization which was the result of enthusiasm rather than reflection, the Japanese government has restored to Chinese traditional medicine a status identical with that granted to western medicine.

The traditional medicine of India, Ayur-Veda (and its variant, *siddha* medicine, in South India), and the schools that are specifically Arab, Persian and Muslim (the *unani* for instance) have also spread widely (Ayur-Veda spread as far as Mongolia and Siberia), and if numerous countries applied their teaching over many years, it is doubtless because they found it satisfactory.

Besides, discontented patients have many ways of showing their feelings forcefully: among the Badaga of South India, the witch-doctor who did not succeed in curing a patient was often put to death together with his family.

Sir William Jones has written with regard to the nomenclature of plants as given in pre-sixth century Sanskrit texts that Linné himself would have adopted it had he known the ancient language of the country. Shankara who, according to his disciples, lived at the time of Caesar, and according to our Indianists in Charlemagne's time, wrote: 'The sperm cell represents in miniature all the organs of the procreating body and contains potentially the whole organism which is to develop from it'. Sharaka Samhita, fifteen centuries before Harvey, explained clearly: 'From this great centre (the heart) leave the vessels carrying blood to all parts of the body—blood which is the nourishment of life in all animals and without which life would stop. It is this element which will feed the foetus in the womb, which flows into its body and then returns to the heart of the mother'.

Spiritual cure or cure by prayer, which has been brought into fashion in the West by Christian Science, has long been practised by Buddhists. In Cambodia it has actually become a therapeutic method, in China it was introduced by T'ang-shan She, and in Japan by Tathagata Yakushi, whose twelfth century statues can always be recognized by the medicine jar they hold. It is also one of the great principles at the basis of shamanism.

The horoscope, which is now being used by many a European

practitioner, plays an important part both for the diagnosis and the choice of the therapeutics.

As for hospitals, in Asia they are an extremely ancient institution. In Mesopotamia, two thousand years before our era, temples were medical as well as religious centres and saw to both the physical and the spiritual needs of the people. In China, free clinics meant for the sick were set up very early; in about the year 300 B.C., asylums were organized for the blind, the deaf and dumb, the crippled, the mad, the old and invalid, the poor and the wretched. In Hangchow in the thirteenth century there were seventy dispensaries which distributed medicines at a very low price. In India, from the fifth century B.C., the Buddhist spirit of charity led to the opening of hospitals, clinics and asylums for the sick, the aged or those in want. One of those opened by the King Parakrama in the twelfth century contained hundreds of rooms; every patient had a male and female nurse who shared the day and night watches. In Ceylon, in the first century B.C., King Dutta-gamini had declared on his deathbed, for the sake of posterity: 'I arranged in eighteen localities for the running of hospitals provided with supplies and open to invalids; I also gave them the necessary staff and medicine for the use of the practitioners'. In the twelfth century King Jayavarman VII alone founded hundred and two new hospitals. Persia already had hospitals in the third century A.D. and by the sixth century they were widely renowned; her model institutions received rich as well as poor patients, gave them medical treatment, food and accommodation of excellent quality; when poor patients left the hospital they were supplied with clothes and a sum of money. These same hospitals were specialized in the clinical training of students. Baghdad in the twelfth century could boast of sixty hospitals. It is in fact with the incentive of the Middle East, and in particular Persian medicine and Arab medicine which is based on the former, that magnificent hospitals, directed by Muslim doctors, were set up as far away as Cordoba and Seville.

However, and quite naturally so, it is in the agriculture of Asia that we find the most highly developed techniques. In a minority of cases it is true that the land was fertile enough and the population sparse enough for the necessary results to be obtained without much effort, for example by cultivation on denshired land or *ladang*, but man had mostly to scratch his subsistence from the soil by heroic labour. This was particularly the case almost throughout China, Indo-China, India, etc. However, it was not just a matter of physical labour; antiquity already possessed voluminous works on agricultural science; in China for instance, the *Ts'i-min yao-chou* of *Kia-Sseu-Hie*, which goes back to the sixth century, embraces both rural economics and the feeding of the population.

One of the most spectacular manifestations of this science is the building of terraces for irrigated cultivation in hilly areas, particularly for rice-fields. Gigantic terraces are to be found from the Philippines to Borneo, from the Shansi to Lebanon. Even in the plains, irrigation has to be minutely organized by a whole system of little dykes and canals which, already in ancient times, reached a high degree of perfection in Persia, in the seventh century in Turkmenistan and Arabia, in the eighth century in north-west Turkestan and in the regions near Mongolia occupied by the Wigurs, throughout the Chinese plain from the time of the Warring Kingdoms, even though this is represented as a period of anarchy by traditional history. Irak, Syria and especially Persia have vast networks of underground canals, the *qanat*, which are very ancient and which are to be found as far as Chinese Turkestan, where they are called *kariz*. Attempts have been made to see an allusion to well digging and irrigation in the Biblical Genesis, but these are rather fanciful interpretations, which endeavour to bring the scriptures down to a purely material and historic level.

In order to conserve water for use in the right seasons, immense dams had to be constructed sometimes. That of Nimrod on the Tigris remained in operation for three thousand years, and there were others in Susiana from the most ancient times; that of Marib in Southern Arabia, built in the remotest past, was still in operation in the sixth century. From the fifth century B.C. in Ceylon there were reservoirs with a perimeter of sixty kilometres which irrigated some thirty thousand square kilometres. The distribution of the valuable liquid had to be cleverly regulated (in Agfhanistan, the witch-doctor settled disputes regarding irrigation). But above all, such organization required a faultless understanding between neighbours, and this is doubtless one of the reasons for the existence of these orderly societies which fill us with wonder.

While we are compelled to admire these irrigation systems, we are inclined, on the other hand, to regard as 'primitive' or 'backward' many of the tools or methods of cultivation used by Asia since time immemorial, although—let us not forget that—she still has the merit of having invented them; thus we see the image of what is probably a plough on a Sumerian seal discovered in the royal cemetery of Ur and dated 3500 B.C.—and it was probably no recent innovation even at that time.

Our pride and self-respect might not be satisfied, however, when we note the results of some of the improvements we try to make.

In Burma, deep ploughing broke the crust which used to retain moisture in the rice-fields and the hoeing of the hevea plantations reduced the quantity of rubber produced by the trees. In Turkey, when the peasants had been convinced that they should remove all stones from their fields, it was noted that the harvest was not so good because the land dried up too quickly. When the Kelabites of Borneo were persuaded to sow only one species of rice, carefully selected and easy to clean, in place of the mixture they had been using up to then, beri-beri broke out among them. The introduction of the iron plough in the Uttar Pradesh in India has dislocated the close relationship between the farmers' families and those of the carpenter who built and repaired the wooden plough, and whenever the new instrument needs repair, long journeys have to be made over bad roads in order to find the specialist, which means a waste of valuable time during the very short period when ploughing is possible, and also a danger to the harvest.

The main crop over a large part of Asia is rice (it seems that it was introduced from India into China over four thousand years ago) and so its cultivation has been perfected to a very great degree. Asia has two thousand varieties, including this strange floating rice, with a stalk which grows with the rise of the flood waters as long as ten yards. There are often two rice harvests, but there is one curious point—although the second harvest may be an innovation, as among the Lepanto of Luzon, one of them only has kept its magico-religious character and is accompanied by various ceremonies. Rice has also been used in the Far East since the third century B.C. to obtain maltose by the germination of gluant rice and for making rice alcohol, rice beer, etc. In Borneo the latter is supposed to supplement the diet very usefully.

It is from Asia that we have come to know many very valuable plants: cotton, which came from Viet-Nam and was introduced into China in the seventh century; tea, known in China since the seventh century and in Japan since the eighth; coffee which, although it apparently originated in Ethiopia, came to us through Asia, etc.

As for animal husbandry, in Asia it has actually been a science for thousands of years and it is esteemed much more than agriculture. From the Neolithic period the Chinese have raised *maiali* and dogs for edible purposes. The horse was domesticated, in Elam for instance, in prehistoric times, and the Hyksos used horses for warfare eighteen centuries before our era; it seems that the steppe civilization was the first to harness them, and this custom then spread south-westwards towards the Caucasus and Iran and south-eastwards towards China. The reindeer was domesticated in

Northern China in the fifth century A.D., and in Siberia the Lapps, the Samoyeds and the Tchuktches knew how to castrate it. It is from Asia that we have learnt to raise pigs, sheep and goats. It is also clear that the Japanese have been domesticating horses, fowl and cormorants since mythological days. On the shores of the Mana the beaver was apparently domesticated by the Siberians. We know how silk was brought into Europe by the missionaries, but what is less known is the care with which the worms were treated: the Kirghiz women used to let the cocoons hatch in little bags which they carried between their breasts or in their armpits! Similarly, artificial incubation of eggs is already mentioned in China in 1585, and it was commonly practised in Viet-Nam by heating the eggs in a wood or coal stove in a bed of rice husks, and this method was seventy per cent successful. In Cambodia, for four million inhabitants, there are 1.5 million oxen and 600,000 buffaloes.

The works on *ayur-vedic* medicine teach how to treat sick cattle, horses and elephants, and in the fourth century of our era Buddha Dasa had set up a veterinary service in Ceylon. Familiarity with animals sometimes reaches incredible degrees: the Bedouins of Roub-el-Khali (Arabia) are able to recognize by its footprints a camel they have seen only once, and they can tell whence it comes and which is its master's tribe.

With regard to the production of manufactured goods also we were nearly always behind Asia until the seventeenth century. Paper, used in China before Christ, was brought to Baghdad under Al-Mansour at the end of the eighth century. It was used immediately for the development of mathematics, astronomy, philosophy, etc. China knew xylography before the eighth century. The first Japanese printing press dates back to 770, under the Empress Koken, and the first mobile characters were used in China in around 1045. In 1404 Korea was manufacturing characters in cast bronze. The scholarly emperors of that time could have 300,000 characters cast at one time.

In China neolithic pottery had attained such a degree of perfection that thicknesses as small as half a millimetre could be achieved. Early in the third century A.D., in the Fu-nan (South Viet-Nam), the people knew how to work glass. We have not yet succeeded in achieving the quality of weaving that has long since been obtained in the carpets of the Near East, Persia or China (Turkmen carpets were already famous in the twelfth century) or that of the Kashmir shawls. The silks of Merv (or Mari in Turkmenistan) were famous a thousand years ago.

As for fuel, coal was extracted and used in China from the fifth century of our era, and Japan at present uses a hundred different species of charcoal.

As regards metals, bronze was apparently used in China, Syria and Mesopotamia in the third millennium B.C., and in Tepe-Sialk (Persia) traces of metal utilization are found that date from the fourth millennium. In Viet-Nam, during the so-called Dongsonian civilization, which is placed by authorities between the fourth century B.C. and the first century A.D., there was considerable development in metallurgical techniques. From the fifth century on the Hindus were able to produce an iron column over seven metres long and weighing over six tons in 99.72% pure metal, which we managed to make in the west only a hundred years ago. In Japan the bell of Todaiji (Nara), cast in 733, weighs thirty-seven tons, is four metres high and 2.70 metres in diameter. The statue of Tran-Vu, cast in the seventeenth century by Viet-Namese bronze-workers in a mould made by the Chinese, weighs four tons.

In the chemical industry it is Asia that invented sugar, camphor, silver nitrate, alcohol, potassium, ammonia and the principal acids as well as many processes.

In the field of transport many Asian peoples have obtained amazing results through their own efforts. Of course there are very 'backward' areas; a French traveller not so long ago reported that 'China, over immense spaces, is a country without roads and at the same time a country without a single wheel . . . in 1955 millions of men used nothing but paths . . . made by bare feet, just wide enough for one man moving in single file . . . not a single beast of burden, not a vehicle' (Guillain). Besides, the oriental still has the habit of walking long distances. To go on pilgrimages, to buy or sell products, he readily walks for days, often loaded heavily, and covers amazing distances in this way; he sees nothing abnormal or dishonourable in having to use his physical strength—an essential part of his capital—in order to draw a cart or carry loads.

Nevertheless, roads and chariots have a very long history in Asia. Among the Sumerians there is a miniature representation which goes back to 3,000 B.C., of a harnessed chariot drawn by four donkeys. In China the Lung Shan culture, which is pure neolithic and goes back to two millenia before the foundation of Rome, has left drawings showing horse-drawn carts. In China, again, the emperor made it compulsory for the axles of carts to be of identical size so that the grooves would be the same distance apart everywhere and the same vehicle could be used throughout the whole country. In 220 imperial roads were built fifty paces wide, planted with trees, raised in order to avoid floods, with lowered sides and a central alleyway reserved for the sovereign. A similar arrangement is still to be found in Turkey. Apparently, these roads connected the capital with the utmost limits of the Empire.

The Persian roads were in no way inferior to those of the Roman Empire. In the sixth century B.C., Darius I had a road 2,400 kilometres long built from Sardis to Susa, with military armed posts, very fine inns, etc., at intervals all along it.

It is therefore even more surprising to see so many Asians apparently ashamed of transport that is not up to modern western standards but is still in use. Although an Arab readily lets himself be photographed with his horse, he feels insulted when we try to photograph him with his camel. At the Imperial Palace in Tokyo the Japanese giggle at the fact that fifty years ago the emperor still had horses in his stables.

With regard to water transport, it is from Asia that we learnt to use the compass; it was known from the late twelfth century, at least for navigation (Chinese geomancians had already been using it for a long time) and also the astrolabe, which was used by our mariners from the tenth to the thirteenth centuries. The exploits of the Phoenicians are well known. The Chinese had a closely knit navigation network and were probably initiated by the Persians and the Indians. Even canals connecting two seas were dug twenty-five centuries before Ferdinand de Lesseps: in the sixth century B.C., Darius completed or reopened the canal which made it possible for ships to go from the Mediterranean to the Indian Ocean, and a century later it was a Persian, Artachaees, who had a canal dug across the isthmus of Mount Athos for Xerxes' fleet. As for nautical qualities, Chinese and Viet-Namese ships were able to stand the competition of European shipbuilding until today. In the twelfth century the Viet-Namese junk of the Bayon was provided with a rudder system which was to be known in Europe only a century later.

With regard to pure science, the Asians were just as much ahead of us. It is from Turkmenia, one of the oldest civilizations of the world, that we received Al-Khoresmi, who supplied us with the basis for algebra. The Indian, Bhaskara, discovered the principle of differential calculus five centuries before Newton. A thousand years before Christ the Chinese were studying the path of Jupiter, and in the eighth century B.C. they were able to predict eclipses. In the following century Babylonian astrologer-astronomers discovered the laws followed by the movements of the planets known as 'vagabond' and were also able to predict solar and lunar eclipses. In the tenth century A.D., in Persia, Habash al-Hasib measured the earth's diameter and determined the distances between the planets as well as their diameters. In the following century, in the same country, the scholars (including Omar Khayyam) drew up a calendar more accurate than the Gregorian. In the eighteenth century, the *Chou-li tsing yun*, a work on astronomy written in China at the order of Emperor K'ang-H of the Ts'ing comprised fifty-three volumes plus a critical study of the various systems applied both in the East and the West.

In the period between the great Merovingian empire and the building of cathedrals, Muslim scholars were already laying the foundations of chemistry, optical science, mechanics and other elements of our modern scientific era.

The Chinese encyclopaedias preceded that of Diderot by a thousand years, and the one prepared at the order of Emperor Ming Yung Lo has no less than 12,000 volumes.

However, it is not possible to establish a cause and effect relationship, as our western logic would expect, between the scientific knowledge of the Asians and their research methods on the one hand and the remarkable technical results they have obtained on the other hand. That is because Asians take into account certain other factors, and all we can say of the latter is that their action is not immediately apparent to us.

A given technique may in fact comprise two parts: one that is empirical in origin and objectively efficient and another which is ritualistic and magical. The latter may seem practically useless to our eyes, but the Asian craftsman or engineer sometimes attaches a decisive importance to it. We have already dealt with medicine and we shall speak later of architecture. In a Chinese treatise on the method of using waterways there is contained, apart from ideas on hydraulics and civil engineering which might fill any European scientist with enthusiasm, a whole series of instructions on the best way to counter the hostility that might be shown by the water spirit in a particular place. Nevertheless, it is clear that the Muslims, for instance, took the experimental method in science much further than the Greeks and the Alexandrians.

It is in the fire arts that the magic part acquires predominance. In the year 636 the standard of the Persian Empire was the banner of the smith Kawe, *diarafch-i-Kawiyani*. There are innumerable Chinese or Japanese stories in which, in order to obtain a perfect welding or a perfect alloy, the smith himself or his wife or both or a young virgin would throw themselves into the furnace. In 1468, when the Great Bell of Seoul was cast, a child had to be thrown into the molten metal. There are cases in China where the bellows had to be operated by 300 boys and 300 virgin girls. Besides, according to Chinese tradition, the potters' god himself, T'ung, throws himself into the fire so that the pots may be perfect.

It is amusing to note that some of the methods common in various Asian countries, which formerly seemed childish to us, have just been rediscovered by our labour and efficiency experts. Thus, the Chinese had understood the part that could be played by singing and music in human productivity, and they used to allow workers to enjoy a relaxing rhythm, especially if the latter were engaged in such hard labour as the construction of the Great Wall of China.

What we have said regarding material wealth and its contribution, education and the direction it should take, science and technology with their consequences, health and medicine, illustrates the peculiarly Asian attitude to problems of progress and tradition.

The 'traditionalism' preserved by Asia for so many centuries and to which, in spite of appearances, she has remained faithful to a large extent, is not, as is generally believed, a lazy and passive inertia. It is a tendency that has been carefully thought over and deliberately chosen, requiring from its adepts an effort as intense and continuous as the western type of progress in our twentieth century.

This traditionalism comes from a deep-rooted belief in a 'golden age' which existed in the beginning; all the changes that have occurred in the course of human evolution have gradually forced us away from this age and any further change would remove us even further. The only real 'progress' which would be to our interest would therefore consist in going backwards in order to come closer, individually or collectively, to this paradisiac state which has been lost and partly forgotten Inasmuch as such a return is only possible for a privileged few and through harsh asceticism at that, we others must do our best, and for as long as possible, not to slide further down the slippery and fatal slope on which we have had the misfortune to embark.

Not only the strict traditionalist Lao Tse, but also Shri Aurobindo, one of the great champions of an evolution which is to lead mankind well beyond its present state, have emphasized these principles.

The following six main ideas may help us to understand the behaviour of our Asian cousins : —

1. *Asia is by no means static and never has been.*—The theory of immobile Asia, so long accepted in the West as an axiom, has always been strongly rejected by the Asians themselves and also by those who have studied Asia objectively and intelligently. Even in the most technical fields, it is from Asia (as we mentioned earlier) that we took most of the great inventions prior to the eighteenth century. To accuse Asia of being static because the various human groups

living there have long preserved many of their traits and customs and have not undergone the same evolution as we have recently experienced is like accusing Europe of being static because for over one and a half millenia she has rejected neither the Gospel nor the geometry of Euclid.

2. *Asia, however, often places progress in a context different from the one in which we seek it.*—The Asians primarily seek inner peace (of course with a few notable exceptions) and even today, even after the smallest trip 'east of Suez', we cannot help noticing that they have nearly always been able to acquire and retain it better than us. They know how not to increase their needs beyond what can be satisfied (of course, inasmuch as they have not been touched by our civilization), and they almost always decide to undertake an effort only after having carefully weighed it against the satisfaction expected from it.

They really have an art of living, an art of making better use of all that life gives them, without trying to embrace as much as possible—like a painter who tries to make good use of his colours rather than collect the greatest variety and the largest quantity possible on his palette. For traditional Asia progress consists above all in achieving ever greater perfection in this art of living.

3. *Traditional Asia is content with its lot and does not seek to alter it.*—When a man is at peace with himself, writes Lin Yutang, he has difficulty in understanding the enthusiasm of youth over all that is progress and reform. For Okakura Kakuzo, the words, 'he has become modern' means 'he is now old and disillusioned'.

4. *Asia shows a great reasoned attachment to tradition and a certain mistrust of anything that goes against this tradition or jeopardizes its existence.*—Even in philosophical and religious matters the master always tries to prove that he has remained faithful to the most ancient tradition. Jesus Christ showed himself to be a true Asian when he repeated that he came, not to destroy, but to accomplish what had been prophesied. In India, even to this day, a new doctrine is not taken into consideration unless it can be supported by Vedic texts. Confucius never replied to questions with the words 'I know' but said 'I have been taught'; indeed, the Chinese regard him as the most perfect example of the national wisdom because nobody credits him with an original thought. It has been said that the Arab practises the fetichism of the ancient and that his natural indolence leads him to let himself 'slide down the slope of a present paved with the past' (Charles).

There are sentimental reasons for this: 'If we love what is old,' say the Chinese, 'it is not because it is old but because it is eternal.' For the Tibetans tradition is a manifestation of heaven's will—and if the Viet-Namese did, indeed, shrink behind a wall of tradition during the French occupation, it is because with their hurt pride they were suspicious of all the innovations introduced by the conquerors.

But there are also reasons of simple common sense. A custom would not have lasted for centuries or millenia if it had not produced good results, and even if its *raison d'être* has been forgotten, that is no excuse for wishing *a priori* to reverse it just because it is old and to replace it by another one which has not yet proved its worth. The Hindus point out with visible pride that the social system of castes is the only one which has survived for four or five thousand years. A Cambodian proverb says: 'Do not reject the crooked path, do not take the straight path; take only the path shown by your ancestors.' The Japanese follow the instructions given by the oldest masters without ever challenging them.

Of course, this could lead very far, if common sense were not used. Thus, early in this century the Buryats used to think that an old gun was always better than a new one, 'because it has been killing for a longer time'—but these are very exceptional cases.

5. *Asia places the Golden Age in the past and not in the future as we are taught to do.*—This belief in a remote past when virtue, peace and happiness reigned unmixed, seems general throughout Asia. It is to be found in China, depicted by erudite writers who preface the history of the royal dynasties with that of the three August Ones and the five Sovereigns who used to manifest their holiness; Tchoang-Tse says that it was the age of perfect unity and union; for Confucius, it was the time when life was simplest and our needs the fewest. For the Japanese, it was Jindai, the age of the gods, which lasted 1,792,470 years. For the Samaritans and the Jews it was the paradisiac stage which we lost through our own fault. For the Ismaelians, humanity today is not at the summit of progress but has descended from a higher level. Mazdaism aspires to a return to the original state. For the Hindus the remote past was the era of the great sages, the rishis, direct descendants of the gods, who, by their purity, lucidity and high-mindedness, were able spontaneously to see truth without getting lost in the maze of research and reasoning; disease, hunger and passion were then unknown. For the Jains the epoch of omniscience and final liberation came to a close with the successor of Mahavira, Jambu. For the Persians, under Jamshid's reign, there was neither disease, death, envy, vice, hunger, nor thirst.

If we have kept only a general recollection of this age without any details, according to Tchoang-Tse, it is merely because everything was so simple then that there was no salient event.

'Civilization', as we know it, was for man the beginning of degeneracy, even if it was not the direct cause, as Lao Tse and his disciples maintain. 'When has the world ever not been decadent?' asks a Japanese (Okakura Kakuzo). In the fourteenth century a Mohammedan, Ibn Khaldoun, exclaimed: 'Civilization is Evil personified.' That is why the fundamental and even sole aim of any real progress has to be either to return to the primordial state of unity without opposition or conflict, as counselled by the Taoists, or else, if the loss is irremediable, to replace it as best we can with a surrogate which at least offers some advantages by way of compensation—which is recommended by the Confucians.

Finally, let us not forget that, although it might seem marvellous and perfect, the Golden Age is not the final point of regression, the ultimate goal fixed by Asia for herself. Beyond this state there is a higher one still, ineffable, where all duality disappears. Although this is recommended for varying and sometimes contradictory reasons, the goal pursued remains the same; we are constantly and strongly reminded that the Sage—be he Taoist, Hindu, Buddhist, Sufi or any other—can, in fact, reach this supreme, original state, and we are given countless instances.

Although in various regions we find some slight evidence that such a period could have existed, its historical veracity is only of secondary interest. What is important, even if this is only a relatively recent ideal projected into the past, is this belief in a lost Golden Age, for it is this which determines to a large extent the Asian attitude towards what we call progress.

6. *Asia is nonetheless capable, if she wants, of evolving faster than we ever did.*—Asia lacks neither initiative, dynamism, willpower, nor intelligence. This has become dramatically apparent in our own times, when we see countries which, not long ago, were still at the stage of the Middle Ages or the Bronze Age catch up with us and cover in ten to thirty years the ground we took several centuries to cover in the technical, economic, political and military fields. Examples are so fresh in our minds that there is no need to mention them here. Of course, we help them a great deal by generously allowing them to take advantage of our recent discoveries and inventions achieved by our hard labour over the last 200 years or so. Nevertheless even if it is only a matter of assimilation or adaptation, this is a striking confirmation of this fact that we have long refused to admit: If Asia, which was so far ahead of us in the most materialist fields for centuries, subsequently and for a long time refused to embark upon the mad race for progress as we conceive it, it was by deliberate choice and not because of any congenital incapacity. In our days, Japan, India, Soviet Asia have numerous

eminent scholars and scientists who contribute to the progress of human knowledge in those very fields where we thought we enjoyed total and final exclusivity.

CHAPTER XIX

Art

I am much more anxious to be in unison with nature than to copy her.
GEORGES BRAQUE

FOR traditional Asia, subject to a few notable exceptions, the idea of 'art for art's sake' is absolutely incomprehensible. A work of art must have an aim and its value is appreciated inasmuch as it succeeds in attaining this aim. Now what is this aim?

Generally speaking, it may be said that the artist's intention is to discover, translate and make us perceive the divine or the harmony which shows itself in the world through rhythm, and to enable us to be an active part of it. It may therefore be said that Asian art is essentially religious in the widest sense of the term.

It has been affirmed, without exaggeration, that Muslim art, including music, is theological. In India, art is only 'a concrete aspect of religion'.[1] And this is even truer for Tibet, where sculpture, for instance, is a religious art, subject to the strict requirements of dogma. A great connoisseur of Far-Eastern art (Cranmer-Byng) has written: 'The great art of the Far East is religious since it is concerned with that which underlies the form of things, with the revelations of light and rhythm which belong to reality alone.'

This trend is apparent in the choice of subjects and in the manner of treating them. It has been said quite rightly that 'the contribution of China to the cause of man is to be sought in the profound recognition by her artists of the divinity latent in all environment, the secret life which awaits the discovery of adventurers in harmony'.[2] For the Taoist artist—and which Chinese artist is not one?—'the subject of a poem or a painting, taken from an unreal and fugitive world, is unimportant; but the rhythm of the verses and the strokes of the brush are able to express, outside time and yet in a concrete manner, a state of personal intuition which is a singular and permanent reality'.[3]

In India and throughout South-East Asia all the arts, from archi-

[1] Marchal. [2] Cranmer-Byng.
[3] Marcel Granet.

tecture and sculpture to music, dancing, theatre and painting, in their noblest and their commonest forms, have as their sole theme the life of the gods, the legendary heroes and the mythical beings.

What differentiates art from philosophy is that the latter lays down laws while art seeks to bring us into contact with the profound reality, to bring us into harmony with nature through a particular detail. An old precept of Chinese art is that 'we should show the large in the small and the small in the large, provide for the real in the unreal and for the unreal in the real'.[4] This is doubtless what should be understood by the assertion of a Chinese scholar to the effect that the art of his country does not aim at domination over nature but at harmony with nature.

Under these circumstances, it is quite natural that very many oriental artists should be recruited from monasteries in China,[5] Thailand[6] and other countries. Even if he were a layman, the artist had to have not only religious knowledge but also deep spiritual experience. Coomaraswamy noted that men who have not seen the ancient gods have shown themselves incapable of depicting them. Anyway, the very practice of art was for the artist a spiritual experience in the same way as prayer or asceticism. In Japan every art, major or minor, has to lead to a total shedding of the ego in the artist, to complete self-control, and through ever-increasing perfection in execution to the purification which is the essential aim of the national religion, Shintoism. This is probably true, to a certain extent, *mutatis mutandis*, of the Buddhist countries. The Thai artist aims only at serving and exalting his faith—and this explains why he makes no effort to adapt himself to the taste of the public, as a European artist teaching in Thailand (Silpa Birasri) noted somewhat dismally.

Consequently, very broadly speaking, it may be said that in Asia every artistic effort aims at enabling the one who undertakes it to perfect the art of living and that, on the other hand, every work of art is the fruit of magic or religious inspiration which must be obeyed, thus producing the equivalent effect on the admirer.

It is only natural, indeed, that the work of art, being thus linked to religion and to the supernatural, should possess an actual magic potential. The latter, exercised mostly through the hidden or apparent rhythm which animates the work, may be brought into action consciously and deliberately by the spectator, or without his knowledge, or even against his will, but in all cases it is the

[4] Lin Yutang.
[5] Particularly the landscape-painters of the twelfth century, mostly Buddhist monks who lived in their temples among the hills and pine forests.
[6] Where it applies also to handicrafts and science.

object that holds the power and receptivity is not always required from the person exposed to its good or evil effects.

In the sixth century B.C. the Chinese Hsieh Ho already spoke of the essence of art as being the vital movement of the mind through the rhythm of things, and this 'rhythmic vitality', *ch'iyun sheng-tung*, the highest ideal of Chinese art, has the same value in all Asian art. 'All problems of art are problems of rhythm'.[7] It is through the use of rhythm that the Chinese artist can instil life even into that which is inorganic: its bronzes, its pottery, its enamel. It has even been contended that this preoccupation explains the predominant importance attached to consonants in the Near and Middle Eastern alphabets, but this is perhaps somewhat far-fetched.

This active nature of creative art is recognized not only in music, as we shall see later, but also in techniques as varied as flower arrangement, calligraphy, and the tea cult, all used systematically, even in our own day, in certain prisons and reformatories in Japan.

In the bulk of Asia the different arts are much more closely interconnected than they are in the West, not only at their very foundation, in having the same goal and a common source of inspiration, but also in the techniques used—which have the same basic rules but vary only in their details—and finally in that many artists practise several arts simultaneously and indiscriminately. An ancient, sacred Hindu text, the Vishnu-Dharmottara, maintains that 'he who does not know the science of dancing will have difficulty in understanding the rules of painting'. Under the T'ang, the declamation of Buddhist texts was accompanied by the showing of relevant paintings. The same word, *pien*, is used for the texts of popular literature and their illustrations. 'Poetry without words' is a metaphor used for painting. Besides, in the China of the Great Age, the same man was often a poet, musician, painter and also philosopher and politician.

Surprisingly for us, the two poles of art in Asia are perhaps dance (we shall revert to that later) and calligraphy.

The latter, in countries using the Arabic alphabet or Chinese ideograms and also, to a lesser degree, among the users of the Sanskrit (*devanagari*), Burmese, Siamese, Tibetan and other alphabets, is closely connected, in spirit and in technique, with painting, and it is often difficult to draw a clear boundary between the two. In Japan, the same word, *kaku*, means both painting and writing, and in China, both together form a single concept which is seldom subdivided. In the countries using the Arabic script, decorative or even figurative compositions are made with lines of script, and calligraphy is used for creating real works of art.

[7] Lin Yutang.

Similarly, calligraphy is connected with sculpture and architecture and, in Muslim countries, supplies them with many of their decorative motifs and a style to go with the decoration. In China, according to a very competent Chinese (Lin Yutang), 'there is . . . not a single type of Chinese architecture, whether it be *p'ailou*, the pavilion or the temple, whose sense of harmony and form is not directly derived from certain types of Chinese calligraphy'.

In another direction, calligraphy is very closely linked to literature, and particularly to poetry; in a Chinese or Japanese poem, the graphic presentation, with its infinite subtleties, is almost as important as the inspiration and cannot be dissociated from it—which makes translation almost impossible. Practically the same may be said of a text written in Arabic characters, whether the language be Arabic itself or Persian or Urdu or any other. Calligraphy thereby naturally touches upon singing, music, theatre and finally the dance.

This interpenetration continues even in fields which we generally regard as being outside art proper, classified by us either under handicrafts or as simple entertainment which we could hardly raise to the dignity of art.

The activities in this category are innumerable. Without mentioning sports and games, to which we shall return later, there is a multitude of art forms peculiar to the East. Perhaps the greatest variety is to be found in Japan. To mention only a few examples: paper cutting, *kirigami* (also practised in China); paper folding, *origami*; incense smelling, *kiki-ko*; flower arrangement, *ikebana*, which is fourteen centuries old; kitchen and table art (kitchen 'aesthetics' are practised in various other countries such as Cambodia); and, above all, the art of serving tea, *chanoyu*.[8] For *ikebana* and *chanoyu* an apprentice generally has to learn for successive five-year periods; all the great masters acquire national fame and go down to posterity in the same way as great painters or poets.

Handicrafts also are inseparable from art. In Viet-Nam, to quote only one example, the mason is also necessarily a sculptor, mosaic-worker and painter, the carpenter is also a cabinet-maker and wood-carver.

Any activity worth cultivating may be taken as seriously as a real art. When a Chinese reads Li Li-Weng's essay on the 'Art of the Siesta', he does not regard it at all as a joke but rather as the very useful teaching of a connoisseur.

This infinite range of artistic fields, plus the fact that most Asians have preserved a strong sense of quality and believe in devoting time to the true enjoyment of life, explains why a much larger

[8] For a description, see particularly Okakura Kakuzo and Fujikawa.

proportion of people than in the West indulge in some form or other of art.

One of the most striking examples in Japan is doubtless that of poetry. Not only does every Japanese, before dying, sum up the essentials of his life's experience in a short poem, *ji-se*,[9] not only does any visitor to a place of great beauty have to set forth his impressions in a poem to be left there as a keepsake, but everybody, even the humblest—servants, taxi-drivers, barbers—compose *hai-kai*. During the last World War, when a number of stories were prohibited because they did not exalt the virtues required under the circumstances, the story-tellers, upon the proposal of Mumeian Nomura, buried them with great pomp in the Honpuji park and built in their honour a mausoleum which they visited every year in order to pray to the stories.

It has been said that for the Japanese true ethics are aesthetics; it is not excessive either to maintain that the real religion of the Chinese is an art—the art of living. Poetry holds an eminent place in all classes of Chinese society. Under the Empire the examinations which opened the way to administrative careers included poetry tests and the time spent by state officials in the practice of an art (poetry, painting, calligraphy, etc.) was regarded as a contribution to the progress of the national culture and was not supposed to be deducted from leisure time. Early in the second century B.C. there was in China a Director of Music who was a senior state official and, at about the same time, the Chinese explorers who went to Central Asia collected melodies there.

In the fourteenth century, in Korea, any cultured person had to be able to compose poems under any circumstances, and not so long ago the examinations for admission to administrative posts included poetry tests as well. At the other extremity of Asia, the Kazakhs have such love and respect for art that their great national hero, Jambul Jambaev (late nineteenth century) is a poet.

Invested with such an important mission, art, although it is widespread, cannot but be imbued with great dignity. Evidence of this is to be found in the interminable list of Asian sovereigns who have left behind works that are much esteemed and rightly so. Here are a few examples:—

In Japan the Emperor Meiji composed over 20,000 poems, two of which are posted up every day in the temple dedicated to him in Tokyo.

[9] We are told about the extreme case of Oto Dokan, the famous builder of the great Tokyo castle, who, assassinated, had a couplet shot out at him by his murderer and, before succumbing, found the energy and the presence of mind to improvise a couplet in reply (Inazo Nitobe).

In the second millennium B.C. tradition says that the Korean kings, Keija and Yuri, composed very fine poems, as also did their successor, King Mu in the seventh century.

In China it is the Emperor Shun who is said to have written the most ancient poetry. In the third century A.D. Ts'ao Ts'ao, King of Wei, and his two sons Ts'ao Pei and Ts'ao Tche, were among the greatest Chinese poets. The Emperors Wu and Chien Wen of the Liang were the best poets of their time, as well as Tchao Ming, son of Wu, and later, the Emperors Heo-tchou of the Tch'en and Yang Ti of the Suei. The latter in fact was so jealous of his fame as an artist that he put to death the great writer Hsieh Tao Heng, who was said to be a better poet than himself. In the eighth century the Emperor Hiuang-tsong was a talented poet and musicion, and the verses of the Emperor Ming Huang are still famous. At the end of the tenth century the Emperor Li Kiu and his son Li Yu left behind poetry of value, likewise the Emperor Hui Tsung in the twelfth century, who was at the same time a great painter. In the seventeenth century it is the Manchu emperors Kang-hi and K'ien Long who were particularly noted for their works, the latter being reputed to have written over 30,000 verses.

In Tibet the Dalai Lama Ts'ang-Chang Jamts'o (seventeenth and eighteenth centuries) has left poems which are still much appreciated.

From the time of the Tran until the last dynasty the Viet-Namese Emperors composed collections of poems and were among the greatest Chinese language poets of their country. In Cambodia in the nineteenth century the king, Ang Duong, was a distinguished poet.

The King of Afghanistan, Ahmed Shah, who, in the middle of the eighteenth century, five times conquered a large part of India, is the author of a book of odes in Pushtu which is full of mystical effusions and which has been the subject of much commentary.

In the Ottoman Empire most of the Sultans received an education combining that of a poet and a warrior. The type of the 'possessor of the sabre and the pen' (sahibu seyfu kalem) had through the centuries become the ideal of the political authorities, who felt themselves compelled to be not only patrons of art, but thinkers and artists themselves. Not long ago, the verses composed by the greatest Sultans were published and republished—those of el Fatih Mohammed II, the conqueror of Constantinople, and of Soleiman the Magnificent, both of whom wrote philosophical poems in Turkish, Selim I, known as Yaouz, who wrote verses in Turkish and Persian, and many others.

The preparation of the artist for his work is extremely long and careful. It would seem that, in many cases, the long preparatory period required is intended more to exacerbate the desire to learn than to teach. We are told that when Chensiang wished to learn to play the sithar, he first spent three whole years merely practising dexterity and touch, without playing a single tune. Not long ago, when a young Japanese wished to learn the samisen, he had to wait for months at his master's before being allowed to touch the instrument, and even then he could only do so in secret. It is common for a learner of calligraphy to spend a whole year in learning how to rub his stick of Chinese ink in the bowl before being allowed even to touch a brush.

This is only a sign, one of the most superficial ones, that the training of the Asian artist includes an extremely large share of work within the mind, for the artist has to 'know' what he will be called upon to depict before being allowed to do so, whatever his technical qualifications may be. In the sixteenth century Tung Ch'i-Ch'ang, one of the greatest Chinese painters and calligraphers, used to say: 'How can one produce paintings before having read ten thousand books and travelled ten thousand li?'[10] Furthermore, this preparation often demands knowledge and practice of various rites which have to remain secret.

The Committee of Mores and Customs of Cambodia wished to learn the methods and rites for casting and tempering swords, an art which used to flourish in the recent past in Cambodia. After an advertisement in the papers, a caster appeared. He took six months to decide finally to submit to the questioning. After a few days he refused to continue, having fallen ill with an attack of fever which he regarded as a punishment by the spirits for his treachery.

However, this goes even further in the moral and spiritual fields. Wen Chen-Ming used to say: 'He whose moral standard is not high will lack style in his art.' In thirteenth century China painting and calligraphy were forms of religious asceticism; an ecstatic delirium was needed for the calligrapher or poet, who was master of his art. The Chinese artist, according to one of our own contemporaries (Lin Yutang) is a man at peace with nature, free from the chains of society, who does not surrender to the attraction of gold and whose mind is deeply immersed in the mountains, rivers and other manifestations of nature. Above all, in his breast there must be no evil passions. The artists of almost all the Asian countries would probably accept this definition.

This general training does not dispense the artist from having to undergo special, intensive preparation for each work. Among the Saora the painter must see his painting in a dream. A Chinese

[10] Lie Tse.

painter who had been ordered by a patron to paint a picture representing a cock had asked for a full year to execute it; once this period had expired the customer was unpleasantly surprised to see that the work had not even been sketched, but in front of him, with a few strokes of the brush, the artist produced a masterpiece; for a full year he had permeated himself with that which is essential in the being he had been asked to reproduce, and then, having lived through this experience, it was easy for him to execute it perfectly. Whether this story is true or not, it is typical of the attitude of the artist in Asia.

It also often happens, as Coomaraswamy points out, that before undertaking his work the artist should perform certain rites to attenuate the influence of the conscious will and to liberate the subjective faculties, which are better able to identify themselves closely with the model. In the sixteenth century the Korean poet, An-sook-Poong, asked to design a name for placing above the gate of the Mulberry Palace, first purified his body for a hundred days by refraining from all meat. The Japanese blacksmith of old had to purify himself for twenty-one days by continence and vegetarianism before being able to reflect his soul in a sword he had made himself; that is how this sword was able to cut through iron. These examples are by no means exceptional.

Respecting his work in this way, the artist also respects the tools used for it and to which he often ascribes a life of their own. This is especially the case with musical instruments, which are actually sacred in character; moreover, their shapes and sizes are determined according to laws of a mystical order.

In Laos these instruments possess a soul, *khwan*, just like men, and care must be taken not to displease them; various rites are performed to propitiate this soul with offerings of candles, food, flowers, incense, etc.—and the *khene*, once consecrated, can even establish communication between the world of the spirits and that of men.

In China, the harp of Peiwoh was said to choose its own theme— and if the table lute, *ch'in*, measures exactly 3.66 feet, it is because the year has at the most 366 days; it has five strings because there are five elements; its upper part is round to represent the firmament, and its base is flat to represent the ground; the thirteen studs stand for the twelve moons and the intercalary moon. When the calendar was reformed in 104 B.C. the whole system of measurements was readjusted and particularly that of the sound tubes determining the musical scale.

The importance of rhythm accounts for the great part played by percussion instruments. In Asia, the drum displays a variety and refinement that we can hardly imagine, and it is not unusual to attend solo performances with a single drum which can last for hours. The manufacture of the drum is a special ritual process. In Laos, where the drum can be good or evil according to its size, its *khwan* is breathed into it when the last peg is placed.

This attitude to musical instruments is not an isolated case. In Thailand the farmer's cart also has a *khwan* like many other inanimate objects. The Japanese solemnly bury broken needles and celebrate special services, *kuyo*, in their honour, in Buddhist temples; when the harvest is good they make offerings to their scarecrows and farming tools in order to thank them for their co-operation. In India, if one enters a modern tailor's shop early in the morning on certain days, one sees the tailors offering incense and flowers to their sewing machine; the Mala weavers worship their loom before starting work; the Madiga tanners do the same for the pot in which they place their tannin; the Kallan devote a special day to the worship, *ayudha puja*, of their tools; and before beginning their tilling, the Lingayat celebrate a cult for their buffaloes and their plough. In Viet-Nam the pots which can no longer be used are not thrown away but hung on sacred trees—and in the late nineteenth century, the Viet-Namese Emperor, Tu'-Du'c, ennobled his inkpot.

In the art of hunting and warfare, the weapon is profoundly revered. We have seen earlier what personality may be acquired by a Japanese sabre. In North Laos, the A Kha make offerings to their cutting implement every year at the end of the Mia Cu festival. The Cambodian worships the buffalo-leather lassoes used for hunting the elephant.

However, all this is nothing as compared to the actual worship of the master who taught the art practised. In all the countries, wherever photography is practised, it is extremely unusual for the artist not to have his master's portrait permanently beside him and often also a relic of his. Before starting any work he addresses a prayer to his master and asks for his protection.

This master may, of course, be a man, living or already dead, but it may also be a more or less mythical being or a lesser god. The Viet-Namese wrestlers, before a fight, pray to the spirit of the *dinh* and mention all the prizes they wish to win, and the Siamese boxers do the same.

The master's attitude towards the disciple is just as familiar, and it is common for him, in various arts, sports, games or crafts, actually to adopt as his son the person whom he has initiated.

In view of the goal pursued in the work of art, it nearly always has an esoteric character, in the sense that its most immediately apparent meaning is only the most superficial and exoteric one.

This holds good not only for the objects which have a sacred or ritual character in themselves, or which, like dancing, are directly connected with religion. It applies practically to any work of art and probably also to every feature of each work. Even those that seem solely decorative and aesthetic to our eyes hold many other messages which the enlightened can decipher to the extent that they are initiated. It has been said that in Muslim art 'the abstract reality of a final universe has more authority than living reality'.[11] To quote an extreme example at the other end of Asia, in Japan, where every art form and every form of entertainment is or was esoteric, the technique of folded paper, according to a great authority on Shintoism, 'has a cosmogonic meaning'.

It is this same esotericism which provides the explanation for certain apparent imperfections which we think are due only to the negligence or the incompetence of the worker or the artist, or even to an interruption of the work brought about by a change of dynasty or by lack of funds. A striking example is given by the countless cylindrical cavities of uniform depth and diameter which are scattered all over the sculptures and bas-reliefs of the Angkor temples. Our archeologists explain them as being necessary in order to have a hold on the stones when these are lifted, forgetting (a) that many of these orifices are to be found right in the middle of a royal or divine figure and (b) that some small stones have a large number of these holes, even if they have been used close to the ground, while very heavy blocks, placed very high up, have none. It is really inconceivable that the great artist who built these sacred edifices should have been so casual about this particular point. However, even if we are convinced that these holes correspond to some kind of law or fact that was not to be disclosed to the multitude, it does not help us to understand their meaning—and perhaps we shall never know it.[12]

It should not, however, be concluded that these hidden truths always express themselves by a uniform symbolism. Although the symbol used is almost always connected by an occult link with what it represents, it varies easily, in space and time, according to its environment. Thus, in the sacred dances of South-East Asia,

[11] Von Grünebaum.

[12] One may venture to assume the same with regard to Pre-Columbian America, where curious projections are to be seen on certain Mexican pyramids and on the immense stone blocks used by the Incas (for instance, at Ollantai-Tambu). There again our archaeologists lazily explain that the workers used these for transport, or to support the scaffolding—and then forgot to remove them! Schwaller de Lubicz has explained similar anomalies in Egyptian temples.

symbolic representation by *mudras* is not always the same. Dhanit Yupo mentions the choreographic representation of a deer in a forest: in India the dancer extends the thumb and little finger and keeps the other fingers bent; in Thailand, in the olden days, he would open both hands and place them before him, palms forward; now, in Thailand, he extends the index and middle fingers of each hand, stretches his arms downwards as far as possible, then raises the index and middle fingers until they are at waist level, etc.

However, the style, the treatment and most of the details of each work of art are generally determined by extremely strict traditional rules, as may be expected in areas where this work pursues a ritual or magic aim and where the transmission of the art, at any rate, is more or less esoteric. Muslim tradition prohibited the representation of living beings, and so, in Iran and elsewhere (particularly in Isfahan at the 'Ali Ghapu) when birds were painted, in the most natural positions, a line was drawn across their throats to show that they were dead.

Even in popular drawing, in Cambodia for instance, no individual fancy is allowed to manifest itself and the artist obeys strict rules. Ever-mobile nature may be interpreted according to the hour and the mood, but the world of the gods is fixed forever, eternal and immobile; and woe betide the hand that would change the line thus drawn by tradition. In the Siamese images of Buddha, if the sculptor shows some originality, it is done 'in spite of himself'. Even in composition there are complicated rules to be observed. In the Indian and Cambodian frescoes and bas-reliefs showing scenes from the *Ramayana*, every scene has to be 'closed in on itself' by the eyes being directed and the bodies leaning towards a central point; the composition focusses inwards upon a single motif; and therefore the juxtaposition of episodes does not cause any confusion in the mind.[13]

Coomaraswamy, recognizing that in Japan, for instance, the art which is seemingly most spontaneous is the result of the most minute and formal technique, admits that perhaps the deepest inspiration not only goes together with such formalism, but even needs it. In any case, this is in keeping with an art which is generally more hieratic than naturalistic, in dancing and theatre—even the more recent styles such as the Japanese *kabuki*—in sculpture and landscaping, in painting where our concepts about perspective clash with those of the Asians—an art where, generally speaking, the absence of symmetry is far from being an enslavement to the model. Even if this trait may not be, as some Indians elegantly put it (S. K. Tagore), 'a feature of the Infinite', it is regarded as an aes-

[13] Bernard-Thierry.

thetic obligation, just as Chinese calligraphy explicitly teaches.[14]

Besides, the artist constantly borrows from nature, and for the unenlightened eye he seems to be copying it continually; but his effort often seems gauche and clumsy to us because we are unable to distinguish his interpretation of the theme and his specific aim which goes beyond the nature that is visible to the human eye. All the arts of Asia include, in the *decor* proper, certain motifs drawn from flora and fauna expressing the exuberance and prolific nature of life; even when stylizing, the artist adopts a conception which breathes life into inanimate objects and turns plants into animate beings.

Anyway, the *leitmotiv* constantly found in all the arts, in the instructions of all the great masters, is that the artist must succeed in discerning, choosing and expressing the essential, and in order to do so, he must master all that is non-essential until he can eliminate it, but in such a way that the work which emerges suggests the whole while giving free play to the imagination. That is why it has been said that Western art aims at expressing differences, individuality and localization in time and space, while oriental art aims at expressing indifferentiation.

While it is nearly always possible in the West to know who was the model of a painter or a sculptor, however allegorical his composition might be,[15] or which landscape served as his background, even if it is only a small fragment seen through a window in an Italian Renaissance painting, it would be unthinkable to try to discover who had posed before an Indian or Indonesian sculptor, a Chinese painter, a Persian miniaturist or an Indo-Chinese ivory-carver. Of course, one of the reasons for this is that many figures or scenes are taken from the world of the gods, the demons or the dead, and even when the events in question took place on earth the heroes were all divine, like Krishna or Hanuman, or even supra-divine, like Mahavira or Gautama Buddha. In any case, they were always fully idealized or transposed into the abstract, like Lao Tse or Bodhi-dharma.

All this leads to extreme subtlety. Unless one is deeply initiated into the niceties of oriental art or, what is rarer, one has an instinctive feeling for it, it is impossible to appreciate these works properly. The tourist strolling through a Japanese department store sees little

[14] When Lin Yutang writes that this absence of symmetry is a character of nature, he means thereby that symmetry in art would cut us off from our harmony with nature.

[15] With a few, very rare exceptions, the Christian artist who represents a Christ on the cross always has one or more models, and he reproduces even their anatomical peculiarities.

vases made of bamboo placed side by side, some of which are a thousand times more costly than the others, and he fails at first to see the reason. Another westerner, even though he may be enlightened and gifted with acute artistic sense, will admire a calligraphy which to a Persian or a Chinese is cheap and clumsy. The refinements of Hindu, Arab or Japanese music can only be appreciated after very long training, even though the pleasure they give us from the very start might mislead us into thinking that we 'understand' and like it.

It has been maintained, not without foundation, that oriental art has one dimension more than ours, for while a western work of art fixes one instant, Asian art evokes a movement. This is illustrated by the fact that the Japanese Buddhist Kegon sect considers that 'only the flower that falls is the total flower'.[16] But these are ideas, and it is difficult for the westerner to see them in concrete form.

Some of the processes used seem, to our eyes, to stem more from psychological than from aesthetic motives—for instance, the interminable repetition. Particularly in Buddhist art, which is certainly not the only case, the same statue is frequently repeated in actual 'litanies of stone' in a hundred or a thousand copies placed side by side; this is to be found in China (e.g. the Caves of the Thousand Buddhas in Yun-kang), in Japan (e.g. the 1,000 Jizo and the 500 disciples of Buddha in the Gohyaku-rakan). The same applies to the statues of the Tirthankaras which fill the temples and other holy places of Jainism, although there are distinguishing features which escape the uninformed observer and which make it possible to find out which among the twenty-four great Jains is represented by a particular statue. The same process recurs in the Muslim philosophic texts of the Kalam and in the Buddhist *suttas*. There are actual mental laws of repetition. R. Schwab has very clearly shown, with the help of examples taken from the *Thousand and One Nights*, the force of conviction that insistence based on repetition has in Asia— it is as if the object would exist with more certainty if it were named several times.

The very size of the work is often of great importance in the eyes of its admirers. The Japanese are proud of their Dai-butsu of Kamakura, which is sixteen metres high, the Jains of their Gomateshvara of Sravanavelagola which measures eighteen metres, and the Hindus of their crouching Nandin of Mysore which measures five metres. In Afghanistan, the two gigantic Buddhas of Bamiyan are respectively fifty-three and thirty-five metres high, but the Chinese pilgrim Hieuen-tsang, in the seventh century, reported having seen, in the same spot, a sleeping Buddha 300 metres long. Early in the fifth

[16] Shimizu.

century the Chinese pilgrim Fa-hien spotted on the right bank of the Indus, in the valley of the Dards, a seated statue of Maitreya thirty-six metres high and three and a half metres from one knee to the other. Of the immense monolithic Buddhas of Yun-Kang in China the nose alone is two or three metres long. At the Wan San Pet of Ayudhaya (Siam), there is one bronze Buddha probably dating from the seventeenth century, which measures ten metres from knee to knee. These dimensions are not only symbolic and show as physically very big those beings who greatly exceeded the rest of mankind on other levels (the Buddha as well as Adam, according to certain commentators of the Koran, are reputed—a curious coincidence—to have been sixteen feet tall), but they perhaps also reflect a belief that these beings were indeed gigantic.[17]

In this connection, it may be mentioned that in jewellery the accumulation of a quantity of precious stones in one single object often seems more important than their aesthetic arrangement—e.g. the Thai crown jewels at Ayudhaya, the treasures of the Rameshvaram temple, etc.

In many cases the artist does not sign his work. The great majority of ancient sculptors are strictly anonymous and this applies to many other arts. This has sometimes been ascribed to the Buddhist influence, which is hostile to any expression of the individual personality. It is indeed largely responsible, but expressed a feeling common to the whole of Asia. The artist feels that he has been entrusted with a mission which is beyond his control, thinks that he is guided by gods or masters, that he is subject to strict rules and has to conform to venerated patterns, and he is therefore often under the impression that he is no more than an instrument. Very often, also, in India for instance, he signs the name of the God who has inspired him or simply incorporates his work in that attributed to his master, human or mythical.

This is by no means a trick, as we are inclined to think, but only a sign of humility or rather, as they would say, of honesty. Granet has stressed the anonimity of the Chinese thinker and he has written quite rightly : 'As questions of time or persons have no importance for anyone who believes in direct communication with the divine, these works are ordinarily just placed under a sacred patronage and are neither dated nor signed unless the signature and date are forged'. Similarly, an expert on Hebrew thought[18] regards the latter not so much as the product of individual genius as the result of a social fact.

[17] It is interesting to note the same conceptions among the early Christians, who imagined Jesus as a giant.
[18] P. Edouard Dhorme.

Moreover, in many cases the artist, on principle, does not aim at perfection. In the Far East there is a tendency to look down a little on the cult of perfection because it is the 'cult of what is finished', what is limited, since it is supposedly impossible to carry it further or to do better. This leads to a curious paradox: that which is perfect, therefore limited, cannot be divine. In the construction of the tea-house, which represents one of the summits of Japanese art, something is always intentionally left unfinished or imperfect. In the great temple of Iyeyas in Nikko, one of the superb white columns which support the great Yomei-mon Gate was carved upside-down so as not to provoke the jealousy of the gods against the family whose ancestor is worshipped in this temple; this pillar is called *mayoke-no-hashira*, the pillar which turns misfortune away. Similarly, at the opposite end of Asia, in Islam, an irregularity is always left—as if accidentally—in a corner of the Muslim prayer carpet, for it is up to the One and Only God to finish and perfect every human piece of work.

In Asia, men and women of all social classes have a remarkable thirst for aesthetic sensations and, generally speaking, know how to savour them better than westerners do—perhaps because they respect them more deeply. The great Indian sage, Shri Aurobindo, wrote, 'A masterpiece of oriental art must be contemplated in solitude, in the isolation of the self, at times when we can indulge in long and profound meditation, when we feel as unburdened as possible of the conventions of material life.' One of the greatest connoisseurs of Tibet, Govinda, speaks of the enjoyment of contemplating a finished work of art and retrospectively feeling the creative urge which produced it.

The strength of religious feeling in Asia and the respect for authority naturally means that the work of art enjoys even greater prestige because of its sacred character and its historical association, if any, with great men of the past.

On the other hand, the exotic nature of a work of art does not seem to imbue it with any additional value in the eyes of the Asians as it does with us. If some kinds of western art—for instance the French impressionists—do enjoy immense popularity almost everywhere in Asia, it is not because they come from afar but because they strike a chord in the Asian soul. Apart from a few cases of this kind—which are rare—we must be wary when orientals express admiration for our art. Unless they themselves have had a long initiation, all they are trying to do is probably to impress us by showing how similar they are to us—to them, this is synonymous with being 'modern'—and delving a little deeper one sees that our art has not really caused any vibration in their souls. An important exception has to be made, however, with regard to our literature which, even through often disconcerting translations, awakens great enthusiasm. It is interesting to note, for instance, that the works of Victor Hugo and Tolstoy are as well-known and appreciated in Asia as they are in Europe—and films based on them are immensely and genuinely successful.

In some Asian countries great value is attached to the fact that a work of art is old. In the thirteenth century there was an active trade in antiques in Hangchow. Often the actual age of the object is specified, but the grounds for such assertions are equally difficult to check and to believe. Besides, this does not interest easterners who, as we have seen, have a conception of history different from ours. The same person can well say about a statuette in his possession : 'It is five hundred years old' and a fortnight later, 'It was made for my grandfather' without feeling that the two statements are incompatible. In the bazaars, the 'antique' dealers who use old moulds for casting bronzes or terracotta have great difficulty in understanding why their Western customers are so interested in the period when a particular piece was made.

The Orientals regard as pure childishness our scholars' efforts to date accurately works of all kinds; the only result, from their point of view, is to take away the joy derived from deep communion with the works examined.

On the other hand, the idea that an artist might copy from an already existing work mostly shocks them. I know cultured Orientals who have been scandalized to see artists producing counterfeits by copying old paintings in our museums.[19] These two reactions are not as contradictory as they seem at first sight. To follow a tradition faithfully and even servilely in all its details is not at all the same thing as to ignore one's own inspiration, (within the context of this tradition, of course) in order to usurp the inspiration of others.

Throughout the orient it is inconceivable that appreciation of a work of art should be allied with thoughts of its commercial value, as we increasingly tend to do under the North American influence. Beauty cannot be evaluated quantitatively, even less in terms of money.

This leads to the conception that the person who most appreciates a work of art is the one who deserves to possess it—one could almost

---

[19] This attitude is in no way incompatible with the need for the student painter to practise by copying, which is normal in Japan (e.g. in the Kano School) and in China, where it has even been maintained that when we come across pre-Ming paintings they are certainly copies.

say 'the one who is entitled to possess it.' This is probably what accounts for the fact that in the East, when someone admires an art object in one's possession, the custom is to offer it to him.

Asia differs from us also in the manner of drawing from the work of art the maximum of what it can give us and, consequently, also in the manner of presenting this work. The western art object tries to call attention to itself both by its own peculiar features, such as its subject, and by certain accessories, such as the frame of a picture. If we want to enjoy the inspiration communicated by the object in order to pass to a higher plane, we have to detach ourselves from it, shut our eyes in order to withdraw attention from the material object—for instance, from the stained-glass window of a cathedral. The oriental art object, on the contrary, invites us, by contemplating it directly and uninterruptedly, to transcend its form and its limits. Before a Japanese painting representing a few waves on the shore, framed in a narrow strip of dull silk, there is no need to shut one's eyes in order to see, feel and hear the whole ocean. The Muslim who prays in the Mosque of Sheikh Lutfallah in Isfahan can let the divine influx flow down into him while keeping his eyes fixed on the polished tiles, while the Catholic who prays in the Cathedral of Chartres is more tempted to let his glance turn inwards as soon as he feels himself carried away by the atmosphere.

Therefore, in the West, we endeavour to supply an appropriate environment for the work of art, in order to bring out its beauty by emphasizing, complementing and prolonging it, as it were, and we avoid any clash with discordant promiscuity. In furnishing we seek unity of style, just as we do when composing an architectural unit. At any rate, we are anxious to remove all that would not be in keeping with the object—for instance, we demolish the battered houses that used to cling to the great cathedrals.

In Asia the idea is to isolate the object completely from all that might cause aesthetic sensations other than those provided by it, even if these sensations are perfectly matched and in keeping with each other. This result may be obtained either physically or mentally. Physically, it is done by isolating the object completely from any other object which might draw attention, particularly if it is more or less of the same nature. The most typical example is the Japanese *tokonoma*, a niche hollowed out in a bare wall and in which only one object is placed at a time (a vase of flowers, a painting, some calligraphy, etc.); and there is only one single *tokonoma* in the room, often in the whole house. To traditional Asia, our museums of painting and sculpture, where we pile together many works of art in the same room on the pretext that they belong more or less to the same school, the same country or the same period, is barbarous. When the Asians, imitating us, build museums, their rooms seem nearly empty to us; many of the western visitors to the Japanese pavilion at the Brussels Exhibition thought that it was not yet finished.

Alternatively, the work of art is provided with an extremely discreet accompaniment, so that one's attention has to be drawn to it especially in order to perceive its beauty—for instance, the strips of precious materials in very subdued tones which border Japanese, Mongol and Tibetan paintings, the dark wood supports which hold the Chinese ivories, jades and crystals.

Mentally, the object can be isolated from all that surrounds it without taking the trouble to remove physically whatever clashes with it. The Japanese seem to have a special faculty for not seeing what should not be seen. This explains why stage-hands in the theatre can move about in order to place a chair, arrange a dress, smooth a hair-style right in the middle of the action and merely cover their faces with a black gauze veil, sometimes not even that. Similarly, in the finest parks, arranged with the subtlest artistry, ugly poles are often to be seen planted in the earth in order to hold up a trunk or a branch. In the most ancient and most sacred temples of which the Japanese are justly proud, next to the venerable and refined buildings, we find huts of white wood housing the guardian who sells postcards; horrible signboards are placed at the foot of the most beautiful works of art. People seem to fear the proximity of beautiful things, which might distract attention, but not of ugly ones, because they just do not see them, e.g. '. . . the Japanese, when they build their towns, seem to derive a secret pleasure from making them hideous, as if to protect their treasures by surrounding them with ugliness'.[20]

This is no exception. The Imperial Palace of Tokyo seems indifferent to the corrugated iron shacks nearby and Hindu temples of the greatest prestige are in no way affected by the crowds of lepers and beggars milling around them. The great sacred Buddha of Ayudhaya (Thailand) has been surrounded by a hideous concrete protection without any protest, and nobody seems to be indignant at the fact that the purest masterpieces of Asian architecture have filth all round them.

Our Asian cousins know full well how to ignore surroundings that shock us and they are able to do this because they are trained to withdraw into meditative contemplation where they isolate the object and mentally eliminate all that surrounds it. Moreover, this mental operation, which is so difficult for us, can be prepared long ahead, as when a Japanese makes various cleverly ordered stops

[20] Fosco Maraini.

357

before entering the 'tea chamber'. It has been said that with regard to furnishing for instance, or menu-making, the Chinese and Viet-Namese, *inter alia*, 'have juxtaposition but no composition'[21]. The same remark could be applied to many other cases.

It is true, nevertheless, that in Asia one frequently finds works which are artistic to a greater or lesser degree and which seem to be real 'hodge-podge' in our eyes—even among the works that are most highly venerated and appreciated from the artistic point of view. The *gopurams* of south India, the sculptures of the Cambodian temples, the ornamentation in the Siamese temples, the marble ceilings of the Jain temples on Mount Abu, the inside of the Tibetan temples with their lanterns and their bags of cloth or paper, the Hindu altars overloaded with statues, objects and offerings—all these seem in rather bad taste if we apply our most elementary aesthetic criteria to them. At a Japanese table cultured and enlightened Europeans are unpleasantly surprised to see plates of different material and style next to each other.

Actually, these exceptions confirm the rule. Indeed, it may be said that we have here a very subtle and clever process which seeks to awaken in us a series of impressions forming a whole; the work of art is not a particular part, even less a particular detail, however beautiful, but the whole. If one could find an informant who is both qualified and willing—which is a rare combination, for generally they are not particularly anxious to explain what they think we are congenitally incapable of appreciating—one would understand how all these very heteroclite items have been methodically combined in relation to each other, not simply lined up like the statues in our museums and churches, but arranged in organic patterns in a whole which constitutes the actual unit, the work of art as such—like so many spots of colour on a great painting.

Besides, Asians generally take great care in choosing the right moment for presenting a work of art. In Japan, not only is there a season for *kabuki*, another for puppet shows, another for wrestling shows, but it would be unthinkable to have a snowscape painting exhibited in summer or that of a blooming tree in winter.

The reluctance felt by the Asian to explain the secret beauty of a thing to a person he deems incapable of truly appreciating it naturally goes hand in hand with a similar unwillingness to show works of art to laymen. He particularly fears that such intrusion into the life of the work might deprive it of some of its 'electric charge' as it were. 'Beautiful pictures,' one Japanese[22] writes explicitly, 'may be degraded by the admiration of the vulgar.'

While in the West, both in shops and in homes, people are anxious

[21] Don-quan-tan.   [22] Okakura Kakuzo.

to exhibit the finest objects they possess and to keep in the background those of lesser quality, the oriental readily displays the mediocre but does not disclose his greatest treasures without first having seriously 'tested' his visitor. Several visits are necessary before a Japanese, Chinese, Indian or even an Arab antique dealer would show his most valuable articles. In a Japanese home, whether rich or poor, the valuable vases are carefully packed in many pieces of cloth and in wooden boxes which, in turn, are stowed away in cupboards, to be taken out religiously, only before a very small group, and for short periods of time. The finest of Hindu statues are protected by many barriers, and the nearer the barrier is to the object the more insurmountable it becomes. Although the many obstructions through which one has to work one's way before being able to see a work of Chinese art have another explanation, they nevertheless make any approach difficult. We shall later see another striking example of this in the case of music.

For easterners the sacred or religious work of art—and we have seen that these are the most frequent—does not have to be in good physical condition in order to keep its value. Not only in the ruins of buildings, but also in western-style museums, flowers, fruit, incense and other offerings are to be seen placed in pious homage before mutilated statues or even before bare pedestals. In India, Thailand and elsewhere, statues are often covered with successive layers of votive oil, sacred pastes, etc., which make it impossible to recognize them.

It is interesting to note in this connection that for most Asians a painted or carved image of God, which has been 'animated' by a special ceremony remains 'animated' as long as another ritual ceremony has not 'disanimated' it, and it therefore keeps all its power till then. The case of the Buddha statues is a different one, at least among many Buddhist peoples that regard Buddha as a man and not as a god; furthermore, those Buddha statues that are no longer worshipped 'die'. In Laos those statues that had been dragged away from the temples, spoilt and pillaged, also become 'dead' Buddhas, p'a chao tai leo, but this only means that they are 'dead to good', i.e., they can still do evil and they do so because they are angry at the treatment they have had to undergo.[23]

Architecture in Asia, at least as much as the plastic arts, but for different reasons and in different ways, is guided by reasons that are not of a material order as we understand it. The buildings to be inhabited by princes or people, those where they will pray, those where they will fight the enemy, those where they will sleep their last sleep, have to be set up and arranged in relation to one

[23] Henri Roux and Tran-van-chu.

another in such a way as to enjoy the protection of the beneficent higher powers by following the main trends of nature and its laws.

A knowledge of the celestial bodies and of the earth determines the site and orientation of the buildings, the date and time for starting the work and even the proportions, size and inside arrangement, sometimes even, as in the case of Lamaist monasteries, the place from which the stones used should be extracted. The site is chosen upon the imperative recommendation of geomancians who have previously found out the exact points that are auspicious or inauspicious for the purpose.[24] The exact azimuth of the sunrise at the equinox or the solstice, the cardinal points and even the magnetic north pole, the position of Mecca, the tombs of the ancestors, the telluric and cosmic currents revealed by occult processes, all supply precise directions towards which façades, doors, windows, inner shrines should be turned. The same preoccupations reappear throughout history and in nearly all Asian countries. In China under the Shang dynasty, 4,000 years ago, important private homes were all made to face the magnetic north—which leads to the assumption that the compass was known! It was a Persian astrologer, Naubakht, who in the eighth century directed the construction of Baghdad. In 1805 the plan made by French engineers for the fortress of Hanoi had to be altered in accordance with the data provided by the occultists.

Finally, it often happens that when the work is to be started, or at a specific stage in its progress, the earth and the deities inhabiting it are propitiated with sacrifices which, in extreme cases, may even be human. This practice lasted a long time in Japan. It seems to have begun in the fourth century—in imitation of a similar Chinese practice—when the Emperor Nintoku had persons and animals buried alive in order to ensure the solidity of his dykes— and continued till the sixteenth century in the case of fortresses (cases are known where this procedure was used in order to obtain more water for a pond). The persons used were known as 'human pillars', *hito-bashira*, and were generally volunteers. Thus, when the Matsue castle was built, a young girl was buried in its foundations. In Laos, in the sixteenth century, a young woman many months

---

[24] 'In China, not only are the geomancians consulted in order to find out whether a particular site is suitable for the tomb or house to be built, but they are also familiar with the processes which make it possible to turn an orientation which is, in fact, irregular, into one which is correct according to religious law; for this it is enough to build screens and obstacles or to change the aspect of the ground (for the shape of the irregularities of the ground have a symbolic value) or to qualify the directions of the immediate space by means of appropriate emblems' (Marcel Granet).

pregnant, Sao-Si, threw herself into the ditch dug for the construction of the Vieng-Chan temple. In ancient Palestine, it seems that a human sacrifice had to be made by anyone who wished to lay the foundations of a house. Even if many such traditional stories are not true they are nevertheless evidence of a deep-rooted preoccupation.

Modern easterners who denounce geomancy (the Chinese term for it is *feng-shui*, which means 'wind and water') as a superstition, nonetheless acknowledge that it has 'great spiritual and architectural value',[25] for the rules drawn from it find a valuable and minute application even in the details of architecture. Indeed, the goal of architecture is in most cases to achieve as full a harmony as possible with nature, either in its superficial appearance or in its rhythm and its deeper aspect, or else in its fundamental essence, and in order to do so it is indispensable to be acquainted with the secrets and laws of nature and their action on men.

The observance or non-observance of the type of rules we have mentioned may, in the case of a home, 'have a great influence, good or evil, on the future of the whole family which is to live there'.[26]

In India, Japan, China, Viet-Nam and many other countries, the most honoured place is set aside for the family altar on which are placed divine or sacred pictures or the tablets of ancestors. The spirit of the house, of course, plays a paramount part, especially in Indo-China. In Thailand, for instance, even before building a house a site is chosen for setting up the chau thi, a little temple for this spirit, *phra phum*. This has to be done by a competent person, and then the house must never throw its shadow on the *chau thi*. In North Laos, in a *Tsa Khmu* house, two packets hanging on both sides of the hearth are the tangible form of the Roi Gang, the spirit of the house; one must not sit on them or use them for anything but offerings. In Viet-Nam, it is this spirit which, at the end of the year, reports to the Jade Emperor on all that has happened in the family. Among the Yakuts, the 'spirit of the cabin' is depicted as an old woman, Nyaha Haraksin, who lives under the central pillar. In Japan a chicken is buried under one of the pillars of the house in honour of the family spirit.

In Asia, although it is difficult to have privacy from the other members of the family, every effort is made to defend this house from outside influences which might bring evil. In both China and Viet-Nam it is protected from indiscreet glances—which might always be the evil eye—by baffles and screens which actually have a magical function. In Viet-Nam and in Japan hedges or tufts of bamboo fulfil the same purpose. In the Muslim countries the family

[25] See Lin Yutang. [26] Pierre Huard and Maurice Durand.

conceals its life behind the walls of the house, in the maze of blind alleys and little lanes of its quarter; the house mostly has only one door facing outwards, opening on to the opposite wall of a narrow passage, and no outside window.

In Japan, when a guest departs, however honoured he may be, the mistress of the house throws salt on the threshold in order to eliminate any evil he may have brought with him. In fact, this concern for the purity of the threshold is very widespread; both in China and the Muslim countries very great care must be taken not to step on it.

Within the house everything has a magic and ritual value. In Chinese countries the building itself is less important than the terrace supporting it and the roof covering it, for they define its relationship with the earth and the sky respectively. The house is naturally built with material which is found locally and is therefore less expensive—daub or crude brick in the Middle East, India, China, and among the Kirghiz; wood in the forested countries such as Viet-Nam, Cambodia, Indonesia, Laos and the Philippines; bamboo in Japan; stone in mountainous countries like Lebanon, Tibet and Nepal. The roofwork is also made from local products: grass, palm leaves, wood waste, flat stones, etc.

Such dwellings are sometimes very durable; daub houses are sometimes several storeys high and can be used for a century. In the thirteenth century, the poorer quarters of Hangchow used to have daub houses eight and ten storeys high, and in Arabia daub houses with five and seven storeys lasted for centuries; in the Hadramaut, a region considered very primitive, the houses of Shibam, made of earth, have six floors on the average. However, as the raw material costs nothing, and there is abundant and free labour available—the only condition being reciprocity—these houses are abandoned without regrets whenever they are spoilt, and new ones are built a little farther away.

Many peoples live in caves where they are sheltered from extreme temperatures, rain and snow. There are millions in Shansi, and Mao Tse-Tung spent a part of his youth in one. On the other hand, in various regions dwellings are raised on stilts or pilotis in order to protect them from floods or wild animals. There are many such houses throughout Indo-China, the Philippines, Japan, etc.

Finally, in numerous Far Eastern countries we find large 'floating villages', composed solely of house boats: e.g., in China, where certain Tanka were not even allowed to settle on dry earth and where a part of the population of thirteenth century Hangchow lived thus in boats; at Aberdeen in Hong Kong; in Bangkok and the whole of southern Siam; in Tokyo; in the whole of the Red River delta in the Viet-Nam; and even in Saigon itself, where they were driven away not long ago so that foreign visitors should not be shocked by such an 'uncivilized' (*sic*) sight; in the Vietminh between the upper region and Hanoi. The building of these boats is often accompanied by the same precautions and the same rites as those which go into the building of a house on firm ground, and they are decorated with the same offerings made to their deity of flowers and other objects.

The peasant's or the ordinary worker's home is nearly always poor and empty to a degree that is disconcerting for the unenlightened westerner. This is doubtless due to the incredibly low standard of living, but it may also be prompted by a concern for cleanliness, which is difficult to maintain in the midst of piles of furniture, utensils, materials, and by a certain taste for simplicity, even among the well-to-do. It is a conscious aesthetic preoccupation which makes the Japanese peasant keep his home as simple as possible. However, there are exceptions, as in Viet-Nam.

In some countries, the component parts of the house are endowed with a certain personality. Thus, in a Burmese home certain pillars are male, easy to live with and harmless, while others are female, dispensing honours and happiness. In Viet-Nam the roof purlin is called life, *sanh*, and the lower beams are named in accordance with an age-old order : *tat* or *lao* (infirmity, old age), *benh* (disease) and *tu* (death).

As for the palaces of oriental princes, the luxury and the splendour which have inspired poets and writers all over the world are not just the product of imagination. To quote only one example, a Singhalese sovereign of the late twelfth century apparently built a palace with 4,000 apartments, a considerable number of dance halls, votive pyramids, monasteries and temples.

The rules of architecture governing the construction were obviously connected with the function of the chief in the society. In South-East Asia the palace frequently represented the Mount Meru, centre of the world according to Hinduism. The 'cosmic' architecture of the ancient Buddhist kings were 'only an arena for the development of Law and for the awakening of all things within its radius'.[27]

The palaces can only be rivalled by the splendour of the temples of the various religions. The building of the latter—and that of the palaces to a lesser degree—is evidently preceded and accompanied by more magic rites than the construction of a simple dwelling house. It varies a great deal, of course, according to the god to be

[27] Pierre Mus.

worshipped and the sect which will use it.[28] For instance, the Tibetan monastery of Samye, founded by Padmasambhava, represents the image of the universe; another temple, a Hindu one, is built on the plan of the *yantra* (geometric symbol) of its divinity; a mosque in Isfahan, the Mesjed-e-Shah, exalts the glory of its patron king, while another neighbouring mosque, the Mesjed of Sheikh Lutfallah, will fill the visitor with the meditative tranquillity characteristic of its patron saint.

As for the fortresses of Asia, from the Babylonian *ziggurat* to the Hindu royal *meru*, from the Viet-Namese citadels built on hills to the Chinese Imperial *tai*, they had to fulfil the strategic purpose assigned to them, based on conditions determined solely by astrology and geomancy; they were therefore never designed isolatedly, but according to their site with which they had to be closely related. By means of appropriate digging work, the king who had the fortress built managed to dominate the country by making himself master of its hidden forces. The building work done seems incomprehensible and incredible today if we remember the means and techniques said to be prevalent at the time. In the citadel of Ho in An-Ton (Viet-Nam), some of the blocks of the South Gate, laid in the fifteenth century, weigh sixteen tons. The Great Wall of China, built twenty-two centuries ago and always well maintained since, is 5,000 kilometres long.

From the most ancient times Asia has had immense cities. At Yang-Shao-Ts'un (China), a neolithic town of twenty-five hectares has been discovered—in other words, twelve times the size of the largest in Europe at that time, and it was 'of extraordinary density'.[29] A century later, in the same country, there were towns like Liang-Ch'eng of double the area. Archaeologists have brought to light in the Indus valley the ruins of two great cities, Mohenjo-Daro and Harappa, which are certainly prior to the third millennium of our era. Early in the same millennium Uruk's fortifications extended over a dozen kilometres or so, and in the seventh century B.C., Babylon used to cover an area of over twenty-five square kilometres. In ancient China the people lived in fairly impressive townships. In 1275, Hangchow, which was then the largest and the richest city in the world, had a million inhabitants. In our days about twenty-five Asian cities have over a million inhabitants, a figure which Tokyo, now the largest city in the world, had already attained in 1868.

In many of these towns, architecture and town-planning had reached a remarkable degree of development, the social organization

[28] The best study in a European language is that by Stella Kramrisch.
[29] Gélinas.

was minutely regulated, the arts flourished, and religious practices were very similar to those of today. The houses of the fifth millennium B.C. which have been exhumed by the excavations of the Mossul area were built on the same plan and with the same materials as those of our time in the same area; it should not, however, be concluded, as the great English architect, Woolley, wisely points out, that Asia is 'immobile', but rather that already in those days, a satisfactory method had been found. In China under the Shang, 4,000 years ago, there were special mains for drinking water and drains for sewage disposal. In the Chinese town of K'aifong, in the eleventh century, 'the Imperial Way was 300 yards wide. On both sides there were covered galleries where the merchants . . . were allowed to sell. Black lacquered barriers and a double red barrier divided the avenue from north to south. The central passage, reserved for the emperor, was banned to the people and to horses. Two small canals ran along these galleries; lotus flowers had been planted in them and along their banks were plum, peach, pear and apricot trees so that in spring it looked like a brightly coloured embroidery'.[30]

Until very recent times the site and plan of these towns, like that of individual houses, was strictly based on centuries-old traditions born of experience and familiarity with nature and perhaps also astrological and geomantic considerations (which are undistinguishable from tradition), although their influence was not always perceptible to the uninitiated. Thus the whole of Peking is arranged around a north-south axis, invisible on the terrain, which goes through the imperial throne, the central pavilion of the Coal-Hill and the Drum Tower. The walls of certain Chinese towns were built on the pattern of the Great Bear and the Little Bear. Although certain spaces remained unoccupied for reasons which are not apparent to us, it might well be because they were on the same line as a temple or were too close to some subterranean dragon.

But while the orientals jealously protect small art objects, even against glances which might pollute them, they often show amazing negligence when it comes to large works—monuments, for instance. Nothing is sadder than to see Turkish or Arab palaces and the great buildings of China or India falling to pieces for want of the most elementary care. When European archaeologists, without even risking anastylosis techniques, as in Borobudur or Angkor, make timid attempts at restoration, or take steps to preserve the monuments, only those Asians who are trained in our school see the advantage of their work. For Asians, generally speaking, a building is meant for a specific use, limited in time, and once this mission

[30] Tong, II, 1, 12.

has been fulfilled there is no reason to prolong its existence arbitrarily, even less to resurrect it from its ruins, except for purely lucrative ends, in order to attract foreign tourists with strange and incomprehensible tastes. In Islam, even the town of sojourn, the princely pleasure residence, was forsaken as readily as it was built.

Besides, in many countries there is a tradition that requires a house to be abandoned when its owner dies. Even today, in Persia, the man who inherits a house from his deceased father prefers to build a new one of his own rather than use the old one which, unrepaired, soon falls into ruin. In India the Kurumi leave a house empty as soon as a death occurs in it, and the Savara of Kolakotta burn these houses every two years at the Karja festival. Among certain Tatars it is a general custom to destroy the houses of those who are dead. Among the Ainus, also, a hut is burnt if someone dies in it. In Japan, according to Shinto tradition, any dwelling place has to be evacuated when its principal inhabitant dies; similarly, when the precincts of a temple have been desecrated by somebody's death, no sacred festival is held there for a month; and the sixty times that the capital had to be moved successively doubtless have a religious significance connected with pollution by death. Among the Bratskains of Siberia, upon the death of the peasant whose name was given to the village, the latter received another peasant's name.

However, our anxiety for preservation has its Asian equivalent in their concern for 'continuity'. Here, as in the field of logic or ideas, the oriental is afraid of immobility, crystallization, mummification; he does not want life to stop flowing freely. In Japan it is customary to rebuild the Oho-yashiro every sixty-one years (this has been done some thirty times already, according to tradition) and the great temple of Ise every twenty years. In many such cases a sacramental value is attached to the material from the old building, which is used again for the new one—often placed on a different site which is probably never chosen at random.

We have seen that in art the communion between man and the cosmos—and consequently between man and the divine—is achieved above all through rhythm. Now it is obviously in dance and music that this rhythm is predominant and most visible. Both arts are therefore particularly valued in Asia; it is through them that the performer as well as the spectator are steeped in the rhythm of the world, in the music of the spheres, and participate in cosmic life and in the divine impulse. In China their function was to balance the world and to tame nature for the benefit of man. This function of rhythm partly explains the importance ascribed in many Asian disciplines to breath control (Pranayama among Hindus, breathing art among Taoists, etc.), for this is the 'sole and first, simple and *total* element of rhythm'.[31]

Magic incantation was and still is the prototype of musical art in all countries; but in Asia it is perhaps even more apparent than elsewhere. In ancient China—where, as we have seen, the Yueh Fu or Department of Music existed even before our era—music was the art by which the sages propitiated heaven and earth, established contact with the manes, pacified the people and made nature follow her course. Popular music still has a ritual function in Cambodia. The sage Lie Tse gives us specific examples: 'When P'ao-pa touched his sithar,' he tells us, 'the birds used to dance and the fishes leap.' What is even stranger, he describes another musician in the following terms: 'We were in the midst of spring; Cheu-wenn touched the *chang* string (of his sithar) which corresponds to the autumn season; immediately, a cold wind blew and the fruits ripened. In autumn, when he touched the *kiao* string which corresponds to the spring season, a warm wind blew and plants flowered. In summer, when he touched the U-string which corresponds to the winter season, snow began to fall and waterways froze. In winter, when he touched the *tcheng* string which corresponds to the summer season, lightning flashed and the ice melted.' But there is no need to go back so far to a past in which we can only believe with some qualification: not long ago it was easy to find in India ecclesiastical and lay musicians whose call brought forth even the wildest of beasts.

Therefore, the choice of music, song and also dance does not depend on the mood or the fancy of the performer or his audience. It has to be made strictly according to the season, the day, the hour, the weather and, of course, it depends also on the aim pursued. One of the most characteristic or at least scientifically well explained examples is that of the Hindu *ragas* and *raginis*—but it is certainly not the only instance. To take another example in a completely different region, among the Tunguz, in the 1820's, it was still a sin to sing at night.

In some countries the esoteric character of music is evidenced by the secrecy that surrounds it, not only when teaching, but also when performing it—to such an extent, that in some cases it must not even be heard by our physical sense of hearing. For the Taoists, 'the best music is silent'.[32] We see that this is not just a metaphor, since in Japan, at certain Shinto festivals, even now 'silent concerts' are held. The musicians, the members of those families traditionally entrusted with particularly sacred music, make all the gestures required by the score but without drawing the least sound from

[31] Marcel Granet. [32] Marcel Granet.

their instruments, for fear that unworthy ears might absorb the mysteries transmitted by this music.

Rhythm is to be found in an even purer state in dancing, and that is why the latter is regarded in Asia as an art (and therefore as a magic art) *par excellence*, and the accompaniment is intended primarily as a source of inspiration for the dancers. In India the great God (Maheshvara) Shiva, in the form of Natarajan (Master of Dance), creates and destroys worlds by dancing to the sound of his little drum, *damaru*.

There are very many religious fraternities which use dancing to obtain ecstasy. They existed in China. There were many in Japanese Buddhism since the end of the sixteenth century; they used to practise the *odori-nembutsu* or *nembutsu-ko*,[33] and a post-war Japanese sect which has nothing to do with Buddhism or any other recognized religion, the *Odoro-shukyo*, relies essentially on dancing to obtain salvation; in the same country, the adepts of the *Tenri-kyo* have to dance several times a day to the sound of a big drum—which doubtless causes some inconvenience to their neighbours! Among the Muslims, the dancing Dervishes, while they are not confined only to the Asian continent, have many adepts there. Among the Jewish Hassid dancing, as a manifestation of love and joy, is said to spiritualize the body by making it participate in the fervour of the mind. The great Hindu sage Ramakrishna often fell into a state of ecstasy, *samadhi*, while dancing before his disciples; and his compatriots, the *pashupata*, regularly resort to dancing. Like the African, the Asian regards prayers expressed by dancing as a contact with the sacred, with the invisible world of his gods and ancestors. Besides, it may be said generally that classical ballet, in India and Tibet, in Cambodia, Thailand and Japan, and often also in China, is essentially an offering to the gods—and that is perhaps why it resists foreign influences better than most other forms of art.

In China old men dance the complex *t'ai chi ch'uan* which keeps them in harmony with the cosmic order.[34]

In Asia, since magic plays a considerable part in war strategy and tactics, the fighting being directed against both the enemy and the forces of evil, dancing naturally holds an eminent place. At the beginning of Chinese history Yu the Great, in order to open the pass of Houan-yuan, danced the bear dance. This same Yu knew how to dance the steps which neutralized the *tche'e-mei*, the ferocious spirits of the marshes and the hills, or the dance which was able to domesticate the Three Miao, make them give up their barbarian ways and pay their tribute to the capital. In traditional China the

[33] Mock Joya.
[34] V. R. Burckhardt gives an interesting description of it.

Great Chief was expected to do the same, for a demiurge's deeds can only be performed through dancing—and any true chief *must* be a demiurge!

This combination confluence of religion, warfare and dancing in a vast magic complex is a practically constant occurrence. In traditional China, 'arms of war and arms of dance were all one'.[35] In Vat Ph'u (Laos), when a buffalo is sacrificed, there is a great sword dance.

The search for harmony with the cosmos through music and dancing is also supposed to help eliminate the discordance which is thought to be a cause of individual disturbances of a physical type, for instance. Prophylactic or therapeutic music is widely used throughout Asia. In ancient China there was not a single poet, painter or philosopher who did not play the lute in the hope that he would thus develop his vital forces and prolong his life. On the psychological level, for the Confucians, not only does music bring about 'harmony of the voices', but it also 'makes sentiments concur'.[36] When it is perfect there is no discontent; it is the principle of mutual affection—and indeed, the degree of perfection in a man's singing makes it possible to estimate his value as a man.

Our scholars are constantly pushing back the date of the literary monuments of Asia. Very probably there was an Armenian literature even before the fourth millennium, a literature which in turn was the product of centuries of intellectual, artistic and religious life. Madras prides itself on having had a Tamil Literary Academy from the fifteenth century B.C. until the second century A.D. As for the Asian sacred texts, which are among the most important literary monuments, many date from before the invention of script.

Literature in all its forms, from song to poetry, and from theatre to story-telling, plays a paramount part in the whole of the orient. Here, of course, there is no question of 'animation' as in the plastic arts, or of rhythm as in the case of dancing and music, but something just as powerful: the word.

Hinduism teaches that the name of god is identical with God.[37] The Japanese identify *kotonaru*, God, Kami and speech, and that is why, as Fujisawa the philosopher tells us, they are so parsimonious with their words. It is striking that in the Koran, the Bhagavad-Gita and St. John's Gospel,[38] the first word should be the one for the name, the Word. In many accounts of creation the spoken word

---

[35] Marcel Granet.   [36] Marcel Granet.
[37] Ramdas. Cf. Ramakrishna: 'He and His Name are identical'.
[38] St John was a Gallilean, i.e. an Asian.

appeared first and gave birth to the rest. Of course, this speech is not identical with the words composing our language, but the latter is descended directly from it, sometimes through the 'primordial sounds', *sphota*, the seed words, *bija-mantra*, etc. In Hong Kong the Scandinavian Lutheran missionaries were very clever when, following Chinese custom, they translated by 'tao' the term *logos* in St John's Gospel, and this translation can be justified if we delve into an esotericism that is quite alien to Lutheran teaching. No Asian is surprised by Victor Hugo's line: 'For speech is the Word, and the Word is God'.

In most Asian conceptions, the name, as we have seen, is closely linked with whatever makes a thing what it is; and the use of this name confers an actual power upon the bearer. Now this power is even greater when we come nearer to the original word, either by means of syllables (in India, a particular god is identical with a secret and sacred syllable pertaining to him) or by letters of the alphabet as in the Hebrew Kabbal, in Muslim mysticism and in the Hindu and Buddhist Tantras. For in those languages which have a sacred script, to pass from the spoken word to the written word is not a degression, as in the other languages. In Japanese there is a science of the 'soul of the word', *genrei gaku*, by means of which it is possible to enter into communion with the very heart of the word; and in India, the whole science of sacred formulae or words, *mantra*, seeks the same purpose, but achieves more specific and conclusive results.[39] Even in Chinese the visible nature is only an image of the subtle meaning of the invisible word. In Islam, where the Arabic script has kept the actual power of a talisman, the literary language is really a divine emanation, for speech is still allied to ritual, and even illiterates are fascinated by the newspapers which, by procuring them visual and tactile sensations, supplement their

---

[39] The theory of the *mantra* is that it is a word of power born out of the secret depths of our being where it has been brooded upon by a deeper consciousness than the mental, framed in the heart and not constructed by the intellect, held in the mind, again concentrated on by the waking mental consciousness, and then thrown out silently or vocally—the silent word is perhaps held to be more potent than the spoken—precisely for the work of creation. The *mantra* can not only create new subjective states in ourselves, alter our physical being, reveal knowledge and faculties we did not before possess, can not only produce similar results in other minds than that of the user, but can produce vibrations in the mental and vital atmosphere which result in effects, in actions and even in the production of material forms on the physical plane . . . The Vedic use of the *mantra* is only a conscious utilization of this secret power of the word. (Shri Aurobindo.)

emotions and their auditive recollections and unleash their imagination.[40]

The magic value of the letters composing the written word is particularly apparent in the Jewish Torah, where every letter is regarded as a real living being which played an active part in the creation of the universe. The same may also be said perhaps of the *devanagari* script which is the one used for the sacred Hindu texts and of the Arabic alphabet used in the Koran.

When speech is associated with music and song, as is normal in Asia, it has even greater value. For Confucius poetry is only an accessory to melody, and singing is only a lyrical recitation. The singing of sacred texts is, *par excellence*, the offering to be made to the gods. All sacred scriptures of Asia, from the Koran to the Hindu Vedas and Upanishads, the Buddhist Sutras and the Shinto Norito must be sung or chanted according to complicated melodies and are said to lose much of their value unless this is done.

Even the most profane song is an effective way of achieving harmony with the cosmos. In the case of the Afghan, for instance, it is a veritable passion, and it has been written (Darmesteter) that for him it is the clearest, the sincerest expression of the national character. The Laotian sings under any circumstances—when chopping wood in the forest or plucking flowers, when leading his buffalo to the paddy fields or when enjoying his leisure at sundown on his doorstep; song and music are for him a necessary accompaniment to any festival. Besides, the true singer in Asia is mostly inspired. In Tibet the bards who, even to this day, sing the epic of Guesar of Ling, claim that they have not learnt the text by heart but have been directly inspired by the hero.

Even without its musical accompaniment, poetry possesses immense magic power. It is poetry that has served as a means of expression for the great mystics of Persia, and all the great masters use it widely everywhere. It has been said that it is only in the realm of poetry that the Turkmen people were conscious of their unity,[41] and that in China 'poetry has taken over the function of religion . . . in so far as religion is taken to mean a cleansing of man's soul, a feeling for the mystery and beauty of the universe, and a feeling of tenderness and compassion for one's fellow-men and the humble creatures of life'.[42] It is in their poetry that the Chinese reveal themselves most fully.

Mahmud of Ghazni, in the early eleventh century, although he showed himself to be a cruel tyrant, actually had a Ministry of

[40] Raymond Charles.   [41] *Encyclopaedia of Islam.*
[42] Lin Yutang.

Poetic Affairs at his court and maintained 600 poets to whom he dispensed millions of gold pieces—and as we have already seen, even the greatest sovereigns did not disdain to indulge in this art themselves. For many Asians, poetry is, in fact, the most natural form of expression; many of the finest Chinese poems are simply familiar letters addressed to friends.

As for the theatre, which simultaneously uses speech in its poetic form, music and dance, it is, of course, a privileged art form. Whether it be of the most ancient traditional kind (puppet shows were known in ancient China) or relatively recent in style (Japanese No was developed only in the fourteenth to fifteenth centuries), it has always aroused passionate interest.

Even if it does not always revive pure and simple mythological episodes (as it does in India, Tibet and elsewhere), divine or semi-divine beings play a primary and decisive part anyway.

Whether the actors are professionals or amateurs, the performances are generally much longer than in the West. In Indonesia or India, for instance, they might even extend over six or seven consecutive nights, from sunset to sunrise. Traditionally, from Mai-mutchen to Ceylon and Bali to Persia, they are financed by art-patrons and the people may attend free of charge.

We have already seen how story-tellers are normally responsible in the East for much of what we call public education. The subject-matter of the stories is, in fact, nearly always taken from the national store of mythological, religious, philosophical and historical literature; but the story-teller, although sometimes he does nothing but recite his tale, usually develops, embellishes, animates and even mimes it. He is a true artist. Asians are irresistibly attracted to him; they collect round him and drink in the words of this magician of sorts and never forget them. The people listening to Mohammed preaching would sometimes leave him in order to listen to his 'rival', Nadr ibn al-Harith, who merely narrated the tale of Rustam and Isfandiyar. Throughout Islam, the *qaccac* enjoy almost incredible prestige and are absorbed with passion.

Musicians, singers, actors and story-tellers are associated with most large festivals, but they are not the only form of entertainment. Sports and games are also in demand and appreciated at least as much as in the West. One might be tempted to think that the predisposition to gaiety and laughter is a healthy way of counter-balancing the invasion of life by the religious preoccupation, but actually the latter cannot be very clearly distinguished from the former. In Asia religion has nothing austere about it, for the Asians joke with their gods and have fun in their company. In fact, games, and sports even more so, aim at an inner purpose more often than we think.

Games like chess (which was invented in China and which is played even by the Tunguz with mammoth tusks), and also cards, are great favourites in Asia. In Japan and China the scholarly *go* or *wai-chi*, which is played on a sort of chequer-board, is so popular that one often sees games of it being played on the pavement, and the Japanese national champion holds an eminent place in protocol; he normally adopts as his son the player who is next best after him. In Viet-Nam the noble *to tom*, which has been simplified for modern use into *mah-jong*, requires an unimaginably difficult science. In Japan, the great masters of the spinning-top game form real dynasties by successive adoptions, and all the members bear the same name, Matsui Gensui, which is followed by a serial number, just like sovereigns.

Animal fights also fascinate many spectators—camel fights in Pakistan; cock-fights in Siam, Cambodia, among various Indian tribes, and in different provinces of China; fish fights in Japan; buffalo fights in Afghanistan; bird, buffalo, cricket and pig fights in the Fu-Nan; and these are only illustrations. They may even be connected somehow with the decorative motif of animals fighting or facing each other so common from the Central Asian steppes to Indo-China.

Of course, these fights, as in the West, offer opportunities for betting, and in very many Asian countries, games of chance, which take a great variety of forms, are a true passion in all classes of society. The Koran has had to forbid them, for the Arabs used to go so far as to wager the members of their families, particularly in lotteries where a camel was the prize. This love of risk is not alien to the Asians' attraction to sports events such as Japanese wrestling, *sumo*, or Siamese wrestling. But in Asia there is actual and authentic veneration for certain sports.

In Japan the *sumo* matches of old often take place at religious festivals and are an offering to the gods, *kami*, and the title of *yokozuna*, which is the highest in this sport and which is seldom conferred, is equivalent to a title of nobility.

In classical China archery tournaments, which were formal like a ballet, were regarded as a great test of nobility, a test for the sovereign himself. In Japan this art is even today, as it was formerly in India, regarded as being of considerable spiritual value. In Krasnoyarsk a reliable traveller reports the following exploit which is described in many sacred scriptures and which seems to be nothing but a hyperbole of oriental poetry: riders at full gallop break an arrow in flight with another arrow shot a few moments later.[43]

The quality most appreciated in this art is often self-control and absence of excitement, as in Japanese *judo*, stick-fencing in Afghanistan, etc.

Not only through such a variety of arts, but also in life at every instant, the incessant search for beauty is a characteristic feature of most Asian peoples. In the West, generally speaking, we think that a large part of our gestures and the objects around us have an exclusively utilitarian aim and are therefore not subject to any aesthetic consideration, whereas the Asian does not make this distinction between the useful and the beautiful. That is why an ecstatic admiration of nature in all its aspects, an infinity of minor arts, games that are pleasing to the eye, refinements of etiquette and politeness permeate their whole life and universe. Okakura Kakuzo spoke of the 'worship of the beautiful among the humdrum of everyday existence'. Lafcadio Hearn used to tell us: 'The Japanese sees in nature all that has remained invisible to us for years, and he reveals to us aspects of life and beauty of form to which we had been absolutely blind previously'. And he warned us, saying: 'As long as you will not have understood that a big, rough stone can flatter the aesthetic feeling more than a carving on steel, that it is an object of everlasting beauty, you will not understand how the Japanese sees Nature.'

Although Japan is one of the most striking examples, it is by no means basically different from the rest of Asia. Under the Sassanids, the king used to be escorted on his hunting expeditions by male and female musicians.

[43] See in this connection the remarkable booklet by H. Herrigel: *Zen in the art of archery.*

Postscript

At the end of a work such as this, the reader will probably expect to find conclusions and even predictions. He will be disappointed. To express an opinion on Asia—the many Asias—or to wish to predict subsequent development, even in the near future, would be as presumptuous and futile as to apply the same exercises to mankind as a whole! Our personal temperament, our optimism or our pessimism, our aspirations and our ideals, our individual conception of the progress or regress of the human race and the human individual—and also our pride or our humility—colour both our view of our Asian brothers and our expectations, good or bad, from our increasing contact with them.

In the foregoing pages we have only attempted to help westerners of good will to understand a little better the reasons for all that in Asia seems strange or disconcerting to us, but we have refrained from passing any judgement on values. The explanations we have given are doubtless not the only ones possible, but it is more than likely that each one of them, taken separately, would receive the approval of an immense majority of Asians who have remained faithful to their traditions—even if none of them might be able to subscribe unconditionally to *all* that we have advanced. If we have helped a few to have a sounder idea of whatever they may have learnt from other reading, without showing blissful idolatry or nervous irritation before anything that is unfamiliar or unacceptable according to some of our criteria, our purpose will have been achieved.

VANDOEUVRES, 1959

Bibliography

Adivasis (New Delhi, Government Publications Division, 1955).
African Worlds (Oxford University Press, 1954).
Aitareya Brahmana (Cambridge, Mass., 1920).
Ame de l'Iran (L') (Paris, Albin Michel, 1951).
ANAND (MULK RAJ).—*Kama Kala* (Genève, Nagel, 1927).
Apastamba-Dharmasutra (Oxford, Sacred Books of the East, 1898).
ARBERRY (A. J.) *et alii*. *The Legacy of Persia* (Oxford, Clarendon Press, 1953).
ASHVAGOSHA.—*Buddhacharita in Journal Asiatique*, 1892.
ASTON (W. G.).—*A History of Japanese Literature* (London, Heinemann, 1899)
AUBIN (EUGÈNE).—*La Perse d'aujourd'hui* (Paris, Colin, 1908).
AUROBINDO (SRI).—*Thoughts and Glimpses*, Calcutta, 1950.
— *Essays on the Bhagavad-Gîtâ* (1938).
— *The Significance of Indian Art* (Pondichéry, 1947).
— *Three Upanishads*
— *Letters of Sri Aurobindo* (Bombay 1949-1958).
— *The Life Divine* (Sri Aurobindo Library, New York, 1951).

BALKHI (ABU ZAYD AL.).—*Le livre de la Création et de l'Histoire* (Paris, Ecole des L.O.V., 1899-1901).
BARBOSA (DUARTE).—*Description of the coasts of East Africa and Malabar . . .* (London, Hakluyt Society, 1866).
Basic Terms of Shinto (Tokyo, 1958).
BASTIAN.—*Die Völker der östlichen Asien* (Leipsic und Jena, 1866-1871).
BATCHELOR (JOHN).—*The Ainu of Japan.*
BAUDESSON (H.).—*Indo-China and its primitive people* (London, Hutchinson, 1919).
BECK (LILY ADAMS).—*The Garden of Vision* (London, Ernest Benn, 1933).
BENNABI (MALEK).—*Vocation de l'Islam* (Paris, Le Seuil, 1954).
BERQUE (JACQUES).—*Vers une étude des comportements en Afrique du Nord in Revue Africaine* (Alger, Société historique algérienne, 1956).
Bhagavad-Gîtâ.
Bhagavata-Purana.
BIDDULF (JOHN).—*Narodi naceliaouchtchie Hindu-Kush* (Ashkabad, 1880).
BISHOP (MRS.).—*Korea and her neighbours* (London, 1898).
BLACHERE (RÉGIS).—*Dans les pas de Mahomet* (Paris, Hachette, 1956).
BLOFELD (JOHN).—*Gateway to Wisdom* (London, Rider).
BLEICHSTEINER (ROBERT).—*L'église jaune* (Paris, Payot, 1937).
Bombay Presidency (Gazetteer of the) XV (1883).
BUCHANAN (FRANCIS).—*A Journey from Madras through the countries of Mysore, Canara and Malabar* (London, Cadell and Davies, 1807).
BURCKHARDT (TITUS).—*Introduction aux doctrines ésotériques de l'Islam* (Lyon, Derain, 1955).

BIBLIOGRAPHY

BURCKHARDT (V. R.).—*Chinese creeds and customs*, 2 vol. (Hong Kong, South China Morning Post, 1953-1955).
Burma facts and figures (Calcutta, Orient-Longmans, 1946).
BUSH (LEWIS).—*Japanalia* (Tokyo, Okuyama, 1956).
BYNG (CRANMER).—*The Vision of Asia* (London, Murray, 1932).

Catholic Encyclopedia (New York Encyclopedia Press, 1913 sqq.), 17 vol.
CAUSSE (A.).—*Israël et la vision de l'humanité* (Strasbourg, Istra, 1924).
Census of India.
CHAMBERLAIN (PROF. B. H.).—*Things Japanese* (London, Murray, 1905).
CHAPPE D'UTEROCHE (ABBÉ).—*A journey into Siberia* (London, 1770).
CHARLES (RAYMOND).—*Le droit musulman* (Paris, P.U.F., 1956).
— *L'âme musulmane* (Paris, Flammarion, 1958).
Chinese Literature (Peking, 1955, 4th edition).
CHRISTIAN (JOHN LEROY).—*Modern Burma* (Berkeley, Univ. of California, 1942).
CLAEYS (Y. C.).—*L'Annamite devant la mer.*
COEDES (G.).—*Les états hindouisés d'Indochine et d'Indonésie* (Paris, de Boccard, 1948).
COLLIER (D. M. B.) and LT.-COL. C. L'ESTRANGE MALONE.—*Le Mandchoukouo* (Paris, Payot, 1938).
COMBARIEU (J.).—*Histoire de la musique* (Paris, Colin, 1953).
CONFUCIUS.—*Analects.*
COOK (CAPTAIN JAMES).—*A Narrative of the Voyages round the world, performed by Captain James Cook.*
COURANT (MAURICE).—*La Sibérie, colonie russe* (Paris, Alcan, 1920).
CROOKE (W.).—*Popular religion and folklore of Northern India* (Westminster, 1896), 2 vol.
— *Natives of Northern India* (London, Constable, 1907).
Cullavagga (London, Humphrey Milford, 1916-1917).
Cultural Heritage of India (Calcutta, Belur Math, o.d.), 3 vol.
CURTIN (JEREMIAH).—*A journey in Southern Siberia, the Mongols, their religion and their myths* (London, Low, 1909).
CURZON (LORD).—*Persia and the Persian question* (London, Longmans, 1892).

DANNAUD (J. P.).—*Indochine profonde* (Saïgon, 1954).
DARMESTETER (JAMES).—*Lettres sur l'Inde* (Paris, Lemerre, 1888).
DAVIDSON (BASIL).—*Turkestan alive* (London, Cape, 1957).
DAVIES (R. A.) and STEIGER (A. G.).—*Soviet Asia* (London, Gollancz, 1944).
DEBNICKI (ALESKY).—*The Chu-shu-chi-nien* (Warsawa, 1956).
DELAPORTE (LOUIS).—*Mesopotamia* (London, 1925).
DEMIEVILLE (PAUL).—*Le Concile de Lhassa* (Paris, P.U.F., 1952).
Dhammapada. (Paris, Geuthner, 1931).
DHORME (P. EDOUARD).—*La poésie biblique* (Paris, Grasset, 1931).
Dictionnaire d'histoire et de géographie ecclésiatiques (Paris, Letouzey, 1930).
Dinshah Irani Memorial Volume (Bombay, 1943).
Doctrine (The) of Tenrikyo (Tenri, 1954).
DOLLOT (RENÉ).—*L'Afghanistan* (Paris, Payot, 1937).
DONNER (KAI).—*La Sibérie* (Paris, Gallimard, 1946).
DOUGHTY (CHARLES M.).—*Arabia deserta.* Passages selected by Edward Garnett (London, Penguin, 1956)
DOURNES (R. P. JACQUES).—*Populations montagnardes du Sud Indochinois* (Lyon, Derain, 1950).

DRESCH ET BIROT.—*Méditerranée et Moyen-Orient* (Paris, P.U.F., 1953-1956), 2 vol.

DUBOIS (J. A.).—*Moeurs, institutions et cérémonies des peuples de l'Inde* (Paris, 1825).

DUCROCQ (GEORGES).—*Pauvre et douce Corée* (Paris, Champion, 1904).

EHRENFELS (BARON U. R.).—*Kadar of Cochin* (Madras University, 1952).

EITEL (DR ERNEST).—*Feng-shui* (London, Hong Kong, 1873).

ELLIOTT (SIR HENRY M.).—*Memoirs on the History, Folklore and Distribution of the races of the N.-W. provinces of India* (London, 1869).

ELLIS (HAVELOCK).—*The Dance of Life* (London, Constable, 1923).

ELMORE (WILBER TH.).—*Dravidian gods in modern Hinduism* (Madras, Society for India, 1925).

ELWIN (VERRIER).—*The Baiga* (London, Murray, 1939).
— *Myths of Middle India* (Oxford University Press, 1949).
— *Tribal myths of Orissa* (Oxford University Press, 1954).
— *The religion of an Indian tribe* (Oxford University Press, 1955).

EMBREE (J. F.).—*A Japanese village, Suye Mura* (London, Kegan Paul, 1946).

Enciclopedia (Espanola) universal illustrada (Bilbao, Espasa-Calpe, s.d.), 88 vol.

Encyclopaedia Britannica (1947 edition), 24 vol.

Encyclopaedia of Religion and Ethics (Edinburgh, Clark, 1908-1926), 13 vol.

Encyclopédie de l'Islam (Leiden, Brill, 1913-1938), 5 vol.

Engi-shiki (Tokyo).

ENTHOVEN (R. E.).—*The tribes and castes of Bombay* (Bombay, 1920-1922). 3 vol.

Epigraphia indica.

Eranos Jahrbuch (Zürich, Rhein, 1952).

ERMAN (ADOLPH).—*Travels in Siberia* (London, Longman, 1848).

ESQUER.—*Essai sur les castes dans l'Inde* (Pondichéry, 1870).

ETIEMBLE.—*Confucius* (Le Club français du livre, 1956).

FABER (ERNST).—*The famous women in China* (Shanghaï, 1890).

FARIS (BISHR).—*L'honneur chez les Arabes avant l'Islam* (Paris, A. Maisonneuve, 1932).

FERRIER (J. P.).—*Caravan Journeys and Wanderings in Persia, Afghanistan Turkistan, and Beloochistan* (London, 1856).

FLORENZ (KARL).—*Nihongi, Zeitalter der Götter* (Tokyo, 1901).

FOCILLON (HENRI).—*L'art bouddhique* (Paris, Laurens, 1921).

FONG (H. D.).—*Industrial organization in China* (Tien-tsin, Chihli Press, 1937).

FORKE (A.).—*Lun-Heng, Selected Essays of the philosopher Wang Ch'ung* (M.S.O.S., 1911).

France-Asie (Saïgon).

FRASER (JOHN FOSTER).—*The real Siberia* (London, Cassell, 1902).

FRAZER (SIR JAMES GEORGE).—*The golden bough* (London, Macmillan, 1951), 13 vol.

FRYER (DR JOHN).—*A new account of East India and Persia: being nine years' travel, 1672-1681* (London, Hakluyt Society, 1909-1915).

FUJIKAWA (ASAKO).—*Cha-no-yu and Hideyoshi* (Tokyo, Hokuseido, 1957).

FUJISAWA (CHIKAO).—*Introduction to the study of . . . Kotonarism* (Tokyo, 1954).

FURNIVALL (J. S.).—*Colonial policy and practice* (Cambridge University Press, 1948).

BIBLIOGRAPHY

GALBRAITH (WINIFRED).—*The Chinese* (London, Penguin, 1943).
GANDHI (MAHATMA).—*Letters to the Ashram* (from Yeravda Mandir).
GARDET (LOUIS).—*Introduction à la théologie musulmane* (Paris, Vrin, 1948).
GAUTIER (E. F.).—*Moeurs et coutumes des musulmans* (Paris, Payot, 1931).
Gazetteer of India (Imperial) (London, Trubner, 1885-1887), 14 vol.
GERNET (JACQUES).—*La vie quotidienne en Chine à la veille de l'invasion mongole* (Paris, Hachette, 1959).
GIBB (H. A. R.).—*Modern Trends in Islam* (Chicago, 1947).
GILES (HERBERT A.).—*Religion of ancient China* (London, 1905).
GINSBURG (NORTON).—*The pattern of Asia* (Engelwood Cliffs, 1958).
GLASENAPP (HELMUTH VON).—*Brahma et Bouddha* (Paris, Payot, 1937).
— *Die nichtchristlichen Religionen* (Frankfurt a. M., Fischer, 1957).
GMELIN (J. G.).—*Voyage en Sibérie* (Paris, Desaint, 1767), 2 vol.
GOBINEAU (COUNT DE).—*Les religions et les philosophies dans l'Asie centrale* (Paris, Didier, 1866).
GOUROU (PIERRE).—*L'Asie* (Paris, Hachette, 1953).
GOVINDA (LAMA ANAGARIKA).—*Foundations of Tibetan Mysticism* (London, Rider & Co., 1960).
GRANET (MARCEL).—*Festivals and Songs of Ancient China* (London, Routledge & Sons, 1932).
— *Danses et légendes de la Chine ancienne* (Paris, Impr. Nationale, 1925).
— *La Pensée chinoise* (Paris, Albin Michel, 1934).
— *Chinese Civilization* (London, Kegal Paul & Co., 1930).
— *La religion des Chinois* (Paris, P.U.F., 1951).
GRANQUIST (HILMA).—*Birth and childhood among the Arabs* (Helsinfors, Söderström, 1947).
GREEN (O. M.).—*Japan 1945-1949* (New York, Wilson, 1950).
GREKOV (B.). et IAKOUBOVSKI (A.).—*La horde d'or* (Paris, Payot, 1939).
GRENARD (F.).—*Baber first of the Moguls* (London, Thornton Butterworth, 1931).
GRENIER (JEAN).—*L'esprit du Tao* (Paris, Flammarion, 1957).
GRIFFITHS (THE REV.).—*Religions of Japan*.
GRIFFITHS (WALTER G.).—*The Kol tribe of Central India* (Calcutta, Royal Asiatic Society of Bengal, 1946).
GROOT (J. J. M. DE).—*Les fêtes annuellement célébrées à Emoui* (Paris, Leroux, 1886).
— *The religious systems of China* (Leiden, Brill, 1892-1910), 6 vol.
GROUSSET (RENÉ).—*Histoire de l'Asie* (Paris, P.U.F., 1941).
— *L'Empire des steppes* (Paris, Payot, 1952).
— et Georges DENIKER.—*La face de l'Asie* (Paris, Payot, 1955).
GUILLAIN (ROBERT).—*The blue Ants* (London, Secker & Warburg, 1957).
GUILLERMAZ (PATRICIA).—*La poésie chinoise* (Paris, Seghers, 1957).
GUITERMAN (ARTHUR).—*Betel Nuts* (San Francisco, Elder, 1907).
GUNTHER (JOHN).—*Inside Asia* (New York, Harper, 1942).

HAIDAR BAMMATE (GEORGES RIVOIRE).—*Visages de l'Islam* (Lausanne, Payot, 1946).
HALFORD (AUBREY S. and GIOVANNA M.).—*The Kabuki Handbook* (Tokyo, Tuttle, 1956).
HALL (H. FIELDING).—*The soul of a people* (London, Macmillan, 1906).
— *The inward light* (New York, Macmillan, 1908).
HAMBIS (LOUIS).—*La Haute-Asie* (Paris, P.U.F., 1953).

HARA (KATSURO).—*An Introduction to the History of Japan* (New York and London, G. P. Putnam, 1920).

HARRER (HEINRICH).—*Seven Years in Tibet* (London, Rupert Hart-Davis, 1953).

HART (HENRY H.).—*Poems of the hundred names* (Stanford University Press, 1954).

HAWKESWORTH (JOHN).—*An Account of the Voyages . . .* (London, 1773).

HEARN (LAFCADIO).—Complete works.

HEDIN (SVEN).—*Through Asia* (London, Methuen, 1899).

— *Adventures in Tibet Towards the Holy City of Lassa.*

HEISER (VICTOR GEORGE).—*An American doctor's Odyssey* (New York, Norton, 1936).

HERBELOT DE MOLAINVILLE (B. D').—*Bibliothèque orientale, ou Dictionnaire universel contenant généralement tout ce qui regarde la connaissance des peuples de l'Orient* (Paris, Comp. des libraires, 1697).

HERBERT (HUGUETTE ET JEAN).—*Dans l'Inde. L'accueil des dieux* (Paris, Aubier, 1959).

HERBERT (JEAN).—*Asien* (Zürich, 1957).

— *Glossaire du Raja-Yoga et du Hatma-Yoga* (Paris et Neuchâtel, 1944).

— *La notion de vie future dans l'hindouisme* (Paris, Adyar, 1944).

— *Spiritualité hindoue* (Paris, Albin Michel, 1947).

— *Aux sources du Japon. Le Shinto* (Paris, Albin Michel, 1964).

— *Yoga, christianisme et civilisation* (Alger, Messerschmitt, 1950).

— *La mythologie hindoue, son message* (Paris, Albin Michel, 1953).

— *Banaras, a Guide to the Panchkroshi Yatra* (Calcutta, Saturday Mail Publications, 1957).

— *L'anatomie psychologique de l'homme selon Shrî Aurobindo* (Lyon, Derain, 1960).

— *Les dix tableaux du domestiquage de la vache* (Lyon, Derain, 1960).

—et Huguette GHAFFAR.—*Premier Album de mythologie hindoue* (Lyon, Derain, 1955).

HERRIGEL (E.).—*Zen in the art of archery* (London, Routledge & Kegan Paul, 1953).

HERRIGEL (G.).—*Zen in the art of flower arrangement* (London, Routledge & Kegan Paul, 1958).

HIRATA (ATSUTANE).—*Tamano Mi-hashira* (1813).

— *Tamadasuki* (1924), 10 vol.

HOADE (FR. EUGÈNE).—*Guide to the Holy Land* (Jerusalem, 1946).

HODSON (T. C.).—*The Naga tribes of Manipur* (London, Macmillan, 1911).

HUARD (PIERRE) *et* DURAND (MAURICE).—*Connaissance du Viet-Nam* (Paris et Hanoï, 1954).

HUART (CLÉMENT) *et* DELAPORTE (LOUIS).—*L'Iran antique. Elam et Perse* (Paris, Albin Michel, 1943).

HUISH (MARCUS B.).—*Japan and its art* (London, Batsford, 1912).

HUNG LOU MENG.—*The dream of the red chamber* (London, Routledge and Kegan Paul, 1958).

IBBETSON (D. C. J.).—*Outlines of Panjab Ethnography* (Calcutta, 1883).

INNES (C. A.).—*Malabar and Ajengo* (Madras, 1915).

IKBAL (SIR MUHAMMAD).—*The Reconstruction of religious thought in Islam* (London, 1934).

JACOBY (ERICH H.).—*Agrarian unrest in South-East Asia* (New York, Columbia University Press, 1949).

BIBLIOGRAPHY

JAQUEMONT (VICTOR).—*Letters from India* (London, 1934).
JAIN (JAGDISH CHANDRA).—*Life in ancient India as depicted in the Jain canons* (Bombay, New Book Company, 1947).
Jataka mala (Oxford, Clarendon Press, 1882-1885), 3 vol.
JAUSSEN (ANTONIN).—*Coutumes des Arabes au pays de Moab* (Paris, Gabalda, 1908).
Jewish Encyclopaedia (New York and London, Funk and Wagnalls, 1901-1906), 12 vol.
JOCHELSON (WALDEMAR).—*The Koryak* (Leyden, 1908).

KAEMPFER (ENGELBERT).—*The History of Japan* (Kyoto, Bunji Yoshida, 1929).
KAIBARA.—*Onna Daigaku.*
Kalpasutra (jain) in Indian Antiquary, XXXI
KANAMATSU (KENRYO).—*Naturalness* (Los Angeles, 1956).
KANEKO (PROF.).—*Engi-shiki Norito Ko.*
KAWAGUSHI (SHRAMANA EKAI).—*Three years in Tibet* (Paris, Adyar, 1909).
KELMAN (JANET HARVEY).—*Labour in India* (London, Allen and Unwin, 1923).
KHANYKOV (Y. VLADIMIROVITCH).—*Bokhara, its Amir and its People* (London, 1845).
KIM (CHANGSOON) *et alii.—The culture of Korea* (U.S.A., 1945-1946).
KISA'I (MUHAMMAD BEN 'ABDALLAH AL-).—*Qiçaç al Anbiya* (Leyden, Eisenberg, 1922-1923).
KOBAYASHI (B.) (pseudonym of J. E. de Becker).—*The nightless city, or the History of the Yoshiwara Yukwaku* (Yokohama, 1899).
Kogoshudi, Gleanings from ancient stories (Tokyo, Meiji Japan Society, 1925).
Ko-ji-ki, in Transactions of the Asiatic Society of Japan, Supplement to vol. X (1883).
Koran (George Sale, 1877).
KRAMISH (STELLA).—*The Hindu Temple* (Calcutta, 1946), 2 vol.
KREMER (ALFRED VON).—*Kulturgeschichte des Orients unter den Chalifen* (Vienna, 1875-1877), 2 vol.
KUMARAPPA (BHARATAN).—*Capitalism, Socialism or Villagism?* (Madras, Shakti Karyalayan).

LABBE (PAUL).—*Chez les lamas de Sibérie* (Paris, Hachette, 1909).
LABOURT (ABBÉ JÉROME).—*Le christianisme dans l'empire perse sous la dynastie sassanide* (Paris, Lecoffre, 1904).
LACOUAGE (R. P. GASTON).—*Dans l'Inde de St François-Xavier* (Toulouse, 1931).
LAMOTTE (ABBÉ ETIENNE).—*Le traité de la grande vertu de sagesse de Nagarjuna* (Louvain, Museon, 1944-1949).
LAO-TZU.—*Tao Te Ching* (London, Allen and Unwin, 1959).
Larousse du XXe siècle.
LATOURETTE (KENNETH SCOTT).—*The Chinese, their history and culture* (New York, Macmillan, 1949).
Laws of Manu (The) (Oxford, Clarendon Press, 1886).
LEBLOIS (GEORGES-LOUIS).—*Les Bibles et les initiateurs religieux de l'humanité* (Paris, 1883-1888), 4 vol
LE FANU (WILLIAM J. H.).—*A manual of the Salem District.*
LEGGE.—*Travels.*
LEGRAS (JULES).—*En Sibérie* (Paris, Colin, 1899).
LI-CH'IAO-PING.—*The chemical arts of Old China* (Easton, Pa., 1948).
LILLEY (W. A.).—*India and its problems.*

Littératures anciennes, orientales et orales (Paris, N.R.F., 1956).
LO-CHUN.—*Peasant women and hand-weaving in Kiangyin*, 1938 (reprinted in Agrarian China, Chicago).
LOUBERE (DE LA).—*Du royaume de Siam* (Amsterdam, 1691).
LOUNSBERY (GRACE C.).—*Buddhist Meditation in the Southern School—Theory and Practice for Westerners* (London, Kegan Paul, 1935).
LOUO KOUAN-TCHONG.—*Le roman des trois royaumes* (Saïgon, France-Asie, 1958).
LOWELL (PERCIVAL).—*Occult Japan*. (Boston, Houghton and Mifflin, 1888).
LUBAC (HENRI DE).—*Aspects of Buddhism* (London and New York, Sheed & Ward, 1953).
LUKNITKY (PAVEL).—*Soviet Tadjikistan* (Moscow, 1954).

MABUCHI KAMO.—*Complete works* (Tokyo).
MACDONALD (DAVID).—*The Land of the Lama* (London, Seely and Co., 1929).
MACPHERSON (CAPTAIN).—*North Indian Notes and Queries, II.*
Madras Census Reports, 1891 and 1901.
Madura District (Gazetteer of the).
Mahabharata (Calcutta, 1930), 11 vol.
Maitri Upanishad (Calcutta, Biblioteca Indica, 1935).
Majjhima Nikaya (London, Oxford University Press, 1888-1902), 3 vol.
MALAVIYA (PANDIT MADAN MOHAN).—*The immanence of God.*
MALCOLM (SIR JOHN).—*A memoir of Central India* (London, 1823), 2 vol.
MARAINI (FOSCO).—*Meeting with Japan* (London, 1959).
MARTINI (R. P. GIOVANNI FILIPO DE).—*Histoire nouvelle et curieuse des royaumes du Tunquin et de Laos* (1666).
MASSON-OURSEL (PAUL).—*La pensée en Orient* (Paris, Armand Colin, 1949).
MATEER (REV. SAMUEL).—*The Land of Charity* (London, 1871).
— *Native Life in Travancore* (London, Allen, 1883).
MA TOUAN-LIN.—*Ethnographie des peuples étrangers à la Chine* (Geneva, Georg, 1876-1883), 2 vol.
Matsya Purana (Allahabad, Sacred Books of the Hindus, 1916).
MATTHEWS (RODERIC D.) and MATTA AKRAWI.—*Education in Arab countries in the Near East* (Washington, American Council of Education, 1949).
MEAD (MARGARET) *et alii.*—*Cultural patterns and technical change* (Paris, U.N.E.S.C.O., 1953).
Mémoires de la Délégation en Perse (Paris, 1900-1949), 31 vol.
MENDOZA (R. P. DUAN GONZALES DE).—*Ein neuwe . . . Beschreibung des . . . Königreichs China . . .* (Frankfurt a.M., 1589).
MEYER (J. J.).—*Sexual Life in Ancient India* (London, Routledge, 1930).
MIAGKOFF (E. D.).—*Tableaux de la vie russe* (Lausanne, 1916).
MILLIOT.—*Introduction à l'étude du droit musulman* (Paris, Sirey, 1954).
MILNE (MARY LEWIS).—*The home of an Eastern clan. A study of the Palaungs of the Shan States* (Oxford, 1924).
Mission lyonnaise d'exploration commerciale en Chine (Lyon, 1898).
MITFORD.—*Tales of old Japan* (London, Macmillan 1886).
MOCK (JOYA).—*Quaint customs and manners of Japan* (Tokyo, the Tokyo News Service, 1951-1955), 4 vol.
Mong leang leou (1275).
MONIER WILLIAMS.—*Religious thought and life in India* (London, Murray, 1883).
— *Modern India and Indians* (London, 1893).
MONTAGU (IVOR).—*Land of blue sky* (London, Dobson, 1956).

BIBLIOGRAPHY

MOSTAFA (MOHAMED).—*Unity in Islamic art* (Cairo, 1958).
MOTOORI (NORINAGA).—*Complete works* (Tokyo).
MUHYI-D'DIN-IBN 'ARABI'.—*La Sagesse des Prophètes* (Paris, Albin Michel, 1955).
MUIR (J.).—*Original sanskrit Texts* (London, Trubner, 1972 sqq.), 5 vol.
MUKERJI (DHANA GOPALA MUKHOPADHYAYA).—*My Brother's Face* (London, Thornton Butterworth, 1925).
MURDOCH (JAMES).—*A history of Japan* (London, Kegan Paul, 1926), 3 vol.
Mysore Census Report, 1901.
Mythologie asiatique illustrée (Paris, Librairie de France, 1928).
Mythologie générale (Paris, Larousse, 1963), 2 vol.

Naissance du monde (La) (Paris, Le Seuil, 1959).
Nihongi, in Transactions and Proceedings of the Japan Society (London, 1896), 2 vol.
NITOBE (INAZO).—*Bushido* (London, Putnam, 1905).
— *Editorial jottings* (Tokyo, Hokuseido, 1938), 2 vol.
NIVEDITA (SISTER).—*The Web of Indian Life* (London, Longmans Green, 1904).
NOBEL (PROF. JOHANNES).—*Central Asia: the connecting link between East and West* (Nagpur, 1952).
Norito, A new translation of the Ancient Japanese Ritual Prayers by Donald L. Philippi (The Institute for Japanese Culture and Classics, Kokugakuin University, Tokyo, 1959).

OKAKURA (KAKUZO).—*The Ideals of the East* (New York and London, E. P. Dutton & Co., 1920).
— *The Book of Tea* (Edinburgh and London, T. N. Foulis, 1919).
O'MALLEY (L.S.S.).—*Indian Cast Customs* (Cambridge University Press, 1932).
ORTIZ (PADRE THOMAS).—*La practica del ministerio* (Manila, 1713).
OSGOOD (CORNELIUS).—*The Koreans and their culture* (New York, Ronald, 1951).
Outline of Shinto teaching (An) (Tokyo, 1958).

PANIKKAR (K. M.).—*India and China* (Bombay, Asia Publishing House, 1957).
PAVIE.—*Etudes diverses* (Paris, Leroux, 1898).
PELLIOT (PAUL).—*La Haute-Asie* (s.l.n.d.)
PERRY-AYSCOUGH and OTTER-BARRY.—*With the Russians in Mongolia* (London, Lane, 1914).
Philippines (The), visitors' handbook (Manila, s.d.)
PHILIPS (M.).—*Evolution of Hinduism* (1903).
PHIPSON (E. S.).—*Tribal beliefs concerning tuberculosis in the hills and the frontier-tracts of Assam* (Assam Government Press, 1939).
Pindanijjutti (Bombay, 1918).
PLANHOL (X. DE).—*Le monde islamique, essai de géographie religieuse* (Paris, P.U.F., 1957).
PONSONBY-FANE (R. A. B.).—*Studies in Shinto and Shrines* (Kyoto, Kamikamo, 1957).
POSDNEIEW.—*Skizzen des Lebens der buddhistischen Klöster und der buddhistischen Geistlichkeit in der Mongolei in Denkschrift Kaiserlichen Geographischen Gesellschaft, Ethn. Skt., XVI* (St. Petersburg, 1887).
Présence du Bouddhisme (Saïgon, France-Asie, 1959).
Présence du Cambodge (Saïgon, France-Asie, 1955).

Présence du Royaume lao (Saïgon, France-Asie, 1956).

PRISSELKOV.—*Des iarlyks khaniaux aux métropolites russes.*

PRODAN (MARIO).—*Incontro con l'arte cinese* (Milano, Martello, 1956).

P'U SUNG-LING.—*Liao chai chih i* (Strange stories from a Chinese studio). Translated and annotated by Herbert A. Giles (London, de la Rue, 1880)

RADCLIFFE-BROWN.—*The Andaman Islanders* (Glencoe, Free Press, 1948).

RADD (A.).—*Guide à travers l'Union soviétique* (Berlin, Neuer Deutscher Verlag, 1928).

RAGHU VIRA.—*Chinese poems and pictures on ahimsa* (Nagpur, International Academy of Indian Culture, 1954).

— and CHIKYO YAMAMOTO.—*Ramayana in China* (Nagpur, 1938).

RAMAKRISHNA (SHRI).—*L'enseignement* (Paris, Albin Michel, 1949).

RAMDAS (SWAMI).—*Carnet de pélerinage* (Paris, Albin Michel, 1953).

RANASINGHE (C. P.).—*The Buddha's explanation of the universe* (Colombo, L.B.M. Fund, 1957).

RASHID ED DIN TABIB.—*Histoire des Mongols de la Perse* (Paris, Imprimerie royale, 1836).

RED CROSS (General Report of the League of Red Cross Societies for 1952-1956) (Geneva, 1957).

REINACH (SALOMON).—*Orpheus: a general history of religions* (London, Heinemann; New York, Putnam, 1909).

REMUSAT (ABEL).—*Histoire de la ville de Khotan* (Paris, Doublet, 1820).

— *Nouveaux mélanges asiatiques* (Paris, Dondey-Dupré, 1829).

RENAN (ERNEST).—*Studies of religious history* (New York, 1864).

RENOUVIER (CHARLES).—*Introduction à la philosophie analytique de l'histoire* (Paris, Leroux, 1896).

REVON (MICHEL).—*Le shinntoïsme* (Paris, 1907).

RIALLE (GIRARD DE).—*Mémoire sur l'Asie centrale* (Paris, Leroux, 1875).

— *La mythologie comparée* (Paris, 1878).

RICE (PERCIVAL S. P.).—*Occasional Essays on Native South Indian Life* (London, Longmans, 1901).

RICHTE (REV. G.).—*Castes and tribes found in the province of Coorg* (Bangalore, 1887).

RIEDE (J. G. F.).—*De sluik—en kroesharige rassen tusschen Selebes en Papua* (The Hague, 1886).

Rig-Veda (Paris, Bibliothèque Internationale Universelle, 1870).

RISLEY (SIR HERBERT H.).—*The tribes and castes of Bengal* (Calcutta, 1891), 2 vol.

RIVERS (DR. WILLIAM H.).—*The Todas* (London, Macmillan, 1906).

ROBERTSON SMITH (WILLIAM).—*Lectures on the Religion of the Semites* (Edinburgh, 1889).

ROCKHILL (WILLIAM WOODVILLE).—*The land of the lamas* (London, Longmans, 1891).

ROOLVINK (DR. R.). et alii. *Historical Atlas of the Muslim peoples* (Djambatan and Amsterdam, 1957).

ROUX (COLONEL HENRI) and TRAN-VAN-CHU.—*Quelques minorités ethniques du nord-Indochine* (Saïgon, France-Asie, 1954).

ROY (ANILBARAN).—*Mother India* (Calcutta, Gita Prachar Karyalaya, 1935).

ROY (DILIP KUMAR).—*Among the Great* (Bombay, Nalanda, 1940).

RUSSELL (R. V.).—*The tribes and castes of the Central Provinces of India* (London, Macmillan, 1916), 4 vol.

BIBLIOGRAPHY

SABIR (C. DE).—*Le fleuve Amour* (Paris, Kugelmann, 1861).

Saddharma Pundarika Sutra (Kyoto University, 1949).

SAMIOS (ELÉNI).—*La sainte vie de Mahatma Gandhi* (Gap, Ophrys, 1940).

SANTIDEVA.—*Bodhicharyavatara.*

Satapatha Brahmana (Oxford, Sacred Books of the East, 1882-1899).

SAUVAGET (J.).—*Relations de la Chine et de l'Inde rédigée en 851* (Paris, Belles-Lettres, 1948).

SCHINTGER.—*Forgotten kingdom.*

SCHMIDT (RICHARD).—*Beiträge zur Indischen Erotik* (Leipzig, Lotus, 1902).

SCHUON (FRITHJOF).—*Les stations de la sagesse* (Paris, Correa, 1958).

SCHWEIGER-LERCHENFELD (AMAND FRH. VON).—*Die Frauen des Orients.*

SCOTT (SIR GEORGE).—*The Burman, his life and notions* (London, Macmillan, 1910).

SEAL (B. N.).—*Positive sciences of the Hindus.*

SELIGMANN (C. G. S.).—*The Weddas* (Cambridge University Press, 1911).

SEWELL.—*A forgotten empire.*

SHAGINYAN (MARIETTA).—*Journey through Soviet Armenia* (Moscow, 1954).

SHAH (V.) and SHAH (S.).—*Bhuvel socio-economic survey of a village* (Bombay, Indian Society of Agricultural Economics, 1949).

SHANKARA.—*Hymnes à Shiva* (Lyon, Derain, 1944).

SHIH KUO-HANG.—*China enters the machine-age* (Cambridge, Harvard University Press, 1944).

SHIVANANDA (SWAMI SARASVATI).—*La pratique de la méditation* (Paris, Albin Michel, 1950).

SHKLOVSKY (I. W.).—*In far North-East Siberia* (London, Macmillan, 1916).

SHORTT (DR. JOHN).—*An account of the tribes on the Neilgherries* (Madras, 1868).

SINGH (MORAN).—*Kabir, his biography* (Lahore, 1934).

Sineca franciscana, Vol. I (Florence, 1929).

Skanda purana (Bombay, 1877).

SKEAT (WALTER WILLIAM).—*Malay magic* (London, Macmillan, 1900).

SKROSYREV (P.).—*Soviet Turkmenistan* (Moscow, 1956).

SLEEMAN (SIR W. H.).—*Rambles and recollections of an Indian Official* (Westminster, 1893).

SMITH (ARTHUR H.).—*Village life in China* (Edinburgh and London, 1899).
— *Chinese Characteristics* (Edinburgh and London, 1900).

SNOUCK HURGRONJE (C.).—*Het Gajöland en zijne Bewoners* (Batavia, 1903).

South Arcot District (Gazetteer of the).

South East Asia Round Table (Bangkok, 1958).

SRINIVAS (M. N.).—*Religion and Society among the Coorgs of South India* (Oxford, Clarendon, 1952).

SSU-MA CHIEN.—*The Life of Confucius according to the historical accounts of Ssu Ma Chien (Shi Chi).*

STADLING (J.).—*Through Siberia* (Westminster, Constable, 1901).

STARK (FREYA).—*The Southern gates of Arabia* (Hardmondsworth, Penguin, 1945).

STELLAR (G. W.).—*Beschreibung von dem Lande Kamtschatka* (Frankfurt and Leipzig, 1774).

STUART (SIR HAROLD ARTHUR).—*North Arcot* (1894).
— *South Arcot.*
— *South Canara* (1895).

Study in human starvation.—2. Diets and deficiency diseases (American Geographical Society, 1953).

SUZUKI (DAISETZ TEITARO).—*A miscellany on the Shin teachings of Buddhism* (Kyoto, Shinshu Otoniha Shumusho, 1949).
— *Essays in Zen Buddhism* (London, Luzac & Co., 1927-1934).

Taittiriya Brahmana (Mysore, 1908-1921), 4 vol.
TATTVABHUSHAN (PANDIT SITANATH).—*Brahmasadhan* (Calcutta, B. M. Press, s.d.).
Thailand Culture Series, I-XVII (Bangkok, 1950-1954).
THAKORE SAHEB (of Gondal).—*A short history of Aryan medical science* (London, Macmillan, 1896).
This is Japan, Number 5 (1958) (Tokyo, Asahi Shimbun, 1958).
THOMAS (BERTRAM).—*Arabia Felix* (London, Cape, 1932).
THOMAS (BRINLEY), editor.—*The Economics of international migration* (London, Macmillan, 1958).
THOMPSON (VIRGINIA).—*French Indo-China* (New York, Macmillan, 1937).
THURSTON (EDGAR) and RANGACHARI (K.).—*Castes and tribes of South India* (Madras, 1909), 7 vol.
TISENHAUSEN (V.).—*Documents se rapportant à la Horde d'or* (St. Petersburg, 1884).
Tong king mong houa lou (Shanghai, 1956).
Transactions of the Asiatic Society of Japan.
Transactions of the Bombay Geographical Society.
TRUMBULL (H. C.).—*The blood covenant* (London, Redway, 1887).
TULSIDAS.—*Sri Ramacharitamanase* (Gorakhpur, Gita Press, 1949-1951), 3 vol.
TYABJI (RAIHANA).—*L'âme d'une Gopî* (Gap, Ophrys, 1938).

VACHOT (CHARLES).—*La guirlande des lettres* (Lyon, Derain, 1959).
Vajrasuchika Upanishad (Bombay, 1925).
VALLEE POUSSIN (L. DE LA).—*Dynasties et histoire de l'Inde depuis Kanishka jusqu'aux invasions musulmanes* (Paris, Boccard, 1935).
VALMIKI.—*The Ramayana* (London, Shanti Sadan, 1952-1959), 3 vol.
VAMBERY (ARMIN).—*Bokhara Története* (Pest, Rath, 1873).
VAN AALST (J. A.).—*Chinese music* (Shanghai, 1884).
VENKATA RAMAMURTI (G.).—*The Savara.*
VIGHNESHWARA.—*Sotto voce* (Madras, Paul, 1959).
VILLETARD DE LAGUERIE.—*La Corée, indépendante, russe ou japonaise* (Paris, Hachette, 1904).
VINOBA BHAVE (ACHARYA).—*La révolution de la non-violence* (Paris, Albin Michel, 1958).
VIVEKANANDA (SWAMI).—*Complete works* (Mayavati, 1924 sqq.), 7 vol.
Vizagapatam District (Gazetteer of the).

WADDELL (L. A.).—*Among the Himalayas* (Westminster, 1899).
WARD (LIEUT.).—*Manual of the Madura District* (1824).
WENSINCK (ARENT JAN).—*Tree and bird as cosmological symbols in Western Asia* (Amsterdam, 1921).
WERNER (E. T. CHALMERS).—*Myths and legends of China* (London, Harrap, 1922).
WIEGER (LÉON).—*Les Pères du système taoïste* (Hien-hien, 1913).
WILKEN (G. A.).—*Das Matriarchat bei den alten Arabern* (Leipzig, Schultze, 1884).

BIBLIOGRAPHY

WILKS (COLONEL MARK).—*Historical sketches of the South of India* (London, 1810-1817).

WILLETTS (WILLIAM).—*Chinese Art* (Harmondsworth, Penguin, 1958).

WILLIAMS (HARRY).—*Ceylon, pearl of the East* (London, Hail, 1950).

WING-TSIT CHAN.—*Religious trends in modern China* (New York, Columbia University, 1953).

WISER (W. H.). and WISER (C. V.).—*Behind mud walls* (New York, Friendship Press, 1946).

WOOLLEY (SIR LEONARD).—*Excavations at Ur* (London, Benn, 1954).

WRANGEL (DE).—*Le nord de la Sibérie* (Paris, d'Amyot, 1843), 2 vol.

Yaçna, (Bombay, Nirnaya-Sagar, 1886).

YANG (MARTIN).—*Chinese Village* (New York, Columbia University Press, 1945).

YOUNG (E.).—*The kingdom of the yellow robe* (Westminster, 1898).

YUDKEVITCH (LEV.).—*At the gates of Hindustan* (*Tadjikistan*) (Moscow, Federatsil, 1932).

YUTANG (LIN).—*My country and my people* (London, Heinemann, 1930).

— *The importance of living* (London, Heinemann, 1938).

YVON (R. P.).—*A l'assaut de la jungle* (Dinard, 1940).

INDEX

INDEX

389

INDEX

INDEX

INDEX